POPULAR TELEVISION AND FILM

POPULAR TELEVISION AND FILM

A READER EDITED BY
TONY BENNETT, SUSAN BOYD-BOWMAN, COLIN MERCER AND
JANET WOOLLACOTT
AT THE OPEN UNIVERSITY

BFI Publishing

in association with
The Open University Press

First published in 1981 by the British Film Institute
127 Charing Cross Road
London WC2H 0EA
in association with
The Open University Press

British Library Cataloguing in Publication Data

Popular television and film.
   1. Television programs—Addresses,
essays, lectures
   I. Bennett, Tony
   791. 45   PN1992.5

ISBN 0 85170 115 9 (hardback)
     0 85170 116 7 (paperback)

Set in Baskerville
Printed by Tonbridge Printers Ltd, Tonbridge, Kent

Contents

Acknowledgments   viii

Preface   ix

PART I: GENRE

Introduction   3

1/STEPHEN NEALE
  Genre and Cinema   6

2/MICK EATON
  Television Situation Comedy   26

3/GEOFFREY HURD
  The Television Presentation of the Police   53

4/Parodying Genre: The Case of *Gangsters*   71

5/PAUL KERR
  Gangsters: Conventions and Contraventions   73

6/RICHARD PATERSON
  Gangsters: The Pleasure and the Pain in the Text   79

PART II: THE DISCOURSES OF TELEVISION

Introduction   85

1/STUART HALL, IAN CONNELL, LIDIA CURTI
  The 'Unity' of Current Affairs Television   88

2/CHARLOTTE BRUNSDON AND DAVID MORLEY
  Everyday Television: *Nationwide*   118

3/Introduction: Television and the World Cup   142

4/COLIN MCARTHUR
  Setting the Scene: *Radio Times* and *TV Times*   144

5/ANDREW TUDOR
  The Panels   150

6/GEOFFREY NOWELL-SMITH
  Television—Football—The World   159

7/CARL GARDNER AND ROBERT YOUNG
  Science on TV: A Critique   171

PART III: POPULAR FILM AND PLEASURE

Introduction   197

1/STEPHEN HEATH
   Jaws, Ideology and Film Theory   200

2/LAURA MULVEY
   Visual Pleasure and Narrative Cinema   206

3/COLIN MACCABE
   Realism and the Cinema: Notes on some Brechtian Theses   216

4/RICHARD DYER
   Stars as Signs   236

5/THOMAS ELSAESSER
   Narrative Cinema and Audience-Oriented Aesthetics   270

PART IV: HISTORY, POLITICS AND CLASSICAL NARRATIVE

Introduction   285

1/COLIN MCARTHUR
   Historical Drama   288

2/The *Days of Hope* Debate: Introduction   302

3/COLIN MCARTHUR
   Days of Hope   305

4/COLIN MACCABE
   Days of Hope: A Response to Colin McArthur   310

5/COLIN MACCABE
   Memory, Phantasy, Identity: *Days of Hope* and the Politics of
   the Past   314

6/KEITH TRIBE
   History and the Production of Memories   319

7/JOHN CAUGHIE
   Progressive Television and Documentary Drama   327

Film and Television Availability Note   353
Index   355

Members of the *Popular Culture* Course Team

Authors

Tony Bennett,
Course Team Chairman
Tony Aldgate
Geoffrey Bourne
David Cardiff
Alan Clarke
Noel Coley
James Donald
David Elliott
Ruth Finnegan
Francis Frascina
John Golby
Stuart Hall
Graham Martin

Colin Mercer
Richard Middleton
David Morley
John Muncie
Gill Perry
Bill Purdue
Carrie Roberts
Paddy Scannell
Grahame Thompson
Ken Thompson
Bernard Waites
Paul Willis
Janet Woollacott

Other Members

Jane Bailey — Course Manager
Susan Boyd-Bowman — BBC Producer
Kate Clements — Editor
Tony Coulson — Liaison Librarian
Liz Lane — Editor
Vic Lockwood — BBC Producer
Robert Nicodemus — Representative from the Institute of Educational Technology, the Open University

Lesley Passey — Designer
Mike Philps — BBC Producer
Sarah Shepherd — Editor

Acknowledgments

The editors would like to thank all members of the Open University Popular Culture course-team for their help in shaping this Reader, particularly Alan Clarke and John Muncie for suggesting articles for inclusion within it. Thanks also to the contributors for agreeing to allow their work to be re-published in an amended form, and to Edward Buscombe and Geoffrey Nowell-Smith of the British Film Institute for their very helpful and constructive role in preparing this Reader. John Taylor, of the Open University Publishing Division, should also be mentioned for his positive role in liaising between the Open University and the British Film Institute, as should Deirdre Smith for her patience and exemplary typing skills. Above all, however, thanks to Jane Bailey, Course Manager at the Open University, for both her efficiency and her dedication.

The publishers gratefully acknowledge the following for permission to reprint copyright material:
Screen and the authors for 'Television Situation Comedy' by Mick Eaton, 'Television—Football—The World' by Geoffrey Nowell-Smith, 'Visual Pleasure and Narrative Cinema' by Laura Mulvey, 'Realism and the Cinema: Notes on some Brechtian Theses' by Colin MacCabe, '*Days of Hope*' by Colin McArthur, '*Days of Hope*: a Response to Colin McArthur' by Colin MacCabe, 'History and the Production of Memories' by Keith Tribe, 'Progressive Television and Documentary Drama' by John Caughie; the author for 'Genre and Cinema' by Stephen Neale, © BFI Publishing; the author and Edward Arnold Ltd. for 'The Television Presentation of the Police' by Geoffrey Hurd; the authors for '*Gangsters*: Conventions and Contraventions' by Paul Kerr and '*Gangsters*: the Pleasure and the Pain in the Text' by Richard Paterson; the authors and the University of Birmingham for 'The "Unity" of Current Affairs Television' by Stuart Hall, Ian Connell and Lidia Curti; the authors for 'Everyday Television: *Nationwide*' by Charlotte Brunsdon and David Morley, © BFI Publishing; the authors for 'Setting the Scene: *Radio Times and TV Times*' by Colin McArthur and 'The Panels' by Andrew Tudor, © BFI Publishing; the authors for 'Science on TV: A Critique' by Carl Gardner and Robert Young; the author and *The Times Higher Education Supplement* for '*Jaws*, Ideology and Film Theory' by Stephen Heath; the author for 'Stars as Signs' by Richard Dyer, © BFI Publishing; Thomas Elsaesser for 'Narrative Cinema and Audience-Oriented Aesthetics'; the author for 'Historical Drama' by Colin McArthur, © BFI Publishing; the author for 'Memory, Phantasy, Identity: *Days of Hope* and the Politics of the Past' by Colin MacCabe.

Preface

The expansion of film and television studies over the past decade has been dramatic. Whether as separate areas of study or as components of courses in other subject disciplines, film and television now occupy a central place within the curricula of most institutions of higher and further education and are increasingly studied within secondary schools of all sorts and sixth-form colleges. Equally important, perhaps, the study of film and television has clearly severed the connections which in the 50s and 60s bound it, in a relationship of tutelage, to the more established disciplines, particularly literature. Indeed, the relationships between these have been, in some respects, noticeably reversed. Less inhibited by prevailing orthodoxies or by vested professional interests, recent debates in film and television studies have proved remarkably open to new influences with the result that those working in these areas have often pioneered theoretical developments that have been only belatedly registered within more traditional disciplines.

The readings collected in this volume are designed initially for use by Open University students in association with the television programmes produced for the Open University course on Popular Culture (U203). However, they are also intended to service the development of film and television studies more generally by making available — both to teachers and to students — a range of materials that is representative of recent work on film and television, particularly the latter. The emphasis throughout is placed not on the structures of broadcasting or the film industry, but on the structures of the texts which broadcasting institutions and the film industry circulate. Applying the techniques of structuralist and semiological criticism, as well as perspectives derived from recent developments in psychoanalysis, across a wide range of television programming — and a smaller range of films — the readings collectively offer an integrated perspective on the formal structures and mechanisms which typify the more influential forms of popular film and television.

Although the focus within each part of the Reader is different, all of the readings share a common concern with the ideological and political significance of the areas of television programming or film practice with which they deal. In the first Part, where the stress is placed upon television fiction, Stephen Neale's general theoretical analysis of the concept of genre and of its applicability to film and television paves the way for a consideration, by Mick Eaton and Geoffrey Hurd respectively, of the generic conventions of television situation comedy and police fiction and of their political and ideological articulations. Part I concludes with an examination of the case, exemplified by the series *Gangsters*, that a radical breach with dominant generic conventions is a necessary pre-condition for the production of politically progressive forms of television fiction.

The second Part of the Reader, by contrast, is concerned primarily with non-fictional areas of television programming; although not without remarking the extent to which these have been influenced by the narrative conventions of the dominant forms of television fiction. The areas of programming examined within this part — current affairs programmes, magazine programmes such as *Nationwide*, televised soccer, science documentaries — are uniquely televisual. They are, that is to say, peculiarly the products of television itself: new cultural forms which have few parallels or roots elsewhere. It is in these areas of programming that the apparatus of television is arguably mobilized in its most distinctive forms. It is also in these areas that television most conspicuously offers itself as a transparent medium, a 'window on the world', seemingly simply passing on to the viewer as economically as possible the given subject matters with which such areas of programming deal: the news, current affairs, sport, contemporary developments in science. The essays collected in this Part of the Reader dispute this medium's image of itself, pointing to the various editorial processes, signifying conventions and modes of address through which television constructs and mediates the 'realities' it allegedly simply reports, 'reflects' or transmits to the viewer.

Part III, a collection of readings addressing the subject of pleasure, moves away from television to the cinema. The central concern of these readings is with the means and mechanisms whereby popular films give rise to pleasurable responses of varying sorts on the part of the spectator. Owing to its peculiar — some would say inordinate — susceptibility to the influence of contemporary debates within psychoanalysis, the question of pleasure has occupied an important place within film theory over the last decade. Not just abstractly, however; it has been, above all, questions concerning the *politics* of pleasure that have occupied the centre of critical attention. The essay by Stephen Heath, which introduces this Part, illustrates, in an informative discussion of *Jaws*, the relevance of psychoanalysis to the study of pleasure and the relevance of both to questions of politics. This is followed by Laura Mulvey's seminal analysis of the ways in which dominant cinematic conventions install the viewer in a position of 'dominant specularity', affording a pleasure which derives from the control associated with the subordination of the image to his or her fetishistic gaze. In his essay on 'Realism and the Cinema: Notes on some Brechtian theses', Colin MacCabe mobilizes the psychoanalytic concepts introduced by Heath and Mulvey in a critique of the classic forms of realist narrative characteristic of the popular cinema. He argues that these efface their own political character in placing the viewer in a fixed position of knowledge from which the meaning of the narrative seems obvious, transparent, as if a literal transcription of reality rather than a constructed re-presentation of the real. An extract from Richard Dyer's book *Stars* concludes Part III, offering a forceful reminder that the forms of pleasure engendered by specific films cannot be understood independently of the patterns of identification that are operative within them by virtue of the star system — itself a kind of massive meta-text, elaborated across and informing the structure of the specific texts of individual films.

Finally, in Part IV of the Reader, we return to television again, and specifically to questions concerning the politics of television fiction. The readings collected here debate the case for and against attempts to use the dominant realist forms of television to convey a politically progressive content. The issues involved here are posed with particular regard to the area of tele-history, the dramatized reconstructions of the past which constitute such a staple component of television fiction. The debate centres around the much-celebrated serial *Days of Hope,* first broadcast in 1975, with Colin McArthur arguing the case for 'progressive realism' of this type whilst Colin MacCabe, with the qualified support of Keith Tribe, argues the contrary view in insisting that progressive television must break with the conventions of realism rather than attempt to 'fill' them with a 'left-wing' political content. In the concluding essay, written some time after the other readings in this Part, John Caughie takes a more balanced view, agreeing with many of Colin MacCabe's criticisms of progressive realism but nonetheless defending the work of politically committed television dramatists who make use of realist forms as a by no means negligible achievement when viewed within the prevailing context and institutions of television.

There are, of course, many areas of film and television that are not dealt with in this Reader; just as there are many articles which we would have liked to have included but did not have space for. Nonetheless, although not in a fully comprehensive way, the readings contained in this volume are representative of the more challenging and innovative approaches currently discernible within film and television studies — approaches which, in their commitment, strongly suggest that film and television are far too important to be simply left to professional film-makers and broadcasters and need constantly to be openly and critically debated.

PART I
GENRE

Introduction

The concept of genre has received relatively little serious attention in the recent history of film and television criticism; somewhat surprisingly in view of the central role that generic conventions play in organizing viewers' expectations. Cinema-goers and television viewers are probably more consciously aware of the differences which distinguish genres one from another than they are of any other sets of differences — those between realist and non-realist forms, for example — within both film and television as well as, of course, between them. Although we may not be able to formalize them, an implicit understanding of the differences between science fiction and historical romance, or between situation comedy and the crime series, constitutes a minimum condition for 'successful' viewing. We know, in each case, what to expect: what type of narrative will be on offer, how it will be resolved, what types of excitation and suspense will be associated with the unfolding of the narrative, and so on. In short, generic conventions both define for the viewer and install her or him within particular regimes of pleasure; they codify our viewing in pinning down the forms of pleasure it might be expected to engender.

In 'Genre and Cinema', Stephen Neale redresses this critical neglect of genre, attempting to re-think the concept in the light of the contributions made by semiology and psychoanalysis to the recent development of film and television theory in this country. Disputing earlier definitions according to which genre had been viewed either simply as a framework for organizing relationships of repetition and difference in the cinema or as an agreed code between film-maker and audience, facilitating the effective communication of intentions from the one to the other, Neale contends that 'genres are not to be seen as forms of textual codifications, but as systems of orientations, expectations and conventions that circulate between industry, text and subject'. The distinguishing features of a genre, he argues, depend less on formal properties of a particular type than upon the ways in which particular formal elements — which may be shared with other genres — are combined or articulated with one another across a range of related film practices, written into the structures of the narrative and the modes of address employed as an integral part of the cinema seen as, in Christian Metz's terms, a 'machine' for regulating the orders of subjectivity. 'As well as providing a means of regulating desire across a series of textual instances, and of offering an ordered variety of the discursive possibilities of cinema itself,' he writes in concluding the monograph from which the above essay is taken, 'genres also provide a means of regulating memory and expectation, a means of containing the possibilities of reading'. (Stephen Neale, *Genre*, BFI, 1980, p.55.)

Neale's essay is followed by two contributions which examine the distinguishing characteristics of arguably the most popular genres of contemporary television: situation comedy and the police series. It is also worth noting that these are distinctively *television* genres: they may have roots in pre-televisual forms and parallels and echoes in contemporary non-television forms (most notably film; especially in the film offshoots of television series such as *The Sweeney* and *Whatever Happened to the Likely Lads*); nonetheless, their provenance is, properly speaking, television. Mick Eaton gives this consideration central importance in his analysis of situation comedy, defining his concern as being with 'the specifically televisual parameters of these half-hour dramas ("the situation") rather than on questions of what makes them "funny" ("the comedy")'. Taking issue with the view that situation comedy can be regarded as merely a development from the earlier traditions of variety theatre and vaudeville, he argues that the distinguishing features of situation comedy — in particular, the requirements of a 'situation' that can be returned to, week after week, without any ultimate narrative resolution — derives uniquely from the specific requirements and structure of television. The argument is developed across a wide spectrum of situation comedy ranging from *The Burns and Allen Show,* which represented a formative moment in the history of the genre, to the more recent examples of *Going Straight* and *Come Back, Mrs Noah.*

In 'The Television Presentation of the Police', Geoffrey Hurd considers the television genre that has been perhaps most heavily and most contentiously invested with the demands of realism: the police series. Arguing against reflection theories, he contends that 'the police series does not simply reflect the social work of policing but must actively construct a coherent version of social reality within which the playing out of the nightly drama of law and order can be contained'. It is within this constructed world that the police series handles 'the contradictions and tensions which are the currency of policing'. Focusing particularly on *Z Cars* and *The Sweeney* and on the different means by which they establish their claims to realism, he outlines the ways in which these series fictively negotiate and imaginarily resolve a series of ideological tensions which have their roots in real social oppositions and contradictions.

Neale's contention that genres consist of 'systems of orientations, expectations and conventions that circulate between industry, text and subject' is, of course, as true of television as it is of the cinema. In the schedules of the BBC and the ITV companies such labels as 'drama', 'soap opera', 'situation comedy' and so on function as easily identifiable markers through which programme planners seek to produce an audience and, once produced, to limit and condition the possibilities of its response, the forms of its pleasure. Yet, particularly since the 60s, television has generated a series of parodic forms, particularly in the sphere of satire, where such series as *Monty Python's Flying Circus*, Spike Milligan's *Q7*, *Rutland Weekend Television* and, more recently, *Not the 9 O'Clock News* owe much of their comic effect to their open flirtation with audience expectations, parodying the established genres of television by carrying their conventions to excess, thus exposing their artifice. Parody has also frequently been an important instrument in the stock of devices at the disposal of radical film-makers and producers, a means of rupturing the expectations engendered by the dominant genres and of liberating the audience from the cinematic or televisual 'machine' by placing it on the threshold of new orders of signification.

Paul Kerr and Richard Paterson consider the possible effects of formal strategies of this kind in relation to *Gangsters*. Originally a single play produced for the *Play for Today* spot in 1975 by the B B C Regional Drama Department at Pebble Mill, Birmingham, the success of this play gave rise to two subsequent series — each of six episodes — in 1976 and 1978 respectively. A 'take-off' of the realistic crime thriller, *Gangsters* breaks virtually every rule in the book: it subverts conventional forms of identification, eschews narrative closure, constantly disavows the claims of realism in revealing — indeed, wallowing in — its own fictive and constructed nature. *Gangsters* is by no means the only instance of contemporary popular television which turns its face resolutely against conventional genre expectations; it is, however, the series within which this project has been perhaps most consistently and most extremely realized — a fact which, as Richard Paterson concludes, 'makes it an important text in terms of television'.

Genre and Cinema

The cinema is not simply an industry or a set of individual texts. Above all, it is a social institution. As Christian Metz writes in 'The Imaginary Signifier':

> The cinematic institution is not just the cinema industry (which works to fill cinemas, not to empty them), it is also the mental machinery — another industry — which spectators 'accustomed to the cinema' have internalised historically and which has adapted them to the consumption of films. (Metz, 1975, p.18.)

Not only a set of economic practices or meaningful products, cinema is also a constantly fluctuating series of signifying processes, a 'machine' for the production of meanings and positions, or rather positionings for meaning; a machine for the regulation of the orders of subjectivity. Genres are components in this 'machine'. As systematised forms of the articulation of meaning and position, they are a fundamental part of the cinema's 'mental machinery'. Approached in this way, genres are not to be seen as forms of textual codifications, but as systems of orientations, expectations and conventions that circulate between industry, text and subject. [. . .]

GENRE AND NARRATIVE

Narrative is always a process of transformation of the balance of elements that constitute its pretext: the interruptions of an initial equilibrium and the tracing of the dispersal and refiguration of its components. The system of narration characteristic of mainstream cinema is one which orders that dispersal and refiguration in a particular way, so that dispersal, disequilibrium is both maintained and contained in figures of symmetry, of balance, its elements finally re-placed in a new equilibrium whose achievement is the condition of narrative closure.

Two points are important here. The first is that the 'elements' in question, their equilibrium and disequilibrium, their order/disorder, are not simply reducible to the signified components of a given narrative situation, nor are they solely the product of the narrative considered as a single discourse or discursive structure. Rather, they are signifiers articulated in a narrative process which is simultaneously that of the inscription of a number of discourses, and that of the modification,

6

restructuration and transformation they each undergo as a result of their interaction. The second point, following on from this, is that equilibrium and disequilibrium, order and disorder are essentially a function of the relations of coherence between the discourses involved, of the compatibilities and contradictions that exist between them. Moreover, a definitive equilibrium, a condition of total plenitude, is always an impossibility. Disequilibrium, particularly in the form of dramatic conflict, is actually a means of containing that impossibility: it sutures* a lack which, if the equilibrium were to be simply maintained, would insist all the more strongly, all the more uncomfortably in the interstices of an ever more frenzied repetition.

Genres are modes of this narrative system, regulated orders of its potentiality. Hence it may be possible to begin here to indicate some of the elements of their specificity, some of the ways in which particular genres function simultaneously to exploit and contain the diversity of mainstream narrative. Firstly, it is necessary to consider the modes in which equilibrium and disruption are articulated, and the ways in which they are specified, represented differently and differentially, from genre to genre. In each case, the marks of generic specificity as such are produced by an articulation that is always constructed in terms of particular *combinations* of particular types or categories of discourse. The organisation of a given 'order' and of its disruption should be seen always in terms of conjunctions of and disjunctions between multiple sets of discursive categories and operations. For example, in the western, the gangster film and the detective film, disruption is always figured literally — as physical violence. Disequilibrium is inaugurated by violence which marks the process of the elements disrupted and which constitutes the means by which order is finally (re)established. In each case, equilibrium and disequilibrium are signified specifically in terms of Law, in terms of the presence/absence, effectiveness/ineffectiveness of legal institutions and their agents. In each case too, therefore, the discourses mobilised in these genres are discourses about crime, legality, justice, social order, civilisation, private property, civic responsibility and so on. Where they differ from one another is in the precise weight given to the discourses they share in common, in the inscription of these discourses across more specific generic elements, and in their imbrication across the codes specific to cinema. Of course, there are other genres which deploy figurations of violence. But the difference resides in the nature of the discourses and discursive categories employed in the specification of the order disrupted and the disorder instituted by that disruption.

For instance, violence also marks the horror film, most evidently in

---

* In anatomy, suture refers to the stitching together of the lips of a wound in surgery. In psychoanalysis it refers to the juncture of the imaginary and the symbolic. For a further elaboration in this latter context see Stephen Heath, 'Notes on Suture', in *Screen*, vol.18, no.4, Winter 1977/78 as well as the essays by J. A. Miller and J.-P. Oudart in the same issue.

films where a monster — werewolf, vampire, psychopath or whatever — initiates a series of acts of murder and destruction which can only end when it itself is either destroyed or becomes normalised, i.e. becomes 'the norm', as in some of Polanski's films (*Rosemary's Baby, Dance of the Vampires*) or in Herzog's *Nosferatu*. But what defines the specificity of this particular genre is not the violence as such, but its conjunction with images and definitions of the monstrous. What defines its specificity with respect to the instances of order and disorder is their articulation across terms provided by categories and definitions of 'the human' and 'the natural'. The instances where the 'monster' is not destroyed but ends instead by pervading the social fabric in relation to which it functioned as 'monster', thus becoming integrated into it, becoming normalised, constitute a special option for the horror genre, testifying to the relative weight of discourses carrying the human/nature opposition in its discursive regime, relativising or even displacing entirely the Law/disorder dichotomy in terms of which violence operates in the western, the detective and gangster films. The monster, and the disorder it initiates and concretises, is always that which disrupts and challenges the definitions and categories of the 'human' and the 'natural'. Generally speaking, it is the monster's body which focuses the disruption. Either disfigured, or marked by a heterogeneity of human and animal features, or marked only by a 'non-human' gaze, the body is always in some way signalled as 'other', signalled, precisely, as monstrous. A variant on this is the inscription of a disruption in the spatio-temporal scales governing the order of the 'human' and of 'nature', producing figures such as giants — be they animals or humans — or, alternatively, homunculi, dwarfs, and so on. In other words, the order involved here is explicitly metaphysical. Moreover, narrative disruption and disequilibrium are specified overtly in terms of discursive disjunctions between 'the empirical' ('the real') and 'the supernatural' ('the unnatural'), as well as between the concatenation of diegetic events and the discourses and discursive categories used by the characters (and, often, the audience) to understand them. *Psycho* is a perfect case in point. The events that occur are 'explained' in a way which upsets conventional categories of character motivation and sexual identity, although in this instance the 'metaphysics' are given a 'scientific' rather than a religious character. The latter tends to predominate in the gothic horror film — such as *Dracula,* or *Frankenstein* — where 'unnatural' acts of brutality and destruction, 'impossible' metamorphoses of identity, 'supernatural' happenings of all kinds, defy the principles both of common sense and of science — at least as these are defined in the films. Hence the narrative process in the horror films tend to be marked by a search for that discourse, that specialised form of knowledge which will enable the human characters to comprehend and to control that which simultaneously embodies and causes its 'trouble'. The function of characters such

8

as the psychiatrist in *Psycho* or Van Helsing in the *Dracula* films is precisely to introduce and to articulate such a discourse.

In the musical and the melodrama, violence may figure in an important way, as it does for instance in *West Side Story* or *Written on the Wind,* but it is not a defining characteristic as such, either in terms of the register of disruption or in terms of its diegetic specification. In both genres the narrative process is inaugurated by the eruption of (hetero)sexual desire into an already firmly established social order. That is to say, the discourse of the law and 'criminality' is marginalised although by no means eliminated, while the metaphysical discourse of the horror genre is either refused entirely or explicitly designated as phantasy. The role of the policeman in *West Side Story* and that of the court in *Written on the Wind,* when compared to the roles these agencies of the legal apparatus play in *Anatomy of a Murder* (each in its own way a family romance), illustrate the difference in status of the legal discourse in the different genres. In the melodrama and the musical, the eruption of sexuality is not inscribed primarily across the codes of legality, as it can be in the thriller or the detective genre, and even, occasionally, in the western (e.g. *Stagecoach*). On the contrary, the disequilibrium inaugurating the narrative movement is specified as the process of desire itself and of the various blockages to its fulfilment within an apparently 'common sense', established social order. In other words, the process of desire in melodrama interrupts or problematises precisely the order the discourse and actions of the law have established in the face of 'lawlessness' and social disorder. Melodrama thus puts into crisis the discourses within the domain circumscribed by and defined as the legally established social order, the kind of order instituted at the end of westerns and detective films. Melodrama does not suggest a crisis of that order, but a crisis within it, an 'in house' rearrangement.

In short, it should be clearly understood that in each example mentioned here, I am not referring to elements which, in and of themselves, are absolutely exclusive to particular genres. Generic specificity is a question not of particular and exclusive elements, however defined, but of exclusive and particular combinations and articulations of elements, of the exclusive and particular weight given in any one genre to elements which in fact it shares with other genres. Heterosexual desire, the element mentioned here, is of course by no means exclusive to the musical or to the melodrama. But the role it plays in these genres is specific and distinctive. Not only does it have a much greater functional role in the generation of the narrative, not only does it provide the motivation for the actions of the principal characters, it also occupies a central as opposed to a secondary or peripheral place in the discursive ensemble mobilised and shaped by these particular genres. In short, its presence is a necessity, not a variable option.

In the musical, desire and satisfaction are generally signified in terms of two sets of discursive oppositions: firstly, that between the private and the public, and secondly, that between social success and failure. Each of these two sets is then articulated across a scale whose polar instances are harmony on the one hand and discord on the other.

Harmony and discord are terms used to specify aspects of equilibrium and disequilibrium in music. In this context, they are used to suggest that it is the specific inscription of music as the determining principle in the arrangement of sound-image relations as well as of relations between elements within the image that distinguishes the genre as such. It is the specific inscription of music into the plurality of discourses that constitute the text which ultimately shapes, determines and marks the register in which equilibrium and disequilibrium achieve their most intense expression and in which narrative resolution finally occurs. In other words, sequences of song and dance represent a shift in the regime of the narrative discourse, marked, for example, by a different articulation of body and voice. These sequences, this 'other' regime, woven into the narrative, allow a particularly intense and coherent statement of the conflicts, tensions and problems that traverse the narrative as a whole. They also, at certain points in some musical films, represent the terms of a resolution to these conflicts, tensions and problems; in the 'Dancing in the Dark' sequence in *The Band Wagon,* the fact that Cyd Charisse and Fred Astaire dance together so perfectly indicates that their initial hostility to one another will be and to a large extent already has been resolved in terms of a rhythmical interaction of their bodies. Whether such a resolution occurs in all song and dance sequences or not, the point here is that these musically determined sequences, in their completion and perfection, represent the discursive mode in relation to which resolution or lack of resolution are to be measured and through which stability and equilibrium are ultimately to be achieved.

Of course, the body and the voice are not the only elements involved here — decor, colour, dress, camera movement, editing and so on are all involved; all are transformed and integrated, all are subject to an explicitly aesthetic form of organisation in so far as it is music which governs the arrangement of signifying relations between and within images as well as between image and sound. This may be why the musical has come to be regarded as the most 'stylised', the most 'aestheticised' of genres, and why it is marked by the constant presence of discourses on art, entertainment and show business.

Finally, the different forms of comedy work by specifying disruption in relation to discourse itself. Crazy comedy tends to articulate order and disorder across the very mechanisms of discourse, producing incongruities, contradictions and illogicalities at the level of language and code, while social (situation) comedy, on the other hand, tends to specify its disorder as the disturbance of socially institutionalised discursive hierarchies. It is important to stress that these two forms are indeed only tendencies. There are overt social implications in much of the comedy of Chaplin, the Marx Brothers, Tashlin and Hawks, just as there are frequent instances of a play with the logical mechanisms of discourse in Lubitsch, Capra and Sturges. But nevertheless the two types of comedy remain distinct as specific emphases and tendencies.

Paul Willemen has pointed to the mode of operation of crazy comedy in his discussion of the workings of the gags in Tashlin's cinema. He stresses in particular the extent to which these gags are dependent upon specifically semiotic sets of logic, the extent to which they function by treating the elements in a situation as units of a language:

> . . . there are a great number of gags based on variations of the basic forms of combination. If we accept that the basic forms of combination consist of the bringing together of two or more items to produce a new structure, then a variation is constituted by such gags as the baby getting lost in the powder in *Rock-A-Bye-Baby* or the man in a plaster cast disappearing in *The Disorderly Orderly*. The plaster cast gag is not merely a form of subtraction, because the viewer is not supposed to consider the unfortunate invalid as a composite of parts of equal value — plaster cast plus man. In the same way, neither is a powdered baby regarded as a combination of two elements of equal value, either of which can be withdrawn from the equation — the baby without the powder/the powder without the baby. In this way, Tashlin's gags of this kind literally deconstruct, disassemble visual/semantic units. [Willemen, 1973, pp.122–4.]

At the purely verbal level, where mechanisms of this kind are at their most overt as operations of discourse, one could point to a number of examples in the Marx Brothers films, where dialogue follows a logic of its own, thus leading to semantic and dramatic absurdities: 'I know where the suspects are: they're in the house next door' — 'But there isn't any house next door' — 'Then we build a house next door'. As detectives in *Animal Crackers*, they reason their way from 'This portrait was painted by a left-handed painter' to 'This picture was eaten by a left-handed moth'.

Many of Chaplin's gags, to return to the situation level, are dependent upon a mixing of the registers of behaviour and action. The meal of boots in *The Gold Rush* is a classic example, as is the making of the bed in a water-filled trench in *Shoulder Arms*. Both depend upon a logic in which behaviour is both logical and illogical, both appropriate and inappropriate given the situation in which it takes place. In both instances, however, there are also overt 'social' implications to the gags and to the structure upon which they depend.

Social comedy proper proceeds by mapping the field of a socio-discursive order, a field whose nodal points tend constantly to be those of class and sexuality. The order is disturbed in order for its hierarchy to be re-arranged. The establishment of a new, 'better' hierarchy is the condition of narrative closure. Capra's films are particularly clear examples. Thus both in *Mr Smith Goes to Washington* and in *Mr Deeds Goes to Town* the initial narrative equilibrium is specified in markedly 'social' terms (in *Mr Smith* it concerns political institutions and is centred on the Senate; in *Mr Deeds* it concerns wealth, particularly as centred in and distributed by financial institutions). That equilibrium, centred in each case in the city, is presented as both corrupt and unjust and yet as normative within its milieu. A naive, 'idealistic' character comes from outside and operates, in narrative terms, to re-order the initial elements so that the final equilibrium is different, and to focus that re-ordering as ethically necessary. The outsider is the bearer of a discourse which, in its contrast with the city discourses, produces humour and comedy, and which in its principles articulates the terms in relation to which the final equilibrium is to be measured.

GENRE, NARRATIVE AND SUBJECT

Narrative is not simply a product or a structure, nor even a process of production, an activity of structuration. It is both a process of production and an activity of structuration, but it is so in and for a subject. The subject is a function, or better, a functioning of signification. Different modes of signification produce different functionings of subjectivity, moving the subject differently in their various semiotic processes, producing distinct modes of address. Mainstream narrative is a mode of signification which works constantly to produce coherence in the subject through and across the heterogeneity of the effects that it mobilises and structures. Specifying its effects as narrative functions, pulling those functions into figures of symmetry and balance, mainstream narrative binds together, implicating the subject as the point where its binding mechanisms cohere, the point from where the deployment and configuration of discourses makes 'sense'. The subject thus is 'carried through against the dispersion, the multiple intensities of the text of the film'. [Heath, 1975, p.99.]

Coherence, therefore, is not simply a fact of closure, of the achievement of the stability of an equilibrium, of the production of a final unified position. It is also and equally a fact of the process which leads to that closure, of the balance of the movement of positioning that disequilibrium itself involves. Its operation is complex and multiple rather than simple and single. Narrative disruption, for example, does not involve the disturbance of one subject position as such, but rather the disturbance of a set of positions, the production of a disphasure in the relations between a plurality of positions inscribed in a plurality of discourses. The coherence of mainstream narrative derives largely from the way in which that disphasure is contained as a series of oscillations

12

that never exceed the limits of 'dramatic conflict' (that never, therefore, exceed the limits of the possibility of resolution), and from the way in which such conflict is always, ultimately, articulated from a single, privileged point of view.

Fundamental, then, to the economy of the subject in mainstream narrative, to the economy of its mode of address, is the achievement of the maintenance of a coherent balance between process (enunciation) on the one hand, and position (enounced) on the other. But this economy can be structured in a variety of ways. Genres represent systematisations of that variety. Each genre has, to some extent at least, its own system of narrative address, its own version of the articulation of the balance. Each genre also, therefore, engages and structures differently the two basic subjective mechanisms which any form of the balance involves: the want for the pleasure of process, and the want for the pleasure of its closure.

For example, consider the detective film and the characteristic mode of its narrative address, suspense. Suspense is not, of course, exclusive to the detective genre, but it is nonetheless essential to it, tying in as it does with a narrative structured around the investigation of the principle of narrative disorder itself in the sense that the enigma is a mystery, an 'incoherence' functioning as the trigger for a story, which, as it unfolds, eliminates the enigma and comes to an end when its disorder has been abolished. The narrative of the detective genre thus directly dramatises the tension inherent in the signifying process through the mobilisation of a series of discourses concerned specifically with the Law, with the symbolic and with knowledge. What the enigma-investigation structure serves to effect is an amplification of the tension inherent in all 'classic' narratives: the tension between process (with its threat of incoherence, of the loss of mastery) and position (with its threat of stasis, fixity or of compulsive repetition, which is the same thing in another form). This tension, which informs all semiotic systems in so far as they are grounded in desire, realises itself in two distinct forms of pleasure: firstly, pleasure in process in the face of the potential 'boredom' of stasis; and, secondly, pleasure in position in the face of the anxieties potentially attendant on unlimited process. The amplification of this tension is largely due to the fact that the detective film dramatises the signification process itself as its fundamental problem: the Law is at issue directly in the investigation, that is to say, in the play between two fluctuatingly related sets of knowledge, that of the detective and that of the audience. In the detective film, the detective *and* the audience have to make sense of a set of disparate events, signs and clues. The 'risk' for the detective being represented in the narrative is a risk of violence and death. The risk for the audience is a loss of sense and meaning, the loss of a position of mastery. On the other hand, though, for the audience the process of the narrative is the primary source of its pleasure. The viewing subject is thus suspended in a structure which stretches the tensions of classic

13

narrative to breaking point though never, axiomatically, beyond it.

There is an important dimension to suspense, and indeed to narrative address in general, which, again, the detective film illustrates particularly well. Narrative is always and essentially a means of organising and articulating process, of organising and articulating both the temporal flow of the text, and the flow, the fluctuation of the subject within it. In the words of Stephen Heath, narrative is thus always and essentially:

> a system which, positioning and effecting, is a ceaseless performance *of the subject in time for the reality given, of subject-time.*
>
> The performance of subject-time is itself a complex time, phasing between two constant moments that — these remarks concern classic narrative cinema, the commercial exploitation of film — are layered together : the subject-reflection and subject-process (the layering and balance of the two being the film's performance of subject-time). The subject-reflection is a narrative effect (or series of effects): in the movement of the chain of differences — the flow of multiple intensities of image and sound — the narrative defines terms for the movements of the chain, specifies relations and reflects a subject as the direction of those relations, produces the coherence of view and viewer. . . Going along with the subject-reflection, the subject-process is just that: the *process,* all the elements of the system in its production-performance, the whole apparatus of the representation: is a *multiple circulation,* the perpetual movement of difference . . . [Heath, 1977, p.9.]

Mainstream narrative regulates complexly the times of its semiotic processes by balancing, on the one hand, points of advance in ceaselessly pushing the flow of text and subject forward, and, on the other hand, points of recall in ceaselessly containing that process in figures of repetition, folding it back on itself into the retrospective coherence of memory. But it can do so in a variety of ways, through a variety of modes of address institutionalised in a variety of genres.

Returning to the detective film, the function of the enigma is to structure the generation of suspense, but it achieves this not simply by articulating the narrative as a puzzle, but also by specifying the puzzle in particular temporal terms. The enigma focuses two initially separate times, the past time of the story behind the crime and the present time of its reconstruction. Indeed the enigma in many ways is that separation of times. Eventually, the two times are brought together coherently and the enigma is resolved. A coherent memory is thus constructed across the separate instances of the story of the crime, the story of its investigation, and the process of the text itself: the memory constructed within the film duplicates the memory constructed by the film. This temporal duplication, the creation of a double temporal tension, is precisely that which marks and generates the tension referred to earlier. It is therefore also

14

that which marks and generates its suspense, the temporal dimension of which has been outlined by Barthes as follows:

> On meeting in 'life', it is most unlikely that the invitation to take a seat would not immediately be followed by the act of sitting down; in narrative these two units, contiguous from a mimetic point of view, may also be separated by a long series of insertions belonging to quite different functional spheres. Thus is established a kind of logical time which has very little connection with real time, the apparent pulverisation of units always being firmly held in place by the logic that binds together the nuclei of the sequence. Suspense is clearly only a privileged — or exacerbated — form of distortion: on the one hand, by keeping a sequence open (through emphatic procedures of delay and renewal) it reinforces the contact with the reader (the listener), has a manifestly phatic function; while on the other, it offers the threat of an uncomplicated sequence, of an open paradigm (if, as we believe, every sequence has two poles), that is to say, of a logical disturbance, it being this disturbance which is consumed with anxiety and pleasure (all the more so because it is always made right in the end). [Barthes, 1978, p.119.]

This point, apparently so banal, is in fact fundamental not only for understanding the economy of pleasure in the mainstream text, but also for understanding the function of genres themselves: genres institutionalise, guarantee coherence by institutionalising conventions, i.e. sets of expectations with respect to narrative process and narrative closure which may be subject to variation, but which are never exceeded or broken. The existence of genres means that the spectator, precisely, will always know that everything will be 'made right in the end', that everything will cohere, that any threat or any danger in the narrative process itself will always be contained.

Suspense is equally as powerful and equally as characteristic, with respect to generic address, both in the gangster film and in the thriller. These genres, however, inscribe their suspense differently, through different narrative structures and in conjunction with different diegetic conventions. Suspense in the gangster film derives from an amplification of the tensions of narration, not by augmenting the threat of incoherence through the constitution of the narrative as a puzzle, nor by specifying that tension across a temporal axis of past and present. Instead, it is achieved, firstly, by identifying the necessity for the existence of the narrative with the existence of the gangsters' activities while identifying the necessity for narrative closure with the existence of the Law. In the gangster film, of course, the Law tends to be specified in terms of a particular, datable, historical law, such as prohibition. The Law in the detective film is less specific, coming often to function as the signifier of symbolic Law itself. The pleasures and anxieties of position are thus made more complex by being articulated across an ideological division between the legal and the illegal. Since the former provides the grounds for a primary identification with the narrative as such, and since the latter provides the grounds for secondary forms of identification, a series of potential gaps and contradictions opens up, across which narrative and subject are suspended. Secondly, suspense is achieved by structuring the narrative across an axis of present and future. One of the major activities in which the gangsters engage is planning — the planning of robberies, assassinations, vendettas, and so on, of activities which will serve to sustain and increase individual as well as corporate wealth and power. The narrative and its subject are thus constantly anticipating. It is the play with this anticipation, the tension in the potential or actual difference between what is planned and what occurs, which provides a major means by which suspense is engendered and articulated in the gangster film, both at the micro-narrative level (the level of scene or segment) and at the level of the structure of the narrative as a whole.

Suspense involves a particular form of affect, what Barthes has called a 'thrilling of intelligibility' [ibid, p.119], and it is to this form that the generic label 'thriller' refers. The thriller in fact may involve a variety of narrative structures and may create its suspense in various ways. It may borrow elements from the detective film: the positioning of an enigma — Hitchcock's McGuffin — and the use of an investigative structure; or it may borrow from the gangster film, playing off identification and pleasure by focusing much of the narrative on the activities of a criminal protagonist; or it may use elements and structures of its own. One of the commonest of these involves the placing of its protagonist in a position such that he (or, occasionally, she) is under threat both from a set of criminals and from the Law. Examples here would include Lang's *Woman in the Window*, Sirk's *Shockproof* and, of course, many of Hitchcock's films — *Strangers on a Train, The Thirty Nine Steps, North by Northwest* and so on. This increases not only the danger to the protagonist, but also the number and complexity of the tasks that have to be performed if all the ends of the story are to be brought together coherently, if the narrative is to end 'satisfactorily'. Thus the wish for the narrative to continue is articulated across the fact that this involves a considerable number of risks, while the wish for it to end is articulated across the fact that the complexity of the situation in which the protagonist finds himself has fully to be worked out. Whatever the structure, whatever the specificity of the diegesis in any particular thriller, the genre as a whole, unlike that of the gangster or the detective story, is specified in the first instance by its address, by the fact that it always, though in different ways, must have the generation of suspense as its core strategy.

Other genres are marked by other modes of narrative address, other ways of articulating the two 'wants' of narrative, suspending the subject

16

in other structures of affect. In comedy, for instance, the mode of affect is laughter, a release of pleasure which comes from a structuring of the two narrative wants and pleasures across the point of intersection of two (or more) discourses, of two (or more) discursive structures or regimes, together with the economy, the appropriateness — the wit — with which the contradictions and resistances generated between them are overcome. This may occur firstly through a 'triumph' over that which is represented to be resisting, as, for example, in many of Buster Keaton's films, where what is signified as resisting is often, simply, 'reality'. Here laughter comes not only from the overcoming of the resistance, but also, and primarily, from the fact that that overcoming involves a drastic (but coherent) re-ordering of the logic of the discourses which, together, define the field and order of 'reality' in the film concerned. Alternatively, and secondly, it may come about through the 'triumph' of that which resists (as, for example, in a banana peel gag). Laughter here stems in particular from the way in which an anticipation of the inevitable is played across the specific temporal articulation of the event anticipated, from, precisely, the timing of the gag, joke or comic scene, the temporal — and logical — economy with which it is structured and realised, the suspense it embodies. Excellent examples of this type of comedy where gags are as it were telegraphed in advance but achieve their effect exclusively through timing, through the variations of the 'delay' between cause and effect, are to be found in Blake Edwards' work, and particularly in the *Pink Panther* series. [. . .]

Finally, the musical, though not perhaps associated with any particular mode of affect, has a particular form of address which stems from its balance of narrative and spectacle. As Patricia Mellencamp has noted, moments of spectacle, generally in the form of singing and dancing, are always separated off, to some degree at least, from the linear flow of the story. [Mellencamp, 1977.] These moments are moments of intense gratification and pleasure, realising the desire for coherence and process simultaneously in a harmony of bodily movement, voice, music and *mise en scène*. They tend to occur in particular at points of stress (whether for the characters, the narrative or the subject and its pleasures and desires), thus contributing towards an economy which in many ways is the antithesis of that of the genres of suspense: 'These breaks [in the narrative, instances of spectacle] displace the temporal advance of the narrative, providing immediate, regular doses of gratification rather than delaying the pleasures until The End.' [Ibid., p.92.]

Spectacle itself, however, cannot be sustained for any length of time without variation (otherwise the lack at the base of its apparent plenitude would begin to insist, thus disturbing the gratification). Hence the necessity, as far as mainstream cinema is concerned, for the narrative to return in order to provide that variation in a time that extends beyond that of the 'spectacular moment' itself. Therefore, rather than the two being in conflict, with spectacle 'subverting' narrative, as Mellencamp tends to argue, they in fact function to reinforce and support each other, the 'deficiencies' of the one being minimised by the 'virtues' of the other, and vice-versa. Moreover, in providing two registers of discourse within the overall coherence of a contained textual system, the musical doubles the possibilities of its semiotic effects while simultaneously doubling the forms of their coherence. Doubling the play of its desires and pleasures, it simultaneously doubles the modes of their binding together. [. . .]

FETISHISM

Fetishism is a psychic structure which psychoanalysis has shown to be founded upon the disavowal of sexual difference. As such, it 'turns' on the privileged signifier of that difference (presence/absence of the phallus) and characteristically involves a 'splitting of belief' as in the phrase: 'I know very well this is so, and yet . . .' Cinema activates fetishistic structures in a number of ways. Firstly, the cinematic signifier itself is such that it initiates an oscillation in the 'regime of credence' which it provokes or allows. The cinematic signifier is perceptually present, but it nevertheless exists as a trace of absence. As Metz put it: 'The actor, the decor, the words one hears are all absent, everything is recorded . . . it is the signifier itself . . . that is recorded, that is absence.' [Metz, 1975, p.47.] As such, the very status of the cinematic signifier inaugurates a 'splitting of belief', the regime of credence that can be characterised as 'I know very well, and yet . . .' (I know this is only cinema, and yet it is so 'present' . . .). Of course, there are other aspects of cinema, particularly of narrative-figurative cinema, which implicate viewers in fetishistic structures such as the use of stars' faces, representations of the female figure, uses of dress, etc. These aspects of cinema have been examined by Laura Mulvey and Danièle Dubroux, among others. [See Mulvey, 1975 and Dubroux, 1978.] In this context, the main point to note is that fetishism is a structure involving the production of regimes of credence and as such has a part to play in the 'reality effect' of cinema as well as in the establishing of the conventions of verisimilitude. Metz made the provision that:

> the precise nuance of the regime of credence that the spectator will adopt varies tolerably from one fictional technique to another. In the cinema, as in the theatre, the represented is by definition imaginary; that is what characterises fiction as such, independently of the signifier in charge of it. But the representation is fully real in the theatre, whereas in the cinema it too is imaginary, the material being already a reflection. [Metz, 1975, p.66.]

In mainstream narrative cinema, intent on the production of the

18

viewer's adherence to a coherent and homogeneous diegesis, the fetishism of the signifier becomes further implicated in the fetishism of fiction itself:

> The audience is not duped by the diegetic illusion, it 'knows' that the screen presents no more than a fiction. And yet, it is of vital importance for the correct unfolding of the spectacle that this make-believe be scrupulously respected (or else the fiction film is declared 'poorly made'), that everything is set to work to make the deception effective and to give it an air of truth (this is the problem of *verisimilitude*). [Ibid., p.70.]

This 'problem of verisimilitude' is in fact complicated by the existence of genres, as each genre has its own particular conventions of veri-similitude, over and above those of mainstream narrative fiction as a whole. As Metz implies, verisimilitude is never a question of 'fidelity to the real' (however one defines the real). It is always a function of systems of credibility, of modes of fetishistic belief. Within the overall framework of the 'regime of credibility' that mainstream narrative cinema itself represents, one in which the fetishism of narrative fiction is reduplicated by the fetishism of the cinematic signifier, genres function so as to provide and to institutionalise a variety of the possibilities of fictional credibility allied to a variety of the possibilities of 'cinematic credibility', thus binding the two together all the more strongly as the very ground of cinematic address, as the very basis of the relations between cinema and its spectators.

It should firstly be noted that some genres are conventionally considered to be 'more fictional' than others. Gangster films and war films, for example, tend to be judged according to strict canons of realism, whereas the musical, the gothic horror film and the phantasy/ adventure film (i.e. films like *The Thief of Bagdad* or *Jason and the Argonauts*) are recognised as either being more 'poetic' or else as involving more of the faculty of 'imagination', as being closer to 'phantasy' than to 'reality'. This difference stems to a large degree from the status accorded the codes and discourses involved in the two kinds of genre. Those involved in the latter, more immediately 'fictional' genres are always already socially defined as 'fiction' in one way or another. That is to say, these genres consist of bundles of discourses already defined as pertaining to the domain of the subjective, to the domain of imagination and phantasy. At most, they are characterised as represent-ing not factual reality but poetic or psychological realities. As the cinematic signifier is fictional from the outset, a property reinforced by the codes and discourses which combine to construct 'narrative fiction', these social definitions that precede the circulation of any given cinematic genre or text, in their turn reinforce this already double

19

fictionality. Each of these three layers activates and strengthens the fictional potentialities of the others. However, in genres such as war films or gangster films, a number (by no means all) of the discourses and codes deployed overlap with discourses involved in genres socially defined, perhaps not quite as scientific or documentary, but at least as non-fictional, e.g. newspaper reporting, sociology, the adoption of the 'press release' or of the front page headline style characteristic of, for instance, the work of Sam Fuller. In this way, connotations of 'non-fiction' spill over into or become attached to certain genres because some of their component discourses are also produced, classified and circulated by institutions whose business is supposed to be 'facts' and 'truth' rather than fiction and phantasy. This helps to explain why different genres appear to favour different types of source material to legitimise their fiction and anchor their regime of credibility. One type of genre, the less insistently 'fictional', will rely more on pronouncements by state agencies, government documents, history books, biographies, newspapers and newsreels, backed up with blueprints, maps, scale models, etc. On the other hand, the kinds of legitimating documents and references employed in the predominantly 'phantasy' genres will tend to be ancient texts, parapsychological treatises, myths, folklore, religion, etc. In the former, the fiction is balanced across the marks of a socially verified truth, while in the latter it is articulated in terms of socially classified phantasy. The two instances, however, do cross one another in genres like science fiction and psychological horror, where the elements of fiction and phantasy are intermingled with discourses marked as science, i.e. as non-fiction.

Of course, the 'realistic' genres do not involve total belief in the accuracy or the reality of their modes of characterisation, nor in the veracity of their narrative events or diegetic details. The division of belief inherent in all fiction still operates. But the mode of authenticity involved, the regime of credibility inaugurated, produces a balance of belief attenuating or deflecting to some extent the fiction's obvious fictionality, minimising the 'danger' of the spectator being caught in the contradictions lying at the heart of the division itself, the contradictions the 'split' is there to disavow. Of course this 'danger' still remains present and can never be evacuated totally. It can surface whenever there is a clash between the demands of authenticity and those of narrative fiction, which is quite a common occurrence in a genre such as the epic, where the 'reality' of the past that forms the diegetic pretext is so different, so other, so distant, that many of the codes and discourses needed for its construction are either lacking altogether in any verifiable form, or are constantly at odds with the demands of the cinematic institution. The details of costume and decor may be 'right' (though there is always some degree of compromise between 'historical accuracy' and current fashion), but the codes of speech, behaviour and character motivation are often so 'evidently' those of Hollywood rather than those of 'the past' that the balance between the two is easily upset. For example, Howard Hawks makes this point in an interview with Peter Bogdanovich in *Movie*, where, referring to *Land of the Pharaohs*, he complains:

> I don't know how a Pharaoh talks. And Faulkner didn't know. None of us knew . . . It was awfully hard to deepen [the scenes] because we didn't know how those Egyptians thought or what they said . . . You kind of lose all sense of values. You don't know who somebody's for and if you don't have a rooting interest, and you're not for somebody, then you haven't got a picture. [*Movie*, no.5, 1962, p.17.]

Generally, though, the balance in these genres is easily managed. The danger is more likely to occur in the genres of 'phantasy', where all the levels involved are heavily invested with marks of the fictional which in turn demands rigorous conventionalisation together with complex signifying strategies if the requirements of credibility are to be fulfilled. It is no accident, therefore, that these genres have persistently been marginalised, relegated to the realms of escapism and utopia (as has the musical) or classified as suitable mainly for children and adolescents. Nor, incidentally, is it any accident that they provide the ground for certain forms of cinephilia, where a fetishistic desire to know 'all about' cinema is concentrated in those forms of cinema in which fetishism is 'most evidently' at work, and in which it is most likely to be 'exposed' as such. The horror film, the phantasy/adventure film and the science fiction film in particular seem to involve special demands on the spectator's faculties of belief and on the cinema's capacities for sustaining it. The degree of 'success' with which this is done is measured by the degree to which particular modes of affect — horror, anxiety, fear, wonder — are supposed to be experienced by the spectator. This in itself is indicative of the degree to which these genres are concerned with fetishism and fetishistic modes of belief. Horror, anxiety and fear are all linked to the problematic of castration, while 'wonder' is a function of a division of belief so strong that it often requires the imaginary attribution of two spectators, one of whom is completely duped while the other 'knows better' and is not taken in at all. Alain Bergala, writing about the nature and function of 'children's films', makes the point very clearly:

> The term 'children's film' in fact functions as a standard of belief, designating a regime of make-believe where the child comes to occupy the imaginary position of the ideally naive, credulous spectator who takes images and fictions at face value. A regime very convenient for parents who in this way give themselves the illusion of accompanying their children to the cinema while it is they, as bashful spectators, who

accompany themselves with a false image of childhood as if they dared not occupy the position of the credulous spectator without such delegation. [Bergala, 1978.]

Finally, it is worth mentioning here the case of two genres with a special relationship to verisimilitude and to the fetishistic division of belief upon which its various forms depend, even though that relation does not necessarily entail particular consequences for the cinematic signifier itself. The first is that of the detective film, whose system of credibility as a genre depends upon an opposition between the laws of verisimilitude of the world of narrative and the truth that the unfolding of that narrative reveals. Tzvetan Todorov explained this aspect of the detective genre in the following terms:

The revelation, that is, the truth, is incompatible with verisimilitude, as we know from a whole series of detective plots based on the tension between them. In Fritz Lang's film *Beyond a Reasonable Doubt*, this antithesis is taken to extremes. Tom Garrett wants to prove that the death penalty is excessive, that innocent men are often sent to the chair. With the help of his future father-in-law, he selects a crime which is currently baffling the police and pretends to have committed it: he skilfully plants the clues which lead to his own arrest. Up to that point, all the characters in the film believe Garrett to be guilty; but the spectator knows he is innocent — the truth has no verisimilitude, verisimilitude has no truth. Then a double reversal occurs: the police discover documents proving Garrett's innocence, but at the same time we learn that his attitude has been merely a clever way of concealing his crime — it is in fact Garrett who has committed the murder. Again the divorce between truth and verisimilitude is total: if we know Garrett to be guilty, the characters are obliged to believe he is innocent. Only at the end do truth and verisimilitude coincide, but this signifies the death of the character as well as the death of the narrative, which can only continue if there is a gap between truth and verisimilitude. [Todorov, 1977, pp. 85–6.]

The point here is not that verisimilitude is somehow either ignored or foregrounded as investigated, but that the genre has its own laws of verisimilitude, even if this law is, in Todorov's words, the law of anti-verisimilitude:

By relying on anti-verisimilitude, the murder mystery has come under the sway of another verisimilitude, that of its own genre . . . There is something tragic in the fate of the murder mystery writer; his goal is to contest verisimilitude, yet the better he succeeds, the more powerfully he establishes a *new* verisimilitude, one linking his text to the genre to which it belongs. [Ibid., pp.86–7.]

What Todorov calls anti-verisimilitude precisely constitutes the basis of this genre's specific regime of verisimilitude. The detective genre turns on this splitting of belief, this fetishistic structure duplicating the fetishistic structure already inherent in cinema itself. As Paul Willemen pointed out in a discussion, the 'red herrings' are the explicit signifiers of this process in operation: they are the signifiers attracting or detouring the look in a process where we know very well they are red herrings, and yet . . . As in *Beyond a Reasonable Doubt*, the 'clues' planted are first red herrings for the readers of the *mise en scène*, i.e. the police, but then are revealed to have been red herrings for the viewers. Fritz Lang's film thus becomes, in Paul Willemen's words, a meditation on red herrings. Similarly, in other detective films, suspects are carefully signalled by means of 'sinister' lighting effects, acting tricks such as voice modulation, suspicious 'looks', 'significant' pauses, or camera movements drawing attention to a suspect presence of an unseen observer, or even close-ups of objects. Anti-verisimilitude only functions in relation to the establishment of a truth, and that truth can only be established if the consistency of the fiction is maintained. The convention of anti-verisimilitude means that 'suspension of disbelief', merely a misleading term for the splitting of belief, is actually integrated into the diegesis as a condition of the inherent narrative structure. It is not only the audience which has to suspend disbelief, it is also the character of the detective, the agent of the process of investigation and representative of the viewer in the diegesis, guiding the reading of the 'events'. But the twist lies, so to speak, in the fact that whereas the fictional detective suspends disbelief in order to discover the truth 'behind' the appearance, the spectator suspends disbelief in order to confirm the illusion, that is to say, the illusion of the fiction itself.

This structure of illusion and belief also constitutes the basis of comedy. Comedy always and above all depends upon an awareness that it is fictional. [See Mannoni, 1969.] What comedy does, in its various forms and guises, is to set in motion a narrative process in which various languages, logics, discourses and codes are, at one point or another — at precisely the points of comedy itself — revealed to the audience as fictions. This can occur in two basic forms. Firstly, it can occur in a mode in which the comic text itself periodically stresses its own artifice, in which the comedy stems primarily from the spectator's own credulity. A classic instance of this kind of comedy is Lubitsch's *To Be or Not To Be*, which sets up and constantly shifts between an extraordinarily complex set of layers of artifice and credulity. The opening sequence in particular is exemplary. We are confronted quite clearly by a representation of Adolf Hitler. The figure we see before us is not Hitler himself, but an actor playing Hitler. Equally, however, we are confronted with a desire to suspend our knowledge in order to participate in the construction of a conventional and coherent fiction. After all, there is always a gap between actor and role, especially in instances where the role is that of a real historical figure. [See Comolli, 1978.] There is a clear hesitation here which exists precisely because the gap is not fully closed, as it were, by the address of the text at this point: the parodic commentary prevents that. Similarly, when we move on to what appears initially to be a scene taking place in the headquarters of a Nazi general, there is a hesitation initiated by the fact that there is no textual indication that the scene is not to be read 'straight' — i.e. that it is not to be taken at 'face value' — while on the other hand, the general is played by Jack Benny, the star of the film and known comic actor. It is only when we are shown that the scene we have been witnessing is a theatrical rehearsal that we know definitively that it is not 'real' in fictional, diegetic terms. But then, of course, our belief, our credulity, has only shifted one step back, so to speak, to the level of the meta-scene within which the rehearsal scene has taken place.

The alternative mode of comedy is one that only plays on the languages, the logics, discourses and codes which the text highlights within the diegesis and the fictional characters' relationships to them. This mode of comedy plays on verbal 'wit', confronting or overlaying one discursive logic with another as in Marx Brothers comedies; or plays on disjunctions between discourses, modes of dress, behaviour etc. in different classes or social groups as in the comedy of Frank Capra. In this type of comedy, the spectator is maintained in a continuous and undisturbed mode of belief, against which the modes of belief of the characters in the discourses they inhabit/employ are measured. Although it remains the case that the nature of the spectator's credulity, unquestioned as it may be, is such that a recognition of the fiction as fiction remains far more essential than in other fictional modes.

In both modes, at both ends of the spectrum of comedy, the comic effect itself derives from a triple structure of belief, with credulity, 'knowledge', and fetishism proper as the three constant functions which are disturbed variously across the two basic instances of subjectivity involved: that of the characters in the fiction, and that of the spectators of the fiction.

(Extracted from *Genre,* London: BFI, 1980.)

References

Barthes, R. (1978), 'Structural analysis of narratives', in Heath, S. (ed.), *Image, Music, Text,* London: Fontana.

Bergala, A. (1978), 'Dora et la lanterne magique', *Cahiers du Cinéma,* no. 287, April 1978.

Comolli, J-L. (1978), 'Historical fiction — a body too much', *Screen,* vol. 19, no. 2, Summer 1978.

Dubroux, D. (1978), Review of *Fedora, Cahiers du Cinéma*, no. 294, November 1978.

Heath, S. (1975), 'Film and system: terms of analysis, part I', *Screen*, vol. 16, no. 2, Summer 1975.

Heath, S. (1977), 'Film performance', *Cinetracts*, vol. 1, no. 2, 1977.

Mannoni, O. (1969), 'L'illusion comique ou le théâtre du point de vue de l'imaginaire', in *Clefs pour l'Imaginaire*, Paris: Le Seuil.

Mellencamp, P. (1977), 'Spectacle and spectator: looking through the American musical comedy', *Cinetracts*, vol. 1, no. 2, 1977.

Metz, C. (1975), 'The Imaginary Signifier', *Screen*, vol. 16, no. 2, Summer 1975.

Mulvey, L. (1975), 'Visual pleasure and narrative cinema', *Screen*, vol. 16, no. 3, Autumn 1975.

Todorov, T. (1977), *The Poetics of Prose*, Ithaca: Cornell University Press.

Willemen, P. (1973), 'Tashlin's method: an hypothesis', in Johnston, C. and Willemen, P. (eds.), *Frank Tashlin*, Edinburgh Film Festival, 1973.

Television Situation Comedy

There has been virtually nothing written about the television situation comedy as a specifically televisual form.* The debates conducted from within the television industry tend to centre around questions of how 'realistic' or 'true to life' the situations and characters in such shows are; this was exemplified in the debates about racial, ethnic and gender stereotyping at [the 1979] Edinburgh Festival. Such arguments embody certain assumptions about the audience which need constant interrogation. In academic work on television the situation comedy has been all but ignored, which is surprising in view of the specifically televisual nature of the parameters of the situation comedy and of what one television practitioner (Michael Grade) has called the audience's 'insatiable demand for comedy'. [. . .]

Although in Raymond Williams' book *Television, Technology and Cultural Form,* there is some discussion of the antecedents of the situation comedy, it is seen largely (and, I would argue, ineffectively) in relation to the variety-sketch; there is no discussion of the situation comedy itself, in spite of Williams' own recognition of it as an 'effectively new form', a product, as it were, of that innovating form of television, namely 'television itself'. [Williams, 1974, pp.76-7.] Therefore, the focus of this article will be on defining the specifically televisual parameters of these half-hour dramas ('the situation') rather than on questions of what makes them 'funny' ('the comedy'). It must be stressed, however, that this attempt is not to be seen as part of an unmaterialistic project to define a 'single, coherent language' of television (where 'language' is made to equal 'transparent message-bearing vehicle', and where concessions towards semiotics are made only to recuperate the terms of bourgeois aesthetics in the instatement of 'the code' as a stylistic unit). Rather, it is an attempt to arrive at a base which simultaneously shifts the emphasis from discussion of television comedy either in terms of its antecedents (a 'history' of the 'forms' of 'popular entertainment') or in terms of its quality (either 'as television' or 'as comedy') and equally provides a grounding against which the heterogeneity of television's

---

* I am very grateful to the staff of the Comedy Department at the BBC Television Centre for allowing me to view their tapes, and to Erich Sargeant of the BFI for his technical assistance.

output in its specific instances can be related. The dangers of such an enterprise seem to me to be as follows: the heterogeneity of television's output must be related to what Heath and Skirrow have referred to as, on the one hand: 'the range of codes and systems at work in television over and across its matters of expression', and, on the other hand, to 'the particular inscriptions and movements of subject and meaning and ideology'. [Heath and Skirrow, 1977, pp.9-11.] If the first of these terms — the range of codes and systems — is undervalued then there is a danger of a possible collapse back into a debate over the ideological (never defined) 'message' or 'effect' of a particular programme, manifested, for example, in such questions as whether Alf Garnett's/Archie Bunker's character had any effect on 'deep-rooted attitudes' or whether they serve to 'reinforce bigotry and prejudice'. If the second — inscriptions and movement of subject and meaning and ideology — is under-valued then the danger is of a return to a formal aesthetic reading of the 'television message'. There is, however, a third danger which is harder to guard against: any reading of an instance of television in its production of meanings should be consistent with analysis of the actual conditions of production (defined in the widest possible way) within the television companies themselves. As information in this area seems difficult to obtain the contribution of this article to the project of a construction of a materialist reading of particular instances of television practice is presented as tentative in every aspect but one: the need to shift the terms of emphasis, analysis and definition away from those already provided by the television practitioners themselves.

We must have certain reservations about the establishment of 'television studies' as 'academically available as a new and self-centred discipline'. [Ibid., p.9.] While much of film studies has allowed itself to be involved with film history (a history which must always be unhistorical if it fails to deal with the presence of the spectator), work on television's past should be conducted in relation to the defined ideological demands of the present. Perhaps it is even a blessing in disguise that so little television archival material is available for study. The past is effaced by television as it happens — our memories involve us in the television's present by the constant re-inscriptions of its past (immediate and distant). This point will be developed more fully below in relation to two series — *Come back, Mrs Noah* and *Going Straight*. Bearing these remarks in mind, it is necessary to look briefly at an instance of television's situation comedy past in order to complicate Williams' proposed evolutionary model and to see the situation comedies of the past in relation to a model of the television situation comedy which I will attempt to develop.

The 'situation comedy' functions as a category in both BBC and IBA handbooks and in the structure of the television companies themselves as a species within the genus 'Light Entertainment', of which the other species is 'Variety'. In view of this it might be seen unsurprising that Williams concentrates on an unproblematic 'evolution' of both the solo turn and the variety sketch into 'situation comedy'. [Williams, 1974, p.66.] Moreover, this 'evolution' is 'essentially unevolved', merely adapted to fit the demands of an 'altered technology and the altered relations with audiences which television involved'. However, the specificities of these 'altered relations' need to be outlined before any further work can be done, and it is clear that they will not be arrived at merely by reference to an 'altered technology'. The techno-teleological problematic Williams advances here may perhaps fit the variety show, but it will certainly not suffice for the situation comedy.

It is necessary to go beyond his remark that 'a significant proportion of what might abstractedly be classified as television drama is composed in effect of variety-hall sketches' if we want to avoid returning to either a technological determinism which considers 'the forms of television' (and, in consequence, its forms of organizational structure) as a product of that medium's technology, or an uncritical 'abstraction' which sees 'television drama' solely as 'drama' on 'television' (a position implicit in much of what passes as television criticism in newspapers). Indeed, when Williams goes on to say: 'But in some very significant and popular cases, from *Steptoe and Son* to *Till Death Us Do Part*, to *All in the Family* an effectively new form has been created and needs to be separately considered' [ibid., p.66] it becomes clear that the use of variety-theatre antecedents alone is inadequate for that consideration. Whilst it may be a convenient 'rule-of-thumb' to consider that the nearer a television situation comedy is to a variety show solo-turn the more diffuse and indefined its paradigmatic situation may be (examples from the not too distant past might be Frankie Howerd's *Up Pompeii* and *Whoops Baghdad*, and going further back, *Here's Harry* with Harry Worth — where the 'situation' of the show is brought much more in line with the pre-defined talents of the particular performer, so that Howerd constantly addresses the audience directly, going through the motions of his 'turn' rather than satisfying the demands of a coherently constructed situation), the 'alteration' of such a turn from its antecedent form is irreducible to technological explanations.

The search for antecedents throws up other questions: What is the relation of the 'evolved' forms to the 'unevolved forms'? How does the relation of these forms with the variety-theatre sketch articulate with their relation to other instances of television drama not concerned with 'making the audiences laugh'? How does the television situation comedy relate to and differ from its other possible antecedents: the radio comedy,

British films of the 1950s? (I'm thinking specifically of Boulting Brothers' *Private's Progress* and *Brothers-in-Law* which provided the model for the television shows *The Army Game* and *Brothers-in-Law*, a practice, incidentally, still common in the States, witness such shows as *M.A.S.H.* and *Paper Moon* and the childrens' weekly comic, with its stable characters/situations each with its 'page-slot'.) Such questions cannot even be broached unless we have some idea of the television situation comedy as a defined species, and even then the answers would provide us with very little material for the interrogation of the present concerns of the situation comedy.

The Burns and Allen Show, a CBS show of which 239 programmes were made between 1950 and 1958, is an example of one of the earliest television situation comedies using established vaudeville characters. If we look closely at the development of the show we can see a process which is in no way an 'adaptation' or 'evolution' of vaudeville material to fit the technological exigences of television, but a repositioning of the spectator in relation to this material, a repositioning which cannot be explained by any McLuhanesque resort to 'the demands of the medium'. In the earliest series the show is obviously and markedly split between the first two-thirds which is a domestic situation comedy whose little narrative is played out, then immediately before the last set of commercials a female announcer says 'George and Gracie will be back to do one of their vaudeville routines'. Following the commercial break Burns and Allen return to do just that, for the final third of the half-hour slot. The last third of the show involves a filming of this routine: this requires a static long-shot by a single camera, with the stars standing on stage in front of a closed curtain — the way they would be seen on a vaudeville stage — the act is transferred 'directly' into the home. The first two-thirds of the show sets them in a domestic situation centred around the stock sets of the rooms of their Manhattan apartment. The important thing to note is that there is no discrepancy between their characters in the vaudeville routine, and their characters in the domestic situation. George is still dry, wise-cracking and laconic, and Gracie the woman with a logic of her own, causing confusion (and comedy) by the misunderstandings generated by the lack of that logic's intersection with other characters in the drama, but outside the central family situation. (Some of these 'outside' characters are regulars, such as Blanche and Harry Morton, the neighbours. Others are involved for one episode only — delivery boys, sales people, their son's new girl friend, and others — but all are caught up in the narrative to the extent that they are caught in the operations of Gracie's idiosyncrasies.) George is the only one who understands Gracie's logic and so remains unaffected and amused by the confusions it causes in others. Thus the classic paradigm of the upper-middle class domestic situation comedy is adhered to — the difference between this and a contemporary British example such as

Happy Ever After lies crucially in the fact that the show is built around (scripted, stage managed, etc.) the audience's supposed recognition of George and Gracie as vaudeville stars (familiar also from their radio shows) and a knowledge of their stage characters and routines (George as straight-man to Gracie's improbable stories about her 'kooky' family) which stipulates both the maintenance of these characters in the 'situation comedy' segment of the show, and the need to finish the show with a film of one of these very routines. So, in this early series the situation comedy and the vaudeville routine exist side-by-side. The difference with something like *Happy Ever After* is that the audience's supposed recognition of Terry Scott and June Whitfield (playing characters called 'June' and 'Terry' in the series) depends on a knowledge of their faces, characters and performances in other television situation comedies (e.g. Terry Scott in *Hugh and I*, June Whitfield in *Beggar My Neighbour*) not from any other variety situation. Indeed, Terry Scott's most famous 'vaudeville' character is of a little boy.

In the later series of *The Burns and Allen Show*, however, we notice some differences. George and Gracie have moved to California — the action now centres around the stock-sets of their Beverly Hills apartment, and of their neighbours', again the Mortons. The basic situation of the show remains unaltered despite the geographical shift. (People from outside coming into contact with Gracie's strange logic, George in perfect control refusing to be drawn into the resulting chaos, refusing initially to play the role of a *deus ex machina* who could clear up the mess right from the start and thus defuse the narrative development of the show). However, the show has changed in one fundamental way: the vaudeville routines which closed the earlier series and which provided the point of reference of the audience's recognition of Burns and Allen as stars have vanished completely (although George and Gracie do appear right at the end of the show to 'sign-off' with their vaudeville catch-phrase — 'say Goodnight Gracie' and so on; but crucially this now occurs on the balcony of their home, rather than on a vaudeville stage) and a new technique has emerged: when things start getting out of hand George will turn to the audience and say something like: 'Well, Gracie seems to have got herself into a mess again — I think I'll watch this with you', at which point he turns on his television set and apparently watches the next scene of the situation comedy drama, usually taking place in the stock-set of the next door neighbour's house.

This shift could be considered in several ways. It could prove Williams' point about 'adaptation' — the vaudeville routines disappear because they use up material too quickly, because they make for 'uninteresting' television. Therefore, the play with the television set comes in as a plot device to move the action along, giving George something to do, to keep him on set at times when he is not necessarily involved in the action and to preserve his laconic character in the absence of the vaudeville routine. Seen in this light the *Burns and Allen Show* represents a gradual but uncomplicated alteration or adaptation of the vaudeville routine to fit the demands of an altered technology. Alternatively, grandiose claims could be made for this as an 'alienation-effect' intervening to subvert the audience's relationship with their own television set. Or, without going that far, it could be seen as merely play, a comic device* whose non-naturalism can be explained by the BBC's notion that 'you can get away with more in comedy' (as in the more recent *Monty Python's Flying Circus* with its continual visual jokes not only on the forms, but also on the flow of television; false-endings, and so on).

Neither of these claims, however, would seem to deal adequately with this device and its historical location in the early days of television. Fundamentally, the device serves as a means of establishing, as a constant source of reference and plenitude, the immediacy of the television image — George watches what we watch as we watch the immediacy and democracy of television. In this early example of a television situation comedy we witness an inscription into the text not only of the television set as a necessary domestic appliance, but also the television viewing situation as guarantor both of the truth of the narrative and of the necessity of watching. George needs to watch it to equip himself with knowledge the other characters do not have — it is his, as it is our 'window-on-the-world'. Placed firmly in the centre of the domestic situation it is the channel through which he receives information about this domestic situation. Far from being an alienation device this particular piece of play serves to establish George as the index of our identification (the inscription into the text of the television-viewer) positioned, as Heath and Skirrow have argued, as 'a citizen in a world of communication' [op. cit., p.58], part and parcel of the process of socialisation of family life, of democracy, centre stage in the drama, laughable or not, of life. In this particular instance the device is blatantly, and perhaps successfully, executed, but when we come to look at *Come Back, Mrs Noah*, a BBC situation comedy from the summer of 1978, we will see a similar process in operation although now more can be taken for granted, taken 'as read' — the image of ourselves as television-viewers, however, needing continually to be re-affirmed.

So it becomes clear that during this 'adaptation' a fundamental change has occurred from 'George Burns the vaudeville comedian' to 'George Burns the situation comedy star', even though the routines and characterisation are not that different at all. What is changed has been effected through our repositioning and inscription as television viewers — consciously and blatantly undertaken at this stage perhaps because of the need to familiarise 'the audience' with television as an appliance and

---

* Indeed, as potential for comedy it is a very successful device — for example, George occasionally accidentally tunes into a 'real' television show, usually that of his show-biz 'rival' Jack Benny, just when he is making a quip about Burns.

as a medium, a familiarisation executed by allowing us to look at ourselves looking. Clearly, this process cannot be reduced to any technical aesthetic explanation of 'the demands of one medium over another'.

TOWARDS A TYPOLOGY OF THE SITUATION COMEDY*

The necessity to recognize television as signifying practice — a concentration on production as opposed to communication — must allow us to deal with the forms of television (in this instance the 'effectively new form' of the situation comedy) in their formal effectivity, not as aesthetic device or evidence of televisuality. Situation comedies are *series*, as opposed to *serials* and, before a typology of their varieties can be attempted, some of the parameters of the demands of the time-slot must be considered, if only because the idea of the series is such an all-pervasive consciously-held motivating force on the production of television programmes. 'There is within television as it exists at the moment . . . an inbuilt tendency towards the series, towards an idea that is capable of reproduction' [Alvarado and Buscombe, 1978, p.3], a reproduction justifiable in terms of capturing an audience, controlling a time-slot, winning the ratings battle. But more than this the series demands a constant repetition viewable across the terms of the single programme, the single series, the single evening's viewing, leading to Heath and Skirrow's characterisation of 'the central fact of television experience' as 'flow and regularity' ('television, the singular plural') a fact again ultimately irreducible to economic notions of 'the ratings battle' or aesthetic notions of 'limiting conventions' or 'formulae'. In a search for the general conditions of the series we must never lose touch of the signifying value of such conditions, the heterogeneity of their instances.

Phillip Drummond has characterized the series in the following way:

> Less over-flowing, more strictly episodic than the amorphous 'serial' (for instance *Coronation Street* or *Crossroads*), but noneless insufficiently discrete to impede the elaboration of a (more or less) continuous internal 'mythology' and hermeneutic for the series as a whole, particularly focused by the perpetuity of certain characters. Thus the overarching syntagmatics of the series as a whole, synchronizing motifs of the series dispersed along its linearity, may provide a form of 'overdetermination' for intra-episodic narrative and dramatic cruces. The extents to which the series 'forgets', that is to say 'suppresses', this synchronicity will naturally be of equal signifying value. [Drummond, 1976, pp.19-20.]

* Credits of British situation comedies can be found in 'Sit-com index' compiled by John Wyver, *Edinburgh International Television Festival 1978 — Official Programme.*

The 'situation', to fill the demands of the time-slot, the demands of constant repetition of/in the series, needs to be one whose parameters are easily recognizable and which are returned to week after week. Nothing that has happened in the narrative of the previous week must destroy or even complicate the way the situation is grounded. There are obvious exceptions to this: *The Fall and Rise of Reginald Perrin* for one. While classifiable as 'situation comedy' this could not be classified as a series — it started out rather as a serial with a definite temporal and narrative thrust. On the other hand many shows demand, even though the weekly show is a discrete unit, some sort of narrative progression across the series — the idea that the characters have progressed and developed because of learning from their past experiences in the interests of dramatic realism. For example, in *Whatever Happened to the Likely Lads* there was a definite temporal development underlining the narratives of each individual programme: the events leading up to Bob and Thelma's wedding, the honeymoon, the move to the new house, and so on. However, when we look closer at the series *Going Straight* (by the same script-writers, Dick Clement and Ian La Fresnais) which also has some temporal development, it will become clear that this never occurs at the expense of the rhythms and problematics of the individual half-hour slot and never leads to revelation of knowledge which would provide for an ultimate narrative closure to those problematics.

This means, as I have already, albeit tangentially, tried to demonstrate in relation to *The Burns and Allen Show*, that every situation which is established needs to have a fairly rigid inside/outside dichotomy which operates across the levels of characters, stock-sets, use of film-footage (for outside locations) as opposed to studio video-filming, and so on. That is, the dichotomy affects every aspect of the production down to its finest budgetary details. In its least complicated manifestations, events from the outside can be allowed to enter the situation to provide for a weekly narrative development, but these events/characters have to be dealt with in such a way that the parameters of the situation are ultimately unaffected by either their entry or expulsion so that the situation can be maintained and taken up again the following week. This structure, which will be demonstrated with examples from *Going Straight*, seems less to reflect a conservatism about the content of the shows (the above remarks have no necessary implications on what 'issues' are defined as 'inside' and what as 'outside' — the ideology resides institutionally in the structure); rather it would seem to be a demand of the time-slotting system — the series being such that its basic parameters can be taken up without change, without narrative progress from week to week. Thus, in a six-week situation comedy series such as *Going Straight* there will be six individual dramas, each with its basic narrative development with rhymes and repetitions sustained by running characters, stock sets, basic situational problematics and in which the narrative 'closure' at the end of each programme is 'open' enough to allow structural repetition across the series.

When we attempt to construct a thematic typology of the situation comedy series we find that the two basic situations used continually over the years are 'home' and 'work'. Again, this seems explicable not, as the practitioners would argue, in terms of a focusing of attention on an assumed 'reality' of a sociologically assumed 'audience', whose predominant ideological concerns centre around questions of the family or of work. Rather it would seem that these basic situations provide material for the constant repetition of character and theme, and fit the economic demands of the company's budget in allowing for the use of stock sets, and little or no use of filmed footage. The constant repetition and familiarity — the timeless nowness of television situations — is reflected in the titles of many shows, such as *Happy Ever After, Till Death Us Do Part, Are You Being Served?, The Train Now Standing, Meet The Wife*. Whenever verbs are used in the title of the series they are always in the eternal present. An exception to this is *Whatever Happened to the Likely Lads?* the implication in the title being that this is a question we have asked ourselves about our old favourites since we last saw them. The show, because it was revived after several years' absence, played on the past/present dichotomy continually; the past of the show being the memories of the previous series. Similarly, out of the index for situation comedies over the years there are virtually no shows set in the past. This seems surprising in comparison with the drama departments' almost obsessive pre-occupation with rifling the past. It is even possible to find examples of series set in the past in other usually contemporary genres such as the police series, for example *Sherlock Holmes, Lord Peter Wimsey, The Mind of Mr J G Reeder* and *Sexton Blake*. It could be argued that these, with the exceptions of the latter two, are actually adaptations of novels or short stories and, as such, are to be classed as 'classic serials', much the same as *The World of Wooster* and *The World of Wodehouse* for the comedy series. However, the situation comedy format usually demands contemporaneity. Apart from the Wodehouse adaptations the two other classes of series set in the past are the two Frankie Howerd vehicles (*Up Pompeii* and *Whoops Baghdad*, already mentioned as vehicles for Howerd's stand-up routines) and the recent series, all of which can be seen as spin-offs of the original model *Dad's Army*, viz: *It Ain't Half Hot, Mum, Backs to the Land* and *Get Some In*. All these shows concern aspects of service experience, though none are directly involved with the dramatic possibilities of 'men-at-war' — this is left to the drama and documentary productions. *Dad's Army* involves a Home Guard battalion in a Sussex village, *It Ain't Half Hot, Mum* (the title referring, obviously, to letters back home) a troupe of service entertainers in India in the Second World War (written by the same script-writers, Jimmy Perry and David Croft). *Backs to the Land* is about Land Army women, and *Get Some In* (its television model is *The Army Game*) about National Service conscripts in the 1950s. Structurally, all these shows have much in common with the paradigm of the 'work' situation. Why should these thematic concerns and historical locations provide the focus for the statistically minute percentage of situation comedies set in the past? The shows *Backs to the Land* and *Get Some In* are the Anglia and Thames responses to the ratings success of *Dad's Army*, but there is a sense in which the past that is drawn on in these series is not just a past that can be related to by the television viewer ('It was just like that when we were Land Army girls/National Service conscripts') but is rather the past of the character in a television family situation comedy: Mum as a Land Army worker and Dad as a private before they married, settled down and became Terry and June or George and Mildred or whoever. It would seem that television continually re-instates the terms of its own past, its own memory and our memory of it. The past which the novelistic of television (as memory-spectacle) continually re-appropriates is not only the re-imaging, the 're-membering', of the individual in terms of the coherence of his or her past, it is also, and crucially, the re-affirmation and re-positioning of the individual in relation not only to the past *in* television, but also to the past *of* television, and the past or present of the memory or actuality of him or herself as 'television viewer'. [See Heath, 1976.] Interestingly, the only situation comedy which, to my knowledge, is set in the future, *Come Back, Mrs Noah* (to be discussed more fully below) articulates convincingly with this argument. The jokes in the series set in war-time make continual references to rationing, the deprivations of the past, and so on, whereas the jokes in *Mrs Noah* betray a preoccupation with the technological excesses of the future. Both, however, draw on a 'Britain Can Take It', 'England in a crisis' ethos, as if both the past and the future articulate with the present of television viewing in terms of the former being 'just like now but less so' and the latter 'just like now but more so'.

THE HOME AND FAMILY PARADIGM

It is not the concern of this article to deal specifically with fiction's investment in family romance or the centrality of representations of the family in ideology. Rather it is to sketch some parameters of the treatment of the family as part of the 'situation' in situation comedy: the model situation which deals with the family as an insular unit and establishes the family as an index of an 'inside/outside' structure of situation comedy. The most typical of the family shows are obviously *Till Death Us Do Part* (the title expressing the endurance of the comic possibilities of the family) and *All in the Family* (whose title expresses its boundary: we do not have to look outside the family for comedy or drama). Other shows place more emphasis on relations between the family and the outside world, usually with neighbours: *Love Thy*

Neighbour; Beggar My Neighbour; Meet the Wife — an invitation, introduction to the outside world to be drawn into the family drama; and *My Wife Next Door* where the inside/outside structure is fused. In these series the outside elements are essentially institutionalized in stock sets and running characters, the focus of the situation being the way one family unit reacts to another. The ideology held by the institution of television as a machine for the production of meaning is that the family is a sufficiently stable situation, settled enough to be able to bear repetition and to deal with the onslaughts of the outside in a recognizable, characteristic way. If a structural change has to take place it happens before the series begins, or between series. Thus in a series like *The Very Merry Widow*, with Moira Lister, the death of her husband occurs before the series begins and the situation of the series is her coping with bereavement. Again, when the situation changes, new series (spin-offs) may result: thus the change from *Man About the House* to *George and Mildred*, where two characters from the former show now constitute their individual family unit outside the parameters of *Man About The House.**

This is obviously very different from the narrative unfolding of the soap opera, whose structure allows no gaps in the temporality and where the basic situation needs to be broader, encompassing more central characters who can be developed, written out, through time. The parameters of the soap opera are liable to be a street, a motel, a small village community rather than an individual family unit, a specific place of work, a couple of friends, and so on.

WORK

The parameters of a place of work constitute an almost perfect paradigm for a television series, be it a drama series (such as *The Brothers*), a police series (such as Dock Green police station) or situation comedy. The situation demands a stability of character and problematic (doctors *always* heal patients; people working in a store *always* serve customers) and a clearly defined boundary between staff and customers, doctors and patients (allowing for a continual turnover of the latter who can enter and leave the situation naturally — the difficult customer, the patient with an unusual complaint, and so on). The situation also allows for the representation of class differences through its treatment of the different hierarchical grades, ranks, of the running characters. In this model's

---

* Cf. Johnny Speight's remarks on this in relation to *Till Death Us Do Part*: '*Till Death* came a little unstuck when Dandy Nichols wanted to leave the series. She was so much a part of the show. I decided the only solution was to kill her off and do a new series with Alf looking around for a new wife. The BBC wouldn't hear of it. They said the death of Alf's "silly old moo" would upset too many people. In the end we had her going off to Australia. But it was unreal. People knew that a woman like her wouldn't just up and take off for Down Under. The series ended.' *Daily Mirror*, Thursday, 28 September, 1978, p.13.

purest form the action takes place within the confines of the work situation, with only marginal reference to the lives of the characters outside (*Are You Being Served?*, *The Rag Trade*). Other situation comedies incorporate aspects of the home/work dichotomy (for example, *On the Buses* with its stock sets of the depot and Reg Varney's house), others even fuse the terms of this dichotomy completely, often by dealing with the 'small family-firm' (for example, *Fawlty Towers*, *Steptoe and Son*) where emphasis can be switched from one pole to the other, perhaps allowing for greater flexibility (the television prototype of this being *The Dick Van Dyke Show*).

THE THIRD MODEL

This model betrays structural elements of both the home and the work paradigms and usually concerns a group of diverse people somehow connected in a situation outside that of their work-place. It usually concerns the home, but not the family except tangentially as part of the 'outside', for instance, *Man About the House*, *Rising Damp* and *Come Back, Mrs Noah*, where the situation concerns a group of diverse characters orbiting the earth in an accidentally launched space-station, a situation which provides little scope for boundary flexibility!

CHARACTERS

The necessity for the continuity of character and situation from week to week allows for the possibility of comedy being generated by the fact that the characters are somehow stuck with each other. In the family situation this is obvious (we think of 'we choose our friends, but fate gives us our relations': also the possibility for in-law jokes — are they family or not-family?) At work it usually turns around the possibility that we can choose our jobs, but not the people we work with no matter how glamorous our job may be (as in *Doctor on the Go*). It is as if the formal necessities of the series provide the existential circle from which the characters cannot escape. We think of Harold Steptoe continually threatening to leave his father (a possibility the series could never allow, but continually took into account) or the literalisation of this demand in *Porridge*: by setting the situation in a prison the characters had no possibility of escaping the parameters of that situation; when Fletch-Ronnie Barker eventually gets paroled, a new series, a new situation is created — hence *Going Straight*.

'GOING STRAIGHT'

The series *Going Straight* illustrates many of the general remarks made in the previous section but has also been chosen because its initial paradigm is somewhat more complicated in its development than many of television's situation comedy offerings. Some initial points need to be made. First, situation comedies are often characterized from within television as being specifically 'the brain-child of a writer'; the writers of this series are Dick Clement and Ian La Frenais, known for their ratings and critical successes, *The Likely Lads* and *Porridge*. Second, the idea for *Going Straight* is a direct spin-off from *Porridge*, which itself was a 'vehicle' for Ronnie Barker. *Going Straight* therefore carries, in spite of the change of situation, a set of familiar running characters: Fletch/Barker himself, his cell-mate Godber and his daughter Ingrid (familiar to us through her prison visits). Therefore, it carries with it a memory of the hermeneutic of the previous series, which provides a double-definition of the 'inside/outside' structure: the first is the one between series (inside prison/outside in the world: *Porridge/Going Straight*); the second the one set up by the problematic of the show, which will be dealt with later. The show also carries with it an initial hermeneutic question, which is easily established because of our knowledge of the previous series; as the *Radio Times* put it: 'He is determined to go straight . . . but will he?', a question the series will be asking throughout its six-week run. Thirdly, as a series, a specific time-slot, *Going Straight* must present itself as 'an idea capable of reproduction'. However, as part of that idea grounds itself on a memory of the past (we know that Fletch used to be in gaol — now he is not) a temporality is, of necessity, set up. Therefore, the scriptwriters have to deal with this temporality without destroying, or even altering, the parameters of the situation.

It is necessary at this point to describe an episode from the series in some detail in order to arrive at the terms of this paradigm and then to see how it is maintained from week to week. The episode chosen is the third to be broadcast: 'Going Sour', which went out on Friday, 10 March 1978 in the 8.30 pm slot, and was retransmitted on Friday, 3 November 1978 at 8.00 pm. The third show of the series was chosen to demonstrate how the rhythms, repetitions, movements of a series continue across its developments. It might be thought that this could be demonstrated in relation to the first episode of a series: in this case the first episode of *Going Straight* dealt with the transition from inside to outside and took place almost completely on the train from Slade prison (site of *Porridge*) to Fletch's London home (site of *Going Straight*).

'GOING SOUR' — BRIEF PLOT DESCRIPTION

No formal analysis of this episode was possible so this description tends to foreground narrative and script at the expense of other factors.

Credits. The credits of the series both establish the inside/outside theme (the film of Fletch being released from prison and looking bewildered at his first view of the outside world) and also emphasise the regularity and flow of the time-slot. Also, the title of the series (*Going Straight*) articulates with the title of each of the episodes (which all start with the word 'going') in creating both a direction, a duration and a memory (of Fletch when he was in prison and therefore not going anywhere). The theme-tune, sung by Barker, emphasises the patent hermeneutic of the show ('He is determined to go straight . . . but will he?') and refers to that determination, which will continually come under assault:

I'm going straight I am, straight as an arrow,
I've paid me price and done me time,
I'm going straight I am, back on the straight and narrow
And I don't mean straight back to crime.

Scene One. Stock set of Fletch's living-room. Jokes to reinforce Fletch's maladjustment to outside life (Fletch is up at seven putting up shelves — 'I learned carpentry in the nick' — which later fall down) and his lack of status in the family (his lack of conversational rapport with his son Raymond, compared with his role as 'father-figure' to Henry Godber in the 'nick').

Scene Two. Stock set of the kitchen. More assaults on Fletch's lack of position and status outside the prison world he is used to. Fletch's reference to the 'attitude of cynicism and mistrust around in this country'. Assaults on his manhood and demonstration of his inadequacy: daughter Ingrid asks him to do the shopping. Narrative prepared by her giving him money, which his pride declines — she puts it under the Jubilee tea-caddy. Ingrid questions Fletch about his apparent lack of sex-drive, preparing the way for his encounter with Penny.

Scene Three. Set of café run by Dante, an Italian, where a tripartite schema of middle-aged male sexuality is drawn up, Fletch's lack of sexual appetite ('that stuff they put in the prison tea must be starting to work') contrasting with Dante's brazen masculine sexuality and Perce, the milkman's, position as butt for jokes about his sexual possibilities on a milk-round. A narrative device to test the hermeneutic of the series enters at this point in the figure of Penny, a teenage runaway, whom Fletch stops from stealing Perce's money-bag. Fletch is in a position to re-establish his role as an old lag with a knowledge of the world in relation to Penny, but also to diffuse the jokes about his sexual inadequacy. His lack of status and manhood is over-ridden in the knowledge and experience he can give Penny.

Scene Four. Stock set of Fletch's living-room. Penny tells her story — the entry of an ideological issue 'teenage runaways' into the hermeneutic which is established as 'Will Fletch be able to re-establish himself as a figure of wisdom, status and authority in a world which is incomprehensible to him?', reinforcing the overall hermeneutic of the series 'Will Fletch succeed in his determination to go straight and withstand the onslaughts of a cynical and distrustful world?'. The 'I don't care' attitude of Penny is equated by Fletch with the general mood of the times, but here he can intervene with his own story and advice and stop Penny following the same course as himself. Comedy is virtually forgotten in this scene through the need to recreate Fletch as a father-figure.

Scene Five. Stock set of Fletch's kitchen. Ingrid returns and Fletch explains Penny's presence. Ingrid responds as if Fletch has made sexual advances to her which allows Fletch the opportunity of a soliloquy emphasizing the importance of helping people, maintaining he was 'just trying to help somebody — an alley cat, a little waif and stray'. As he delivers this speech there is a short cut back to the sitting-room where we see Penny stealing Ingrid's purse. It is at this point that the first narrative movement of the show is concluded: Fletch's attempts to withstand the cynicism of the world have again come under attack. Fletch has re-established his role as father-figure, a possessor of knowledge in relation to young people (a role he had inside, but which his family deny him) only to have this attempt exposed as naïvety — the world has made a fool of Fletch again — he would be better off inside.

Scene Six. Stock set of the kitchen after a passage of time. Fletch's face betrays the shattering of his faith in human nature. Ingrid's attempts to cheer him up are in vain as he adopts the attitude of cynicism he was earlier trying to combat ('my lost faith in human nature won't be restored by watching Orient play Mansfield Town'). At this point, Arthur (Penny's stepfather) enters with Penny who has returned the purse (she 'thought better of it'). Fletch is obviously overjoyed as it is clear he had been listened to — Arthur wants to thank Fletch alone in the sitting-room and Penny remains in the kitchen.

Scene Seven. Stock set of the kitchen. Fletch again with Ingrid, but this time in high spirits. At this point Fletch delevers a speech which needs quoting in full since its direction is that of the series week after week. Fletch says:

> I bet missionaries feel like that — I mean it can't be all beer and skittles out in the jungle with the heat and the titsy [*sic*] flies. When one day in come a group of young warriors — throw down their spears and say 'we want to learn the catechism' — then they eat him.

That this speech is a model for the drama as a whole becomes clear when immediately afterwards Fletch decides to take the whole family out for an evening at the pub using the money which Ingrid offered him in Scene Two and which she left under the Jubilee tea-caddy. Of course, when Fletch looks for it, it has gone ('Gor blimey — she's pinched the fiver!'). The scene ends and the credits come up ('You have been watching . . .') on a freeze of Fletch's face as the cynicism of the world pours down on him again — thus making for the final movement of the narrative which allows the re-instatement of the series' problematic: 'He is determined to go straight . . . but will he? (in such a cynical world)'.

The structure of this episode (which is the structure of each episode of the series) could be expressed diagramatically thus:

Initial Paradigm — The memory of 'Porridge'

Inside
Fletch in prison
[father/authority-figure]

Outside
Fletch on the outside
[outsider, with no sexual, economic or familial status — no knowledge of how things work]

Secondary Paradigm — The hermeneutic of 'Going Straight'

Inside
Fletch's code of conduct
[trust, resolve to go straight, naïvety, yet need to display knowledge]

Outside
Fletch's attitude that cynicism and distrust are prevalent in the world — the world's conspiracy to think the worst of all his intentions. (This allows for weekly entry of narrative elements: Penny in 'Going Sour', the con who offers him a job in episode 6, and so on)

Movement of this episode through these parameters:

Naïvety and knowledge of Fletch

Cynism and distrust of the world

Fletch the father-figure

Penny the runaway

Fletch taking Penny under his wing

Penny stealing the money

Penny returning the money
(now she's 'going straight')
(Fletch as 'missionary')

Penny pinches the fiver
('Then they ate him')

Freeze-frame on the disillusioned Fletch. The question of the series remains open: 'he is determined to go straight — but will he?'

41

It is clear that the narrative of each episode of the series must not allow for a resolution of the two sides or the problematic/hermeneutic of the show would be eliminated, another 'situation' would have to be established, another series written. Every episode ends with the freeze-frame of Fletch's disillusionment — the flow of the series (though not, of course, the flow of television — 'now it is time for the *Nine O'Clock News*') is held in abeyance until the same time next week when the terms of its movements, its rhymes and repetitions, will be re-activated in its regular time-slot. The organization of the novelistic and the organization of television harmonise — at the point at which Fletch tries to re-establish his position as father (by taking the whole family out for a celebration and footing the bill) this is confounded — it is not a possibility or it would finish the series with three weekly time-slots left to be filled.

Any attempt to deal with television situation comedy written at this time must consider the remarks of Norman Lear at the 1979 Edinburgh International Television Festival; and if only because his speech was greeted so enthusiastically by British television practitioners and was widely reported in the press, it deserves to be contextualized here. Lear's speech and most of the ensuing debates at Edinburgh centred predominantly, at least in the sphere of situation comedy, on the need to incorporate the 'issues of the day' into the half-hour comedy slot. Norman Lear's proud list of 'toppled taboos' achieved in his shows bear witness to this:

> For the first time we saw: married couples in the same bed. Our stories dealt with death, infidelity, black family life, homosexuality, abortion, criticism of the economic and foreign policy, racial prejudice, problems of the elderly, alcoholism, drug abuse, menopause, the *male* mid-life crisis. Such health issues as heart disease, hypertension, breast cancer, lung cancer, mental retardation, depression, manic depression, plastic surgery and more. [Lear, 1978.]

The task of the 'concerned' member of the 'creative community' of television practitioners becomes to find the humour inherent in 'whatever life struggle is going on around me'. Here we see the language of heroism in the service of getting 'substantive content' onto television: the braveness of the shows dealing with contemporary issues; the temerity of the network-programmers in finding them too hot to handle. For Lear, the alternative is clear: those programmes which do not deal with the 'real problems of life' are 'shouting the largest message in the world'; they are, by omission, saying:

42

You have no race problems; there is no economic concern in the nation, we are *not* in trouble in Vietnam; everyone does have an equal crack at medical attention; there are no problems with the poor or the elderly or the uneducated — and all mothers and fathers and children live in absolute harmony.

Clearly, this position contains fundamental assumptions about the role of television in society, and about the nature of the audience. If, as Heath and Skirrow have argued, television is 'an apparatus for the production and the reproduction of the novelistic' which 'serves to address the problem of the definition of forms of individual meaning within the limits of existing social representations and their determining social relations, the provision and maintenance of terms of social intelligibility' [Heath and Skirrow, 1973, pp.58-9], then we can initially contextualize Lear's call for a greater 'realism', a greater 'humanism', a greater degree of 'substantive content' in television situation comedy as a call for an organization of the television novelistic which takes a greater account of contemporary issues. This position necessarily assumes that society and television are two wholly distinct realms: one concerned with 'reality' — the domain of the 'real problems of life' — the other somehow concerned with reflecting that reality, whilst not being part of it. Television exists outside society and is answerable to society only to the extent to which television adequately reflects its concerns. The idea of the process of representation as something which exists outside society can be seen in the assumptions which are made about the audience. The audience of television exists to be 'entertained, informed, offended and provoked', by seeing its problems ('the real problems of everyday life') reflected in the television programmes it chooses to watch (a mass audience, composed of 'citizens of a free society' exercising their rights as individual consumers). The notion of 'entertainment' itself is always defined in opposition to 'work', to 'everyday life'. For example: 'After the tensions and anxieties of everyday life, people welcome the opportunity to sit down, relax, and *be made* to smile and laugh' (*IBA Handbook 1978*, section on situation comedy, p.89, my emphasis).

Thus, these assumptions are belied by the practice of television, by the constant and relentless need of the programmes we watch to inscribe the television viewer into the organization of the novelistic. Constant and relentless because as a process it is incapable of final closure: it is readable across the individual shows, series, evening's viewings, and so on, but can never hold us there as it is part of the more general process by which we are constituted as social beings, one which the very forms the situation comedy takes seem designed to reinforce.

So, in conclusion, I have chosen to look at some aspects of the organization of the novelistic in a show which apparently eschews any humanistic treatment of 'hot' social issues, from a need not to be sidetracked into dealing with the 'treatment' of those issues. Although the section of the programme to be considered does contain tangential references to industrial unrest, immigration, rising population, technological progress, and so on, it does so only in relation to the continual re-inscription of the television viewer into the text of the programme, *Come Back, Mrs Noah* — the apotheosis of the citizen in a world of messages.

'COME BACK, MRS NOAH'

Come Back, Mrs Noah is set in the year 2050, and stars Mollie Sugden as the Housewife of the Year, accidentally launched into space. One element of its inter-textual references is its specific relation to other television programmes, both science-fiction, for instance *Star Trek*, *Dr Who*, and science-documentary, for instance *Tomorrow's World*. However, as already mentioned, the show is bound up in references to the past: the theme music is a deliberate recreation of 1920s or 1930s music, Mollie Sugden as a television figure embodies characteristics of a cultural past (fat women in sea-side postcards, a northern accent, jokes about knickers, and so on) as well as a television past (playing Mrs Hutchinson in *The Liver Birds* and Mrs Slocombe in *Are You Being Served?*). The show is a vehicle for Mollie Sugden as the space station is a (literal) vehicle for the parameters of the situation. *Come Back, Mrs Noah* was scripted by Jeremy Lloyd and David Croft (who also scripted *Are You Being Served?*), the latter of whom was the co-writer of both *Dad's Army* and *It Ain't Half Hot, Mum* and also produced all the above shows. The title itself defines the parameters of the show: *Come Back, Mrs Noah* referring not only to the attempts to get the module back to earth again, but also, through the use of the imperative, suggesting a calling-back, an interpellation back to the terms of our comprehension of the present/past, away from the fear of the technological excesses of the future, whose terms are continually being lampooned.

The first pilot show of the six-week series was shown in February 1978 as a 'taste of things to come' — the rest of the series was to be shown, as it were, in the future — and was then repeated as a preview to the other five episodes in July 1978. I have chosen a section from the second episode, 'In Orbit' (broadcast on BBC 1 at 6.30 pm on Monday, 17 July 1978) for, although this is the second of the six shows, it acts, in effect, as the first of the new series. The first show 'introduced' the characters and situation and provided the diegetic explanation as to how they managed to be marooned in space — the rest of the series involves their adventures up there and the attempts to get them down. However, before that is possible the characters and the situation have to be redefined — re-presented — to us and the terms by which that is achieved will be the focus of this analysis.

Episode 2: 'In Orbit'

I Shots 1-3

Shot	Time*	Description	Dialogue
1	3.75	*Farandwide* Titles — music fade into	

'Nationwide' *end title*

Shot 1

2	91.5	MCU of *Farandwide* announcer reading the news	*Farandwide Announcer:* 'Hello, good evening and welcome to the 7,582nd edition of *Farandwide* for today, Thursday 23rd June 2050. In tonight's programme we will be taking an in-depth look at proposals for the new London Airport — in the Orkneys.† And on the Industrial front† at the British Leyland Robot Factory — arm and leg fitters have been laid off due to a strike in the tool room. But first† the subject that's on everybody's lips: the accidental launching of Britannia 7, Britain's multi-million pound space station from the Pontefract International Space Complex — otherwise known as PISC. There were angry scenes† in the Commons today as various motions were tabled by the joint Labour-Con-
		No camera movement in this shot but periodically at points† news stills are flashed behind him onto a screen: †photo of Orkneys †photo of outside of a factory	
		†photo of space station	
		†photo of House of Commons	

---

* In this and the following tables shot times are given in seconds.

| Shot | Time | Description | | Dialogue |

Shot   *Time*   *Description*   *Dialogue*

servative opposition.
Speakers pointed out that so
far we had managed to put
into orbit two mathemati-
cians, one cleaner, a BBC
reporter and a housewife —
at a total cost of 700 million
pounds. Was this a good way
of spending even our vast
resources? In reply the
Prime Minister said that he
had already set up a Royal
Commission to look into the
whole matter. This is the
strongest measure any Government could take short
of actually doing something

†picture of boxing ring   about it. And now sport† —
Britain's heavyweight cham-
pion, Ram Jam Patel last
night retained his world-title
against the Italian, Ping-
Dong Schlossnoy . . .'

Shot 2

Shot 2a

Shot	Time	Description	Dialogue
3	6.75	LS inside module from behind of four characters watching the screen: Mrs Noah; Clive (BBC Reporter); Carstairs and Fanshaw (mathematicians)	*Mrs Noah:* 'How can they talk about sport when we're marooned up here 350 miles above the earth?'

Shot 3

The programme re-introduces and re-instates its parameters through a news programme. *Come Back, Mrs Noah* went out after *Nationwide* and the *Farandwide* logo and theme music is identical to that programme — already we are inscribed into the text as television watchers: the news as our source of information on the issues of the world/*Farandwide* as our source of information on the issues of *Come Back, Mrs Noah*. Reference to contemporary issues in the context of a news broadcast emphasises the future as 'just like today — only more so'. The scene inside the module, with the crew of Britannia 7 watching the broadcast, again puts the screen at the centre of its terms of intelligibility: the two mathematicians belong to the world of science fiction and technology, Clive Cunliffe belongs to the world of broadcasting, Mrs Noah, the Housewife of the Year, is positioned like us, as television viewer.

II Shots 6-10

Shot	Time	Description	Dialogue
6	6	MLS of module from in front with four characters in frame	*Carstairs:* 'Why don't we switch through to mission control — see if they've worked out a way of getting us down from here?'
7	2	As shot 3 with Mission Control on monitor screen	*Mission Controller:* (aside) 'Well, I've got no idea how to get them down.'
8	5	MCU of Mission Control	*Female Assistant:* 'Hm, excuse me, sir . . .'

Shot	Time	Description	Dialogue
9	4	MCU Mission Controller looking and speaking at TV monitors of the module	*Mission Controller*: 'Oh hello Pip-Top-Mish-Con here. Is everything all right? Down here we're straining every nerve to do everything we possibly can.'

Shot 6

Shot 9

Shot	Time	Description	Dialogue
10	3	As shot 8	*Tea-woman*: 'One lump or two, controller?'

Again, the axis of the comedy in this section is on the claims of technology/the reality behind those claims, but information is relayed through the institution of watching — the Mission Controller sees the crew of the module, like us, through a TV monitor (significantly black and white), although his set does more than ours — he can communicate direct.

III Shots 20-21

Shot	Time	Description	Dialogue
20	6	As shot 3	*Mission Controller*: 'We do have some good news for you. We've assembled one or two family and friends at the *Farandwide* studio so you can have a chat with them.'
21	24	MCU *Farandwide* studios — desk with announcer and guests	*'Farandwide' Announcer* (to the guests): 'Well, to put it quite plainly the chances of getting them back alive are very remote, but they don't know that yet. The fact that they're doomed to spend the rest of their lives in that space coffin must never

enter their heads.'
Technician: 'On the Air.'
Announcer: 'Oh God —
Hello Britannia 7, well you'll
be pleased to know that
we've assembled some of
your nearest and dearest in
the studio to pay their last
respects . . . er, to say
hello to you.'

Shot 21

Here, television is not only the medium of communicability, but also the medium of domesticity. The *Farandwide* announcer mediates constantly in the following shots between the crew and their family on earth: stopping the broadcast when Mrs Carstairs breaks down, relaying information about Fanshaw's wife and brother, and so on. Again, the joke about what we are allowed or not allowed to see is used: the knowledge that we are perhaps having the wool pulled over our eyes is part of our definition as television viewers, but it is celebrated here along with every other aspect of that definition/inscription.

IV Shots 29-36

Shot	Time	Description	Dialogue
29	7	As shot 3	'And now here's a lovely surprise for Mrs Noah — we've taken a camera over
30	1.5	cu Mrs Noah	to your very own home, Mrs Noah, where your very own husband is waiting to give you a word of comfort.'
31	1	As shot 29	Mr Noah: 'Hello, love.'

49

Shot 31

Shot	Time	Description	Dialogue
32	2.75	As shot 30	Mrs Noah: 'Ee, look at him.'
33	12	As shot 29	Mr Noah: 'Here I am in our own little nest at number 36. In front of the fire we've shared so often together — I know you must be very worried about me, love, but don't fret — in
34	15	MCU Mr Noah (filmed at home)	England in a crisis there's always a neighbour to help out and I've chosen one from number 38 next door — that's right,
35	1.5	LS of Ivy entering the room	you've guessed it — it's none other than Ivy Basset, so sadly widowed last year.

Shot 34

Shot 35

| 36 | 17 | As 34 with Mr Noah and Ivy in frame | Although we're far apart it's a great comfort to me to know that every two hours |

Dialogue
you're passing over our
little house at 35,000 miles
an hour — so it's goodbye
from me, the cats, the parrot
and all at Number 36.'

Throughout this section the specific televisual references are those
sections on *This is Your Life* where the guest is unable to appear in the
studio and is therefore filmed at home. Mr Noah's diction throughout is
deliberately stilted, as if he's talking to a television camera. Interestingly, the decor of No. 36 and Mr Noah's dress has no futuristic
over-tones ('I'm in front of the fire', 'the cats and the parrot') so that
although the discourse of the future can be contained in the figures of the
mathematicians and the staff of Mission Control, and the discourse of
Mr and Mrs Noah's domesticity is seen to be defined outside that, it
cannot be defined outside the discourse of television itself — the
mediator between Mr and Mrs Noah. The fire Mr Noah is sitting in front
of is in fact the television camera recording his words.

V Shots 42-43

Shot	Time	Description	Dialogue
42	16	As shot 3 — occupants of the module watching *Farandwide* Announcer	'And now a word to you all — keep your spirits up. Remember this is the 21st Century and working on your problems are the scientific brains and resources and the latest technol . . .
		Sign flashes up on screen:	(breakdown)
		'We apologise for loss of sound and vision'.	
43	6	As shot 6: MLS from in front of characters in the module	Clive: 'That's a great relief I must say!'

After this opening the series can, in effect, start with the antics of the
marooned passengers on board the space station and deal more directly
with the sci-fi and technological lampoonings that are the mainstay of its
comic resources. However, we have seen how this requires an instatement of ourselves as television watchers in the present, even at the
expense (for the comedy) of introducing television as something that
goes wrong and something which hides the truth, as well as something

51

from which we receive information and which guarantees, provides the expression for, the family wit. In this programme, almost as literally as in the Burns and Allen shows of the early 1950s, television viewing is inscribed into the situation comedy format, interpellating us into the world of ideas and information and holding us there by a celebration of our own subject position as television viewer.

(First published in *Screen*, vol. 19 no. 4, Winter 1978/9.)

References

Alvarado, M. and Buscombe, E. (1978), *Hazell: the making of a TV series*, London: British Film Institute.

Drummond, P. (1976), 'Structural and narrative constraints and strategies in *The Sweeney*', *Screen Education*, no. 20, 1976.

Heath, S. (1976), 'Screen images, film memory', *Edinburgh Magazine '76*.

Heath, S. and Skirrow, G. (1977), 'Television: a World in Action', *Screen*, vol. 18, no. 2, Summer 1977.

Lear, N. (1978), MacTaggart Lecture at the 1978 Edinburgh International Television Festival.

Williams, R. (1974), *Television, Technology and Cultural Form*, London: Fontana.

The Television Presentation of the Police

THE TELEVISION POLICE SERIES

The television police series has for many years held an important place in the production and consumption patterns of mass entertainment and during the 1970s has achieved a primacy even against its most enduring competitor, the western (Lavers, 1975). The 'new wave' programmes — *Kojak, Starsky and Hutch, The Sweeney* — have regularly made the top five in JICTAR and BBC audience research surveys while still leaving space for one of the longest running series, *Z Cars*. In 1962 the first *Z Cars* series was watched by fourteen million people and in 1977 was still reaching half that number. If we add to this the spin-offs from the programmes — books, games, records, fan magazines, posters, feature films and tootsie pop rolls — the importance of the genre to the economics of the television industry is apparent.

However, although the economics of the industry are an essential aspect of any analysis of the media, the concern here is with the actual programmes and more specifically with the ways in which an image of policing is constructed and mediated through the fictional forms of the television police series. To claim significance for those images is to point to the central issue of the relationship between systems of representation and the place of the media in the production and reproduction of knowledge about society and the relationships between individuals, groups and institutions within it. Writing about film in this context Richard Dyer (1977) has argued:

> No social group can afford to ignore the importance of the cinema. *Although perhaps eclipsed today by television,* it has been for most of the century the mode of communication, expression and entertainment — the 'signifying practice' — par excellence. It has acted as a repository of images of how people are and how they should be, images that are both produced by and help to produce the general thought and feeling of our culture [my emphasis].

Historically, groups and institutions have always been concerned with the images of themselves produced by the media, and the police forces have been no exception to this concern. The chief constable of Lancashire withdrew support from the original *Z Cars* series on the grounds that the presentation of policemen as 'human beings', not immune from the pressures and problems of everyday life, might undermine public confidence, though the decision was later reversed when the success of the series became apparent. Jack Warner, the star of *Dixon of Dock Green,* was honoured by the force for his idiosyncratic personification of the 'bobby on the beat' and similarly John Thaw and Dennis Waterman of *The Sweeney* have been guests at Flying Squad dinners, presumably in admiration of their roles as the violent agents of a ruthless justice. Interestingly, an ex-Flying Squad officer works as programme advisor to the series.

We can assume from this that the images in these cases recapitulate a version of police work that the police can, at least in part, share. Outside the institution of the police force the mode of appropriation of those images into the culture at a conscious level can be indicated by an examination of the 'models for consuming' television provided in the television columns of the daily and weekly press. Of course, this is not to insist on any necessary symbiosis between a television critic's statements about a programme and a viewer's particular reaction to that programme. But it is to suggest that television is a cultural phenomenon that extends beyond the dimensions of a screen-viewer relationship to the wider and more complex sets of interactions within society that operate to produce that relationship within certain frames of reference.

People not only 'watch television' but learn 'how television is watched', both from its position within the culture and the general definitions of its nature which are available. On the one hand there are those institutions which have a specific concern with the medium — the state, press, radio, television itself — and on the other the social relationships of exchange and usage — within the family, education, work — both of which serve to confirm television within certain established patterns of consumption. For example, the artificially balanced duo of 'entertainment' and 'information', a division upon which a great deal of television's self-presentation is based, sites the field of definition within which output is located. Therefore, if one viewer finds a programme 'realistic' and another 'unrealistic', we are not faced with two qualitatively different responses: it is only the fictional output of television which is talked about in this way and it is only certain aspects of that fiction upon which those assessments are based. Essentially, the criteria being employed are the same: how 'realistic' is a programme? The question of the *meaning* of realism is left unstated.

Given this tendency to think about television within already available categories, popular criticism is, not surprisingly, distinguished by a distinct homology of responses to the police series so that a few examples are entirely representative. Richard Hart, in the *Daily Telegraph,* praised *The Sweeney* as 'easily the most believable police series at present on our screens' and in the *Sunday Telegraph* a year earlier (9 November 1975) Philip Purser argued that the series was 'a melodramatization of how most people would like the police to deal with the violent thugs of the world'. Peter Buckman, in *The Listener* (12 February 1976), welcomed the first episode of a new *Z Cars* series by writing that, 'As always, the very real problems the police face were intimately related to individual character, so that one has the feeling of a thriller done in the naturalistic manner of a documentary'. Jack Waterman, writing also in *The Listener,* (15 April 1976) summed up the evolution of *Dixon of Dock Green* over its twenty-one year run: 'It has reflected changes in society, in attitudes to the police, and in the police forces themselves.' The popular critics, working within the consensus categories, share common ground in their belief in the ability of the police series to reflect the social world of law enforcement, to be 'authentic', 'realistic' and even to embody the varieties of attitudes and feelings towards the police that members and groups in society may hold at particular moments.

This [essay] seeks to investigate these received notions of the meaning of the television police series by an examination of the critical foundations of 'reflection', 'authenticity' and 'realism'. What is being challenged is the neutrality of these concepts and their everyday articulation within the television discourse, in other words, seeing them as referring to 'active signifiers', producers of meaning, within a particular programme or sets of programmes. Furthermore, they are active at several different levels — firstly, as conventions and practices at the level of production, the particular way in which a police series is conceived and constructed, drawing on the heritage of realism in the genre through novels, films, radio and other television programmes, but also as the practices which produce these conventions as specific products. Secondly, they are active as constraints, the necessity to include or exclude, to produce in a certain way, in a particular form. And thirdly, they are active at the level of consumption, the knowledge which a viewer brings to a programme, a knowledge of other productions, forms and genres, and the general level of cultural knowledge about both television and the police. While these elements do not allow a precise theorization of the relationship between viewer and programme, they do allow the identification of a 'preferred reading' (Hall, 1977), a dominant discourse which operates to subordinate and make difficult alternative and oppositional readings of the structure, content, form and meanings of any particular programme.

It is when concepts such as realism, authenticity and entertainment are seen as referring to active signifiers within the television discourse that the 'ideological work' of television can begin to be understood.

Stuart Hall (1977), considering one aspect of the relationship between the medium and ideology, writes:

> As social groups and classes live, if not in their productive then in their 'social' relations, increasingly fragmented and sectionally differentiated lives, the mass media are more and more responsible (a) for providing the basis on which groups and classes construct an 'image' of the lives, meanings, practices and values of *other* groups and classes; (b) for providing the images, representations and ideas around which the social totality, composed of all these separate and fragmented pieces, can be coherently grasped as a whole.

The argument developed in this [essay] is that the police series does not simply reflect the social world of policing but must actively construct a coherent version of social reality within which the playing out of the nightly drama of law and order can be contained. Although there are a variety of mechanisms at work in this construction, the concentration here is on the fictional world of the police series, the characters, institutions and groups which compose that world; the sets of relationships between these components; the milieu in which these relationships are placed; and the tensions and alliances which structure those relationships. It is in this sense that Stuart Hall's argument, that the media provide us with knowledge about other groups, is being related to a specific fictional form.

But there is also the second sense, the placing of these components within a unified, intelligible social totality, a 'world of the whole'. Richard Dyer argues that media images are both 'produced by and help to produce' the sum of social knowledge with which we map society and make sense of it. Such a perspective means that the fictional world of the police series must in some way include and handle the contradictions and tensions which are the currency of policing, either by defining them out in such a way that their absence does not question the 'authenticity' of the representation, or by incorporating and redefining them within the structure of the series in such a way that the contradictions are papered over. Therefore, a particular emphasis of this analysis will be to explore the extent to which the fictional world is one in which, as Alan Lovell (1975) has argued in relation to the film *Dirty Harry,* 'social phenomena of different and contradictory kinds are brought together and presented as if they were a unity'.

It must always be remembered that the fictional world is not constructed in isolation and that the police series is not a self-contained, hermetic product. Whenever we watch television drama there is a constant negotiation between the fictional relationships of the programme and some implicit perception of 'real relations'. In our occasional contacts with the police, from crime reports in the press, through the

56

everyday exchange of information, we already have some idea of what the police are and what they do. But it is not a complete picture. As Horace Newcomb (1974) writes, 'It is like another side of our own world, one that we know exists but that we may never see, may experience only in rare moments of extremity'. In this sense Ashley Pringle (1972) has posited a function of the drama series as the completion of the 'half-formed picture' that the viewer has of often unfamiliar sections of society. It is this making complete and the effects of that construction that can be referred to as the ideological function of the fictional world of the police series.

This [essay] is divided into two main sections. In the first part the realism and authenticity of the police series will be examined in order to indicate the major mechanisms in operation and some of the ideological results of that operation. In the second part the structure of the fictional world will be analysed in order to demonstrate the handling of contradiction. In order to concretize the analysis, two programmes have been taken as examples — Thames Television's *The Sweeney* and BBC 1's *Z Cars*.

The police series enters the world of law and order by an initial excision of the two arms of law enforcement which delimit the totality of the legal system — the courts and prisons. Denied access to either, their absence must be resolved within the drama by references that define them as no more than discrete and self-contained institutions within the drive to retribution, absent not only from the fiction, emphasized by their placing within the confines of other genres (court-room dramas, prison dramas) but also from the drama. In the action-orientated *Sweeney*, the moment of capture becomes the moment of conviction, a moment often superseding the legal strictures of society when the death of a villain carries the full weight of a transcendent natural law. In a different but reciprocal movement, in *Z Cars*, with its emphasis not on action but interrogation, the piecing together of evidence in the revelation of truth, the trial is inscribed in the truth revealed. (Here we should note that *Z Cars* was inspired by a documentary on police interrogation methods.) The double actions of capture-conviction, trial-truth are most heavily signalled in those episodes that assign the courts and prisons a central, but absent, function in plot construction: 'A year of painstaking enquiries is wasted when three top villains walk out of court, free men. Jack Regan is determined to ensure a conviction. But no one at the Yard is putting money on it' (*TV Times,* 1977).

The displacement here is transparent. It is not in the courts that convictions are obtained but in the fact-to-face world of police and villains. There is a sneering quality in the phrase 'painstaking enquiries' which serves to instate Regan in his familiar role, the agent of an immediate, self-sufficient justice. We know that the narrative will demand one of two inevitable resolutions — the villain's death in the hopeless moment of discovery of guilt or the assurance of conviction in the inescapable web of evidence which Regan will spin. The prisons serve in their turn as repositories of villains and of plot devices, only to be visited for their stock of informants and snouts, their gates opened only to release characters into the drama. Apart from the occasional reference to 'putting in a good word', the police are seen to have no real influence in the courts, to have no access to the judicial manipulations of trial and sentence. The conflict in which they are engaged is clearer, altogether less confused.

Having excised two thirds of the legal apparatus, an initial fragmentation of the social world of crime and law, the police series must assert its realism in the devices of characterization and models of action, in other words the function of characters and their actions as the carriers of meaning, as the point of identification for the audience. The cinematic mechanism of identification is important in this context and can be described as the existence of an empathy and emotional involvement between an audience and a screen character. But it must also be thought of as a 'double identification with the star and/or character' (Wollen, 1972). So it is not only an involvement with the character a star plays but with the personality of the star in his or her own right and conceived in this sense we can see the significance of Phillip Drummond's (1976) observation on *The Sweeney* that it is only policemen who have 'characters', that criminals, because they are represented by a cycle of cameo actors in opposition to the stability of recurrent police stars, have no 'character'. 'This leads to two ideologically conspicuous results. First, villainy is rendered amorphous, abstract, perhaps anonymous . . . Second . . . the fiction's need to re-mark these "characterless" villains at the level of (especially grotesque or comic) stereotype and iconography'.

The notions of character and stereotyping in this context refer to the regular, week-by-week appearance of police stars as opposed to the cameo actors who appear in perhaps only one episode, yet must fill the social world of the police series by their representation of social and individual types. Obviously the police occupy more screen time and therefore are permitted a more developed character in a variety of situations and social encounters. The cameo actors must rely on crude stereotyping in order for their roles to be immediately identifiable to the audience. This is achieved either through iconography — the visual elements of an individual identity, such as clothes, physical characteristics, social settings, material objects and so on; or by particular behaviour patterns, such as violence, disloyalty, cowardice, irrationality.

The Sweeney's stereotypes are readily identifiable — the sharp clothes, flash cars and prominent 'London' accents of the gangsters, moving in a milieu of drinking clubs, horse races and boxing matches accompanied by the inevitable moll, controlling their crime empires with cryptic commands and sudden violence. Burly muscle-men, unable to take decisions but only orders, broken-nosed and leather-jacketed emissaries of their clean-handed bosses. 'The man wants 'im 'urt, not crippled.' And the snouts, whining, shabby, incompetent, isolated, helpless but ultimately lethal voyeurs in the criminal underworld.

When the analysis of stereotyping is applied to *Z Cars*, the ideological field is extended to encompass all social life outside the regular occupants of Newtown police station, a result of the series format's intention to show police in their day-to-day duties, demanding not only the stereotyped criminal but a stereotyped public — the brusque, man-of-the-world industrialist, self-made, patronising and meritocratic; the pedantic, interfering and uninformed councillor; the effusive jollity of upper middle-class young-marrieds; the paternalistic aristocrat; the harmless deviants and outsiders, tramps, drunks and eccentrics, objects of pity and protection to the police. (In one episode a tramp is arrested to give him a bed on a cold night.) Between public and villains lies a more uneasy world of the apprentice criminal. Two marked stereotypes operate here — the delinquent from a 'rough' home background, heading for trouble but potentially open to control given the right police treatment, free from interfering do-gooders. Secondly, the future villain, often linked to a middle-class family where a muddle-headed liberalism and laxity is the context for future criminality.

But in this drive to establish the police as characters, as the point of identification for an audience, one social group in *The Sweeney* and *Z Cars* is denied character either within or outside the social world of the police. Claire Johnston (1976) has pointed out: 'As the cinema developed, the stereotyping of man was increasingly interpreted as contravening the notion of "character"; in the case of woman, this was not the case; the dominant ideology presented her as eternal, and unchanging, except for modifications in terms of fashion, etc.'

The Sweeney is studded with woman types derived directly from the conventions of the Hollywood film — the vamp, career girl, moll and mother. Often these stereotypes negotiate and exercise power through the manipulation of sexual relations — woman as an instrument of revenge or as the predator. She is, then, frequently the weak link in any criminal organization, open to pressure from the police on the basis of a code of sexual ethics that assumes a greater importance than loyalty or even self-preservation. In contrast, *Z Cars* tends towards the more pliant stereotype of woman as the uncomprehending victim of the world, with no knowledge of the vagaries of human behaviour, unless it is through an undefined intuition. So often we meet women as the mothers of delinquent children, who, when the policeman 'breaks the news', can only reply by crying over the inevitable cup of tea. And the only role that policewomen have is to stand silently by the door of the interview room as these exchanges take place, no more than props that add to the 'realism' of the scene. Women are not only denied character, they are also in one crucial respect denied presence in the fiction. Only one character in both *Z Cars* and *The Sweeney* is married (DCI Haskins and DI Moffat) with a home life occasionally shown in an episode. And in the case of Moffat, his wife is an academic, independent woman, unlikely to place domestic demands on her husband which might intrude on his career. The rest of the main characters in both programmes are either divorced, separated, widowed or unmarried, a trail of broken and unmade relationships presented as a direct result of the pressures and demands of police work. Here lies the definition of the male, professional world of the television policeman.

Given the extent of this paring down of the social world of the police series to a limited number of regular characters, it is clear that the meanings of either programme, the world of the Flying Squad, of Newtown Division, must be carried by the reduction and construction of police work in individual biography. In E. M. Forster's words (1974), there are only a limited number of 'round' characters who must do the work of a series, as opposed to a plethora of 'flat' characters. While both productions deploy individual biography as a major narrative device, the mechanism is in each case accented differently, a difference essential to an understanding of the social world of each programme. The two modes can be termed centred and de-centred biography for *The Sweeney* and *Z Cars* respectively. In order to develop each mode I will discuss them in relation to each programme separately.

CENTRED BIOGRAPHY AND 'THE SWEENEY'

The Sweeney is constructed around the biographies of three main characters introduced in the credits in a hierarchy of screen significance as opposed to rank — DI Jack Regan, DSC George Carter and DCI Frank Haskins. That Regan occupies the lead position is only a reflection of the centrality of his role to the whole series, described succinctly in the cover notes to the second paperback spin-off from the series, *Regan and the Manhattan File*, written by Ian Kennedy Martin: 'Jack Regan is a mean cop in the Flying Squad. He's also the Sweeney's hardest, sharpest and brightest detective inspector. He hates interference, rank, regulations and crime. But most of all he hates to lose.'

This hierarchy of significance is constant with only infrequent foregrounding of either Haskins or Carter and then only to act as the epicentre of Regan's manipulation, their foregrounding the deliberate outcome of his activities and always answerable to his control. For example, in 'Golden Fleece' (October 1975), the plot revolves around the framing of Haskins by a gang intent on taking him out of action and the subsequent investigation by A10 of his alleged corruption. Although Haskins is effectively placed at the centre of the plot, it is only as a means for displaying Regan's skill in clearing him of the charges. Significantly, the villains are allowed to escape only to reappear three episodes later ('Trojan Bus', November 1975), and be snatched by Regan in confirmation of his status.

In contrast, the bureaucratic, authoritarian, father-figure of Haskins, and the sibling, pupil-figure of Carter serve, in their different ways, as supports that sharpen the image of Regan as the tough individualistic, freebooting cop, an image that finds its fictional heritage in the 'hard-boiled' detectives of American crime writers and the gangster and thriller movies of the 1930s and 1940s. He can also be placed alongside the American television cops of the new wave, Baretta, Kojak, Starsky and Hutch. Regan, accompanied by Carter, dominates each episode, isolated in the drama and at the same time isolated in the fictional world which he occupies. The nuclear quality of Regan and Carter's relationship allows them to question the very worthwhileness of the job they do, to see all around them hypocrisy, privilege and deliberate obstruction. The loathing they share for the underworld is matched by their contempt for the world of bourgeois niceties. London, their 'patch', is menacing and dangerous — 'each time I stop a car I don't know if I'm going to get my head blown off or not' — the Flying Squad, their 'home', hostile and envious, and oscillating between these two antagonistic environments Regan finds his satisfaction in the vengeful settling of old scores on the outside, a success rate with which to fend off his enemies on the inside.

The centred biography, deploying in each episode the anomic, isolated, violent, individual, cop-as-hero, demands an anomic, violent and antagonistic world for that hero to occupy, to survive in and dominate. Neither is it a world that needs understanding or investigation. In one episode, 'Chalk and Cheese' (September 1975), Carter is forced through his personal involvement to face the question as to why a childhood friend has turned to armed robbery — 'I just don't understand it' — to which Regan replies 'Don't even try, George. It's just human nature.' And later Carter tries to console the friend's father, 'he's sick, pop', but only to be met with the retort 'anyone can find excuses if they try hard enough'. What is resisted and obscured in this world is the intrusion of meaning and, therefore, the people, institutions and events which form that world can only be described, never dissected. In this sense the emblematic violence of *The Sweeney* can be recognized as a descriptive continuo, incorporated in a violent world that has no meaning except its meaninglessness, endlessly and poetically elaborated within every programme, but never elucidated. In a similar context Dick Hebdige (1974) illustrates the preference for descriptive rather than analytical categories when society is faced with the fact of criminal violence:

'You terrorised those who crossed your path and you terrorised them *in a way* that was vicious, sadistic, and a disgrace to society' (my italics). And so the judge deplores the method (the 'way') and ignores the meaning. Society has indeed been disgraced but at a level at once too deep and too close to home to be admitted in court.

The Sweeney marks its violence heavily as method but refuses its substance — the choreographed crazing of shotgun-blasted windscreens, balletic car crashes, iconographical detailing of Lugers, knuckle-dusters and telescopic coshes — in such a way that its presence does no more than confirm our expectations, emptied of its potentially disruptive content. *The Sweeney* is violent but it is not about violence. The nearest Regan gets to philosophizing about the subject is the observation, 'if people carry guns they can end up using them'.

And finally, in this world in which everyone is a potential deviant we come to realize that it is only Regan's deviance that holds the lid on, and when he asks his commander, 'don't you realize it's a war out there?', he only states what we have already seen to be true. The trail of blackmailed and threatened suspects, wrongful arrests, excessive harassment and illegal entries that he leaves behind him in every episode are only the legal casualties of a conflict that extends beyond law to permit society some kind of existence.

'Z CARS' AND DE-CENTRED BIOGRAPHY

In contrast, *Z Cars*, employing the de-centred biography, requires different characters, a different manifest world. Rather than projecting a nuclear family, *Z Cars* is a world of extended relationships, not only within the structure of a single series but in history and memory, a sense of the programme's evolution over fifteen years. The cycle of regular characters that make up Newtown Division — Inspector Lynch, DI Moffat, Sergeant Quilley (promoted in the last series), Sergeant Bowker and PC Render — are foregrounded in turn in different episodes, given space in which to become individual policemen. Often the foregrounding of any individual is signalled in the narrative by some special knowledge of people, crime or location. In 'Whisker's Castle' (1977) Quilley is sent to help a local businessman with the eviction of an eccentric down-and-out from a derelict factory because he knows Whiskers is a local lad and can be trusted to use the personal touch. Or Bowker in 'Rip Off' (1977): 'Bowker and Jack Crawford have met before. Their relationship's very simple: one way or another Bowker's going to nail Crawford, unless Crawford can nail Bowker first' (*Radio Times*).

The sense of history and memory is most directly signalled in an aptly titled episode 'Skeletons' (1977): 'Excavating for a swimming pool, a young couple come across an old trunk buried in their garden. For the police it means old files, old memories and old wounds must be reopened' (*Radio Times*).

As befits a local force, *Z Cars* moves synchronically and diachronically through its narratives, placing its characters at the point of intersection, equipped with identity and memory, able to understand the world in which they live. In an almost direct reference to the universe of *The Sweeney*, Render remarks to Bowker as they arrive at the scene of a juvenile shoplifting, 'so this is where it's all happening', to which Bowker replies, 'what would you rather have, terrorists, machine-guns, hostages?' Render's facetious musing as Bowker goes into the shop, 'I don't know, I don't know', demands that the viewer recognize the imminence of that other world, its possibility, as in other episodes we see police undergoing small arms training or discussing the pointlessness of unarmed combat against a sawn-off shotgun. But it is not this world. 'Real villains', in Inspector Lynch's words, do exist in *Z Cars*, but rarely as anything more than an off-screen reference. Instead we are faced with a parade of 'classic' villains — skilled thieves, con-men, fraud merchants, delinquents and so on. The deviant policeman is as out of place in Newtown as the psychopathic gunman that bursts in on Quilley's attempt to talk Whiskers out of his squat; and when Moffat comes under suspicion of taking bribes (the suspicion cast not by a member of his own force but by a policeman working off his patch), we realize at once that it is not his honesty but his naivety that is in question. As Lynch remarks to a visiting chief inspector, 'We're a happy station'.

Although there is a great deal more that could be said about the manifest meanings of the social worlds of both series, we now have an initial account of the salient features and the demands they make in terms of relationships between the police themselves and between the police and the society they inhabit. Before examining the ways in which these apparently distinct statements of the social process must handle the same sets of contradictions, it is important to note that already, at a 'visible' level, notions of the group and the individual are being articulated in specific ways. In *The Sweeney*, the centred biography inserts an isolated hero into an anomic social world in which individual actions are the only guarantee of effectivity. What is crucial to this placing of the individual is the way in which it everts the actual relationship of the individual to contemporary capitalist society, in other words the separation of the majority of people from the outcome of their actions within the social division of labour. It is a world in which individual actions are effective, a notion of individuality which is at once mythic and ideologically powerful in its implicit dismissal of collective aspirations and actions: 'The individual is something quite new and capable of creating new things, something absolute and all his actions quite his own. The individual in the end has to seek the valuations for his actions in himself' (Nietzsche).

In *Z Cars* the group functions to deny the anonymous world of large-scale organization and its encumbent distortion of personal relationships. Policing is not the organized institution of social control of which policemen are the agents but is translated exclusively in terms of face-to-face relationships, of open eyeball-to-eyeball confrontation, a role personified in the now promoted character of Inspector Barlow. Whereas in *The Sweeney* individuality is sufficient indemnity against bureaucratic rigidity, in *Z Cars* it is the group that subverts that bureaucracy by virtue of its humanizing sets of intra-relationships. This general function of certain groups within mass society has been indicated by Adorno and Horkheimer: 'Many of these newly differentiated groups can be called synthetic; they are planned from above as cushions between the anonymous collective and the individual'.

Initially we can establish some of the major mechanisms by which the police series is constructed and some of the more overt ideological results of that construction. But this is still dealing with the manifest meanings of the series, what is available on the surface. If we consider the notion of the 'half-formed picture' of the viewer, the question is still begged as to how these characters and their social worlds are able to be convincing, how the contradictions embedded within the fictional constructs are prevented from rupturing the coherence of the representation.

CONTRADICTION AND COHERENCE

The social worlds of *Z Cars* and *The Sweeney* cannot simply be imposed upon an audience but must be constructed in such a way that the actions of their inhabitants assume a psychological realism that 'fits in' with our knowledge of policing and, further, are recognizable versions of a social order that can be interpreted as versions of the 'real world'. Of course, realism is a conceptually complex notion that refuses any easy generalizations about the relationship between fictional forms and audience response, in spite of behaviourist-inflected assertions to the contrary. But when a production is described as realistic, or in Richard Hart's words, 'believable', it is not just a question of verisimilitude between a fictional world and an extant real world but the degree to which the production is able to make its reality convincing. To be convincing, the police series must incorporate the antagonisms and contradictions, real or perceived, of policing in England today. In other words, the effective individual of *The Sweeney* or the group-directed relationships of *Z Cars* must exist in a world which is structured at some level according to a consensual understanding of the exchange of power relationships within contemporary society.

It is, of course, necessary for the argument to accept that the police within a class society occupy a contradictory position within class structure and are expected to take action when class tensions erupt into physical violence, attacks on property or the disruption of the normal

64

functioning of the economy. But this perspective should not be taken as a crude dismissal of the police as nothing more than a 'repressive apparatus', to be abolished in any future socialist society. Any society will require a police force to control the activities of both the supportive majority (traffic, emergency services and so on) but also to defend that society against the hostile, the sick and the malicious. What is at stake is the control, organization and accountability of state apparatuses, not the utopian 'solution' of abolition. If the major contradictions of policing in Britain today can be stated as conflict with organized labour and racial groups, that is because those particular antagonisms are inherent in the relations of production which characterize the present mode of capital accumulation.

At a time when such conflicts are becoming more 'public' (Grunwick, Notting Hill) the television police series must reproduce in the structure of its fictional world a coherent account of the patterning of tensions and conflicts within a contemporary society, in order to project its authenticity and realism convincingly while at the same time displacing and referencing-out those more fundamental tensions which are essential to any basic understanding of the role and function of policing. It is the fictional world which, at the level of 'deep structure', performs the ideological work of refracting social reality in such a way that the felt tensions of police work are structured within its organization, but never structural, never threatening the apparent logic and coherence of that construct. Conflicts are contextualised, determined.

Clearly, while both series articulate different accounts of the need for law and order, both have inscribed within them the fundamentally antagonistic relationships which characterize advanced, capitalist societies. If law enforcement was simply presented as an unproblematic engagement with a criminal fringe, the programmes would be creating utopian versions of society, ideal worlds. But if the conflict was presented in all its complexity, the hours spent with the television policemen would be unbearable reminders of the exacerbations of our social structure, no longer to be classified as 'entertainment'. What the television police series must construct, if not an ideal world of policing, is, as Richard Dyer (1977b) has argued in relation to Hollywood thrillers and westerns, a world that can be experienced ideally, in which real contradictions in society can be resolved by 'deploying the constituent elements of a series at points of tension' (Pringle, 1972).

The points of tension within the police series can be revealed by considering the major oppositions identifiable within the programmes, the ways in which they are resolved within the drama and their relation to the structural contradictions which they manipulate and redefine. The set of oppositions listed below was originally developed in relation to *The Sweeney* (Hurd, 1976), but research indicates a much wider application than one specific series:

police v. crime
law v. rule
professional v. organization
authority v. bureaucracy
intuition v. technology
masses v. intellectuals
comradeship v. rank

Police v. crime
This is the starting point for all police series, *The Sweeney* and the criminal underworld, *Z Cars* and minor criminals, deviants and delinquents. The obvious dramatic resolution is the success of the police in containing crime, even though mistakes may be made along the way. But such an initial statement of a police role in an advanced capitalist society denies the wider political, and necessarily repressive, function the police fulfil, as agents of the state, most prominent in relation to organized labour, race and sex.

Law v. rule
This is most obvious in *The Sweeney* and in productions in the same trajectory, in which the short-circuiting of legal niceties is the accepted method for establishing guilt. In *Z Cars* the tension between law and rule is signalled differently by the careful reiteration of the rule-abiding policeman, with only occasional, though significant infringements. For example, in 'Domestic' (1977), Moffat sets up his criminal brother for a beating by a gang. In *The Sweeney* the rules can be dispensed with providing it is for the right reasons, while in *Z Cars* they must be adhered to in spite of the attendant frustrations and loss of effectiveness. When a police constable, interestingly played by a guest actor rather than a regular, over-enthusiastically acts as an agent provocateur, the investigation is called off and the reprimand issued that it was 'bad police work'. But in whatever direction the tension is resolved, its existence serves to render law an abstract embodiment of a natural justice, morally incontrovertible, which often has nothing to do with the rules for its enforcement. And often the crimes committed, involving the most innocent members of the community (the young, the old, the helpless) allow the policeman to step into the role of an avenger, acting on behalf of an outraged moral consensus. Such a representation serves to separate out law from the social and political structure which is inscribed in it, the power and property relationships of society, to sever its practice from its meaning. Justice and law are inviolable, given, not to be confused with the frequently flawed mechanisms by which they are obtained.

Professional v. organization
Regan and Carter are presented as the professionals, their lives defined

66

by their role as crime-fighters. This is the only rationale they have. Opposite them is the organization man whose concern is not the action-orientated fight but the corporate survival of the organization. It is a division between those that do and those that obstruct. In *Z Cars* the group functions as the centre of professionalism, bringing together men who play only the singular role of policemen in society. The self-sufficient individual of *The Sweeney* becomes the self-sufficient group, functioning without the organizational apparatus of a large-scale bureaucratic institution and resenting interference from its occasional envoys into Newtown's affairs. Again, this opposition loses the institutional dimension of policing, asserting the individual rather than the structure he inhabits. The ideological and material structuration of the individual by the organization is elided.

Authority v. bureaucracy

Authority for the professional is not derived from occupancy of a position within the bureaucracy but from his status within the milieu in which he operates. The late DS Stone of *Z Cars* failed to qualify as an inspector but was still 'the best jack on the force'. Both Carter and Regan by nature of their style miss promotion chances which would remove them from the front line and, as Regan scathingly remarks, reduce them to 'pinching bicycle thieves in Pinner'. On his first day as sergeant, Quilley undergoes the unusually violent ordeal of facing a gunman, an event which symbolically restores his professionalism and status, threatened by three stripes and a desk sergeant's docility. Status and power are safely confined to the confrontation on the streets, never allowed to overspill into the complex and shifting patterns of power relationships in large bureaucratic institutions.

Intuition v. technology

What marks the individual is his personal ability, intuition, 'nose'. Policemen continually follow up hunches, develop almost telepathic 'feelings' for a case. Against this is set the organization's faith in technology. In one episode of *The Sweeney*, 'Countryboy' (1975), the plot revolves around a young technology graduate from a regional crime squad sent to help Regan investigate a series of break-ins involving unspecified interference with alarm systems. But in spite of his technical deductions as to the location of the interference, it is only by his accidental befriending of a child with a cut knee that he manages to break the case. Similarly, in *Z Cars*, policing is an intensely human activity not dependent on high-level technology or large-scale operations. An interesting comparison could be made between police films and television series of the 1950s which sought to emphasize the technological infrastructure of criminal investigation and the current emphasis on the human dimension.

Masses v. intellectuals

In line with the emphasis on intuition is the mistrust of intellectuals, characterized as administrators, technocrats, psychiatrists, psychologists, social workers and probably sociologists. The policeman is a man of the people, a member of the mass, although often, as in the case of Regan, an elite member. The intellectual is seen as the preferred agent of the bureaucracy, sometimes well meaning but usually experientially incapable of understanding both the criminal and the priorities of law enforcement.

Comradeship v. rank

Relationships among professionals are defined in terms of their mutual respect as opposed to the organization men among whom relationships are defined in terms of rank. The first-name form of address which is habitual in both series is symbolic of a camaraderie which is juxtaposed to the formal relationships of the men from 'upstairs'.

The structuring of the fictional world of the police series along this set of oppositions, the 'points of tension' in any episode, can be directly related to the 'myth of classlessness' outlined by J. H. Westergaard (1972):

> In so far as power remains concentrated, it no longer derives from the accumulation of private property, but from the control over bureaucratic organizations of diverse kinds — public at least as much as private — in which authority is divorced from wealth. Thus two crucial dimensions of inequality no longer coincide . . . In addition, it is sometimes argued or implied, new dividing lines of cultural distinction or political tension are coming to the fore which bear no relation to the old divisions of economic class or social status — for instance, between adults and adolescents . . . between 'highbrows' or 'egg-heads' and the 'masses', irrespective of social position . . . between professionals and 'organization' men in both private and public administration; and so on.

The articulation of this myth is central to the police series and has three main functions. Firstly, it allows the viewer to recognise in any episode the working through of an ideologically consensual conflict model of contemporary society, to place crime and law enforcement within an already familiar pattern of tensions. Secondly, the characters acting out the drama within the fictional world become psychologically authentic, responding to the pressures and frustrations of these tensions in their relationships. And thirdly, the drama is emptied of its potentially disruptive conflict by divorcing the activity of policing from any class analysis of power relationships within society, reducing policing to a fictional pursuit of natural justice and denying the role of the police as an institution in the maintenance of those relationships. It is this structuring of reality that performs the ideological work of the police series, that endows with meaning and significance the manifest actions of characters within the drama. As Althusser (1969) has argued: 'Ideology is indeed a set of representations . . . They are usually images and occasionally concepts, but it is above all as *structures* that they impose on the vast majority of men.'

CONCLUSION

This [essay] has attempted to analyse the television police series by going beyond what a programme intends to be or say (entertaining perhaps, realistic certainly), to the more important meanings that are embedded in its structures. In the introduction I argued that the police seem to endorse the images of their work provided in the media, and before the impression is left of policemen conspiratorially applauding the ideological displacement at work in the police series, Maureen Cain's (1973) comments on the peculiarly contradictory, and often uncomfortable, position that policemen are placed in, should be noted: 'Policemen need to believe in a largely consensual populace whose values and standards they represent and enforce. It is by reference to this that they legitimate their activities.'

It is the way in which that consensus is constructed in the images of the television policeman that has been the concern of this analysis. And it is important to remind ourselves as well that the larger audiences for these programmes presumably derive a good deal of pleasure from the police series formula. The credit sequences of both *Z Cars* and *The Sweeney* are remarkably similar in terms of the standard elements they contain — strident music, car chases, expectations of violence and the successful capture of villains — and can usefully be read as condensed versions of the general themes and elements to be elaborated in the programmes themselves. If people do find the programmes pleasurable, it is perhaps because the image of policing that they convey fits so well with the ideal image the police have of their own work, what Skolnick and Woodworth (1967) have termed 'the symbolic rights of search, chase and capture'. (Originally published in S. Holdaway (ed.), *British Police*, London: Edward Arnold, 1979.)

References

Althusser, L. (1969), *For Marx*, Harmondsworth: Penguin.
Cain, M. (1973), *Society and the Policeman's Role*, London: Routledge and Kegan Paul.
Drummond, P. (1976), 'Structural and narrative constraints and strategies in *The Sweeney*', *Screen Education*, no. 20, 1976.

Dyer, R. (1977), *Gays and Film,* London: British Film Institute.

Dyer, R. (1977b), 'Entertainment and utopia', *Movie,* no. 4, 1977.

Forster, E. M. (1974), *Aspects of the Novel,* Harmondsworth: Penguin.

Hall, S. (1977), 'Culture, the media and the "ideological effect"', in Curran, J., Gurevitch, M., Woollacott, J. (eds.), *Mass Communication and Society,* London: Edward Arnold.

Hebdige, D. (1974), 'The Kray Twins: a study of a system of closure', Centre for Contemporary Cultural Studies Occasional Papers.

Hurd, G. (1976), *'The Sweeney:* contradiction and coherence', *Screen Education,* no. 20, 1976.

Johnston, C. (1976), 'Women's cinema as counter-cinema', in Nichols, B. (ed.), *Movies and Methods,* Berkeley: University of California Press.

Lavers, S. (1975), 'The detective genre television programme on British television', Dissertation for Polytechnic of Central London School of Communication.

Lovell, A. (1975), *Don Siegel: American Cinema,* London: British Film Institute.

Newcomb, H. (1974), *TV: the Most Popular Art,* New York: Anchor Books.

Pringle, A. (1972), 'A methodology for television analysis with reference to the drama series', *Screen,* vol. 13, no. 2, 1972.

Skolnick, J., and Woodworth, J. (1967), 'Bureaucracy, information and social control: a study of a moral detail', in Bordua, D. (ed.), *The Police: six sociological essays,* New York: Wiley.

Westergaard, J. (1972), 'The myth of classlessness', in Blackburn, R. (ed.), *Ideology and the Social Sciences,* London: Fontana.

Wollen, P. (1972), 'Counter-cinema: *Vent d'est', Afterimage,* no. 4, 1972.

4

Parodying Genre: The Case of *Gangsters*

The following two articles relate to the BBC Television production of *Gangsters*. This production took the form first of all of a 'Play for Today' in 1975, which was then followed by two six-episode series in 1976 and 1978. The play and the series were written by Philip Martin, who had written an earlier 'Thirty-Minute Theatre' production called *Gunplay* in 1971 and a number of scripts for *Z Cars*. David Rose, the Head of English Regions Drama (Television), and also a former producer of *Z Cars*, undertook to produce *Gangsters* for the Regional Drama Department at Pebble Mill, Birmingham. The original Play for Today was the seventh feature-length film to originate from this department, but the serial was the first to come from there. This is significant in itself since the English Regions Drama Unit was only established in 1971. The Birmingham department was established as a direct result of the major 1969/70 reorganisation in the English regions of the BBC. This, in turn, was partly a result of criticisms that the BBC was too London-centred and out of touch with regional differences.*

The Play and the series received a critical panning but high ratings, being described as 'hokum', a 'silly series' or 'like eating curry and chow mein to the sound of a Moog synthesiser'. More sympathetically, it was described as 'James Bond country', as a 'TV strip, probably the first successful one of its kind'. Another critic said that 'it was a relief to have the naturalist illusion punctured . . .' This last point indicates some of the reasons why, elsewhere, *Gangsters* was taken more seriously. It was described, for example, as 'one of the most interesting of recent television productions' by the TV critic John Wyver and led to a day school on the series organised by the Society for Education in Film and Television with West Midlands Arts and the co-operation of the BBC. The articles which follow are edited versions of two of the papers presented at that day school.

The two articles describe how, in various ways, *Gangsters* constituted a *challenge* to many of the dominant forms of television and to the ideological forms which accompany them. Taking the relatively familiar gangster genre as its basis with the apparent hero-figure of John Kline

* Much of the factual information here is taken from the paper presented by John Wyver at the SEFT/West Midlands Arts day school on *Gangsters* held in Birmingham in 1978.

(Maurice Colbourne) at its centre, the play and series develop through a series of intrigues and plots based in the milieu of underground, ethnic Birmingham, through gang-wars, drug- and immigrant-smuggling and prostitution rackets. Also, in the words of David Rose, this must have been the 'first ever television series to have a Pakistani hero . . . played by Ahmed Khalil'. (Interviewed in the *Radio Times*, 1978.) As the series develops, and as the following articles show, more and more aspects of parody of conventional forms are introduced. The gangsters genre is undercut by the 'quoting-in' of elements from Asian films, Fu Manchu and Kung Fu movies, comic-strip titles — 'That's all, folks' — bizarre characters such as the White Devil, dressed as W. C. Fields and played by the author Philip Martin, and by the direct intervention of Philip Martin dictating the script and the action to a scribe somewhere in Pakistan. As you will see from the articles which follow, this breaking of television codes and traditions has a more serious side which opens up some important questions for the analysis of popular television.

Gangsters: Conventions and Contraventions

The production of any televisual commodity (the construction of the text) and equally the consumption of that commodity (the construction of a reading) do not, of course, occur in a vacuum. A matrix of institutional, industrial and ideological conventions pre-exist and to an extent pre-determine their purely textual counterparts. Thus it is important to stress that any discussion of the specific textual structures and strategies of *Gangsters* must take account of the facts of its production, transmission and media previewing. Conventional expectations are generated not only by generic and other textual criteria but also by scheduling, slot and pre-selling. The original, 1975 *Gangsters* was made, shown and seen as one of a weekly anthology of contemporary dramas transmitted on Thursday nights at 9.25 under the general title of 'Play for Today' — an anthology which was at that time dominated by a relatively naturalistic mode of representation. The first serial was preceded by a repeat of this play and its six episodes were spun off in the same slot. The second serial, on the other hand, was rescheduled to Friday nights as a replacement for *Cannon*. All these factors tend to encourage authors and readers alike to 'conventionalise' the text. Thus the previews of the press, *Radio Times* and television itself emphasised the serial producer's background in 'authentic' dramas like *Z Cars*. (How different might the response have been if the second serial, for example, had been presented as a quiz or as surrealistic?)* Once it became a serial the territory of *Gangsters* was no longer restricted to the 'stylish' rehearsal of specific generic conventions but expanded and this enabled the programme to elaborate and embroider conventions of its own. Consequently its project was not only to rehearse but also to review, revise and even reveal and refuse those conventions.

Recently some work has been done in adumbrating the particular conventions which constitute the TV crime fiction genre, most notably in *Hazell: The making of a TV series* (Alvarado and Buscombe, 1978) and *'The Sweeney:* TV Crime Series' (*Screen Education*, 1976). While both

---

* As the serial actually was described in a studio discussion which followed the transmission of the final episode.

studies focus on Thames Television productions (rather than those, for example, of the BBC and/or the regions) and on series (rather than serials or single anthologised dramas) they successfully identify how the genre conventionally works within the confines of the classic realist text.* Briefly the realist crime thriller is comprised of a network of conventional practices including a teleological and formulaic narrative structure (an equilibrium posed, fractured by villainy and recovered by heroism); credible characterisation (a family allegory peopled by coherent, plausibly motivated racial, sexual and class stereotypes, cruder in the background than the foreground); identifiable iconographic elements (as illustrated, for example, by the discussion in both studies of the imagery of the title sequence, emphasising costume, decor and the tools of the hero's trade); milieu (the use of 'authentic' locations, the contrast between class settings, etc.); and finally the film and video conventions for the construction of these fictions (conventions of framing, shooting, lighting, editing, sound recording, composing, narrating, plotting, casting, acting, writing and directing). In realism this latter group engages the audience interest in what is being represented without at any time alerting them to the processes of that representation. Conventionally certain of these characters and settings are granted an authority and an authenticity over and above the rest; music and performance, lighting and camera angle, cutting and voice-over can all contribute to this privileging. This privilege allows for the thriller's climactic apportioning of guilt, etc.

It is worth quoting briefly here from both studies to elaborate a little on these conventions. Thus, in general, 'The *tenure* of the television series . . . depends for its effect on its *intermittence* and its *periodicity* (weekly and seasonal). Compulsively repetitive, it thus plays a simple game of absence/presence, its invariant features (central characters, plot-type, dramatic structure) guaranteeing the success of recognition and identification, with only the rationing of subsidiary variants (villains and their villainies, details of action) forestalling complete redundancy.' (*Screen Education*, 1976, p.16.) This simple game ' . . . works within the dictates of narrative realism, in which both characters and the world they inhabit have an inner consistency and unity' and ' . . . though Hazell speaks to the audience he never looks at it. The convention of virtually all television drama, that the audience is looking in on events rather than having them directly presented to it, is preserved.' (Alvarado and Buscombe, 1978, pp.44, 52.). These conventions: of consistency, continuity, coherence, transparency and unity are realist conventions; they are the source of an important strand in *Gangsters* but they are also conventions which it occasionally refuses and ruptures.

The Pebble Mill Press Release for the second serial announced that:

* See the article by Colin MacCabe in this book for a more detailed explanation of the concept of 'classic realist text'.

74

'As the original Play for Today of *Gangsters* used the idiom of the gangster movie and the subsequent TV series the style of the Saturday Morning Serial, the second TV series retains a more varied form of the cliffhanger endings — this time reflecting some of the "Yellow Peril" and "Fu Manchu" movies of the 20s and 30s as well as referring to the recent wave of "Kung Fu" films.' Rather less sympathetically, in a review of the second serial Richard Last complained that it was like a '. . . compound of leavings from *The Avengers, Monty Python,* early Laurel and Hardy, late Ken Russell, *Who Do You Do?* and *Batman* . . . with a touch of *The Prisoner* thrown in . . . You can't get too many laughs from a W. C. Fields impersonation when it is liable to be followed by painful death and wild realistic grief, or relax with jokes like a tombstone inscribed Sacred To The Memory of Bryan Cowgill when a few frames further on an elderly Asian will be beaten up by white hooligans. Mr Martin was trying to play tennis without benefit of net or marker lines and it can't be done. Without rules of any kind credibility perishes.' (*Daily Telegraph,* 11 February, 1978.)

Just what the status of notions like 'style', 'idiom', 'reflection', 'reference', and the 'realistic' are in *Gangsters* and how the blurring of distinction between them functions are questions which this paper hopes to pose.

The original 'Play For Today' *Gangsters* fits perhaps least problematically within the confines of the classic realist text. Much is made, for example, of the posing of narrative enigmas (who is Khan, etc?), narrative momentum (the lengthy climactic car chase), narrative structure (the twinning and intertwining of individual narrative strands, themes and characters); of credible characterisation and creditable performance (notably in the more 'harrowing' scenes involving physical and psychological pain, the use of authentic street-language, plausible motivation — usually a mixture of greed and desire for revenge — and a wide social panorama). Furthermore all these elements are sealed into a unity by the linking presence of John Kline, a character privileged by the provision of background information, posed against the Law on one side and the gangster jungle on the other, betrayed by his ex-partner but unexpectedly aided by women defecting from the opposition. The audience's appreciation of this rehearsal is guaranteed by an overlay of stylistic flourishes; it is a stylishness orchestrated of rapid cutting, sound overlaps, voyeuristic perspective, hand-held camera, filmic inserts and animations which never disturb the essential consistency and coherence of sound and image. The televisual abberation of these moments tends rather to reinforce the realist unity they temporarily infringe.

Even here, however, there are echoes, moments of reference and quotation which at least on a (safe) thematic level exceed the conventional modes of the realist crime thriller. Thus the intrusion of a series of images and titles from the trailers of Pakistani adventure films (e.g., 'High voltage drama'), the use of Enrico Morricone's 'Dollar' Western music — albeit in the realist narrative function of 'background' for the Maverick Club — together with tight closeups on the eyes (à la Leone), Kline's adoption of two pseudonyms (John Wayne and John Dillinger), the inter-cutting between 'spoken' plot questions and their 'sung' lyric echo in the club, the camera's 'Sting-like' focus on Malleson's shoes as he prowls along the roof of Anne's barge; all such sequences not only interrupt the play's realist project, but also indicate its status as a generic construct, though only by allusion to other genres or to other periods. References are therefore reserved for the western, the musical and the crime thriller of the twenties and thirties.

Such essentially playful and self-conscious elements are retained in the first serial but they remain tangential. Thus in episode one Khan remarks of the police that their dialogue seldom varies — a slightly bizarre and explicitly theatrical turn of phrase, which for a moment fractures the conventions of suspended disbelief. The remark is disarmed in two ways, however; both by means of its place within Khan's characteristic sarcasm and by its status as an aside. Later, while a particularly dramatic sequence of *Stagecoach* is being screened in the Maverick Club, Kline stands between the projector and the screen, throwing his shadow across Wayne's as he describes his desire to '... ride off into the sunset with a crock of gold.' Later still, a gangster board meeting both partakes of and at the same time parodies the language of big business and the stereotypes of 1930s Warners movies when Malleson suggests of Kline that: 'We simply foreclose on his option to breathe.' This particular instance is of some pertinence here as a challenge to realist conventions because Malleson is suddenly making use of a vocabulary which he previously and subsequently lacks. Malleson is not just acting out of character here, he is no longer a coherent character at all. This sequence demands new distinctions: it is necessary to distinguish not only between the reproduction of integrated generic conventions but also between characteral and authorial referees.

In another scene one of the strippers, bored with her routine, drops her hat over the lens of the (voyeuristic) low-angle camera, momentarily materialising the conventionally 'absent' technology. Such moments in the first serial remain as moments, jokes, occasional excesses which function as guarantors of the essentially serious and unmediated quality of the text, exemplified by the relationship between Kline and Anne. Thus in episode six when Sir George is revealed to be both Khan's boss and his quarry the performance of Robert Stephens is a significantly excessive one, signalling a constructed identity. This is the function of his extravagantly eloquent elegy to an (archaic) England of stately homes and tea drinking. Neither Kline nor Anne is ever called on to perform such a self-evidently stereotypical role.

The second serial, however, is convened of so many distinct and discrete textual practices that the construction of an unexceptional (and therefore unexceptionable) centre from which to gauge excesses is made extremely problematic. In the first serial certain stylistic flourishes had been anchored within the credible fiction of a multi-racial immigrant smuggling gang but in the second the Chinese Triad is presented to some extent at least as an anachronism comprised of 'Kung Fu' and 'Fu Manchu' stereotypes. The relatively rounded characterisation of the earlier serial and the play has been replaced by much less 'realistic' characters including, for example, Lily Li Tang, a combination of 'Fu Manchu's daughter', cold bloodedness, bland delivery and ex-Roedean arrogance. Similarly Red Stick's slow motion bionics, Khan senior's Kiplingesque colonialisms, Sarah Gant's apparently infinite allegiances, Kuldip's incoherence and White Devil's impersonation of W. C. Fields all exceed the criteria of realist characterisation. Finally, as Rafiq and Kuldip admit their own role as agents of the Narcotics Squad, Anne's 'disbelief' is destroyed. Significantly, perhaps, Anne, the ex-addict who spoke her mind about Kline's gangsterism and described life at the Nirvana as an 'everyday story of gangsterfolk', is the 'character' designated to walk out of the set into the studio. With the collapse of the coherence of realist characterisation the hero is himself killed off (unheroically) and his ex-partner, Dermot, returns in a wheelchair for the funeral.

A new credit sequence comprised of drugs, dragons and stereotyped silhouettes (as in 'Bond' titles), and an emphatic ambiguity toward character and narrative in the second serial reverse the realist project of the play. The first episode begins with Khan in conversation with an old man as they walk down an anonymous dusty road. This enigma is immediately solved by Khan's establishing explanation of his presence: 'Why not visit you, my father, here in Pakistan?', raising his arm to the land as he speaks. As they continue walking the sound of a typewriter is heard and the voice of a man dictating camera and script directions. The camera then reveals this 'writer' (who is 'played' by Philip Martin, who had taken the role of Rawlinson in the original Play) and thus the 'written' itself as a construct. Later Khan waits at a deserted roadside in a scene which echoes, right down to the use of music, Hitchcock's classic cropduster sequence from *North by Northwest*. Later still an unconscious Kline is rescued in a field by Dan Archer from the radio series and the familiar *Archers* theme music is played. Regaining consciousness in hospital Kline hears the theme music of that programme on a radio held by a window-cleaner. Throughout the episode the dominance of the integrated generic convention of the first serial is replaced by not only textual and characteral reference but also by quotations and the collapse of character itself.

Like character the conventional narrative is fractured in the second serial. Episode five for example opens not with an enigma but rather with a cliché; the discovery of a man holding a gun (Khan) by the side of a body is such a conventional signification of innocence. Later Rafiq rejects Lily's advances by feigning a headache; here a clichéd narrative convention has been inverted. Lily saves Kline's life without any apparent motivation, she is merely fulfilling a conventional narrative function, supplying both 'cliffhanger' suspense and 'romantic' testimony to the irresistibility of the hero. In the last two episodes in particular narrative action is both a reflection of and reflected in quoted conventions. Thus while Kline fights for his life in the Triad cinema Bela Lugosi struggles similarly on screen. A fight in the foyer of the cinema is frustrated by the sheer materiality of spilt canisters of celluloid. A stereotyped blonde usherette looks on with the same bored lack of interest she shows for the films themselves: she does not distinguish between them. Sarah Gant re-enacts a scene from *The Maltese Falcon* and then places that quotation with the words: '*The Maltese Falcon*, Warners, circa 1941'. A telex types out its coded messages on to paper while the screen itself is imprinted with commentary. Lily's excursion into French requires English subtitles; when she switches back to English the subtitles become French. A chanting football crowd is over-dubbed with the words: 'We are the gangsters'. Kline's killer is revealed to be none other than White Devil alias W. C. Fields alias W. D. Fields alias Philip Martin, who had previously 'impersonated' both the 'writer' and Rawlinson.

The second serial challenged the fragile conventions of (in particular) character and narrative which had sustained the illusions of the first. The trajectory, however, retains several significant parallels with the classic realist text. Narrativity and specific characteral voices remain privileged; there is a distinctive demarcation between discrete conventional strands (at least at climactic moments in the narrative); there are enigmas which pose problems for television 'readings' and which are reprised and resolved in the (very literal.) dénouement.

References

Alvarado, M. and Buscombe, E. (1978), *Hazell: the making of a TV series*, London: British Film Institute.
Screen Education no. 20, '*The Sweeney*: TV Crime Series', Autumn 1976.

Gangsters: The Pleasure and the Pain in the Text

The orientation of this analysis of *Gangsters* owes much to the work of Roland Barthes, especially his approach to Balzac's story *Sarrasine* that plots the textual fabric and reads behind the multiple codings to show how a classic realist text is constructed (Barthes, 1975.) Whilst it is not possible to transfer analysis wholesale from literature to the moving image, some of Barthes' observations are suggestive in terms of *Gangsters*.

The opening out of the text *Gangsters* can only be touched upon here, and it is the intention of this paper to pose possibilities, not offer answers, nor to offer a version of the 'story'. However, to ease the difficulties of exposition most of the examples used will be confined to the final episodes of the text (the site of the fully worked-through dynamic of the narrative) placed within the context of the wider play-series frame.

There are many possible entry points to the analysis of a text. For this analysis the starting point is the ultimate seriousness of the text — this will act as the anchor around which this discourse can structure its exposition of the playfulness, pleasure and pain of *Gangsters*, key concepts in an understanding of television drama.

Gangsters ends at the point of pain — the discourse that resides in the complex 'Writing' of the Khans (Old Man Khan and his son) politicises the narrative at the mugging incident, distresses the audience-subject and offers a (the?) 'truth' that uncomfortably pins the comedy and narrative excesses in the final series to its Birmingham-ness and the conjuncture of racial tension; it is used to jolt us out of the pleasures of the text. The forgotten 'truths' of the original play, with sound-over racial jokes offering an ironic jamming to the narrative, together with a racial realism, is suddenly reasserted as the textual excess and comedy play with/for us. This 'truth' of the text is further encapsulated in the authorly (writerly) voice that sets out Old Man Khan's project (to free his son and to see England, land of justice and freedom) while complicating it through sardonic inflections from Kipling's works, and offering a privileged and repeated coda: 'It was not taught by the State, no man spoke it aloud, when the English began to hate'. This voice over — a signification of 'truth'* is bounded, complicated by the quest of both Khans: justice. That is, the text offers its characters in search of traditional conceptions of British justice another reality; in the narrative they are victims of the social climate despite what they seek to implement. Pain in the text is strengthened by the interweaving codes of the narrative. Khan, the policeman attempting to break illegal immigrant rackets, stop corruption in the Midlands, prevent the drug smuggling of the Triad gangs, is realised televisually in very conventional ways (a reinforcement for the audience-subject of an accepted code of crime-breakers). Thus amidst the many anti-conventional strategies used, the complex 'truth' of Khan, signified in many ways, is an important feature of the text. Yet his task, echoed strongly in his Kiplingesque father, is countered, made irrelevant, outreached in the mugging sequence.

However, the multiplicity of the text disallows the simplicity of this one anchoring reading. As in the classic realist text there is an irreversibility of the framework of interpretation (the posing of enigmas, their elaboration, equivocation and eventual solution) and the actions cohere to form an understandable narrative in the text — *Gangsters*. However, the modernist influences which become more replete in the last series make it an incomplete classic text, as the style and the 'writing' stop the narrative drive (through comedy, see-the-point-wit, disabling images) and beg an answer. A reading looks — it looks primarily (traditionally) at character and narrative. But a textual fabric with a complex movement of antitheses, themes, references and connotations rooted in major characters (Kline, Anne, Rafiq, Kuldip, Khan) is interwoven in *Gangsters* by multiple stylisation; an intratextuality of *mise en scène,* joke dialogue, unconventionality of camera use. The pleasure centred in the flow of image and narrative is punctuated by the text's structuration toward a plenitude (a limited plurality) which it foregrounds, desroying the image and the narrative in a final assault in episodes five and six — the excess of White Devil, the death, the funeral, the gravestones.

In the whole text assertion is followed by bracketing, character is contextualised, bent then split or snared, redolent of a classic realist text, but the movement of the image, the chain of signification that is specifically televisual, centres the text and disallows the case of realism. 'The awareness of absence breaks the immediate delight in the image' (Heath, 1977/8); one particular example of this is the absence of the series style in the mugging; the use of the conveniently 'available' reportage style of the mugging disturbs the audience subject. (This oversimplifies the signification of the whole sequence — thus never do you get in television reporting the image of feet kicking at a person accompanied by two bars of 'Land of Hope and Glory'; it is the feel that is right, the approach through the subverted/jokey naturalism of the football crowd chanting 'We are the Gangsters' carries into the filmic

---

* The theoretical background for the notion of 'truth' in the voice of the narrator stems from the debate initiated by Colin MacCabe in 'Realism and the Cinema: Notes on Some Brechtian Theses', reprinted in this book. (Eds.)

devices of the mugging.)

Pleasure is centred in the text's artifice and in the telling of a good tale. Character is important in the text but its discourse is not necessarily dominant. The characters John Kline and Anne Darracott, the complexity of their partnership and of their individual trajectories through the narrative, are important in an understanding of the text. Both characters offer a kind of normality (of characters in gangster stories) that possibly allows a pleasure of identification (cf. Mulvey, 1975). Their enigmatic destinies repose and underpin the narrative continuity and orient the whole text. Their essential goodness (good old-fashioned romance, commitment out of past struggle and despair) is complicated in Kline's quest for 'gangsterism' (the ploy in the text to maintain the deferred denouement; Kline forced to aid Khan in the first series, the magical ingredient of the Chinese paper with details of the Triads in the second series). This is set against Anne's desire to be an honest citizen, and her position of desired woman breaking free of the wretchedness of heroin addiction and then convention (and finally freeing the narrative of pretensions to the real in its dying moments). Kline starts as a marginal character (in social terms) with a background in the SAS, a manslaughter conviction and being *used* to track down illegal rackets, and ends purposely pursuing danger to his death. Anne starts as secretary to the gangster Rawlinson, addicted to heroin, ploy for Kline's death and is traced through addiction and rescue to the preserved woman, who has chosen commitment, and finally survives the narrative. The trajectory through the text is based on Kline's marginality in contact with Anne's desirability, acting through fraught and snared situations.

The more difficult area in the text is race, because on the surface it appears so central for the original play, with a multiplicity of racial groups represented. As already outlined, the sting in the tail is the complex 'truth' of the mugging incident. However, the placing of the other ethnic characters is much harder to trace through the text especially as the complex of codes develops towards its dénouement. As Barthes has noted 'what stands out, emphasizes and impresses are the semes, the cultural citations and symbols', and there is a sense in which characters act as representatives of racial groups in the play and first series, but, as the text progresses, it is the intratextuality that becomes more important than the initial posing. Thus Rafiq, after his initial depiction as a community leader acting with great duplicity in his dealings (involvement with Rawlinson, illegal immigration racket, blackmail), magically aids detection of corrupt leaders in the first series, and after initial co-operation with the Triads, magically evades arrest and ends up (with Kuldip) agent of the US Narcotics Bureau in the second series. The stylisation of camerawork in his house, the jokiness of the scenes, deny the initial trajectory (corrupt community leader) of its force, turning into a comedy of textual acrobatics. Race *is* significant at the end (in the mugging), but the ethnic multiplicity of the characters becomes of the text, not of society. They act as a part of the pleasures of excess in the text. This contrasts with the force of the character Dinah in the original play, whose powerful dialogue is ended by repatriation (in a coffin) at the same time as the deportation of the illegal immigrant.

In the second series the posing of enigmas becomes less important, the cultural references obscured, as actions and the symbolic (the supernatural, the telex, the 'staged' qualities of the signification — through film, subtitling, etc.) dominate the text and its pleasurability through multiple internal complexities. The hardness of the original is almost lost to an elaborate 'See-the-point' exercise; the play becomes playful. But wit and comedy are centred in the unconscious as is our scopophilic delight in looking,* so that in the end the covering over is thrust aside to distress through realism (the mugging). 'The truth is . . . long desired and avoided, kept in a kind of pregnancy for its full term, a pregnancy whose end, both liberating and catastrophic, will bring about the utter end of the discourse' (Barthes, 1975, p.62.). The end distresses, pains our delight in looking; the excess of the justice/England antithesis saturates the text, but is in turn liberated by Anne's liberation of our look.

The last episodes, the final realisation of the enigmas of the idiosyncratic (if heavily influenced in a realist style) original play heavily centred on issues and Birmingham, through the excess and liberation from the conventional mode into the extremes of a surrealist style, are the expression of an un-institutionalized drama, a regional structure unbound and justified. The final reassertion of the televisual version of 'reality', through the complex appropriation of the signifiers of mugging, foregrounds an absence that brings the voice of the real (the author) back to haunt and depress, as despite Anne's liberating look he is seen dictating the end of the script and throwing it to the wind.

Gangsters is a complex text; it raises issues as part of the narrative (drugs, corruption, race, violence) but this does not mean they are argued through (they can't be). However, the progressiveness of form and the stitching in of the absence, a making then breaking of the delight in the image, influenced by filmic reference, the filmic use of video, but thrown away at the end by the final denial of a unity of form (of signification, of the suspension of disbelief), make it an important text in terms of television.

References

Barthes, R. (1975), *S/Z*, London: Jonathan Cape.
Heath, S. (1977/8), 'Notes on suture', *Screen*, vol. 18, no. 4, Winter 1977/8.
Mulvey, L. (1975), 'Visual pleasure and narrative cinema', *Screen*, vol. 16, no. 3, Autumn 1975.

* Scopophilia is a term introduced into film theory from psychoanalysis. It designates, roughly, the psychic pleasure involved in certain ways of seeing and looking at images and relates these to psychic processes.

PART II
THE DISCOURSES
OF TELEVISION

Introduction

In his *Television, Technology and Cultural Form* (1974), Raymond Williams argues that one of the distinctive characteristics of television is the 'flow' of an evening's viewing. Remarking the extent to which viewers tend to watch television for a general period — from *Nationwide* to the *9 O'Clock News*, say — rather than switching on for specific programmes, he also comments on the extent to which, in comparison with the early days of television, the marked punctuation of the transition from one programme to another has all but disappeared as advertisements, trailers, etc., install the viewer in a single, uninterrupted flow of viewing. This tendency (and it is no more than that) to blur the distinctions between different categories of programming has arguably been supplemented by the deployment of related formal strategies and conventions across a wide range of programming. If the development of drama documentary as instanced by such made-for-TV films as *King* (based on the life of Martin Luther King) has witnessed the 'factionalization' of fiction by means of the use of conventions derived from television news and documentaries, or by means of the use of historically pertinent actuality footage, it is no less the case that 'fact' is often fictionalized by the tendency, increasingly prominent in both news and documentary programmes, to bring highly formalized dramatic conventions to bear on the supposedly sober business of 'reporting'. This has never been made so clear as by ITN's coverage of the siege of the Iranian Embassy in 1980, coverage which made that event — or the terms in which it was re-presented on television — virtually indistinguishable from the climactic conclusion expected of a James Bond thriller.

An awareness of the ways in which specific formal strategies, narrative conventions and modes of address — sometimes derived from adjacent areas of television, sometimes distinctively specific — inform the news-current affairs-documentary axis of television has strongly characterized recent research in these areas. Between them, these types of programme account for a significant proportion of television output: Williams estimates that, in March 1973, BBC 1 devoted 31 hours to news, current affairs and documentaries, and a further 23 hours to the broad category of education, out of a total week's output of 100 hours (ibid., p.83). Quite apart from such quantitative indices of its significance, the news-current affairs-documentary axis of television has largely supplanted the role of other media in increasingly setting the agenda for public debate about matters of social and political concern, defining and limiting the terms of such debates as a result of the ways in which certain issues, and ways of approaching them, are selectively highlighted at the expense of others. Not surprisingly, concern about the way in which television exercises this power has always been to the forefront of public debate about the role and responsibility of broadcasting institutions, figuring centrally within both the Pilkington and Annan reports (1961 and 1977 respectively). Such concern, of course, is also reflected in the constitutional requirements of balance and impartiality which govern the operations of both the BBC and, through the IBA, the ITV companies.

The essays comprising this Part of the Reader collectively dispute the widely-held view that the operation of such canons of balance and impartiality ensure a politically neutral role for television. To the contrary, it is suggested that, in the diverse areas in which television seems, fairly evenly and open-handedly, to reproduce the 'real world' to which it refers, the practice of television inevitably intervenes, mobilizing distinctive forms of narration, specific modes of address and types of camera-positioning so as to selectively structure the viewer's orientation to the 'real world' it re-presents. Television, such approaches affirm, is indeed an agent of mediation rather than simply a vehicle for the communication of messages; it installs the viewer within particular positions of knowledge in relation to the discourses it mobilizes in the act of constructing, as the effect of its practices, the 'real' — the image of untarnished reality — which it claims as its warrant. It is, so the readings which follow suggest, largely via the operation of such 'constructive' mechanisms that television achieves a range of ideological effects — all the more effectively because such mechanisms are usually concealed or, more sustainedly perhaps, simply taken for granted.

In 'The "Unity" of Current Affairs Television', Stuart Hall, Ian Connell and Lidia Curti address questions of balance and impartiality head-on. Tracing the history of these concepts, with particular regard to the ways in which they have been interpreted and implemented within current affairs television, they confirm that television is surprisingly true to its word here. The flag-ship of BBC current affairs programming — *Panorama* — is, they suggest, usually scrupulously impartial in giving equal prominence to Conservative and Labour party viewpoints, and according the views of the other political groups operating within the spectrum of consensus politics — the Liberals, for example — a weight and importance roughly proportional to their mass support as evidenced by the ballot-box. The effect of thus implementing the canons of balance and impartiality within the limited terms of reference supplied by consensus parliamentary politics, they suggest, is to reproduce 'the unity of the Parliamentary political system as a whole'. In excluding those views which fall outside the framework of consensus politics (those of communist or nationalist parties, for example) and through its resolute impartiality within the framework of this consensus, current affairs television both seeks to appropriate for itself and in turn reproduces and sustains an ideological view of the state as representing the idea of a general interest over and above competing class or party interests. And

86

this 'ideological effect' of current affairs television, simultaneously fetishizing existing political structures, legitimizing the existing forms of the state and marginalizing political forces operating outside the consensus, is, the authors conclude, 'accomplished, not in spite of its rules of objectivity (i.e., by "covert or overt bias") but precisely by holding fast to the communicative forms of objectivity, neutrality, impartiality and balance.'

Whilst magazine programmes like *Nationwide* have not usually received the same degree of critical attention as that paid to the more serious end of the current affairs spectrum, Charlotte Brunsdon's and David Morley's study of *Nationwide* convincingly demonstrates that the flippant, self-deprecating tones of such immensely popular programmes should in no way beguile us into believing that, as is so often claimed, they are merely innocent family entertainment. Paying particular attention to the direct and homely forms of address which characterize the programme, the informal styles of the presenters and its populist anti-intellectualism, Brunsdon and Morley argue that *Nationwide* pulls the viewer into a relation of identity and complicity with the highly ideologically charged view of the nation — a view of the nation as a unity overriding the class, regional and ethnic differences of which it is comprised — which the programme itself constructs and mobilizes. The essays by Colin McArthur, Andrew Tudor and Geoffrey Nowell-Smith collected under the heading 'Television and the World Cup' perform a similar function in relation to televised soccer.

Finally, in their 'Science on TV: A Critique', Carl Gardner and Robert Young challengingly contest the assumptions underlying the images of science, scientists and scientific progress that are produced by the main conventions governing the representation of science on television. Examining a wide range of science documentaries as well as dramatized versions of key moments in the history of science, such as BBC's highly successful series *The Voyage of Charles Darwin*, Gardner and Young argue that the media construct a view of science as abstracted from social and political processes — developing, seemingly, as a result of its own momentum or as a result of the break-throughs of individual geniuses — in spite of the increasing evidence both that the production of scientific knowledge is a social process and that science, in areas as diverse as medicine and micro-chip technology, is re-shaping our lives in all of its dimensions: social, political, psychological, sexual and environmental. Arguing that there is a pressing need for science, in all of its guises and in all of its implications, to be the subject of informed critical and public debate, Gardner and Young conclude with some suggestions as to ways in which the television coverage of science might be modified in order the better to equip it to meet this need.

Reference

Williams, R. (1974), *Television, Technology and Cultural Form*, London: Fontana.

The 'Unity' of Current Affairs Television

INTRODUCTION

Since the General Election of 1959 (often referred to as the first 'television election'), television has been thought to play an increasingly crucial role in the provision of social knowledge about the issues and events which are pivotal to election campaigns. Three major interpretations have been made of its contributions, and of the relations of television, as an informer, to its sources and audiences.

The first of these is the *conspiracy thesis*. Various authors, especially critical and radical ones, have argued that what we may broadly call 'political communication' is founded on a conspiracy between the State and television. News and current affairs programming is depicted as the public voice of a sectional, but dominant, political ideology, which is reproduced in the media to the exclusion of any other; this area of programming is said to offer, fairly unambiguously, to the public 'the ruling ideology of that class which holds State power'. [...] In essence, the thesis assumes the absolute and undisputed sway of this political ideology over the whole social formation, including its 'ideological apparatuses'. From this position, the broadcaster is conceived as nothing more than the ideological agent of his political masters; and the audience as a mass of isolated individuals deprived of any ways and means to question or resist the former's ideological onslaught. [...] The second interpretation, the *displacement thesis*, [...] transfers the power, elsewhere ascribed to political forces, to the broadcasters, who are presented as the 'new priesthood'. The image of television offered here is that of an independent and prime mover in the social formation. Television is thought not to confer authority on definitions of political situations formulated outside the studio, but rather, of its own volition, to construct these definitions which it then proceeds to present as those of the society as a whole. The logic of this position can be most clearly seen in the recent study of the February 1974 General Election by Trevor Pateman (1974). His central thesis leads him to regard the phrase 'television coverage of an election' as more and more misleading. He argues that television can only be said to 'cover' an election when the campaign has an existence independent of it. For him, the campaign no longer possesses this independence: 'we do not have television coverage *of* an election: we have a *television election'* (Pateman, 1974, p.2).

This study is very important in that Pateman gives due weight to the specificity of television's mode of operation: its 'inflexible formats and ritual repetitions', the use of rapid camera changes, or more than one news reader, and of a variety of other 'attention-holding devices'. It nevertheless glosses over certain vital distinctions. We would agree with Pateman that the devices he isolates and examines do indeed mediate political events such as General Elections. But if we accept that television plays a mediating role, it follows that elections as *political events* remain distinct from their presentation as *television events*. [. . .] Unlike Pateman, we would argue that communications is not the only level on which political parties are formed and operate; that the formation and maintenance of political parties takes place primarily within the institutional framework of the State. This is not to deny that there are *interconnections* between the political system and the ideological apparatuses: but they must be grasped and studied as such, not assumed to be identical.

As with the former thesis, Pateman does not sufficiently allow for breaks or discontinuities at the reception or decoding end of the communicative exchange between television and its audiences. In this respect, he seems to commit the error of assuming that audiences are *always* bound to programming in a transparent relationship; and thus infers audience responses from the nature of the messages they receive. That the broadcaster will *attempt* to establish such a relation of transparency with the audience (what Pateman calls a 'relationship of complicity') [. . .] is undoubtedly true. But, to assume the success of the strategies employed is to ignore the 'crisis of credibility' through which broadcasting is currently passing and thus the lived experiences and complexities of these exchanges.

The third position may be referred to as the *laissez-faire thesis,* typically proposed by broadcasters themselves. In general terms, it is argued that the elections command no special attention, beyond that which television accords any other important moment in the life of the nation. Television does not attempt to shape or mould this event; it simply reflects, as accurately as it can, the development of the campaign as it happens. Nor is the coverage systematically 'biased' in favour of any one of the competing parties. Broadcasters and commentators have emphasised that great care is taken to ensure that all the major parties have equal access to the debate as it appears on television. Programming is conceived, simply, as a 'window on the campaign'; it reflects, and therefore does not shape or mould, the political debate. In short, the objectives of television are to provide *objective information* for the public so that they may make up their own minds in a 'rational' manner.

In the course of this paper [. . .] we shall attempt to pin down more precisely what we see to be the inadequacies of each of these positions. It is our contention that each offers an inadequate explanation of the complex nature of the coverage and of the equally complex relations through which the State and television are interconnected. Each points to some form of unity between the two; but this is conceptually grasped only at the expense of evidence suggesting certain oppositions between the two institutions. Each depicts the circuit of communication about political events as closed up around one 'real' and unambiguous meaning, which flows smoothly, without breaks, discontinuities or oppositions, to the majority of the audience. Our own thesis begins from an essentially different set of premises. In relation to the messages available through television we shall suggest that they never deliver *one* meaning; they are, rather, the site of a plurality of meanings, in which one is preferred and offered to the viewers, over the others, as the most appropriate. This 'preferring' is the site of considerable ideological labour. Furthermore, we shall suggest that the relations between television and the State have a dual character. Television is *both* autonomous and dependent, or to put this another way, it is *relatively autonomous* of the State. [. . .]

THE PROBLEMATIC PRACTICE: BROADCASTERS VS. POLITICIANS

The 'Election' *Panorama* which forms the basis of this study is an instance of Current Affairs programming in a particularly sensitive area of television journalism. News and Current Affairs have always been maintained as separate departments within the BBC; and though there is more co-operation and contact between them now than there was in television's early days, the distinction remains important. It is the institutional expression of the classic journalistic distinction between 'fact' and 'comment'. Of course, Current Affairs, like News, is governed operationally by the same general criteria of impartiality, balance and objectivity; but, unlike News, which is predominantly concerned with establishing the 'facts' of a given situation, Current Affairs is predominantly concerned with exploring and probing situations, to establish the prevailing 'attitudes' and 'opinions' which frame problematic events. [. . .]

The sensitivity of this area stems in part from this distinction. Current Affairs programmes, like *Panorama*, deal with, and invite, comment on controversial issues in the political domain, where broadcasters are most exposed to charges of bias and unfair practice, and where politicians are most alive to the danger of broadcasting's usurping their right to address and represent the electorate directly without the broadcaster's intervention and mediation. Election coverage is a sensitive area in its own right, since it occurs at the very moment when the electorate is 'making up its mind' — an extremely delicate moment in parliamentary democracies. For these reasons, the coverage of elections has always been strictly monitored and limited. [. . .] The nature and extent of the coverage has been the subject, over the years, of quite formal negotiations between broadcasters and the political parties: the coverage is negotiated afresh on the occasion of each election, and is framed, not only by the 1969 *Aide Mémoire* (the details of which are confidential) which governs all ministerial and party political broadcasts, but also by the Representation of the People Act, 1969. Furthermore, the companies of the IBA are expressly required to present the expression of political opinion in 'properly balanced discussions or debates' (cf. Television Act, 1964) while the BBC have adopted this as a self-imposed requirement. Nevertheless, throughout the history of the television coverage of General Elections, both networks have been allowed the editorial autonomy to decide what, precisely, counts as 'proper'. Formulating the agenda for discussion, comment and debate, the right of selecting the speakers and of chairing the debate, have been, as a consequence, in the hands of the broadcaster. [. . .]

This should not suggest that the negotiations between broadcaster and politician have always been perceived by each of them as unproblematic. [. . .] There is a lengthy history of very real antagonism between the broadcaster and the politician, which casts considerable doubt on the thesis that the latter exercises an absolute control over the former at all levels. Politicians, from each of the major parties, have publicly and privately attacked both networks, and particularly the BBC, for their handling of controversial issues, especially during the build-up period to General Elections. The precise character of this attack has shifted over time: the Labour Party, prior to 1966, was comparatively enthusiastic about the general role and performance of the BBC, a position which had changed dramatically by the late 60s with Richard Crossman's public criticism of the BBC's handling of civil rebellion, and the publication of Wedgwood Benn's more extreme thesis that 'broadcasting was too important to be left to the broadcaster' (*The Guardian*, 19 October 1968). We cannot here engage in tracing these and other important points of conflict [. . .] in any detail, except to outline certain of the basic and recurrent themes. These include the perennial charge of 'bias'; the charge that in current affairs programmes there has been an over-concentration on 'comment and analysis' to the virtual exclusion of 'straight reporting' which has resulted in the cardinal sin of editorialising; that broadcasters have acted as a 'pressure group' for certain kinds of social and political change; that broadcasting has trivialised and personalised politics and thus contributed to the erosion of traditional political *mores;* and, in more recent times, that it has contributed to the crisis in established political structures by providing a public platform for the voices of political dissent and opposition. [. . .]

The parliamentary critique hinges on the assumption that the broadcasting authorities, the BBC in particular, are too powerful, too monolithic and have acquired too great a degree of independence.

Television is felt to place itself *between* the politician and the elector, in the absence of any formal responsibility to either. Nevertheless, established political forces have, in the main, stopped short of the suggestion that television should be more directly managed and controlled by the State [. . .] While they have considered ways in which the broadcaster's editorial power might be rendered more 'accountable', [. . .] politicians have for the most part been united behind the line that editorial power should remain in the hands of the professional. What they require is that this should be exercised differently and more circumspectly.

The spokesmen for the BBC have been far from submissive in their replies to this critique. [. . .] To the charge of trivialisation, for example, they have counter-attacked with the suggestion that this stems from the conduct of politicians which appeals to, and nurtures, emotional commitment at the expense of commitment based on 'rationality'. On the issue of responsibility, the [then] Director General, Sir Charles Curran, argued that the BBC has, and fulfils, a responsibility:

> . . . to provide a rationally based and balanced news service which will enable adult people to make basic judgments about public policy in their capacity as voting citizens of a democracy . . . We have to add to this basic supply of news a service of contextual comment which will give understandings as well as information (Curran, 1971). [. . .]

The antagonisms between the broadcaster and the politician are [primarily] rooted in their respective approaches to the public. The divergences between them can be most clearly seen in the context of General Elections. While the politician is manifestly concerned to enlist support to a particular manifesto or Party position, the broadcaster manifestly aims to win the politician *and* the electors to what they consider a rational and intelligible presentation of the issues. Thus the antagonism may be summed up as a conflict between the dictates of 'good television' on the one hand, and the dictates of 'good politics' on the other.

The history of the relations between television and the State is not, however, characterised by conflict alone. Certain symptomatic instances of accommodation can also be isolated, such as the controversy over *Yesterday's Men,* a programme considered by both managers of broadcasting and the managers of politics to have transgressed the underlying rules of good political communication. [. . .] Thus the relationship between the two is complex. This complexity — opposition and difference on the one hand, accommodation and unity on the other — is perhaps best demonstrated in relation to the question of 'bias'. Television spokesmen have rightly insisted that, as a rule, they are not biased in favour of any one political faction. Yet they have not denied that they are indeed biased. Sir Charles has said:

> One of my senior editors said recently, in a phrase which I treasure: 'Yes, we are biased — biased in favour of parliamentary democracy.' I agree with him. It is our business to contribute to the debate by making available to the widest general public the opinions of those who are directly engaged in it. It is not our business to shape the end of the debate. That is for the electorate, guided by the politician (Curran, 1974, p.782).

So, it would appear that the broadcaster and the politician operate, broadly speaking, within the same ideological framework, though they frequently take different positions within it. [. . .] While the broadcaster is not partisan in relation to the 'legitimate' transfer of power from one Party to another, he is partisan in terms of the maintenance of a certain mode and type of institutionalised power — namely the capitalist state as a parliamentary democracy. In this light, the differences and oppositions we have indicated are what have been called 'secondary contradictions' — 'conflicts of mutual indifference'. While they are real differences, they do not add up to fundamental contradictions — contradictions of the structure. [. . .]

CURRENT AFFAIRS VALUES

The distinction between News and Current Affairs programming which we indicated in the previous section is reflected in the differential values which frame the skills and objectives of each domain. [. . .] What is received as 'good television' will vary as between those who are routinely employed in the field of news, and those who are regular contributors to one of the existing current affairs programmes. The criterion of 'immediacy', for example, [. . .] has considerably less relevance for those Current Affairs broadcasters who take on the responsibility 'to inform the audience not only about the immediate dramatic happening, but also about moments and incidents which could lead to tomorrow's headlines' (BBC, 1974, pp.6-7). This does not suggest a complete disregard for the values of news. Indeed, [. . .] at the present time News provides the *baseline*, in the sense that an event or issue must have already passed through the stage of being a 'news story' before it can be passed on and constructed as a 'current-affairs story'. [. . .] Current Affairs is [thus] not wholly autonomous of News, [nor] are they interchangeable or reducible to the other. What then is distinctive about Current Affairs programming?

Typically, a news *story* or 'report' becomes a current affairs *topic*. It becomes a topic by being framed as a question, or set between seemingly alternative or antagonistic propositions. This is particularly true of *Panorama*. In the edition of this programme on the so-called 'downfall' of

Vietnam, the question which established the perspective on the item was delivered after a brief situating introduction:

> The resignation of Thieu then is the end of a long chapter in the book of America's involvement in Vietnam. It's almost certainly the last chapter. We just await now the epilogue as the United States tries to withdraw their own people and some of their dependents and helpers. How then does the United States view the demise of the man they supported for so long? *(Panorama,* 21 April 1975). [. . .]

Current Affairs magazines provide a space in which the broadcaster can set about *filling in the contexts* to events which have been already accredited significance by their appearance on news bulletins, or, as is frequently the case with *Panorama,* by press reports. They do not only register that an event has happened, but go on to *probe* the attitudes and opinions of the actors involved: to put questions to them which the 'average viewer' would put, if he or she could; to test out the arguments held by 'many people' against those held by 'many others'; and to invite 'expert' comment. As a whole, the field can be characterised as providing *informed speculation* about events, with the objective of promoting a 'rational' understanding of the issues involved. [. . .]

Not all the events which are selected and constructed as news stories subsequently become current affairs stories. Nor do those news stories which pass into the keeping of Current Affairs receive attention from all the programmes in this field. Some stories trigger coverage across the full range (e.g. an announcement by the Government on its measures to 'curb' inflation, or on the question of devolution). Events such as these have a more or less guaranteed access to *all* the mainstream current affairs slots, in that they are instances of high controversy between those in authoritative positions; they are, in short, topics which stand high on the agenda of 'legitimate cleavage' in the political domain. Some topics, on the other hand — crime, for example — while receiving extensive routine surveillance in news, rarely set in motion the full Current Affairs apparatus (Hall, *et al.,* 1975). Crime topics will, in the main, go only so far as *Midweek,* whose stock of items contains a higher proportion of 'deviance' topics — moral, political and sexual, as well as the strictly criminal. [. . .] These *differential passages* through the Current Affairs field reveal a process of selection similar to that operated by the newsman in his choice of items from the range of potential 'newsworthy' events in any one day. Just as events do not select themselves for news coverage, neither do they select themselves for current affairs coverage. The selection and placement of topics for current affairs programmes require a process of assessment with its own discrete norms.

'Current Affairs values' is a more complex system of evaluative norms than the system of news values, given the existence of a range of stylistically differentiated programmes (cf. *Panorama Casebook* for a detailed exposition of the stylistic repertoire of current affairs). There are important differences of approach, of 'making sense' and of style, as between, for example, *Nationwide* and *Panorama* or *Weekend World*. [. . .] These differences and oppositions are particularly clear in relation to the communicative role of anchorman/presenter. In general the occupants of this role are not expected to present themselves as especially knowledgeable. This point was emphasised by Robin Day in his estimation of the late Richard Dimbleby's contributions to developing and refining this role:

> Because he is not a keen student of politics or current affairs, he is presented as a sort of Plain Man, who like the viewer, is a bit puzzled by the problems on which these sharpwitted, indefatigable commentators report. The idea is that Dimbleby is 'with' the viewer speaking for millions . . . (Day, 1961, p.183).

Kumar (1974) underlined the importance of this role when he said:

> The people that matter, from the public's point of view, the people who for it constitute 'the BBC' are the regular 'personalities' who increasingly are the familiar 'link-men', the 'anchor-men' of the regular programmes . . . It is these men who map out, for the public, the points of identification with the BBC (p.11).

In short, the anchorman operates principally as a mediator and orchestrator, standing between the audience and its assumed puzzlement, and the reporters whom he 'calls up' or nominates to deliver that 'rational-sense' of the spheres of authority to which they are intimately attuned. Yet there is no single way in which this role is performed; the camera-presence of Michael Barratt (whose image has been described as that of a 'no-nonsense man of the people . . . emphasised in the aggressive set of his shoulders' *(Listener,* 1 May, 1975)) is quite distinctive from David Dimbleby's, in which the declared emphasis is in projecting himself as earnest and sincere. These forms of presenting the self vary, and do so according to the broadcaster's sense of the audience and of the degree and nature of the problematicity of the topic or domain handled by the programme.

Thus, we would suggest that News and the different Current Affairs programmes do not constitute a simple unity, but rather a 'complex unity in difference'. No one approach predominates to the exclusion of others; different styles co-exist in Current Affairs; and the programmes in this area are not a simple extension of the News. Nevertheless, there is a fundamental commitment to *informed speculation* which connects News and Current Affairs; and specifically for the coverage of elections, there are many shared 'preferred forms'. [One] reason for studying the edition of *Panorama* we have selected is that it provides an example of these preferred forms in operation.

Since *Panorama,* of all the current affairs programmes, is the one most sensitively tuned to the 'great political issues' of the moment, it is necessary to sketch in the immediate political context from which the theme of this particular programme — 'What Kind of Unity?' — was adopted. October was the second election [in 1974]. The first, in February, occurred in the middle of the Heath 'emergency' crisis, and as a direct result of the confrontation between the Heath Government and the miners. [. . .] It was thus a 'crisis' election, called to obtain a vote of confidence for the Heath strategy, and announced under the single crisis-theme: 'Who Rules Britain?' [. . .] The Heath strategy was to identify the Conservatives with the 'National Interest', the 'common good', against the sectionalism and 'extremism' of the unions, whom he attempted to present as a threat not just to orderly government under the Conservatives, but also, as he stated in his first election address on television, to the system of parliamentary democracy itself. [. . .] The Liberals, also seeking the 'moderate' middle ground, but at the same time anxious to maximise party advantage, floated the idea of a 'Government of National Unity'. Labour, claiming to be the only party able to get a settlement with the miners, also — but less overtly — jockeyed for a position within the 'moderate' spectrum. It counterposed its 'new deal' with the Unions (in the form of a new 'Social Compact') to the 'conflict policies' of the Tories. [. . .]

The result of the February election was crucial. Labour won, but with an extremely small majority. [. . .] In the immediate aftermath, although the miners' strike was settled, the talk of 'national unity', of 'coalitions' and Grand Coalitions, of compromises and deals, thus continued to command the political field. It became clear that Labour could not govern for long on a minority basis, and that another election, to resolve the statemate, would shortly be called.

In the period between the February and October elections, the economic and inflationary crisis took tangible form and came to dominate the whole economic and political scene. For our purposes, the significance of this was two-fold. First, in the conditions of a 'hung Parliament', the broad political issues — moderates vs. extremists, 'who rules Britain?', who can unite the nation? — become translated from their political to a *narrower* Parliamentary meaning: *which Party* will emerge from the second election with a majority? [. . .] Will another 'hung result' produce some version of a Parliamentary coalition? Will the two-party system survive the challenge from the third and fringe parties which, because of the narrow balance in Parliament, could exert a critical balancing influence (a constraining effect which was, of course, defined as forcing an 'extreme' Labour minority government to act more responsibly and 'moderately')? This narrower definition of the theme is clearly evident in the programme. Second, the *content* of 'unity' was redefined: less in direct relation to the confrontation between Government and unions, and more in relation to the economic crisis. Now it was the economic 'crisis', inflation and its divisive social consequences, which were seen as posing a threat to 'democratic institutions themselves'. [...] This way of posing the issue of 'unity' and conflict thus led to a broader, more abstract polarisation between Order and Anarchy. This second theme, too, can be seen at work in our programme.

In October, Labour decided to go to the country again to seek a mandate. It was armed, now, with a firmer 'Social Contract' agreement with the unions: and with a commitment to seek a national mandate, through referendum, to seal Britain's entry into Europe. Labour thus appealed to the electorate on the basis of itself having the programme to tackle the crisis, of itself being able to 'unify the nation'. The Tories, under Mr. Heath, trying to win back power from a weak base, offered, if elected, to rule 'moderately': specifically, to bring into government members of other parties so as to ensure a broad and unified administration, capable of guiding a united nation and Parliament through the crisis: a government of 'National Unity'. The Liberals, hoping to exploit their small but pivotal role in an almost perfectly balanced situation, called for 'moderation' on all sides, the specific form of which, they suggested, ought to be a 'national' government, which would include them on some agreed basis or programme. [...] The Nationalist parties and groupings [...] all hoped to advance their electoral chances and emerge, in a Parliament similarly unresolved, with an enhanced position enabling them to use their votes, against whichever Party won a marginal majority, to advance their interests.

It was in this political context that *Panorama* chose, for its third and final Election programme, to take up the theme of 'What Kind of National Unity?'. This background helps to explain both *why* this was an issue which *Panorama* thought it could use to orchestrate a wide-ranging political debate between the principal Party contestants, and also why the theme of 'unity', as it was introduced in the opening sequences of the programme, hovers rather uneasily between its wider, political and its narrower, Parliamentary meaning.

THE PANORAMA CASE STUDY

Programme Outline
The edition of *Panorama* which is examined here was screened on Monday, 7 October 1974, three days prior to Polling Day. [...] The

following chart sets out the overall framework of the third programme, giving some idea of what was covered, and how, in each segment:

Preface: Actuality clips of Smith Square with commentary over; actuality clip of Westminster with commentary over; actuality piece to camera by Michael Charlton.

Opening Titles: Graphics depicting the register of a 'one-armed bandit' on which the faces of the main party leaders, and their parties' rosettes 'rolled' round. Closed with title 'The Battle For Britain'.

Segment 1: *Framing the Topic:* piece to camera by Charlton on the theme 'What Kind of Unity?' which opened with a reminder about the 'huge economic difficulties' facing the country; introduction of the 'leading party spokesmen in the studio' (shown); and next, the 'nationalist challenge': report to camera by Denis Tuohy which began with a summary of the February Election results, and with the aid of stills, the seats held by Liberals, Nationalist and Unionist Parties. Actuality clips of Oil Rig with commentary over on the 'nationalist argument'; then into actuality interview with Gordon Wilson, chairman of SNP, on the theme that 'North Sea Oil is Scotland's Oil', and another from Willie Ross for Labour's estimation of the claim. Followed by a further interview clip with Wilson.

This pattern is then repeated for Plaid Cymru.

Back to studio: Tuohy to camera announcing the major parties' proposals for devolution; presented with graphics and commentary over; comes back to Tuohy who moves the topic onto the failure of power-sharing experiment in Northern Ireland which is handled by means of actuality clips and commentary; first interview with William Craig on the nature of his party's position.

The examination of the nationalist challenge concludes on the question of the possible accommodation the SNP and Ulster Unionists might attempt with the major parties.

Back to studio, Charlton to camera on the major parties' responses to the threat to unity, and their prescriptions; Charlton's report interspersed with 'actuality' quotes from each of the three leaders of the major parties, Wilson, Heath, then Thorpe.

Segment 2: *Reprise:* to Robert McKenzie who summarises the main themes to be covered in the interview/debate with James Callaghan, William Whitelaw and David Steele, each second-in-command of their respective parties.

Segment 3: *'Free' Discussion and Debate:* opens with a round of questions to each of the participants on their policies for devolution; on their positions on Northern Ireland; on the 'broader question of the kind of national unity this country's going to have to develop'; which breaks into 'open' debate; then a question directed to Whitelaw on the Tory Party Leadership; and a final question to Callaghan on the

98

proposed date of the EEC Referendum, and what his party will recommend.

Programme Analysis: Signifying Systems and Practices
Though we cannot give a detailed résumé of the method employed to study this particular encounter between the broadcaster and the politician, we shall identify the overall approach, its main components and its conceptual premises.

We do not conceive of News and Current Affairs programming simply as a series of 'windows on the world' which permit a faithful and comprehensive reflection of 'the facts'. The facts must be gathered: hence the coverage of political topics will be constrained in part by the nature of the available sources. Broadcasters must select which facts seem most relevant and important for an intelligible coverage of the topic: hence the coverage they produce will be selective; and the selection process will be constrained in part by their 'news and current affairs values', and by their sense of audience. The facts must be arranged, in the course of programming, so as to present an intelligible 'story': hence the process of presentation will reflect the explanations and interpretations which appear most plausible, credible or adequate to the broadcaster, his editorial team and the expert commentators he consults. Above all, the known facts of a situation must be translated into intelligible *audio-visual signs, organised as a discourse*. TV cannot transmit 'raw historical' events, as such, to its audiences: it can only transmit pictures of, stories, informative talk or dicussion about, the events it selectively treats. So, however a broadcasting organisation gathers, selects and pre-arranges its topics, programme transmission must ultimately assume the form of an audio-visual discourse; and this is a symbolic activity, requiring the intervention or mediation of visual and verbal codes, or what we call the use of *systems of signification*. Current Affairs topics, in short, must be *encoded*, if they are to carry any meanings and be intelligible to audiences. [. . .]

By meaning, we have in mind something more than the literal meaning of the different sounds and images which compose the programme: we use it to refer to both the literal meanings and the more associative or connotational meanings. As we tried to establish in the section on 'Current Affairs Values', programmes in this general area produce for their audiences constructed topics, which are subject, in the course of presentation, to the process we have called *informed speculation*. The aim of the producers of the message is to transmit a meaning which will be 'read' by the audience in much the same terms as those of the broadcasters. [. . .] To put this another way, the broadcasters' objective is to have the audience reconstruct the programme as it has been *ideologically inflected and structured* by them. [. . .]

The broadcasters' encoding practices, therefore, aim at establishing a *transparency* between the presentation of the topic, as embodied in the programme, and the view which their audiences 'take' of it. The broadcaster tries [. . .] to bring the encoding and decoding moments into alignment: it is an attempt to realise a certain kind of ideological closure, and thereby establish a *preferred reading* of the topic. [. . .] However, it is in the nature of all linguistic systems which employ codes, that more than one reading can potentially be produced: that more than one message-structure can be constructed. It follows, in our view, that different audiences, depending on their socio-economic position, cultural position and 'competences', and the interconnections between them, can make more than one reading of what has been encoded. [. . .]

Thus, when we analyse a programme according to the scheme outlined above, what this produces is the way particular codes and their combinations work so as to produce and sustain, not *the* meaning (for there is no such unitary thing), but the *preferred encoding* of the topic. [. . .] Although the TV programme-message is *structured*, and aims for a certain kind of ideological *closure*, it can only be *relatively* closed up around any one reading: and that partial closure is, precisely, the result of the *work* — the ideological work — to which the signifying systems and their preferred *use* in any one instance contribute, and what, in effect, *they sustain*.

APPROPRIATING AND RE-APPROPRIATING THE TOPIC

How, then, is this programme ideologically structured? What is the nature of the 'ideological closure' towards which the programme moves? How closed or open-ended is this 'closure'? And how is the structuring actually affected in the course of the programme? This involves, as we have suggested, looking closely at the *interaction* between what, for purposes of convenience, we distinguish as *contents and forms*. [. . .] By 'contents' we mean the events and developments in the political world *as they become thematised into the subject-matter, the topics, of the programme*. By 'forms' we mean the combination of discourse elements *which are employed, in different parts of the programme, to signify what in fact its content is*. 'The programme' may then be defined as the appropriation of a topic and its selective development and passage through the forms of its signification. We shall take some examples from the two basic 'halves' of the programme — the first, where the topic is elaborated and thematised, principally, by the media men, employing such elementary signifying forms as commentary, scene-setting, compilation film. This part of the programme relies heavily on all those forms which allow the media men to gather up, summarise, select the principal points (themes) which define the topic, which appropriate it into the TV discourse of Current Affairs. This might be called the *informational* side of 'informed speculation'. The second half is where the topic is 'thrown open' for further development in free discussion between participants, under the

100

chairmanship of the broadcasters. This principally takes the form of the TV round-table debate: the *'speculative'* side of 'informed speculation'. The second half not only follows chronologically, but depends, logically, on the first: the topic must be 'established' first — as much as possible through the use of actuality material, to avoid any charge of bias or partiality — in order that the participants can speculate on and around this established base. One must also remark that, if the first half 'takes over' the political subject-matter in the form of a topic and its themes on to the terrain of the media, the second half seems to 'return' the topic to its source — it gives back the constructed topic to the politicians for them to reconstruct and deconstruct as they will — under the controlled conditions, of course, of 'reasonable and rational debate'. [. . .]

SETTING IT UP

Charlton announces the 'Unity' theme in the prefatory film to the programme. This opens with a series of shots of *Smith Square*, headquarters of the two main Parties, described as 'the heart if not the mind of British politics'. Cut to a close-up of the *Houses of Parliament* from Parliament Square:

> Charlton: On the whole Westminster has been accepted as the place and centre of decision and rule for all the United Kingdom. But not so today. Rule from Westminster is challenged in Ulster, in Scotland and in Wales.

Next Charlton *against the background of Parliament,* now viewed from across the river, speaking direct to camera:

> So how is Parliament to accommodate itself to all the rival dissents and discontents in Britain? Behind the campaign arguments we've been listening to about wealth and fairness and justice, stands the nation of Britain itself. Where is the nation going? All the parties call for unity, but what kind of unity do we need?

Following the credits, the first main sequence opens with Charlton, seated at table to left of screen; behind him and to the right, a *Union Jack* with the question 'What Kind of Unity?' superimposed. Charlton, straight to camera:

Shot	Dialogue
2-shot Charlton & caption	Charlton: What kind of Unity? Not for the first time in Britain's history the politicians warn us that this country faces huge economic difficulties . . . and that the only way of fighting the battle is to fight it

101

	together. So each of the parties talks of unity and each has its own prescription for that unity. In a moment we shall be
Cut to 3-shot of Whitelaw, Steele, Callaghan	talking to the leading party spokesmen on why they think they have the best means of achieving it. Calls for unity come at a
Back to Charlton	time when the United Kingdom faces varying degrees of challenge to established rule from Westminster . . .
Caption change to Nationalist posters	Nationalists and Unionists have joined the Liberals in forming a third force in British politics.

There are really two parts to this 'set up'. The first takes over and establishes certain key parameters to the topic for the purposes of Current Affairs exploration: the establishment depends on forging certain equations — to which both spoken and visual discourse contribute:

(Commentary): Westminster — UK — Parliament — nation itself — Unity
(Visual): Smith Square (Parties) — Parliament — Union Jack

These established points of reference, the supports to the concept 'Unity', are then cross-cut by certain challenges:

Nationalists — dissent and discontents — different prescriptions for unity

The topic thus becomes an *issue* for current affairs, a problematic question, by contrasting 'unities' against 'challenges': the Union Jack, with 'What King of Unity?' superimposed, exactly visualizes the topic as a theme for informed exploration, speculation and debate. The topic has passed through these forms into the keeping of the media.

But this passage onto the terrain of the media is immediately followed by *grounding it,* so to speak, back in the terrain from which it originated: 'politicians warn us . . . ', 'each party talks of . . . ', 'we shall be talking to the leading party spokesmen . . . '. This reminds the viewer that, though the parameters of 'Unity', offered by the broadcaster, will frame and organize the passage of the topic throughout the rest of the programme, the topic has its origin in the on-going political debate *outside* the media. It is *politics* which has set the theme *for* the media: and the media definition of the topic will be heavily dependent on the way the subject has already been pre-defined by the primary definers (the main Party spokesmen) in the primary circles of Party and Parliamentary activity. [. . .] Television's 'impartiality' in relation to the topic is *validated* by substantiating that the topic already has a political life outside of television, on which television's treatment ultimately (in the last instance) depends. This privileged and primary determination over the topic by the three major Parliamentary parties is realized visually and verbally, at several points throughout the first half of the programme. After exploring 'the nationalist challenge', the broadcasters summarise, by means of commentary-over-captions, the three Parties' main policies on devolution. Later still, the first half is closed with *direct quotes* on 'their prescription for Unity' from Wilson, Heath and Thorpe. Note that, whereas the main Party definitions are both summed up by broadcasters, and allowed to come over in straight extracted quotes, the Nationalist challenges are *not* allowed to come over straight. They are not accorded the same degree of authority.

Under the heading 'What Kind of Unity?', four quite distinct questions are pulled together into a common theme (thematised) in the course of the first segment: the rise of the small nationalist parties; the possibilities of government by coalition; the problem of Northern Ireland; and the possibilities of Britain remaining in the Common Market. [. . .] The editorial work can, therefore, be seen to reflect or reproduce a *certain political perspective* on the 'unity' issue: one which identifies unity very firmly with two-party rule, a centralised, unitary kingdom under Parliament — 'the place and centre of decision and rule for all the United Kingdom'. [. . .]

This framework can be read as *inflecting* the definition of the topic in the following way. The crisis is a crisis of Parliamentary government, of the established two-party rule from Westminster, and *thus* (therefore) of the nation itself. The 'crisis of unity' is therefore set mainly in terms of the break-up of established party positions and alliances, and the emergence of a new, third force in British politics. The 'hung Parliament' result of the February Election, the comparatively strong showing of the Liberals, the new nationalist parties and factions, and the interim moves by the major parties to counter them and restore or recapture unity, *constitute the relevant dimensions* — the terrain on which the 'national unity' theme is framed and discussed. [. . .] The identification of 'national unity' with the two (three?) party-system is unquestioned. Though exposed to question by the representatives of the nationalist parties this premise is not itself placed under scrutiny by the broadcasters. On the contrary, it is assumed, taken for granted: it forms the *backdrop* against which the broadcaster 'speculates' (sets about exploring and probing the various positions in play). Thus the whole Parliamentary and Electoral framework of relevance is tacitly reproduced here without question, not as an explicit or conscious 'bias' but as the programme's (and the topic's) *raison d'être*. 'Unity' then becomes a question of *how to re-affirm or re-establish the political status quo*. The programme asks 'what kind of unity?'; but it does not question what is understood by unity, what its content is. On the underlying meaning of Unity the broadcasters *assume a consensus*. What is problematic is a divergence at the level of *strategy* — the precise content which each major party gives to the question of unity. [. . .]

PASSING IT AROUND

In the first section, the passage of the topic and its ideological construction as a theme is organized through a complex use of signifying forms. Though 'politics' and 'actuality' provide the essential raw materials of this discourse, the control over its ideological development and inflection is very much in the keeping of the broadcasters. The second segment is introduced by McKenzie, who recaps the main dimensions of the theme, and 'passes the topic' across to the political protagonists. [. . .] What follows is a 'free debate'. But how is the topic *developed* in an organized discussion, where the main participants are political opponents in the week before an Election, each seeking to make the most political advantage by appearing to 'come out best' in the debate, to win arguments, punch points home, better than the other speakers? How is the *control* over the development of the topic managed in a 'free debate'?

In the first segment *control* is in the keeping of the broadcasters and the verbal and visual discourse are tightly bonded: each picture either (with its own actuality sound) conveying precisely the point the broadcaster wants made at that stage in the sequential development, or illustrating a point, which is then made or drawn attention to in the commentary or voice-over. The broadcasters construct the visual discourse parallel to, and complementary with, the verbal discourse by the work of editing, sequencing, compilation of extracts and *assembly*. But in the second segment, live in studio, whose precise point is its *spontaneity*, its unplanned nature, its 'open-ended' outcome, order, control and coherence (including a coherence between what is said and shown) are ensured by the 'live' combination of communicative forms and roles, operating under certain *preferential rules*.

McKenzie and Charlton now occupy new communicative roles. They are no longer presenters, commentators, editors, etc. They have become *chairmen* of the discussion, and thus *initiators* of topics of debate, *monitors* of the course of the debate (its opening, development, smooth closing); above all, *interrogators* of the three main participants. They frame the whole discussion by 'putting the question'. In fact, there are two parts to the discussion: in the first, the broadcasters get the topic 'moving' by putting two questions each, on the topic they have nominated, to each participant, before, second, 'allowing' free debate to range between them. At one level, then, the rules regulate control over *sequencing*. Broadcasters *nominate* speakers, often by name or verbal gesture, by this act *signalling* a move in the sequence to the cameras, who 'follow him over' to the person nominated, ready to catch his reply. [. . .] The chairmen frame questions in a polite interrogative form: 'Could you . . .?', 'Now can I also suggest . . . ', 'How would you define the essence of . . . ?' This is especially the case with the first question, which is intended to *elicit* a general reply, allowing the politician to 'state his or his Party's case', succinctly, but on his own terms. The second question is more of a *polite probe,* pinning the speaker down on some more controversial or inconsistent aspect: 'Now can I also suggest to you . . . ?'; 'Does that mean, does that mean that you . . . ?'. Here the broadcaster-as-interrogator is either 'impartially' putting the questions he imagines his 'informed layman' viewer would like to put to the Party leaders; or clarifying what has already been said by a harder or more searching probe. Since both parts of the questioning take the form of interrogation/reply, the visual sequence is thereby ordered: it, too, consists essentially of 'two-shots', alternating between the two roles, interrogator and responders.

There are communicative roles for the responders, too. They occupy two roles, that of *respondent* to questions put (if directly, by the chairmen), and *protagonists* in the debate with their opposite Party spokesmen. The polite form of the response to a chairman's question is to 'take up' or *accept* the question, and elaborate a reply on the basis of this acceptance. Probing questions may be more difficult; but the polite form of the transition is either to accept, and *then modify* — the 'yes, but . . . ' formula — or politely to *demur*. Thus; [an] example of 'straight acceptance':

McKenzie: 'How would you define the essence of the Labour position?'
Callaghan: 'Well, the essence of the Labour position is that . . . '
[. . .]

Here are two examples of 'acceptances' which also include a demur, the respondent taking up the question, but putting his own, more favourable *gloss* on it:

Shot	Dialogue
Camera still on Whitelaw	McKenzie . . . But does that, does that mean you begin by inviting formally the other major parties to enter a
Cut to 2-shot McKenzie and Charlton	national government in the pattern of say, the 1931
Move into c-u McKenzie	national government?
Cut to m.c-u Whitelaw	Whitelaw: What Ted Heath has said, eh very clearly, is that he would wish to

consult with the leaders of the other
parties and see where that got

The pattern is repeated with the exchange between Charlton and Steele;

Shot	Dialogue
Cut to full shot of table	Charlton: Well before — we must obviously come back I think to ask you who these people might be — but David Steele first of all, your prescription for national unity, isn't it
Cut to c-u Charlton	essentially negative and destructive . . . has provided the political stability which Britain has had over the years
Cut to m.c-u Steele	Steele: Yes but it hasn't provided the national unity and the point I would make to both Mr. Whitelaw and Mr. Callaghan, who are now attempting to don the mantle of national unity

As with Whitelaw immediately before him, Steele accepts the opener
[. . .] and then immediately *attempts to turn it to his advantage* by scoring
points off the other two. [. . .] Both these sets of exchanges conform to
the unwritten 'rules of the game'. The media men have been able to *probe*
and *examine* (interrogators) the claims made by the representatives of the
Conservative and Liberal parties, without having their right to do so
questioned. At the same time Steele and Whitelaw have been able to *take
up* (respondents) and *turn* (protagonists) these questions onto favourable
ground, without challenge from the chair or from the other protagonists.
[. . .]

INFLECTING IT

By obeying the unwritten rules, responding to questions by acceptances,
or polite demurs, taking up the aspect signalled by the chairman and
developing a case in reply, glossing it favourably, the politicians *follow the
rules of good debate by formally putting themselves under the control of the
broadcasting chairmen.* They elaborate their Party-political points *within
this framework of impartial chairmanning and equal, reasonable exchange.* Party
partisanship here operates *under the prescriptive rule* of impartiality and a
balanced exchange of views. However, Party spokesmen are also
representatives of their Parties and opponents of one another. Their
protagonist role must therefore be exercised *through* the mediation of
their roles as respondents and discussants. We have noted the preval-
ence of the 'yes but' form of question-acceptance. This enables

106

participants to take up and follow the broadcasters' lead, *but* then to gloss and inflect the topic — to *reappropriate* it — in such a way as to make it reflect more favourably on their own Party position, less favourably on that of their opponents.

Both Whitelaw and Steele, in accepting the media men's questions, also accept the definition of the unity theme constructed in segment one. In doing so, they have also inflected this overall definition back onto more favourable terrain. Whitelaw re-appropriates the 'unity' topic in the direction of a 'broad-based' Conservative government which would include consultations with the other parties. This is how he interprets 'national coalition government'. [. . .] To give one example (Whitelaw, in response to McKenzie's opener):

> For [our] purposes [we] believe (we) are facing, and I think all the parties agree (we) are facing considerable economic difficulties, and I believe there are: many: people in this country who say, right let: us: work together and why is it if: we: want to work together, unite together, why can't/they/work together.

In this instance, the *favourable gloss* works through the organisation and manipulation of the key nouns and pronouns. The opening 'we' (accepted from the chairman) means Conservatives, while the final 'we' (glossed) means the Nation. It is an effective piece of unity, or consensus/coalition building. We can follow the gloss in this way:

[we, our]	= Parliamentary Conservatives
(we)	= The nation as a whole, all of us together
:we, us, many:	= Conservative voters; the middle ground; The People; the Nation
/they, the politicians/	= Labour, Liberal, Parliamentary Opposition

In terms of definition, this passage works so as to position the Conservative Party on the side of the People; and then to set off the 'us' (the People *and* the Conservatives) against 'them' — Labour and Liberal politicians who are seeking to put Party before and above Nation. In other words, 'Unity' is here being glossed as if synonymous with an obvious and over-riding desire for cross-Class, cross-Party 'National Unity', under Conservative management.

For Steele, the re-appropriation of the topic must also be accomplished in such a way as to provide a favourable gloss for the Liberals. He, too, explicitly touches on the Party-over-Nation mechanism when he says, somewhat later in the programme, to Callaghan:

> Now, what you are really aiming for in this election is a majority which will enable you to go for the policies which are acceptable to the whole

of the Labour Party, to that area of unity, if you like, the Left wing as well as the Right wing, and it is that you are putting above the national interest . . .

Recognising that the Liberals, though they might again increase their proportion of the vote as they had done in February, were unlikely to be able to form an administration, Steele plays his hand very much in terms, not of 'Party' but of the 'will of the People' and the 'will of Parliament'. While there is equivocation each time the mechanics of 'coalition' are touched, this is always covered by an appeal to Parliamentary authority. [. . .]

In coming third, Callaghan has the most work of re-definition to do, especially since his Party's manifesto is opposed to the definitions of 'unity' as some form of coalition which have prevailed up to his entry into the debate. This positioning of Callaghan (last in the sequence of speakers) reflects the rule that it is legitimate to hit the Party in office hardest, though balance is invariably maintained by ensuring that it always has the 'right to reply'. From this position, Callaghan must take a longer, more qualified route to re-appropriating the topic. Thus, in defining the essence of Labour's position, he begins by putting the 'negative case first'; he makes several points against both his opponents. Only then does he move to align the topic to his party's position:

> But you see it's when you get down to the practical issues that you have got to make up your mind, and that is why we in our manifesto, in the point that Mr. Whitelaw picked up, said a coalition fudges the issues. It was in that context we said there is no meeting point.

and later, more emphatically, when he says:

> The idea of national unity is not the supreme idea. The supreme idea is whether a government has the policies that is going to get the country out of the difficulties it is in, without fudging or compromising and that is the supreme idea, that is what the election is about.

Here Callaghan inflects the unity theme into strong, authoritative government and pragmatic effectiveness (i.e. a Labour majority). Only that Party with specific clearcut policies can set about solving the problems; the tendency to converge on coalition as *the* solution is *redefined* here as no solution at all; it is, for Callaghan, the road to ineffective management of the crisis and compromise.

BREAKING THE RULES: WINNING THE GAME

Certain of the preferential rules, which sustain control and development of the topic throughout programmes, are broken in the course of this programme; and this infringement of the 'rules of the game' leads to a suspension of normal communicative roles, role-reversals (participants temporarily taking over the chair, chairmen relegated to silence) and a shift in the control over the topic. The moment occurs in the exchange of questions-and-responses between McKenzie and Callaghan. The opener and response flow smoothly and conform to the typical pattern:

Shot	Dialogue
Camera on Steele	McKenzie: Could we turn to Mr. Callaghan, to Labour's approach to the problems of national unity. How would you define the essence of the Labour position?
Cut to Callaghan	
	Callaghan: Well, the essence of the Labour position is that, eh, putting the negative side first, that the Conservative and Liberal parties are offering the electors a pig in a poke.

But the follow-up is *refused completely* by Callaghan:

	McKenzie: But may I bring your mind to the fact that almost every government in Europe is a coalition . . . Why is it part of Labour party dogma . . .
Cut to 3-shot Callaghan, Charlton and McKenzie	
Cut to c-u Callaghan	Callaghan: . . . This is not Labour party dogma. This has been the constitution of this country, and until the Conservative party fell into its present bedraggled state, they had no interest in a coalition either . . .
Cut to Whitelaw	
Camera is back on Callaghan	Now, now, now come on now don't you try to get me into a position where you're saying this is only Labour party dogma. The Conservatives have argued this for years.

The probe which McKenzie offers is extremely strong; one which is felt by Callaghan *to go beyond the limits* of impartiality and objectivity. This tactical mistake is also recognised by McKenzie himself, following Callaghan's strong reprimand. The break consists of the too clear 'bias' on McKenzie's part, signalled by his use of the provocative word, 'dogma'. [. . .] The word 'dogma' also connotes the charge that Labour's position stems less from a pragmatic concern with the crisis and more from a prior 'ideological' commitment. [. . .]

This break in the rules, registered by the participants' performance, is important in several ways. First, it suggests that although the media interrogator may probe hard with a follow-up question, he can only do so *within certain unspoken but recognised limits.* Above all else he must not reveal his personal perspective, his 'prejudices'; nor must he suggest that the politician's prescription is based on 'prejudice'. Second, it allows Callaghan to *come on hard* and win unexpected ground. As we shall see, it enables him to move into a position where it is *he,* and not the media men, who manages and controls the passage of the topic.

DEBATING IT

The debate component is the moment for the 'free' ebb and flow of discussion within the overall framework of the programme. Normally, media men would only intervene here if it is manifest that a particular protagonist is illegitimately hogging the floor. [. . .] This moment is, therefore, still governed by certain preferential conventions.

Normally, direct exchange between *protagonists* would only occur after the completion of the introductory question and answer exchanges. The break we have noted above brings on this second phase of the sequence *prematurely,* however, with Callaghan appropriating control of the direction of the debate. The 'chair' has been both by-passed and expropriated. This is most clearly revealed when Callaghan now directly *interrupts* Whitelaw (still in his *respondent* role), and puts questions to him direct (i.e. treats him as a *protagonist,* Callaghan now in the role of *chairman*).

Shot	Dialogue
Cut to shot of full table	Callaghan: What about the ballot on the EEC . . .
	Whitelaw: Yes, well I think we are coming back to that (looks to McKenzie and Charlton)
	Callaghan: Would you have a ballot on the EEC
	McKenzie, Charlton: We're coming back to that later
Cut back to Whitelaw	Whitelaw: We're coming back to that later, and I would be very glad . . .
	Callaghan: What about food subsidies. Would you take off food subsidies?
	Whitelaw: Well we have said very plainly on that, and I would make it perfectly clear . . .

In this sequence we can see Whitelaw *attempting to get back* to the orderly flow in his appeal to the chair. But Callaghan, jumping in ahead of the chair's support, fires another question at Whitelaw, who this time accepts. He could have again appealed to the chair, or simply refused to reply. In either case, however, this would have registered a collapse in the face of Callaghan's extremely strong bids.

At the close of this interchange, both of the 'deposed' chairmen succeed in *nominating* Steele back into the floor (restoration of normal control), but Charlton's attempt, following this, to put a direct question to Callaghan is again simply overridden. Despite the fact that Charlton is almost shouting, Callaghan *presses on* with his point (refuses to yield the floor in the normal turn-taking way) about 'the supreme idea'. From this point, Callaghan goes on to *confirm his command of the debate* in two main ways. In the course of emphasising the importance of 'the social contract in a free democratic society', Callaghan takes time out to 'play with' Whitelaw, by undermining his much qualified attempts to be 'rude' ('I find Mr. Callaghan's assertions, if I may say so, very arrogant . . . '). Callaghan accomplishes this by explicitly signalling, and then openly playing with, the fact that two codes are at work — the political code (hard opposition and attack) and the 'Parliamentary debate' code (rudeness is a sort of polite game):

Shot	Dialogue
Camera on Callaghan	Callaghan: The seriousness of this election to me (gestures to Whitelaw) and I'm sure Mr. Whitelaw, however arrogant he may think — he doesn't really think I am
Cut to Whitelaw	but however arrogant he may say I am, he will agree with me that nobody is trying to disguise the seriousness of this. Now
Cut back to Callaghan	where does it lead to? In my judgement unless we can get the country to accept and see the facts . . . the alternative is either anarchy or fascism in this country.

This is one of Callaghan's most powerful bids for the topic; for here the topic is not just being aligned to any one Party's programme or even to the 'nation as a whole'. Rather, the topic-problem is here being defined *as a potential threat to the system of parliamentary democracy as such*. Against this threat, Callaghan has put up the social contract, aligned with a 'free democratic society', as 'the best way of trying to achieve a real unity'. So, the power of the bid and the seizing of an opportunity to have a go at Whitelaw, when viewed together, emphasise Callaghan's supreme command, his sense of the control he has secured. At the end of this statement Callaghan further consolidates this command by 'permitting' Whitelaw to put a question to him:

Whitelaw: Could I ask one thing on this, after that
Callaghan (over Whitelaw): Certainly

111

Here, Callaghan puts Whitelaw down by exploiting his formulation 'could I ask' — i.e. he takes the rhetorical question literally. (His own earlier interventions utilised none of these interrogative markers; he simply fired questions directly.)

It is not just over the other protagonists that Callaghan senses and registers his command, but also in relation to the chairmen. Following Whitelaw's attempted re-appropriation of the topic — which counter-poses 'nationalisation' against 'the social contract in a free democracy' idea — the chairmen once again attempt to wrest control back from Callaghan. This time he does not ignore them, but blocks the intervention in the name of a 'higher duty' — (a more powerful code); the responsibilities of the politician:

Shot	Dialogue
Cut full shot of all	Callaghan: If I may say so Mr. White-law . . .
	Charlton (over Callaghan): If I could put this question to Mr. Callaghan, Mr. Callaghan . . .
Cut into Callaghan	Callaghan: Now, forgive me, because it is Mr. Whitelaw and I who have to account for ourselves to the electors on this.

Charlton immediately backs down in the face of this rebuff, which reminds him of his proper place (broadcaster, chairman) as understood by the politician (protagonist). Callaghan thus retains the initiative by figuratively and explicitly setting 'politicians' roles against 'media' roles.

Toward the end of this sequence on the 'broader question of what kind of national unity', the media chairmen do, tentatively, regain their position, control and composure. It is, however, a difficult re-entry — which Callaghan interrupts again and twists round to his own advantage: so that, by the time Charlton *does* manage to put the question, much of its strength has been dissipated:

Charlton: But could I put to you the point about the social contract which you say is a means of unifying the nation . . .
Callaghan: I'm not sure about unifying the nation . . .
Charlton: But because it's part of the social contract . . .
Callaghan: Mmm . . .
Charlton: I — — it is a divisive issue . . .
Callaghan: Yes . . .
Charlton: . . . Because 18 million people voted against it, judging by the last election
Callaghan: Not against the social contract
Charlton: (firmly) Against nationalisation.
Callaghan: (smiling) Oh, I see, nationalisation.
Charlton: Now, because nationalisation is part of the social contract, is the

112

social contract, are we right in saying, socially divisive? (pause/
silence) Because . . .

Callaghan: Oh. Oh well, the Conservatives don't accept it until they've got to
do it [. . .]

THE 'UNITY' OF CURRENT AFFAIRS

On the basis of this analysis of a *Panorama* programme, we want to try to
formulate certain *tentative* propositions about the 'unity' of Current
Affairs TV, and the nature of the relationship between the media and
politics which *this example,* at any rate, suggests.

Let us start from the 'break in the rules' and 'Callaghan's win' which
has just been described. If television is wholly autonomous and
independent of the political domain, and must exert its control
regardless of who infringes, and maintain a strict and formal impartiality
when it handles politics, why is it that the media Chairmen don't
intervene more sharply on this occasion to restore the normal rules?
[. . .] One reason why the Chairmen struggle for control with
Callaghan, but do not brusquely insist on it, does have to do with the
high status of the accredited and accessed political personnel taking
part. In each case, these are the 'seconds-in-command' of each of three
major Parliamentary parties, the men who have chaired their Party
press conferences throughout the Election campaign. It is also the week
of the Poll itself, when broadcasters must be especially sensitive to the
charge that they are intervening between the representatives of the
People and the Electors.

Another, related reason may have to do with the precise nature of the
balance between the media and politics in Current Affairs television in
general, and especially at election times. Each sphere has its own way of
approaching and appropriating a topic. Each realizes a different
communicative aim — the media, to explain, inform, speculate intellig-
ently about; the politicians, to score points, win arguments and votes,
and mobilize support. Each sphere, however, also operates this difference on the basis of some shared or consensual framework: for only in
this way can they continue to function and exchange in an orderly
discourse on the same terrain. [. . .] To put this point another way:
politicians *require* the media in order to reach the widest audience: the
media's 'audience' is the politicians' 'electorate'. But since, in television,
it is the media which *mobilizes* the audience for the politicians, and
provides the latter with a communicative channel to the audience, the
politician is required to perform, and to realize his own goals, by
operating, broadly, *under media rules.* He must abide by, for example, the
operational rules which enable the media to function as a neutral
instance, even in the highly divisive and contested moment of an

113

election: that is, the rules, sanctioned in the last instance, by the State —
of balance, impartiality, objectivity and neutrality. These 'rules' are
actualised in the programme in the forms of the rules for reasonable
debate, polite interchange, neutral chairmanning, equal turn-taking,
etc. It is indirectly — *through* these 'rules' of neutrality and objectivity —
and only in that way, that the politicians can achieve their own, highly
partisan purposes. [. . .]

Politicians positively (though often, grudgingly) submit to this
equalising and neutral management of the debate by the media, since
this 'equal' regulation, which ensures fair play, provides the most
favourable long term conditions for the reproduction of the existing
structure of political relations: not the relations which favour one party
over another, but those which stem from the nature of the political
system as a whole. This submission to the rules of the media, therefore,
represents the *necessary displacement* of partisan politics onto the terrain of
a more neutral space. Though this limits, in terms of the short-term
advantages, what any one Party can win over another, this displacement
also ensures the long-term viability of the whole political and political-
communication system. But this 'neutral and impartial space' *is itself
granted to the media by the political sphere*. It is determined in the long run, or
last instance, by the political apparatus, operating through another level
of the State. [. . .]

Some such interpretation suggests that the relationship of the media to
the political is remarkably *homologous* to the *general* relationship between
politics and the State itself: in which politics (party practices) accords to
the State (the institutions of power such as Parliament and the Courts) a
certain measure of independence and neutrality, *because* this appearance
is, ultimately, the most effective way in which politics can make itself
effective *through* the State, without appearing *directly* to do so in the
defence of narrow or short-term class or Party advantage. It is clear that
the State, in capitalist societies, is related in complex ways to the
securing of the long-term interests of ruling class alliances. But we also
know that, classically in the 'liberal' capitalist state, and even in its
subsequent modifications, these interests and the class personnel do not
appear directly and in their own person on the stage of the State. The
State is required as a neutral and objective sphere, precisely in order that
the long-term interests of capital can be 'represented' as a general
interest. It is through the 'relative neutrality' of the State — not in spite
of it — that conflicts are settled 'to the profit of the ruling classes'; but in
ways which, because they appear as neutral and general, command the
assent of the nation as a whole. This is the sense in which both Gramsci
and Poulantzas speak of the State as necessarily having a 'relatively
independent' structure. It is by the *displacement* of class power *through* the
'neutral and independent' structures of the State, that the State comes to
provide the critical function, for the dominant classes, of securing power

and interest at the same time as it wins legitimacy and consent. It is, in Gramsci's terms, the 'organizer of hegemony'. If, then, we consider the media in homologous terms, we can see that they, too, do some service to the maintenance of hegemony, *precisely by providing a 'relatively independent' and neutral sphere*. And when we ask what it is that, in their overall tendency, the media reproduce of the ideological field as a whole by their occupancy of this neutral sphere, we would argue that it is certainly *not* the giving of narrow party-advantage to this or that side: it is the *whole* terrain of State power — the underlying idea of the general interest — which is the most significant part of the ideological field which the media reproduce. And this reproduction is accomplished, not in spite of rules of objectivity (i.e. by 'covert or overt bias') but precisely *by holding fast to the communicative forms of objectivity, neutrality, impartiality and balance*. [. . .]

The media do not intervene directly to tilt the balance towards one party or another. On the contrary, their interventions seem overwhelmingly to be ones which preserve and reinforce, wherever possible, their position of 'relative autonomy' from the play of narrow party interest. In so far as we can tell, each of the main protagonists in the programme was given symmetrical visual space in the visual discourse. Despite appearances, each speaks, overall, for roughly the *same* length of time. We are therefore obliged to say that, if by 'bias', is understood the way television, or individual television personnel, might intervene to ensure, unfairly, the predominance of one Party speaker over another, this is an extremely rare, unusual occurrence, out of line with 'normal practice'; it is precisely what the preferential rules are designed to *prevent*. [. . .]

'Bias', however, does not exhaust in any way the relation of TV to the political and politics, and it cannot, on our evidence, be replaced by the equally ideological and inadequate concept of 'absolute autonomy'. We have tried to show that, in its establishment and glossing of the topic of Unity, television *reproduces selectively* not the 'unity' of any one Party, but *the unity of the Parliamentary political system as a whole*. *Panorama*, above other Current Affairs programmes, routinely takes the part of guardian of unity in this *second* sense. It reproduces, on the terrain of ideology, the political identification between the Parliamentary system and the Nation. As a consequence, the agenda of problems and 'prescriptions' which such a programme handles is limited to those which have registered with, or are offered up by, the established Parliamentary parties.

[. . .] The media are [therefore] *not biased* in favour of any one Party: but they *are* biased in favour of the Party-system *as such:* the Parliamentary character, nature and orientation of the Parties: and thus, the identification of the continuation of 'Parliamentary government' with the continuation of 'the unity of the nation as a whole', and the setting off of both against their 'enemies' (whether of the electoral kind or other varieties). [. . .] Media neutrality and independence are therefore quite 'real', in the sense that their function is essentially to try to *hold the ring,* to sustain an arena of 'relative independence', in order that this *reproduction of the conditions of political power can take place.*

As with all types of 'social reproduction' of this kind, no perfect harmony between the parts can be assured. Actual work — difficult, ideological, work — has to be done, in every programme, in every moment of signification, to effect what Althusser describes as a 'sometimes teeth-gritting harmony' between the different branches of the State, which prosper together only through the 'separation of their spheres and powers'. So the antagonism, the surface ebb and flow of power and control, in programmes and about programmes, between the broadcasters and the politicians, is not a 'phoney war', though it may not represent an antagonism or a contradiction of a principal kind. Similarly, since the reproduction of a 'structure in dominance' takes place on the much disputed terrain of politics and the State — that is, on the terrain where the political class struggle appears — ideological reproduction is *always* the result of the contradictory relations of class forces; some of those antagonisms cannot be reconciled or reduced by their projection on to more 'neutral' territory, and space *can* be gained, viewpoints expressed, contradictions emerge which are contradictory to the ones in dominance. Thus the media remains a 'leaky system', where ideological reproduction is sustained by 'media work' and where contradictory ideologies do in fact appear: it reproduces the existing field of the political class struggle in its contradictory state. This does not obscure the fact, however, that the closure towards which this 'sometimes teeth-gritting harmony' tends, overall, is one which, without favouring particular positions in the field of the political class struggle, *favours the way the field of political class struggle is itself structured.*

Our thanks to R. Rusher and R. Powell for their contributions.

(First published in *Working Papers in Cultural Studies,* no. 9, 1976.)

References

BBC (1974), *Tastes and Standards,* London: British Broadcasting Corporation.

Blumler, J. (1969), 'Producers' Attitudes towards TV Coverage of an Election Campaign', Sociological Review Monograph, no. 13.

Curran, C. (1971), 'The Problem of Balance', in Smith, A. (ed.), *British Broadcasting,* Newton Abbott: David and Charles.

Curran, C. (1974), 'Broadcasting and Public Opinion', *The Listener,* 20 June 1974.

Day, R. (1961), *Television: a Personal Report,* London: Hutchinson.

Gramsci, A. (1969), *Prison Notebooks,* London: Lawrence and Wishart.

Hall, S. (1974), 'Encoding and Decoding in the TV Discourse', Stencilled Papers, no. 7, Birmingham: CCCS.

116

Hall, S., Critcher, C., Clarke, J., Jefferson, T., Roberts, B. (1975), 'Newsmaking and Crime', Stencilled Papers, no. 27, Birmingham: CCCS.
Kumar, K. (1974), 'Holding the Middle Ground', *Sociology*, vol. 9, no. 1.
Pateman, T. (1974), *Television and the February 1974 General Election*, London: British Film Institute.

Everyday Television: *Nationwide*

I GOING NATIONWIDE

Nation and Regions: the historical development of the programme

Nationwide was started in 1966 as part of a strategy adopted by the BBC to meet three different needs. First, there was the necessity to build on the 'spot' established by *Tonight,* and to produce a programme which would carry through the solid audiences for the early regional news into BBC1's major evening output beginning at 7 p.m. On the other hand, there was the need to meet the criticism that the BBC output was too much dominated by the metropolis and thus failed to express/deal adequately with the needs of 'the regions'. The 'regionalism' of *Nationwide* was seen as a necessary basis for any sense of national unity in the conditions of the late 60s and 70s — or, as the BBC evidence to Annan put it:

> local and regional services are an essential part of a truly national broadcasting system. (BBC *Handbook,* 1978.)

Finally, there were the recommendations made by the McKinsey Report and developed in the BBC policy document, *Broadcasting in the 70s,* that fuller use should be made of the company's regional studios, allowing for regional specialisation and a 'rationalisation' of resources (and cost-effectiveness).

The regional element has always been crucial to *Nationwide* — the idea:

> is to impress on the viewer that this is a programme which is not dominated by London and which embraces every main centre in the UK. (William Hardcastle reviewing current affairs schedules; quoted in Connell, 1975.)

So much so that when *Nationwide* 'looked at London' in the film 'Our Secret Capital' (*Nationwide* 16/8/76) Julian Pettifer, the presenter, consciously acknowledged the programme's brief by saying:

> On *Nationwide* we try desperately not to be a metropolitan programme. Tonight is an exception. For the next 25 minutes we're looking at life

118

in London: but we offer no excuse, because after all, wherever you live in the UK, London is your capital . . .

Similarly Stuart Wilkinson (deputy editor of *Nationwide*) claimed that:

Nationwide would not be a nationwide programme without this facility to involve our colleagues in the regions. The crosstalk between the regions is the very essence of the programme. (Quoted in Brody, 1976, p.20.)

The programme attempts to construct a close and 'homely' relationship with its regionally differentiated audiences: this can be seen clearly in the programme's self-presentation, or billing, in the *Radio Times*:

Reporting England: Look North, South Today, Look East, Midlands Today, Points West, Spotlight South West. (Radio Times, 29/3/77.)

Today's news and views in your corner of England presented by the BBC's regional newsrooms. Then . . . take a look at the scene *Nationwide. (Radio Times, 13/1/76.)*

. . . present news and views in your region tonight. Then at 6.22 . . . present some of the more interesting stories of life in today's Britain . . . (*Radio Times*, 14/1/76.)

News and views in your region tonight. Then the national scene, presented by . . . (*Radio Times*, 15/1/76.)

. . . present the British scene to the people of Britain . . . (*Radio Times*, 16/1/76.)

Nationwide is positively involved in the search for regional variety: of customs and ways of life. Indeed 'Let's go *Nationwide* . . . and see what the regions think . . .' becomes the characteristic *Nationwide* form of presentation. Thus the programme is able to stress regional differences (different dishes, superstitions, competitions), to present a Nation composed of variety and diversity, but also to unify the regions in the face of National Crises: 'How is Leeds coping with the drought? What about the South-West?' (17/8/76.)

We see variations in regional responses to issues given by the centre: classically, regional variations in the celebration of the Jubilee. But the regional is still contained within the national: regionalism is the life-blood of *Nationwide*, but full-blooded separatist or nationalist movements — such as the Irish Republican Movement — transgress the limits of the *Nationwide* discourse, breaking as they do the assumed frame of the 'United Kingdom'.

Similarly, within the programme, the links over to regions are usually from London, and are used to 'fill out' regional aspects of something of national import; the regions do not usually initiate stories. The regions follow, and are linked to the national news — they pick up stories signalled in the national news and flesh out their significance for the region. The input of 'regional stories' — material drawn from the 'life of the region' — is subordinate to this 'national with regional effects' input; the regional variations are orchestrated from the central London studio base. London is the 'absent' region, the invisible bearer of national unity. It is both technologically and ideologically the heart of the programme. [. . .]

Programme format and slot
The magazine format of *Nationwide* — short items (rarely longer than 10 minutes), light relief mixed in with 'heavy fare' to hold the viewers' attention — 'the Postmaster General mixed with a tattooed cat' (quoted in Gillman, 1975) — is to some extent determined by the slot that the programme occupies: the break between children's TV and the BBC's major evening output. The programme is usually followed by light entertainment, family shows, quizzes or the like — it is a time of evening when, as Michael Bunce (one-time editor of *Nationwide*) put it:

> people have had a hard day's work and when they sit down they don't want a remorseless, demanding, hard tack diet every night. (Gillman, 1975.)

There is, therefore, a deliberate policy in *Nationwide* to include light items, especially when the programme contains some 'heavy fare'. Barratt argues:

> We need some light relief if we are to hold the viewer's interest: there's a limit to the serious fare they can absorb or want to at this time of evening. (Quoted in Brody, 1976.)

These 'common sense' definitions of the nature of the 'slot' — when people are coming in from work, when the whole family including children will be present, when no sustained attention is possible, etc., allow us to construct *Nationwide*'s own sense of its responsibilities and its constituency.

The space from 6 to 7 p.m. does tend also to be populated by domestic serials, comedies, panel games, and *Nationwide* is 'contaminated' by, or actively parasitic upon, these alternative genres, as well as aspects of the time zone preceding the early evening news, that reserved for children's programmes. Thus the history of the time slot makes available a certain range of genres which all have a common sense appropriateness to that hour of the day. This is the basis for some of *Nationwide*'s quality of heterogeneity and also for the oscillations of tone within some of the items.

The Nationwide *style of presentation*

In his autobiography, Barratt spells out a key element in the '*Nationwide* Style':

> The art of communication on any topic — whether it be life itself, or the price of porridge — demands the use of easily understood words, and is greatly heightened by skilful illustration. (Quoted in Brody, 1976, p.24.)

The stress is on direct and effective communication — 'simple language, common language if you like' (Michael Barratt) — getting it across to the people. Thus, when 'heavy' items are dealt with, *Nationwide* is primarily concerned to 'establish the point at the heart of the matter' and concentrate on getting that over, unlike, for instance, *Panorama,* which, after 'establishing the topic', will explore the different perspectives and dimensions of it, offering a range of views and definitions for the audience's 'education'. (Cf. Hall *et al.,* 1976.)

The discourse of *Nationwide* then is relatively closed; the stress on 'making the issues comprehensible', translating them into 'real terms', leaves little space for interpretation. The endeavour for *Nationwide* is to establish the time/place/status/immediacy of events and people involved in them — making these, where possible, concrete and personalised — and to get the 'main point' of an item across to the audience.

In *Nationwide* there is a thread almost of anti-intellectualism; 'experts' are held in some value for what they may have to contribute, but it all has to be translatable into the language of immediate issues and everyday concerns.

Thus, while experts expound on 'the causes of inflation', the *Nationwide* team do their best to find out what inflation really means, how it will affect 'our' day-to-day living, whether anything can be done about it ('Yes, minister, but how will that improve the situation here tomorrow . . .'). The team often expresses 'our' exasperation with politicians by asking them 'down to earth' questions. This can be seen in the different interviewing styles of *Nationwide* and *Panorama*; a *Panorama* interview with the Chancellor will tend to probe and challenge his position with reference to the positions of opposing political parties and economic experts. The challenge put by *Nationwide* interviewers will tend much more to be at the level of practical policy making: 'will it help/work?' and will often take the form of a 'commonsensical' perspective in terms of which politicians of all parties are likely to be seen as culpable. This style of interviewing is directly in the tradition of *Tonight* and its style of popular journalism — once described as the 'discipline of entertainment':

> We are flippant, irreverent, disbelieving when we feel we should be; we refuse to be taken in by pompous spokesmen... (Cliff Michelmore, introducing the programme after summer break, 1961.)

Implicit in this perspective is a populist ideology which takes for granted the irrelevance of 'politics' to the real business of everyday life ('Whichever party is in power I'll still not have a job. Prices will still rise ...') and also takes for granted the disillusionment of the electorate with 'politicians' and their promises.

The 'serious issues' — unemployment, inflation, etc. — which are the basis of most current affairs programming can therefore only enforce attention within the *Nationwide* discourse where they can be shown to have immediate effects on everyday life; when this happens *Nationwide* can wheel in Robert McKenzie and his clipboard and graphics to tell us what this 'IMF loan business' is all about. But, even on such occasions, everyday life and its continuities (nature, sport, entertainment, quirky events) are, within the *Nationwide* world, what 'frame' these issues, and are called upon (reassuringly) to put them into perspective. ('And on this gloomy day, a look on the brighter side'... 'With all this crisis going on one could almost have forgotten that today was Shrove Tuesday'...)

Barratt, the principal anchorman during the period of viewing, presents himself as the embodiment of this 'populist' perspective: a no-nonsense man of the people, stressing down-to-earth common sense, not only by asking questions he thinks the public would want to ask but also, unlike many other current affairs presenters, by adding comments ('Well, they do seem rather daft reasons for going on strike...' *Nationwide* 14/3/73) he assumes the public might make, or at least agree with.

Interestingly, these comments are not seen to transgress the requirements of balance and impartiality. They rest on an image of 'the people' *outside* the structures of politics and government. Precisely because they are made from a perspective at odds with that of parliamentary politics — 'the politicians' as such are suspect from this perspective — these comments do not favour the position of one party against another within that framework. This 'common-sense' critique of 'politics' presents itself as a-political, despite the obviously political content of common-sense wisdom about what 'we all know...' The discourse of *Nationwide*, rooted as it is in this populist 'everyday' perspective on events, undercuts the traditional discourse of parliamentary politics by basing its criticisms on a set of assumptions about 'what everybody thinks'. It is a discourse which poses 'ordinary people' as its source, and thus represents historically-determined and necessarily political positions simply as a set of natural, taken-for-granted 'home truths'.

122

Moreover, the *Nationwide* perspective is legitimated not only through its identification with the content of common-sense wisdom, but also through the forms of discourse in which that perspective is constructed. *Nationwide* employs a kind of populist 'ventriloquism' (Smith, 1975, p.67) which enables the programme to speak with the voice of the people; *i.e.*, to mirror and reproduce the voice of its own audience. *Nationwide* adopts the language of popular speech — the language is always concrete, direct and punchy, with an assumption of and a reference to always pre-existing 'knowledge'. This populist vocabulary is the language of 'common sense' which the programme adopts and transforms, picking up popular terms of speech (much in the style of the *Daily Mirror*'s 'Come off it, Harold . . .'), mimicking phrases and clichés, and putting them to new uses, making them carry the weight of a political message. *Nationwide* often uses, and sometimes inverts, proverbs and clichés, quite self-consciously (the 'postcard shot' of Blackpool; 'when in Rome let the Romans do as you do', 19/5/76; etc.) — grounding its vocabulary in familiar tags and sentence constructions. ('This may look like a load of old rubbish to you . . .', 19/4/76.) The 'persona' of the programme, then, is a professionally formulated reconstruction based in and on 'popular speech' and its sedimented wisdoms. The use of linguistic register is one of the ways in which *Nationwide* constructs 'ordinary people' as the subject of its particular kind of speech.

This 'populist ventriloquism' is a crucial strand in the way the programme attempts to forge an 'identification' with its audience; its project is to be accepted by the audience as their representative, speaking for them, and speaking to them from a perspective, and in a language, which they share. At the same time, this work of constructing identifications is actively denied in the programme: the presenters appear as 'just like us', just ordinary people — who happen to be 'on telly', doing the talking, while we listen. [. . .] *Nationwide*, in short, offers us a 'nightly mirror [rather than a window] on the world'. It presents itself as catching in its varied and comprehensive gaze 'everything' which could possibly be of interest to us, and simply 'mirrors' or reflects it back to us. What is more, it 'sees' these events in exactly the same perspective, and speaks of them in exactly the same 'voice', as that of its audience. Everything in *Nationwide* works so as to support this mirror-structure of reflections and recognitions. The ideology of television as a transparent medium — simply showing us 'what is happening' — is raised here to a high pitch of self-reflexivity. The whole of the complex work of the production of *Nationwide*'s version of 'reality', sustained by the practices of recording, selecting, editing, framing the linking, and the identificatory strategies of producing 'the scene, *Nationwide*', is repressed in the programme's presentation of itself as an unproblematic reflection of 'us' and 'our world' in 'our' programme. *Nationwide* thus naturalises its own practice, while at the same time it is constantly engaged in constituting the audience in its own image. It makes the object of its discourse and practice — the audience — the subject of its speech. The discourse of *Nationwide* thus depends on its ability constantly to reconstruct this imaginary equivalence, this perfect transparency, between the 'us' who are seen and the 'we' who see. What we 'see' and recognise is a reflection of ourselves and our world, caught in the mirror-structure of the screen.

The material of Nationwide: *specificity of news values*

Nationwide is a 'mosaic made up of a variety of interests' where the viewer does not know if s/he will see ' a film of Ulster or a beer-drinking snail' because *Nationwide* has 'no brief other than to be unpredictable, informative and entertaining'. (Quoted in Gillman, 1975.) This is the territory originally 'mapped out' for current affairs TV by *Tonight*:

> *Tonight*'s back . . . the familiar bouncy tune will invite you to look around (with Cliff Michelmore and his team) at the topical, the insignificant, the provocative, and even the sentimental issues of the day. Such is the range of the programme that no string of adjectives will suffice to make a boundary of its activities. (*Radio Times*, 26/8/60.)

Nationwide must be topical, but its material is not the same as the material of the national news. While news programming usually acts as a baseline for current affairs TV there is always a selective translation from the domain of news into that of current affairs; current affairs programmes differing according to whether they have a closer or more distant relation to news output. Items usually have to 'pass through' the news before becoming suitable topics for current affairs TV, but not all news items will survive the transition. For instance 'crime', which is routinely 'news', will only become current affairs material if it involves some special feature, or if the crimes are seen to form some significant and problematic social pattern (such as 'mugging').

The differential relations of current affairs TV to news can be seen, for example, by comparing *Tonight* Mark II — which has a close relationship to news, routinely taking up and developing the immediate background to news items — with *Panorama*, which selects only the 'heavy items' (foreign policy, the budget, incomes policy, etc.) from the news.

Nationwide characteristically has a 'distanced' relation to the 'National News', although all the regional programmes carry local news in the traditional format. The 'newsworthy' items that *Nationwide* sets off against an always taken-for-granted reference point of normality are not those like the unexpected 'big bang' (News) or the world-shattering political development (*Panorama*) nor even the worrying deviant (social problem TV) but the extraordinary, perplexing, various, eccentric

124

quirks of otherwise ordinary people and their lives. *Nationwide* deals in 'human interest' stories. 'Heavy' items like Britain's involvement with the IMF, which are the staple diet of serious current affairs programmes (like *Panorama*), are explicitly featured only sporadically. These problems are, however, routinely recognised, even taken-for-granted, as the familiar background against which more typical *Nationwide* items are foregrounded. *Nationwide* items are often introduced with openers like 'In these days of economic crisis . . .'. When such items are handled, the 'angle' on them will be the search for 'the brighter side', 'what can be done', the 'good news among the bad'.

Nationwide policy in these issues, on the selection and handling of their material, is, at least in part, designed to respond to the fact that, as the BBC Audience Research Department Survey put it:

> Four times as many people mentioned politics as mentioned any other subject as the 'most boring'.

What people wanted of a current affairs programme, according to the Survey, was:

> on the spot film, where the action is, to see for themselves . . . to hear the people who are the subjects of the report telling their own story — not debates and discussions between experts in a TV studio.

Nationwide responds to these demands by placing first and foremost the 'discipline of entertainment' — the focus on the quirky, the fascinating, the sensational as a strategy for holding the attention of the audience, in order to lead them to the 'preferred reading' of a given event: the programme aims to produce 'interesting stories' which will 'grab the audience'. (*Nationwide* producer, quoted in Gillman, 1975.) *Nationwide* doesn't cover areas remote from everyday life (like a *Panorama* special on Vietnam) but visits the places many of us have visited, takes us into the living rooms of ordinary families, shows us people enjoying their leisure time, couples coping with inflation and their new baby. The aim is to be 'a reflection of what you and your family talk about at the end of the day'. *Nationwide* thus occupies a peculiar space in the spectrum of current affairs TV; uniquely, on *Nationwide*, the majority of items are about ordinary people in their everyday lives. These items are always presented with a 'newsy' inflexion, but none the less they overwhelmingly draw their material from the 'normal/everyday' category which usually constitutes the absent baseline against which the 'newsworthiness' of other items is constituted.

It is from this area of 'everyday life' that *Nationwide* routinely produces the bulk of its magazine items: such as the story of the 'man who wrote out the Bible by hand'. (*Nationwide* 2/1/76.) Such stories could not in any sense become 'news' within the dominant current affairs framework of news values. However, these items are the specific constituency of *Nationwide*: the dominant perspective is reversed here. The items generated are from a 'grassroots' level: ordinary people's extraordinary habits/hobbies; or the effects of the state/bureaucracy as felt in the lives of 'ordinary folk' as it impinges on the sphere of private life.

Nationwide roots itself in the 'normal' and the everyday, in a 'consensus' based on what it represents as the 'natural' expectations of its audience. A vast proportion of *Nationwide* stories are simply about individuals 'like you or I', with their special skills and interests. Of course, a story about people doing absolutely ordinary things can't trigger an item on its own — even a magazine item — since it would contain no news potential whatsoever. The absolute norm is invisible in the perspective of news: it is what provides the taken-for-granted background to everything else.

Nationwide, then, is grounded in the obvious, the familiar — but in celebrating this area of everyday life, the programme works on and against this 'norm'. *Nationwide* is constantly discovering that appearances are deceptive: the items often spotlight the special things that otherwise 'ordinary people' are doing. Here, *Nationwide* plays off a range of oppositions around the normal/abnormal, ordinary/eccentric polarities, discovering that the 'ordinary' is never as ordinary as it seems; celebrating the life of the people of Britain through the diversity which the programme finds in the activities of its own subjects/audience. [...]

II COMPONENTS OF THE *Nationwide* DISCOURSE 1975–77

Nationwide *events/links*

> I hope you don't mind me coming into your home in shirtsleeves.
> (Tom Coyne, *Nationwide*, 8/6/76.)

Nationwide is, above all, a friendly programme, where we're all on Christian name terms ('Over to you, Bob ...') where we're introduced personally to new members of the *Nationwide* team and regularly given personal news about those of the team we already know. In 'serious current affairs' programming the presenter's personal life/personality does not intrude into his/her professional role. The *Nationwide* team positively exploit their different and highly developed personas — as *part of* their professional 'style' — commenting on each others' lives, hobbies, attempts to lose weight/give up smoking, etc.; portraying themselves as individuals like us, with their own problems, interests, idiosyncrasies: people who know each other ('Dilys, what about you? Were you a comic freak?') and whom we can know. We get to know 'the team' as personalities — as a family, even, rather like our own: the *Nationwide* family.

126

The audience is constantly involved in the programme. We are invited to participate through letters, choices, ideas, etc., and our participation is acknowledged; we are asked to help (a poor family is shown on *Nationwide* 9/1/76 with not enough furniture — and our response is recorded — 100 'offers of help pour in'; 'The £ in our pockets may be shrinking, but our hearts are as big as ever'). The team give friendly advice, warnings and reminders (don't drink and drive at Xmas; remember to put your clocks on/back, etc.). The team/audience relationship is presented rather like that of the team as guests in our home, us as visitors to their studio/home.

The team is not at all stuffy, they are willing to mess about and 'have a go' — and we are entertained by their, by no means always successful, attempts to deal in unfamiliar contexts. The East Anglian boat trip on the good yacht *Nationwide* (19/5/76) is a classic example — Barratt and Wellings, two members of the national *Nationwide* team, during *Nationwide*'s week in the Norwich studio, are presented 'at sea' on a trip on the Norfolk Broads, skippered by the regional *Nationwide* presenter. The regional presenter is clearly 'at home' in this nautical context, confident and relaxed — our national presenters, though willing to try their best (Barratt gamely dressed in yachting gear, trying to get it right), cannot cope: Wellings is presented as the original landlubber, about to be seasick, unable to understand seafaring terms. He is the most sympathetic figure, standing in for our own ordinary lack of expertise; and in the end it is he who gently dismisses the specialist exercise:

All this 'tacking' and 'avast' and 'ahoy' and left hand down and giblets and spinnakers . . . ludicrous performance.

The team are game to try, and they invite the audience to respond in like terms: viewers' competitions are a *Nationwide* speciality — 'Super-save', 'Good Neighbours', 'Citizen '76', etc. The audience are also invited to participate in the construction of the programme — 'What do you think *Nationwide*'s New Year resolution should be?' (17/12/75), and our participation becomes an item in the programme.

Audience response is scanned: we are shown on the programme both 'some of the Xmas Cards we've received from you' and also the more problem-oriented contents of the '*Nationwide* Letter Box' (29/12/75). *Nationwide* constructs an open and accessible relation to events: we watch members of the *Nationwide* team, who are presented in a self-consciously amateurish manner, participating in a *Nationwide* Showjumping Competition, set up as a parallel to the International Showjumping Competition (17/12/75); or we may see the presentation of *Nationwide* medals to Olympic athletes (15/6/76). We meet not only the 'Midlands Today puppy' (3/6/76) but also the '*Nationwide* horse' (19/5/76) — 'Realin', whose name was itself chosen by us, the *Nationwide* viewers. Val introduces us to the horse, points out how we may recognise it in a race, and explains the factors relevant to racing success. Here we are invited to participate (as surrogate 'horse-owners') in 'the sport of kings' — an area from which as normal individuals we would be excluded — through the mediation of the *Nationwide* team.

Links and mediations. At many points the *Nationwide* discourse becomes self-referential — *Nationwide* and the *Nationwide* team are not only the mediators who bring the stories to us, but themselves become the subject of the story. This is the 'maximal' development of one consistent thread in the programme — the attempt to establish a close, personalised relationship between the *Nationwide* team and the audience. A 'mystery item' (on *Nationwide* 28/9/76) turns out to be *Nationwide*'s own 'tele-test' with an invited audience who submit themselves to the process of research into their comprehension of *Nationwide* items. Here we have invited 'experts' whose views are elicited; but they are subordinated to the direct relation between *Nationwide* and its audience; it is principally a 'participation' item: we see *Nationwide* in reflection on itself, in dialogue with its own audience.

However, this aspect of the *Nationwide* discourse is not sustained only through the manifest content of those odd items where *Nationwide* and its audience have become the subject of its own story — it is also sustained through the 'links' between any and every item in a programme. Here the team appear in their capacity as links/mediators — getting out there 'on the spot', bringing us the variety, topical stories, drama of life in Britain today: bringing the regions to each other and to the centre, the parts to the whole. It is the team who must construct a world of shared attitudes and expectations between us all in order to hold the heterogeneous elements of *Nationwide* together.

Links can be made in various ways — through familiar presenters' faces in the studio, through the extraction of some element from the last item ('it may not be the weather for . . .') linked to an extracted element from the next item ('but it's certainly the right day for . . .'), through the establishing of shared ground between commentator and viewer. The central components of these links tend to be references to a level of shared attitudes towards the taken-for-granted world: concern about the weather, holidays, anxiety at rising prices/taxes, exasperation with bureaucracy.

The audience is constantly implicated through the linkperson's discourse, by the use of personal pronouns: 'tonight we meet . . .', 'we all of us know that . . .', '. . . can happen to any of us', 'so we asked . . .'. The audience is also implicated by reference to past or coming items, which we have all seen/will see, and (by implication) all interpret in the same way. There is a reiterated assertion of a co-temporality ('nowadays', 'in these times of . . .') which through its continuous present/immediacy

128

transcends the differences between us: 'of course . . .' *Nationwide* assumes we all live in the same social world.

The relations between the team and the viewers are constantly mystified in the discourse of *Nationwide*. There is no credit sequence at the end or beginning of the programme; without reference to the *Radio Times*, we can only know them informally and internally, as they refer to each other, people who know each other, so that we too know them like that, like people we already know rather than as presenters/TV personnel. (In their absence, people on the programme are referred to by their full names — 'A report from Luke Casey in Leighton Heath', in the more formal manner of an introduction, but in general these are precisely not the core team.) This already-knowingness, the *Nationwide* team in our living rooms as friends, constantly catches us with them as 'we', in their world, which purports to be nothing more than a reflection of our world.

This can be most clearly seen in the use (*Nationwide* 19/5/76) of 'Let's . . .'. Tom Coyne: 'Let's take a look at our weather picture'; 'Let's go to Norwich'; Michael Barratt: 'Let's hear from another part of East Anglia'. Here, the audience's real separation from the team is represented in the form of a unity or community of interests between team and audience; the construction of this imaginary community appears as a proposition we can't refuse — we are made equal partners in the *Nationwide* venture, while simultaneously our autonomy is denied. This, with its attendant possessive, '*our* weather picture', is the least ambiguous form of the 'co-optive we', which is a major feature of the discourse and linking strategies in *Nationwide*.

Links discourse sometimes seems to be structured in the recognition of the different positions of presenters and audience. Michael Barratt: 'And after *your own* programmes *we* go cruising down the river to bring *you our* third programme from East Anglia.' (Nation/region link.) But this difference is also constantly elided and recuperated:

(1) By reference to a wider, shared context or frame, in which we are all 'we' together: a context which embraces us all, establishing a false equivalence/homogeneity between us, dismantling our real differences of position and power. Here, through this construction, they unashamedly establish us in position in the discourse in a place which enables them to 'speak for us'. For example (19/5/76):

Tomorrow we'll have some sunny intervals . . .

If our society was destroyed, heaven forbid . . .

(2) Through the denial of the inequality of the audience/presenter relationship. Although the form of this relationship is friendly and familiar — conducive to we-ness — it is actually only *they* who can speak

129

and initiate action. Thus, when Michael Barratt says 'so we thought that tonight we'd go racing', although he may strictly be referring only to the studio group, 'we the audience' are implicated because if they go racing, we go racing, unless we switch channels.

This elision, this constant concealing of the one-way nature of the television system in our society, their negotiation of the isolation of their medium, lays the basis for a whole set of ways in which the *Nationwide* audience is implicated in, and identifies with, 'the scene *Nationwide*' (15/6/76).

Identification is also produced and reinforced through the chatty informality of the links. The links themselves are signified as transparent — bearing no substantial meaning of their own, made only of the reference to past or coming items. However, as already discussed, they also signify 'we-ness', which is constantly constructed by both the team and the viewing subject to mean 'nationwideness'. The seemingly neutral links themselves, always carrying this 'other', extra meaning, the 'being-among-friends in one's living room', are constantly contributing to the construction of the meaning of *Nationwide*, which we are always already implicated in, because it is with us, the viewers, that this assumption of intimacy is made. [. . .]

The mechanisms for the construction of the 'co-optive we' depend on and are realised in language: but they do not operate exclusively at the level of language in the narrow sense. In *Nationwide*, we suggest, they are further secured by and through the 'positioning' of the team — the presenters who represent and 'personify' the programme. And this is a feature, not of *Nationwide* alone (where, however, it is a prominent and characteristic presence) but in the discourses of 'popular TV' more generally. The *Radio Times* observed long ago about *Tonight*, the programme which has a key position in setting the terms and establishing the traditions which structure the practice of 'popular TV':

> the items [were] knitted together into a continuous and comprehensive show by a personality, starting off with Cliff Michelmore . . . (*Radio Times*, 26/8/60.)

The *Nationwide* presenters attempt to identify as closely as possible with 'you, the viewers'. The team speak on our behalf, mediating the world to us; they assume a position as our representatives. Lord Hill noted, of *Tonight* (but the observation could easily be extended to *Nationwide*), that the first essential of a reporter is:

> not unselfconsciousness or camera presence, but a total conviction that he represents the absolute norm, and that any deviation from his way of life is suspect. (Quoted in Connell, 1975.)

The team are not stars in the sense of telepersonalities but:

> real people; whole rounded people who ask the sort of questions that are sound common sense — questions that are in the viewer's mind and that he would ask if he was in their place. (Quoted in Connell, 1975.)

Thus, the relationships which are established between programme and audience, which set the viewer in place in a certain relation to the discourse — here, a relation of identity and complicity — are sustained in the mechanisms and strategies of the discourses of popular television themselves, but also by the presenters, who have a key role in anchoring those positions and in impersonating — personifying — them. The linking/framing discourse, then, which plays so prominent a part in structuring any sequence of items in *Nationwide*, and guides us between the variety of heterogeneous contents which constitute *Nationwide* as a unity-in-variety, not only informs us about what the next item is, and maintains the 'naturalism' of smooth flow and easy transitions — bridging, binding, linking items into *a* programme. It also re-positions 'us' into — inside — the speech of the programme itself, and sets us up in a particular position of 'knowledge' to the programme by (also) positioning us with 'the team'; implicating 'us' in what the team knows, what it assumes, in the team's relationships with each other, and the team's relation to 'that other, vital part of *Nationwide*' — us, the audience. For, as the (one-time) editor Michael Bunce put it, it is not only Michael Barratt, or the *Nationwide* team, who decide what goes on the air, so does the audience:

> Telephone calls, telegrams, 1000 letters a week . . . breathe life into the programme and inspire much of what actually gets on the air . . . [the presenters] do not make *Nationwide*. The viewers make it. (Quoted in Gillman, 1975.)

Identification and preferred readings. However, while our participation as audience may be necessary to the programme, 'we' do not make it in a relationship of equivalence with the 'team'. It is the team who control and define the terms of the discourse, and it is the team who signal to us 'what it's all about'. It is the presenters who 'explain' the very meaning of the images we see on the screen. The 'menu' for the 19/5/76 item on the students

> (Tonight we meet the students who built a new life for themselves out of a load of old rubbish. These may look like a few old plastic bags to you, but actually, for a time it was home to them.)

positions viewer, *Nationwide* team and interviewees within a paradox of the programme's own construction.

It is 'we' together who will meet the students, but it is the *Nationwide* team who will offer a privileged reading of the actual significance of the images on the screen, which the audience at home is thus caught into 'reading' as 'a few old plastic bags'. This systematic subversion of the 'obvious' reading an audience might have made of an image, apart from the implications it has for the constantly set-up 'natural' and shared decoding, renders the audience rationally impotent, because the conditions of the paradox are always that it is impossible to know what the image really denotes. The consequent dependence of the audience on the broadcasters' explanation of each little mystery accentuates, in a self-justifying way, the team's role as our 'representatives'.

The presenters and interviewers define for us the status of the extra-programme participants and their views: through these introductions, links and frames the preferred readings or contextualisations of the items and events portrayed are suggested. In the 19/5/76 programme, for instance, we are 'directed' by Tom Coyne's gruff, fair, but 'no-nonsense' manner towards a rather low estimation of the activities of the students who 'built a new life for themselves out of a load of old rubbish'. After all, they cannot compete with the basically 'sensible' perspective expressed in Coyne's final, indulgently-phrased question:

> Now I can obviously see that a student of your age is going to enjoy an experience like this, even if the weather is rough, because it's a lot of fun, but other people want to know what you actually got out of it from an educational point of view . . .?

Moreover, here Coyne not only invokes our views on the matter but implicates us in his. He does not merely ask a common-sense question, but claims to do so on behalf of us; we are the viewers — those 'other people' who 'want to know'.

The world of home and leisure. Let us begin with an analogy between 'the scene *Nationwide*' and Duckburg. Dorfman and Mattelart observe of Duckburg:

> In the world of Disney, no one has to work to produce. There is a constant round of buying, selling and consuming, but to all appearances none of the products involved has required any effort whatsoever to make . . . The process of production has been eliminated but the products remain. What for? To be consumed. Of the capitalist process which goes from production to consumption, Disney knows only the second stage . . . (Dorfman and Mattelart, 1975, pp.64–5.)

Foremost among the areas of life from which *Nationwide* draws its material is the world of 'leisure' — the sphere of culture, entertainments and hobbies. Here we meet individuals in their personal capacities, away from the world of social production; we follow their activities in the realms of their personal life. The nation '*Nationwide*', like the inhabitants of Duckburg, seems to be principally concerned with the process of consumption. Unlike Duckburg though, we consume principally in families — entering the Supersave competition (Monday nights 1975) together, and even enlarging our family size together ('Citizen 76' Monday nights 1976).

The world of home and leisure is by far the dominant single element in the *Nationwide* discourse, accounting for 40% of the items in the sample. [. . .] The first thing to remark is that this 'presence' betokens the almost total absence (except in some local news items) of the world of work, the struggle of and over production. This private leisure-world is a 'free floating' sphere from which the productive base has been excised. This absence extends to production in the family. Although 'Citizen 76' focused on pregnancy and the birth of children, and at Christmas we have shared selected hostesses' Christmas menus ('Christmas Round the World' 1975), the day-to-day labour of childcare and housework, which makes the home a sphere of work and not leisure to most women, is invisible in *Nationwide*. *Nationwide* leaves us suspended in the seemingly autonomous spheres of circulation, consumption and exchange: the real relations of productive life, both inside and outside the home, have vanished.

Nationwide addresses itself (cf., *Radio Times* billing) to an audience of individuals and families, the nation, in their personal capacities. Its transmission time allows it to construct itself/constructs it at the bridging point between 'work' and home (for wage workers). Its discourse is structured through the absent/present opposition between the 'world' and home. This opposition between the public and the private, we would argue, is partly informed by the sexual division associated with 'world' and 'home' (Rowbotham 1973). It is the 'masculine' world of work which constructs the home as a place of leisure, a private sphere where the male labourer has some sort of choice and control, which exists quite differently for women (who may well also be wage workers), as it is their responsibility to maintain this 'tent pitched in a world not right'.

As a family show, *Nationwide* addresses itself to the family together, 'caring and sharing' (Thompson, 1977), a close knit group of individuals, among whom the 'obviousness' of the sexual division of labour emerges as simply different responsibilities, specialities and qualities for men and women. Thus *Nationwide* does not, like women's magazines, address itself primarily to the 'woman's world' of the home, with advice about 'coping' and 'managing' which reveal the contradictory tension of maintaining the 'ideal' 'norm' (Winship, 1978). *Nationwide* doesn't have recipes, dress and knitting patterns or household hints, unless there's something special about them: a man who makes his children's clothes ('Supersave'); if we slim, we slim together, *Nationwide* ('Slim and Trim' March 1977, with *Nationwide*'s 'ten guinea-pig slimmers' — *Radio Times*, 30/3/77). We meet the family together, usually in their home ('Supersave', 'Citizen 76', 'Budget' 1977), or its individuals in relation to their own speciality. Sometimes, for women, this is 'being a wife and mother', as in the interview with the Pfleigers in the 'Little Old England' item 19/5/77, which opens with a shot of Mrs. Pfleiger at the kitchen sink, and is cut so that her answer to the question 'Did you find it difficult to settle in here?' is entirely concerned with household equipment, while her husband gives a more general account of the family's history and attitudes. More usually it is being a wife and mother *and also* being fascinated by lions (19/4/77), being a witch (18/6/76), making a tapestry of Bristol's history (15/6/76).

We are concerned, then, with a discourse which, very schematically, and at a general level, has an underlying 'preferred' structure of absences and presences:

ABSENT :	*PRESENT*
world	home
work	leisure
production ⎱ reproduction ⎰	consumption
workers (functions)	individuals (bearers)
structural causation	effects

There is a concentration on 'the "real" world of people' (Hoggart, 1957) both as a bulwark against the abstract, alien problems of the outside world, and as a moral baseline through which they are interrogated. The effectivity of the outside world is symbolised for *Nationwide* in 'bureaucracy' — faceless men (non-individuals, but still personalised to the extent that it is 'faceless men', not 'the system'), behind closed doors, who have power over 'us':

> Once again, the key decisions were taken behind closed doors, in this case the small branch meetings up and down the country. (*Nationwide*, 15/6/76.)

In relation to these issues *Nationwide* will adopt a 'campaigning' stance — aiming to 'open doors' on our behalf. Thus in Autumn '76 we had the creation of 'Public Eye': a spot in which two team members

> investigate an issue which they feel should be brought under the gaze of the public eye. (*Radio Times*, 3/11/76.)

134

This opposition between we 'ordinary people' and the 'faceless men' of the bureaucracy is close in structure to Hoggart's description of a class sense of 'them' and 'us':

> Towards 'Them' generally, as towards the police, the primary attitude is not so much fear as mistrust; mistrust accompanied by a lack of illusions about what 'They' will do for one, and the complicated way — the apparently unnecessarily complicated way — in which 'They' order one's life when it touches them. (Hoggart, 1957, p.74.)

The difference is that the 'us' *Nationwide* speaks for is not class specific, but 'the nation' of consuming individuals, always already in families. In the example above, the decisions taken 'behind closed doors' were made by workers in Trade Union branches. (Cf., Morley, 1976, section 1.b, on presentation of TU decisions as the sole cause of events.)

Classes do not appear in the discourse of *Nationwide*; only individuals, and these individuals usually appear in relation to the market — in the spheres of exchange and consumption. Thus the image of a group of white male workers with clenched fists standing outside a factory gate (*Nationwide* 19/5/76) is *not* an image of workers victorious in a struggle at the point of production, but that of a group of Pools winners:

> altogether nine people will share the prize money, and for one of the winner's wives, news of the win came as an unexpected but most welcome 44th birthday present. (19/5/76.)

This is not to suggest that *Nationwide* does not, or can never, deal with the worlds of production and hard news, but that when confronted with the need to cover political items, such as the budget or incomes policies, *Nationwide* deals with them where possible by translating them into the context of domestic life; how will such 'political' issues affect the home. The strategy is precisely that of the humanisation/personalisation of 'issues' into their 'effects on people'; or, alternatively, the exploration of the range of people's 'feelings' or reactions to external forces that impinge on them. (For example, the new tax schedule: 'Do you recognise that — one of those nasty PAYE forms . . . an all time grouse . . . along with mothers-in-law' — *Nationwide* 29/3/77.)

Political events then in this discourse have their meaning made comprehensible through their *effects* on 'people', and it is assumed that people are normally grouped in families:

> We . . . look at how this budget affects three typical families . . . 'Ken' feels strongly he's not getting a fair deal at the moment . . . what would you like to see the Chancellor doing for your family and friends? . . . (*Nationwide*, 29/3/77.)

135

Nationwide asks 'home' questions in the world. If we enter into that larger domain, it is to find out what the people in the public world are like — as individuals; for example, that an M P is also a racehorse owner (19/5/76). The structures of ownership and control in society are dissolved into the huge variety of individuals *Nationwide* — it takes all sorts to make a world. Where this type of treatment is not possible, it is because some crisis in that world has made its day-to-day absence no longer tenable in the programme discourse; its effects, at this point, intrude into the concerns of the *Nationwide* World — which at some level involves a recognition of the determinacy of this outside world. But this is precisely registered as intrusion, interruption or inconvenience. (Cf., Morley, 1976, section 5.b on the reporting of strikes as a regrettable disruption of 'normal working'.) [. . .]

People's problems
Nationwide is a 'responsible' programme; it will not only amuse and interest us. *Nationwide* is a programme of care and concern and consistently runs stories on 'people's problems': the problems of the lonely, the abnormal, underprivileged and (especially the physically) disabled. These items account for the third largest part of the sample: 16 per cent ($^{30}/_{182}$). The point here is that *Nationwide* deals with these stories in a quite distinctive way; rather than the discussion between experts that we might get on *Panorama* about the background to some 'social problem' *Nationwide* takes us straight to the 'human effects' — the problems and feelings of the 'sufferers', what effect their disability has 'on their everyday lives'.

Nationwide seems to have a penchant for dealing with cases of physical abnormality: where the 'problem' is seen to have natural, not social origins — blindness, handicaps, etc. The angle they take is usually a 'positive' one: 'look what is being done for these people with new technology'. The social role of technology — of inventions and inventors — is stressed here; useful technology is seen to solve social problems by demonstrably improving the quality of people's lives. This is indicative of *Nationwide*'s concern with 'human scale technology' in 'Britain Today', where, as Tom Coyne says (19/5/76), 'Things are changing all the time' — it is the world of 'new developments', such as an invention which enables blind students to produce 3-dimensional drawings (19/5/76).

Physical abnormality, without its social origins or consequences, is very much part of that 'natural human' world on which *Nationwide* frequently reports, and from which it regularly draws its stock of internally-generated reporters' 'stories'. A London region item on the treatment of a thalidomide child, for example, made no reference to the origins of the case, the contentious question of compensation, or the degree of the drug company's responsibility, or the suppression of the

Sunday Times report. It was concerned, precisely, with finding the means to normalise the life of those affected by thalidomide without reference to the more troublesome question of causes.

The destruction of nature and the effect of natural disability recur again and again: 'Threat to rare birds by egg collectors' (29/3/77); 'Cause for Concern: Christmas pets' (15/12/75); 'Cause for Concern: rare animals' (2/1/76); the problems of 'Hay Fever Sufferers' (9/6/76); the problem of 're-employment of the blind' (3/6/76.) But *Nationwide* is also concerned with other kinds of social misfits for whom something must be done. The problems are 'brought home' to us, and in these areas of 'ordinary human concern', *Nationwide* wears its heart on its sleeve: we see the problem, but we are also shown the positive side — what can be done about it.

Thus we learn of the anguish caused to relatives by 'disappearing people' (1/6/76) but we also meet 'Brigadier Grettin', from a voluntary organisation, who 'devotes his life to trying to find missing people'. We hear of 'old people alone at Christmas' (19/12/75), but also of positive responses: 'six men riding a bike for charity' (19/8/76), people collecting waste, and 'marathon singers' performing for charitable funds (17/6/76).

Nationwide monitors, on our behalf, serious and topical issues — thus not only are there the occasional, 'investigative', reports on the problems of soccer violence (20/1/76) and West Indian children's educational problems (30/3/77), but also responses to 'topical' issues directly affecting us all. So, during the rabies scare, *Nationwide* featured 'rabies remedies' (11/6/76); during the drought, not only an investigation of 'whose responsibility' its problems were (20/8/76), but also practical warnings of 'cuts in our areas' (17/8/76) and of 'diseases from the drought' (20/8/76).

Nationwide's treatment of people's problems is then, immediate: we are shown 'what it means in human terms'. This 'humanising' emphasis can be seen to have its basis in the specific communicative strategy of the broadcasters — in trying to 'get the issue across' what better way than to concentrate directly on the feelings of those immediately involved? However, the consequent emphasis, being placed almost exclusively on this 'human angle', serves to inflect our awareness of the issue; what is rendered invisible by this style of presentation is the relation of these human problems to the structure of society. The stress on 'immediate effects', on 'people', on getting to the heart of the problem, paradoxically confines *Nationwide* rigidly to the level of 'mere appearances'.

The *Nationwide* discourse in this area is in fact structured by two dimensions of the same 'significant absence'. On the one hand the problems that are dealt with are almost exclusively those with a natural, not social, origin — especially problems arising from physical disability. Here the 'problems' generated by the class structure of our society are largely evaded, through the tendency to naturalise social problems. On the other hand the treatment of these problems consistently evades the social determinations acting on the experience of physical problems: thus the items on people suffering from physical disability do not address themselves to the differential class experience of these problems.

The social dimensions of the problem are consistently excised — they are constantly re-presented as the problems of particular individuals, deprived of their social context. Moreover the horizon of the problem is set in terms of what can be done about it immediately — by charitable work, by individual voluntary effort, or by 'new technology'. The systematic displacement of the discourse to the level of individual effort make logical, as one of its consequences, this stress on practical, pragmatic remedies. This is not to deny the importance of these matters, but to point to the absence of any awareness of the need for social and structural solutions to structurally generated problems.

We would suggest that in parallel fashion to the way in which class structure is largely invisible in the *Nationwide* 'image of England' (see following section) — and is only presented through the displaced form of 'regional differences' — in this area of *Nationwide* discourse 'natural disabilities' stand as a similarly displaced 'representation' of the absent level of socially generated inequalities and problems.

The image of England: town and country
The discourse of *Nationwide* takes as a matter of explicit concern and value our national cultural heritage; the category accounts for 17 per cent ($^{31}/_{182}$) of the sample.

The 'culture' in which *Nationwide* deals is of course the cultural heritage of 'middle Britain'; it is decidedly not the up-to-the-minute culture of the pop world (the Sex Pistols made their breakthrough on *Today*, not *Nationwide*) nor the world of 'high culture'. It's the world of the 'Cook Family Circus' (18/6/76) and the anniversary of '30 years since the last ENSA show' (20/8/76). Reunion and anniversary are a recurring thread in the items; it may equally well be 'Pilots in pre-war planes reliving Biggles' (17/8/76), or 'Dakota planes 40 years old today' (17/12/75), or even a Burma p.o.w. reunion (9/1/76). The cultural context is neither the Rainbow nor Covent Garden: it is rather Blackpool (3/3/76) or 'holidays in Spain' (1/6/76). The cultural context is often constructed through the mass of calendar items which punctuate the *Nationwide* year: from the Glorious 12th, to Hallowe'en, Christmas, Ascot, St. George's Day, Midsummer's Eve, etc.

Even when dealing in other areas *Nationwide* consistently inflects the story back towards the idea of a national heritage. Thus, *Nationwide* will not normally deal with MPs' 'campaigns', but they will cover Willie Hamilton when he is attacking the Monarchy (30/12/75) —

Nobody prompted a bigger response from you than Willie Hamilton...
In January we gave him a chance ... and asked you to reply ...

Similarly, *Nationwide* covers, not our general economic prospects in the export trade, but the particular success of Morgan Car manufacturers — a traditional British make (17/8/76); not the economics of the EEC, but

the effects on our great British Institutions of joining the EEC. (15/12/75.)

Here is national(-istic) politics, concern with our craft traditions and national heritage combined in a peculiarly *Nationwide* inflection: an oddly serious, yet self-parodying chauvinism. Wellings:

Here I am in an English garden — flowers, rockery, ... and garden gnomes, good sturdy English gnomes, moulded and painted by English craftsmen ... today their very existence is threatened by imported gnomes — 'gnomeads' ... from Spain. How will the British gnome stand up to the new threat? (*Nationwide* 15/6/76.)

The dominant theme which orchestrates this material (in over half the items — $^{17}/_{31}$ in this category) is based on a concern with 'traditional values'. Primarily this takes the form of a massive investment in rural nostalgia — a focus on the variety of rural crafts; items on the highways and by-ways of the countryside. Implicitly there is a reference to an 'image of England' which is founded in an earlier, traditional and predominantly rural society — a more settled (even an organic) community. (See Williams, 1975.)

Nationwide's peculiar addiction to the rural customs and traditions of 'Old England' finds an interesting counterpart in the cosmology of Disneyland; Dorfman and Mattelart argue that each great urban civilisation creates its own pastoral myth, an extra-social Eden, chaste and pure, where:

The only relation the centre (adult — city folk — bourgeoisie) manages to establish with the periphery (child — noble savage — worker/peasant) is touristic and sensationalist ... The innocence of this marginal sector is what guarantees the Duckburger his touristic salvation ... his childish rejuvenation. The primitive infrastructure offered by the Third World Countries [or, in the case of *Nationwide*, 'The Countryside'] becomes the nostalgic echo of a lost primitivism, a world of purity ... reduced to a picture postcard to be enjoyed by a service-oriented world. (Dorfman and Mattelart, 1975, p.96.)

What *Nationwide* presents is not the rural world of agricultural production and its workaday concerns — today's price of animal feed — but the country viewed from the city, a nostalgic concern with the beauties of 'vanishing Britain . . . the threat to our countryside . . . ever since the Industrial Revolution' (31/3/77). Here we meet the Vicar who is concerned with the future of 'one of the Midlands' most beautiful churches' (31/3/77); the army is praised 'in an odd role — as conservationists' (5/1/76); we pay a touristic visit to Evesham and Stonehenge (18/6/76); to the West Midlands Agricultural Show (19/5/76) and the Three Counties Show (15/6/76): we observe the vestiges of the traditional cyclical calendar of rural life.

We are here presented with a very distinct set of concerns — not the workings of the local social security tribunal but of the 'Forest Verdurers Court' in the Forest of Dean (10/6/76); we learn of the work, not of factory farming, but of seaweed collectors (19/8/76); we are entreated with the problems of 'animals threatened by forest fires' (19/8/76) and see the efforts of forest fire-fighters (18/8/76). It is the world of 'Little Old England' (19/5/76) which may be treated in a 'folksy' way — often with deliberate self-parody and irony — but which is nevertheless secure, and the parody leaves the traditionalism intact.

Thus the approach to the soul-searching, investigative item 'Where have all those nice tea-places gone?' (11/6/76) — complete with music from 'An English Country Garden' — may be tongue-in-cheek, but the subject matter is ultimately accorded serious concern. After all, this is a vanishing part of our national heritage; Frank Bough: 'Does the Tradition not continue anywhere at the moment?'

But this is not all that Tradition has to offer. When the pollen count rises (10/6/76) *Nationwide* sets off the remedies of modern western medicine against the 'traditional hay fever remedies', which are explored in their regional variations around the country. Here the (regionalised) mode of treatment is as important as the subject matter: *Nationwide* uses the form again in the item on 'the ingenious artist' (5/1/76). We move into the realms of art and craft — but more particularly small, home-based craft and craft-industry. We meet individual craftspeople using 'odd materials' and working in 'unusual places' — a painter from Wales who paints family pets on stretched cobwebs, one from Leeds who paints on piano keys and one from Glasgow who paints on the inside of bottles. The *Nationwide* presentation of these activities — remnants of a craft tradition in an industrialised world — is positively celebratory. Bough sums up:

There really is no end to the extraordinarily beautiful things people do in this country. (5/1/76.) [. . .]

(Extracted from Charlotte Brunsdon and David Morley, *Everyday Television: 'Nationwide'*, London: British Film Institute, 1978.)

References

Barratt, M. (1973), *Michael Barratt*, London: Wolfe Publishing.

Brody, R. (1976), '*Nationwide*'s contribution to the construction of the reality of everyday life', M.A. Thesis, Centre for Contemporary Cultural Studies, University of Birmingham.

Connell, I. (1975), 'London Town: A kind of Television Down Your Way', Centre for Contemporary Cultural Studies mimeo.

Dorfman, A. and Mattelart, A. (1975), *How to Read Donald Duck*, New York: International General.

Gillman, P. (1975), 'Nation at Large', *Sunday Times*, 2 March 1975.

Hall, Connell and Curti (1976), 'The "Unity" of Current Affairs Television', *Working Papers in Cultural Studies*, no. 9.

Hoggart, R. (1957), *The Uses of Literacy*, Harmondsworth: Penguin.

Morley, D. (1976), 'Industrial Conflict and the Mass Media', *Sociological Review*, May, 1976.

Rowbotham, S. (1973), *Woman's Consciousness, Man's World*, Harmondsworth: Penguin.

Smith, A. (1975), *Paper Voices*, London: Chatto and Windus.

Thompson, E. (1977), 'Happy Families', *New Society*, 8 September 1977.

Williams, R. (1975), *Keywords*, London: Fontana.

Winship, J. (1978), 'Woman', in *Women Take Issue*, London: CCCS/Hutchinson.

Introduction: Television and the World Cup

Few areas of sporting activity have changed as rapidly or as extensively as football has during the post-war period. Chas Critcher, in a survey of developments within the game since the war, points to a series of radical and often quite fundamental changes in the economics of football, the structures of control within the game, the financing of the clubs, the relationships between clubs and supporters, the shifting status of the player associated with the increased professionalization of the game, the increased importance of international competitions and so on. Undoubtedly the most important change, however, has been the massive development in the amount and nature of televised soccer. Apart from constituting a significant change in itself, television's coverage of football has been deeply implicated in all of the other changes which have transformed the structure of the game. It has been television, perhaps more than any other single factor, which has contributed to the development of soccer heroes as highly paid, international superstars; it has been television which has depopulated the terraces, weakening the connections between local clubs and local supporters by focusing the nation's attention on the annual contest between the League giants; and it has been television that has accentuated the significance of international competitions within the rhythms of the game. Numerically speaking, the typical football fan today is not the partisan supporter on the terraces but the viewer in the living room.

It is, of course, equally true that football occupies an important position within the structure of television practices. In his introduction to *Football on Television*, Edward Buscombe estimates that the BBC and ITV each spent £400,000 on their programmes for the 1974 World Cup, devoting, between them, 135 hours of television to the coverage of this event. 'The BBC claimed', he writes, 'that the Scotland v. Brazil match was watched by a total of 24 million people on both channels, and placed the match third in their list of the top twelve most popular BBC programmes of the year. The World Cup Final came equal sixth' (Buscombe (ed.), 1975, p.2).

The essays which follow deal with television coverage of the World Cup, perhaps the most important instance of televised soccer in the respect that the development of this competition from a relatively minor to the most important event within the structure of the game, its four year climacteric, has been inextricably associated with the development of mass broadcasting. Ranging across both the 1974 and the 1978 World

Cup, the essays consider how the television practices which mediate between the World Cup and the viewer transform the 'raw material' of the football into specific forms of television which have marked consequences for the ways in which the competition is perceived by the viewer and for the ways in which s/he is situated in relation to it.

In 'Setting the Scene', Colin McArthur focuses on the way in which the 1974 World Cup was *pre-constructed* in *Radio Times* and *TV Times*, paying particular attention to the ways in which these 'cued' the competition as concerning, essentially, a contest between a number of individual soccer 'superstars'. Andrew Tudor follows a similar tack in considering the role of the 'panel of experts', a distinctive innovation of television, in selectively concentrating the viewers' attention on particular aspects of the game. Tudor also considers the degree of ethnic stereotyping which characterizes television's construction of the relations between different national teams within international competitions. In 'Television — Football — The World', Geoffrey Nowell-Smith considers — this time in relation to the 1978 World Cup — the way in which television has intervened within and radically re-shaped the structures of partisanship within the game, transforming the viewer from a committed supporter of one team (the position of the fan on the terraces) into an impartial spectator, the subject of a very different form of pleasure. Adopting a rather different stance to that exhibited by Colin McArthur and Andrew Tudor, Nowell-Smith then goes on to consider not the way in which football is signified but the way in which, on television, football functions as a signifier. He does so by examining the way in which the television coverage of the 1978 World Cup was 'overdetermined' by the political question of Argentina. The result, he suggests, was that the elements of the contest — the different teams, different styles of play, the constructed images of different stars and managers — were mobilized as the signifiers of political differences within a discourse that centred on the problem of the connection between the right-wing dictatorial regime in Argentina and the footballing style of its national team.

References

Buscombe, E. (ed.) (1975), *Football on Television*, London: British Film Institute.

Setting the Scene: *Radio Times* and *TV Times*

Popular belief has it that one of the crucial oppositions in categorising films and television programmes is that between 'fiction' and 'actuality'. It is very often felt that while feature films, television drama series and, perhaps, quiz shows and panel games are subject to various structuring mechanisms such as narrative, the use of actors, rehearsals, and so on, the media's coverage of sporting events, public ceremonies and news is unmediated, unadulterated, passed 'raw' to the audience through the 'eye' of the camera. [. . .]

By extension, it might be felt that the characteristic back-up documentation for the cinema and television — various fan magazines and the weekly *Radio Times* and *TV Times* — are also 'factual' productions offering straightforward information about programmes and personnel.

This [essay] challenges the accuracy of the popular position. [. . .] [and] argues that back-up documentation such as *Radio Times* and *TV Times* operate their own forms of structuration on 'reality'. As Stuart Hall has written:

> The raw historical event cannot in that form be transmitted by, say, a television newscast. It can only be signified within the aural-visual forms of a televisual language. In the moment where the historical event passes under the sign of language, it is subject to all the complex formal 'rules' by which language signifies. To put it paradoxically, the event must become a 'story' before it can become a *communicative event*. (Hall, 1974.)

[. . .] This essay examines the 'story' [of the 1974 World Cup] as told by the relevant issues of *TV Times* and *Radio Times* and the *Radio Times World Cup Special*. [. . .]

THE ON-GOING FUNCTION OF *Radio Times* AND *TV Times*

Something more needs to be said about the fact that both *Radio Times* and *TV Times* have identities which transcended the 1974 World Cup, for in a very real sense these journals adapted the event to their on-going identities rather than sought to reveal the peculiar essence of the World Cup.

Radio Times and *TV Times* have a function closely analogous to that of cinema fan magazines in that they treat virtually the entire output of television from drama series to news broadcasts as a set of 'star vehicles'. Thus, the most characteristic 'feature' in both *Radio Times* and *TV Times* is the star biography using the recurrent narrative strategies of that form (of which more later). It is by no means unusual to find a television comedian thus biographised one week and a television newscaster or current affairs pundit written about in exactly the same terms the following week. Clearly this mechanism reinforces the processes of signification in television transmission to further erode the distinction between 'fiction' and 'reality'.

In terms, therefore, of the on-going identities of *Radio Times* and *TV Times* it was to be expected that the 1974 World Cup would furnish another 'star vehicle' and, of course, this was the way the event was 'told'. Insofar as *TV Times* 'told' the event at all, its stars were Billy Bremner and Brian Clough.

Within the heavy coverage of *Radio Times* certain players (and of course 'experts') were designated as 'stars'. There was here a certain contradiction between *Radio Times'* on-going commitment to star biography and its recognition of the particular quality of football as a team game. This contradiction took the form of ostensible discussion of particular teams (Brazil, Australia, Zaire, Italy, Scotland, Uruguay) and *de facto* discussion of particular 'stars' within them. This pattern was reproduced in a more blanket form in the *Radio Times World Cup Special*.

Three players were cast in advance as superstars. Their pictures were on the cover of *Radio Times*: their 'stories' were told in some detail. The three players were Paulo Cesar of Brazil, Giorgio Chinaglia of Italy and Franz Beckenbauer of West Germany. By a peculiar irony, the only one of the three whose actual performance in the competition bore any relationship to the role he was assigned was Franz Beckenbauer and the issue of *Radio Times* devoted to him failed to appear due to industrial action. Both Cesar and Chinaglia receded to obscurity during the competition, throwing some element of doubt on the much-touted 'expertise' of the BBC and ITV and exemplifying a recurrent phenomenon of the competition, the failure of both individual players and teams to conform to the stereotypical roles they had been assigned by 'experts', broadcasting institutions and journalists.

Richard Dyer has discussed, in the context of television light entertainment, the important mechanism whereby certain 'stars' are seen both to be of the people and yet elevated above the people [Dyer, 1973]. This mechanism finds its expression in what is perhaps the most familiar motif of the star biography — the 'rags to riches' motif. It constitutes a central theme in the *Radio Times* stories of Paulo Cesar and Giorgio Chinaglia. Thus, Cesar, 'the waif from a Rio shanty town':

...came from a poor home in Rio... He did not know his father and at eight was adopted by a richer family whom he had come to know. His mother agreed to the move so that he, at least, could leave the *favela* (shanty town). As soon as his success at football enabled him to do so, he moved her out too. Now she lives in the comfortable beach suburb of Leblan, near Ipanema. [*Radio Times,* 8–14 June 1974, p.58.]

and:

His skills mean everything to Giorgio Chinaglia. 'They have made me somebody. If I hadn't been good at football I'd be working in my father's restaurant in Cardiff.' [*Radio Times,* 15–21 June 1974, p.62.]

It is interesting to speculate on the reasons why Cesar and Chinaglia, rather than other individual players, were designated by *Radio Times* as *the* superstars of the competition. It seems clear that Cesar had been stereotyped by journalists to fulfil the role of legendary hero which Pele had played in Mexico in 1970. It is uncertain quite in what context Cesar had been 'named by Pele as his successor' but to the journalistic mind it amounted to a transference of charisma.

In the case of Chinaglia, the central element seems to have been his British connections, the fact that he himself played unsuccessfully in English league football and that his parents still ran a restaurant in Cardiff. This exemplifies further the central theme of this essay that it is less the objective status of the event than its mediation which is important. The clear reference point for all the television coverage and back-up documentation of the 1974 World Cup was the English (*English*, not British) television audience and readership of *Radio Times*. This point of reference is very clear in the coverage given to Scotland, the only UK team in the competition. Billy Bremner was an acceptable 'star' for *TV Times* less for his captaincy of Scotland than for his captaincy of Leeds United, a prominent English club. Also, if the priorities of the *Radio Times* and *Radio Times World Cup Special* can be gauged by examination of their *colour* photographs, then it is clear once more that the point of reference is the *English* readership. The *Radio Times* discussion of the Scottish team carries a large colour photograph of Bremner and his *Leeds* colleagues, Jordan and Lorimer, and the largest colour photograph in the *Radio Times World Cup Special's* discussion of Scotland is of Law and Morgan and stresses their *Manchester* connections.

STEREOTYPING OF TEAMS AND INDIVIDUAL PLAYERS

Just as two of the three players designated super-stars by the *Radio Times* coverage failed to conform to their assigned roles, so too did the most strongly stereotyped teams. West Germany, the eventual winners of the competition, were characterised as the team who had 'peaked' too early

Fig. 2.1: *Bill Tidy's cartoon in* Radio Times, *15–21 June 1974.*

and Brazil (the 'fabulous beach-boys'), having been stereotyped as flamboyant, skilful in attack, weak in defence and wary of physical contact, displayed quite the reverse qualities. Scotland, described as 'Inconsistent. Capable of occasional inspired performances but just as likely to be disjointed, playing without cohesion . . .' [*Radio Times*, 8–14 June 1974, p.17] played a flowing team game distinguished for the maintenance of a consistent texture and standard, their finishing apart.

Where 'hard' information was lacking on any team the coverage fell back on more general racial, national and ideological stereotypes. Thus the three East European teams (Bulgaria, Poland and Yugoslavia) were written about collectively under the rubric 'Iron Curtain Football' (see Fig.2.1) and the descriptions of the Haitian team were determined by popular conceptions of what life in Haiti is like:

> In voodoo-shrouded Haiti where the largely illiterate, secret police-shadowed inhabitants have an unenviable existence, the diversion of the World Cup is sheer magic . . . [*Radio Times,* 15–21 June 1974, p.3.]

Something has already been said about the stereotyping of particular players as super-stars. Just as Chinaglia was 'the Welsh reject who hits goals for Italy' [*Radio Times World Cup Special,* June 1974, p.66], so too was Johann Cruyff 'the world's most expensive footballer' [*Radio Times,* 15–21 June 1974, p.22] and Peter Wilson, the Australian captain, the man who rose from English Second Division soccer to World Cup football:

> . . . his heroes were Denis Law and the Beatles. One thing's for sure. When they gave him a free transfer from Middlesbrough, he never envisaged that he and Law would be playing in the same World Cup. [*Radio Times,* 8–14 June 1974, p.11.]

These stereotypes reveal once more the centrality of the 'rags to riches' motif in the structuration of the event.

SELF-LEGITIMISATION OF BACK-UP COVERAGE

Unlike 'fictional' television, 'factual' television and its associated back-up documentation is prepared to reveal a considerable amount of the process of its own production in the form of the figures who actually structure the event. There is an apparent contradiction here. How can it be maintained — as the ideology of factual television would have it — that the event is presented 'raw' and unmediated when its impresarios are blatantly paraded? The contradiction is only *apparent,* for *by the nature of the presentation* of the impresarios — both in television itself and in the back-up documentation — their roles as impresarios are both celebrated and subsumed within the hegemonic category of 'stars'. The lowest-key level of this process is revealed in the opening page of World Cup coverage in the *Radio Times* which is as much a discussion of the personnel writing and photographing the coverage as about the event itself. However, the process is most blatantly revealed — and the myth of the opposition 'fictional'/'factual' smashed — on the cover of the *Radio Times World Cup Special* which shows Jimmy Hill, arch-expert of the BBC,

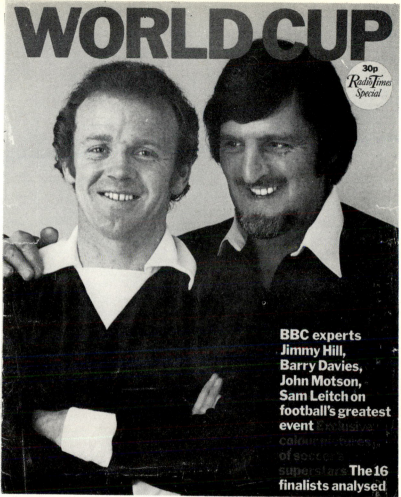

Fig. 2.2: *Cover of* Radio Times World Cup Special, *June 1974.*

in referee's garb, with his arm round Billy Bremner. This single image shouts from the rooftops the message that, in the context of the mass media, an event can *never* be separated from its mediation (see Fig. 2.2).

(Extracted from Edward Buscombe (ed.), *Football on Television*, London: British Film Institute, 1975.)

References

Dyer, R. (1974), *Light Entertainment*, London: British Film Institute.
Hall, S. (1974), 'The Television Discourse: Encoding and Decoding', in *Education and Culture*, No. 25, Council of Europe, 1974.

The Panels

It is hardly in dispute that television, like any other communications medium, stands between its audience and the events it portrays. Whatever the topic, television moulds it to fit a particular means of communication, refines and distills, selects and emphasises certain things at the expense of others. Often that process is quite complex, for style and programming depend on both the overall stream of television and the individual demands of light entertainment, drama, or current affairs. [. . .] Something like the World Cup, however, sets different problems, for it is composed of a highly condensed set of homogeneous events. Whereas the overall continuity of domestic football coverage is limited by the constraints of normal programming, the World Cup is paid enormous attention in a short space of time. So if, as seems likely, sports coverage is just as much concerned to tell a coherent 'story' as any other sort of television, the very condensation of World Cup coverage into a three week frenzy might make that process all the more obvious. [. . .]

But what does 'telling a story' involve? First, and most obviously, it demands that a scene be set; that television constitutes a world within which the story's events may be presented as a coherent development. [Whereas a] work of drama openly offers such a world conventionalised as a 'fictional' construction, [. . .] received wisdom suggests that this mode is in contrast to the treatment of such subjects as current affairs or sport where television's accepted role is to record and reveal 'reality' for us. Received wisdom is surely wrong in this, for in varying degrees television actually *constitutes* the reality which it then purports to reveal. It selects, emphasises, and abstracts long before anything arrives on our screens; how could it be otherwise? So, although events may dictate aspects of television coverage, the coverage itself is made intelligible by television and not by some order inherent in the events. [. . .]

What, then, are the dimensions of the World Cup world [as constructed on television]? What morality does it presuppose? What is its physical, social, and ideological nature? What labels does coverage invoke? How are they interrelated into an intelligible structure, and how, if at all, does that structure develop and change? And [. . .] what sort of machinery does television use in constituting this particular reality? [. . .] The answers to [some of these questions are] to be found in the sort of format that both British channels chose to employ as the main carrier of their interpretations [of the World Cup]: support programmes. In 1974,

150

support programmes, on both channels, were running at up to 30 per cent of total World Cup coverage, and a very large proportion of those programmes centred on the ubiquitous panels. What had been a famous ITV innovation for the 1970 World Cup (the all-action, all-purpose, and, as some crueller observers remarked, all-mouth panel of experts) became the over-fed albatross of 1974.

Quite an odd bird too. Unlike most television 'panels of experts' the football panels did not draw any members from other media — no sports writers, notably enough. Instead they were composed entirely of men from the world of football. The BBC's, chaired by Jimmy Hill, included Bobby Charlton, Frank McLintock, Laurie McMenemy, and Joe Mercer. On ITV, chaired by Brian Moore [. . .] there was Malcolm Allison, Jack Charlton, Brian Clough, Paddy Crerand, Derek Dougan, and Bobby Moncur. In addition both sides had a motley group of football figures on tap in Germany — Alf Ramsey, Bobby Robson, Jock Stein and others. This mixture was welded together in a format of impressive monotony: set the scene before the match; a few passing comments and an instant replay or two at half-time; an immediate post-match post-mortem. Then, later in the evening, perhaps a chance to give a more considered opinion. The internal structure of the programmes was also regular and uninspired. Members of the panel offered their opinions at the behest of the chairman, only occasionally breaking out of Hill's iron control on BBC, though the ITV group found more chance to engage one another under Moore's more sensitive chairmanship. Nevertheless, the structure of the situation did very much bend things toward any chairman who cared to take his opportunities, and, as I shall suggest, Hill was especially successful in imposing his definition of what was important on the BBC coverage.

Now while that may admittedly have something to do with the particular personalities involved, it does also derive in considerable part from the peculiarities of the telexpert role. The accepted convention of television expertise is one of the most widespread in the medium, and the World Cup coverage leant heavily on its most straightforward formulation. [. . .]

THE EXPERT AS SUPERSTAR

As Colin McArthur suggests, *Radio Times* and *TV Times* resemble cinema fan magazines in their concern to cast all their subjects in 'star' terms. The football telexperts continue that trend, not only interpreting football in some such framework, but applying a similar rationale to the ways in which they present themselves. Indeed, the very legitimacy of their opinions and analyses stems in part from their own 'star quality'. Their demands on our credibility depend on our accepting their claims to expertise. But how are we to judge? Television certainly does not subject

151

us to a cumulative process of enlightenment, the persuasive development of which finally convinces us of the expert's mastery of his subject. For that to be the case, [. . .] support programmes would have to focus positively on events, reasoned arguments, supporting evidence, and detailed discussion, instead of making their current superficial gestures in this direction. At present they focus on 'personalities', and there seems little doubt that these telexperts see themselves (and are seen) in 'star' and 'superstar' terms. It is on this *television and showbiz derived* basis that we are asked to accept their claims to expertise, whatever their football successes or — notably — failures.

Such a development is not too difficult to understand; television has shown a well established appetite for experts [. . .]. And football expertise [had] only recently reached the massive proportions of [the 1974 World Cup. In the mid-sixties,] there were only the commentators, and, whatever their individual styles, they did not usually expand their field of operations beyond the immediate demands of the game itself. More extensive analysis was left to the 'quality' press. Perhaps the major break came with David Coleman's expanding image, expecially his personal prominence in fronting *Sportsnight with Coleman.* Apart from those who moved into other areas of the medium (like Eamonn Andrews) he was the first British sports commentator to grow fully into showbiz status *within* television's sporting world. He breached the wall of specialism, and it is notable that it was in his era that the BBC took to grooming candidates taken from football into television's image of expertise. During that transition the whole thing was still characterised by a sense of friendly, slightly diffident amateurism. [. . .] But it was only a brief transition for, to use the expert's favourite term of admiration for footballers, expertise itself rapidly turned professional. So much so, in fact, that this professionalisation came to involve big money and make big news. Though ITV's 1970 panel may have begun the publicity cycle, its climacteric was to be found in Jimmy Hill's transfer to the BBC as the sports studio midfield anchor man. That particular transaction received almost as much publicity as the transfer of an expensive player within the game.

So, somewhere in the early seventies a line was crossed, and demonstrable expertise on football itself ceased to be the *crucial* ground on which we were asked to accept expert opinion. Though most such figures are still drawn from the game, there is no doubt that showbiz standards are increasingly prominent. To some extent that is unavoidable. Television has developed its own styles of presentation which effectively preclude some undoubtedly perceptive and successful footballers, coaches, and managers. Revie and Shankly — for some time BBC stalwarts — were hardly television successes, though between them they have enough football qualifications to command anyone's ear. In contrast, Allison and Clough, whose achievements might best [have

152

been] described as uneven, mastered the television format with ease. This sort of pattern was notably reflected in the 1974 support programmes where effective priority was given to those able and willing to operate within television conventions. [. . .]

Jimmy Hill's chairing of the BBC panel is worthy [of detailed] consideration: it is instructive on the telexpert role in general, and on the capacity of a panel chairman to set a particular pattern for the interpretation of events. [. . .] My notes for the Scotland/Zaire match (14 June) record the first of many similar comments. They read cryptically: 'Hill *obsessed* with Jordan fouling the Zaire goalkeeper', and they go on to note that at this very early stage Hill appeared to be trying to impose his particular perceptual pattern on the four less experienced panellists. Whether Jordan was fouling or not is neither here nor there. What is significant is the inordinate amount of time spent on the question, largely at Hill's insistence. On ITV, consistently more moderate on the fouling issue, the question was not even raised. But BBC discussions did repeatedly focus on fouls, endlessly replayed and reconsidered, and invariably at Hill's instigation. [. . .] And it is a measure of his success in constraining discussion that one of the BBC panel was finally moved to raise the question himself. In the half-time discussion of the Holland/Brazil match (3 July) Laurie McMenemy broke the telexperts united front. Clearly annoyed, he told the nation that he had spent the whole first half of the game listening to Hill shout each time a foul was committed. 'We are getting the game a bad name, emphasising the negative aspects', he added. [. . .]

This sort of forceful selective perception is much more in accord with television's entertainment expectations than with the vaunted aim of 'in-depth analysis'. For the paradigm telexpert is a loquacious, single-minded and infallible guide to right and wrong, truth and lies. His job is to 'mark our card' (as Brian Moore continually required of the ITV panel), and to do so in more than a simple predictive sense. The telexpert is to lend us his framework; we are to see through his eyes. He is to tell the story and we are to listen. As *TV Times* put it on 19 June: 'Tonight, each country should have completed its second game and the form lines are becoming clear. What are the shock results . . . which players have dominated the competition . . . which teams have emerged . . . who are the failures? The ITV panel provides the answers.' [. . .]

I have not recorded my distaste with Jimmy Hill's performance here simply for its own sake, though I have to admit that, in my view, he did destroy what little the BBC panel had to offer. But he is not entirely to blame in as much as the institution of television expertise itself provides the foundations on which he was built. He is significant as a qualitatively typical extreme, not as an individual aberration. By grouping its 'experts' with its 'stars' television lends them total self-confidence and persuades us to see them accordingly. It is this logic that puts Hill on the front cover of the *Radio Times* special with an arm around Billy Bremner, a football 'star' who, interestingly enough, also figured on the front of the *TV Times* with yet another 'star' counterpart: Omar Sharif. This is a perspective which encourages the interpenetration of entertainment, analysis, and outside event, that blurs together the various hierarchies of showbiz esteem. [. . .]

The 1974 World Cup world was above all a product of an expertise growth area. It was presented to us as the what and how of the World Cup, and, though individual contributors did sometimes disagree quite violently, it was bounded by more or less agreed parameters. It is these parameters which define the common world that interests me here. I have suggested the main context in which they are articulated; but what do they involve?

WORLD CUP WORLD

Any medium faces a basic problem of setting and peopling the worlds it constructs. But in some cases the setting itself is not open to much direct manipulation, and most interpretive effort goes into peopling the drama with suitably defined characters. So it is with World Cup coverage, if only because the intractable centre-piece remains the 90 minute football match, an event even more fixed in its own conventions than the television programmes which feed upon it. Television cannot change these basic rules, but it can reconstitute the football world by erecting a superstructure through which the football itself may be viewed. And the most common tool for that purpose — especially in sports coverage — is the stereotype. I do not intend the term to be pejorative. Any attempt to sort out the characters of a television world must use some stereotyping; it must draw on the framework of conventions and images which are assumed to inform the perceptions of the audience. Otherwise it would be unstructured and, in some senses, unintelligible.

But as one might expect, sports coverage does have its own particular specification of the stereotyping pattern, and one which *is* relatively simple. It is defined by two basic dimensions which seem to underlie the main elements of television's sporting world. One of them depends on the particular sport under analysis, and develops — often implicitly — an evaluation of what counts as 'good' or 'bad' football, cricket, or boxing. In English football coverage, for example, great value is placed on goalmouth incident, goals, and committed 'professional' play, an appraisal which is probably an accurate reflection of our general cultural mores about football. Compared to many continental cultures we subscribe to an orgasmic theory of football; the foreplay only has meaning if it is climaxed with goals. It is worth underlining that, whatever television may assume, this is not a universal attitude to the sport; continental crowds appear to place just as much value on the short passing skills of the build-up as on the brief ecstasy of the goal. But it is a view that we tend to take for granted in television definitions of the game simply because it is so familiar to us. Much the same taken-for-granted character applies to the second of the two basic dimensions, this one operating primarily with a series of ethnic and cultural stereotypes. Understandably such divisions are especially prominent in international sport (though there are domestic versions such as North versus South) where the categories are often not so much ethnic *and* cultural as ethnic masquerading as cultural. Though explicit terminology is not commonly racial in its reference, its underlying assumptions may well be: many distinctions prevalent in sports coverage would reduce quite easily to interpretations based upon race.

The single stereotypical group most frequently distinguished in English international football coverage is cast in terms of 'Latin Temperament'. It is an image well bolstered by other elements in our culture, and the many and varied teams of Latin America and Southern Europe are invariably lumped into this one perceptual class. Even the Brazilians have not so much escaped the stereotype as had a transmutation produced specifically for them. Their relaxed, extrovert, attacking football (more stereotypes) is construed as an unusual though intelligible channel through which the Latin Temperament may manifest itself. But, of course, on this reading it would be easy to slip back into the 'real' Latin style, and Brazil's relative failure in 1974 was seen in just this way by television. The recent expansion of world football, though, is going to require some new terms in the language, particularly for the African teams, in relation to whom the usual racial stereotyping is likely to prove embarrassing. It is notable that the commentators and panellists of the 1974 coverage were carefully guarded in the vocabulary they applied to black African newcomers Zaire, generally sticking to ethnically neutral terms of condescension: 'youth', 'enthusiasm', and 'inexperience' were typical. But whatever the immediate problems of such new developments, the general ethnic/cultural stereotype remains *the* interpretive tool of international sports coverage, inevitably reinforced by the nationalism already built into such events as the Olympic Games and the World Cup. The first priority in television commentary is always national interest, and, that established, the second is an ethnocentric classification of the 'rest' in ethnic and cultural stereotypes.[. . .]

For *English* television, specifically, 1974 presented an interesting ethnic problem, one which was finally resolved in a plethora of tartan and the evident belief that Scotland was an England team with accents. But ethnocentrism spreads wider than this straightforward nationalism. Where at all possible the ethnocentric focus is used as a grounding for all other stereotypes, as a measure of difference or of similarity. Television even discovered British players where it could, endlessly reminding us of their existence: Chinaglia, of Italy, came from Cardiff; Babington, of

Argentina, was born of English parentage; and the Australians were heavily bolstered with first generation immigrants. Where direct links were impossible, the indirect and tenuous was in order. In a moment of revealing extravagance (normally he was the most perceptive, restrained, and pertinent of the panellists) Jack Charlton compared Poland's newly discovered 'great style' to that of England in their heyday, while later references even stretched the comparative thread as far as linking the Dutch with Leeds United. I do not suggest that such comparisons are meaningless: only that as short-hand they are very culture-dependent. [...] They serve only to locate us in an ethnocentric perceptual set. Of course it is quite intelligible that domestic experience should inform television presentation, but it is also significant that television seems unable to find a language which transcends such ethnocentrism when the situation requires it. As I have already noted the image of 'good football' incarnated in television coverage is deeply embedded in our own culture. Even near-neighbours Scotland have traditionally been treated as stylistically foreign, making it notable that Joe Jordan attracted so much advance attention from television. Notable because Jordan — perhaps more than any other Scottish player — epitomised the central focus of the 'English style', the strong front runner; something that Scottish football (along with much of the rest of Europe) has never emphasised so strongly. [. . .]

In this way an ethnocentric definition of football style combines with an ethnocentric classification of the larger world to produce the fundamental sporting coverage stereotypes. Indeed, the only other major category apparently independent of this pattern actually incarnates another value so often claimed as typically English: love of the underdog. As with Korea in 1966, so with Zaire, Haiti, and, in part, Australia and Sweden in 1974. But compared to the main dimensions this was only a minor theme, as were the interesting but occasional attempts to define a more extensive social and political context. The only situation in which this was attempted in anything but the briefest compass was the BBC's scene-setting programme (12 June) when David Coleman made a desultory few comments on what he called 'underlying issues': [. . .] West versus East Germany illustrated with standard footage of the Berlin Wall; Chile's game with East Germany as a 'flashpoint' consequent upon recent political events; even a quick reference to Hitler's 1936 stadium. But, apart from a weak joke about Henry Kissinger and a Dutch player called Israel, that was as deep as the well of political comment went on either channel. Even the usual political overtones saved for East European teams (*cf.* Colin McArthur's discussion) were only intermittently invoked, though Poland did have to do a great deal before they finally, and deservedly, escaped the traditional straitjacket. Ethnic/cultural definitions, though widely pervasive, found their most extensive direct expression in the 'Latin/

European' imagery.

Of course, that distinction does indeed have some uses in discriminating football styles; there are definite contrasts between the two groups. But television usage combined explicit evaluations with the stylistically descriptive classification, evaluations which were in turn embedded in a pre-World Cup set of assumptions. In this perspective the Latin was associated with the bad ('cynical', 'dishonest', 'dirty') while the European suggested the good ('professional', 'open', 'disciplined'). Inevitably, for English television, Argentina began the festival marked out as villains. After 20 minutes of the Poland/Argentina game the first clear Argentinian foul (which led to a booking) caused Hugh Johns to invite Sir Alf Ramsey to recall the 1966 'animals' game. Nicely, Ramsey declined, and instead remarked on the cleanness of the Argentinian play thus far. That was on 15 June. Yet eight days later Brian Moore still felt able to say that it was curious how the Argentinians had arrived in Germany with a bad reputation. Hardly curious; it was the media in general, and television in particular, that insisted on conceiving them in this way. For English television, at least, it seems that Argentina will never live down the combination of Latin stereotype and the distant battle of 1966. [. . .]

The sheer simplicity of that Latin image was most succinctly revealed in both channels' penchant for the cryptic scene-setting phrase on the game we were about to watch. For Uruguay: will they show 'enterprise or fear of defeat', 'skill or cynical defence'? Would Argentina 'lose their heads' against Poland? And for a game almost by definition defying discrimination (Italy/Argentina) the English observer could only throw up his metaphorical hands: a 'clash of Latin temperaments'! Of the European teams the treatment of Scotland and Poland was probably the most revealing, partly because both teams proved amenable to analysis and appreciation in terms of the tacitly approved 'English style'. Joe Jordan, as I have mentioned, was a case in point, but it was also notable that Scotland (and Poland in the later stages) were usually allowed a little more latitude than most teams. What was cynical and irresponsible Latin temperament in an Argentinian, Uruguayan, or Italian, became solid professional play in a Scot or a Pole. And while that is easily understood for Scotland (open nationalism, many of the team English club players), Poland seems a bit more complex. I think their treatment derived from their playing football much as traditional English expectations would demand of an England team. Poland could be, and were, seen as a side including strong, though fair, defenders, tireless 'high work-rate' mid-field players, powerful central attackers, and (that much bemoaned absentee from modern English football) wing-play on both wings. Their approach work was quick, unelaborated, and effective; their goals often spectacular and always satisfying. They were the nearest thing to the English dream available in Germany, and in the end (they *did* have to live down the fact that they knocked England out) they were receiving as much attention as the patently outstanding Dutch. [. . .]

So far, then, I have suggested that a particular set of commitments lies behind these common stereotyping processes, commitments which derive in part from the values of English sporting culture and in part from the exigencies of television. I have sketched in some of them, albeit roughly, and I have tried to mention one or two of their more obvious applications — especially in the widespread use of ethnic and cultural stereotypes. [. . .] They do not, however, only manifest themselves in relation to team stereotyping, though that is very important, for they have more indirect channels of expression. For instance, one of the claims made by World Cup support programmes was that they would get at the 'truth' for us; a common claim in all television coverage of the 'real world'. [. . .] In line with this aim both channels have their machinery for presenting and establishing the facts; primarily, of course, the replay. Now, given how much time the panels had available one might have expected to see that tool applied to a wide range of football events; in fact it was dominated by two main uses. One, in replaying goals, saves, and near-misses: goalmouth incident. The other, in arbitrating disputed decisions and in getting the measure of fouls whether penalised or not. Compared to these two the application of replay analysis to other aspects of the game was marginal, an emphasis once more reflecting the major stereotypes. The focus on goalmouth incident (understandable in brief highlights but surely not in the longer panel spots) reflects precisely the English football values I have already discussed; for the English subscribers to the orgasm theory this is the epicentre of the game. The second emphasis (disputed decisions and fouling) reflects more of a television self-conception as 'outside arbitrator', vetting the performance of others, and offering a superior view on 'bad' elements in the game. Here, consistent with the expert syndrome, 'truth' is what the experts say the replays tell us! [. . .]

(Extracted from Edward Buscombe (ed.), *Football on Television*, London: British Film Institute, 1975.)

Television — Football — The World

PREFACE

This article takes as its starting point three observations on the question of television, politics and sport: first, that sport is almost always political and may even — to adapt Clausewitz's dictum on war — be regarded as a continuation of politics by other means; secondly, that the predominant relationship of the spectator to sport is partisan, and takes the form of an identification with a contestant, whether individual or collective; and, thirdly, that sport has been radically changed, in all its aspects, by the advent of television.

Provisional verification — or at least illustration — of these observations is not hard to find. One need look no further than, for example, the 1978 World Chess Championship, in which dour Soviet *apparachik* Anatoly Karpov took on and defeated romantic dissident Viktor Korchnoi, to see a reflection of cold-war politics in its sentimental Carterite guise. Or one might take the case of 'football supporters' who do little to support football but very clearly and vehemently support a team. Or, again, one might point to the way in which in televised games of American ('grid') football the ads are no longer timed to coincide with breaks in the play, but breaks in the play are introduced to coincide with the ads.

Examples could be multiplied indefinitely. [. . .] What this article aims to do, however, is not to confirm these observations but to investigate certain of the conditions of their combination, with a view to re-analysing them in a slightly less *ad hoc* fashion. The re-analysis, which takes as a central focus the 1978 Football World Cup, has no clear-cut conclusions to offer, but it may suggest ways in which the complex television/politics/sport can be viewed less defensively than is usually the case, and can, perhaps, become a productive terrain of struggle.

TELEVISION

In its simplest conception television is a recording and transmitting device which enables images to be made visible in a place other than their place of origin and possibly at another (later) time. It resembles film in that it deals with images, but it differs from film, and resembles radio, in that it allows simultaneity: the television picture can be seen at the moment at which it is made, contemporary with the event of which it is an image. Unlike sound transmission, however, which can be almost neutral in respect of the event recorded (as is the case with a record or broadcast of a symphony concert), television is a process with effects: the television picture is always different from the event of which it is a picture — or, put another way, it is a different picturing from the one that would obtain in the presence of the event itself. Even where one can legitimately talk about events, the television picture is never exactly a reproduction of one: it is always, in some way or other, a *representation*.

The case for television being representation rather than reproduction is, of course, even stronger on those occasions (the majority) when there is no pre-given, 'natural' event to be reproduced but only a series of artificially composed 'pro-televisual events'.* None the less the prejudice dies hard that television is there to reproduce; that its subject is given reality; and that its success or failure is to be measured in proportion to the quantity of this reality that it reproduces without distortion. [. . .]

The effects of the inevitable directionality of the television image are also relevant here. Sound is directionally weak, and modern techniques of sound recording, mixing and playback can give the listener a neutral placement in his or her space indistinguishable from the real thing (no matter, for the moment, that most often there never was a 'real thing', that the sound mixing is pure simulation). The television picture, however, is always *somewhere*, and always presents an 'angle' — a point of view coming from somewhere and directed somewhere. It supposes a spectator directed towards the screen and a camera directed now this way now that to offer the spectator various 'views' of the televisual event. Like film, television is always a question of particular placements and directions (though, unlike film, it allows evasion, since television is so easy *not* to watch). Television, therefore, implicates the viewer in a structure of viewing for which there is no equivalent in the activity of listening to sound.† Essential to this structure are a directional viewing space, and the various directions of view offered by the image emanating from the box. [. . .]

It follows from the foregoing — though the implications remain to be spelt out — that television provides, as part of its mode of operation, a

---

* On the analogy of 'pro-filmic event': whatever is brought together, or finds its way, into the field of view of the video-camera.

† This statement should perhaps be qualified. There are structures of listening and there are differences between, say, listening to stereo through headphones, listening to stereo through loudspeakers, walking about while listening to the radio, moving the radio about, etc. All this goes to show, however, that strictly speaking 'reproduction' is not the only issue in relation to sound either.

special set of placements for the spectator-subject. In particular, a lot hinges on identification. Identification has recently come to be recognized by film theory as constituting a basic mode of relation between spectator-subject and the objects and processes of representation, and all the problems for film theory in understanding the work of identificatory processes apply to television as well. But for television the problems are perhaps even more acute, since the positions open to the tele-viewer are more varied and the heterogeneity of television material and its modes of address harder to overcome. The presupposition of the bulk of fictional cinema (the classic realist text) is of a single dominant speaking voice and a single (collective) addressee — the 'audience'. Whatever the differences between members of the audience, the audience-as-a-whole is the object (generally) of a unitary mode of address, overriding difference. This is not the case for television, with its perpetual meshing of different sorts of programme and its need to confront the social heterogeneity of its component audience. Although television may aspire to homogeneity, it cannot assume it. On the contrary it must operate to produce it. And this means a constant work on the processes of identification, an active production of the identity of the audience itself by means of the introduction of points of identification onto which to pin that identity. This production of an audience, or of an audience-identity and audience-position, is a still unsolved problem for television, and one with important consequences, whether good or bad.

FOOTBALL

With these remarks in mind I now want to examine a TV spectacle which was watched last summer by hundreds of millions of people and which was criticised by various writers — including myself — precisely for its spectacular qualities [see *Time Out,* no. 426, 2-8 June 1978].

This spectacle was the 1978 Football World Cup, held in Argentina, and the criticisms took the line that the televising of the event produced a construction which traduced two realities: that of football and that of the Argentinian dictatorship. It was unequivocally argued that television was a construction, but a wish subsisted that it was less of one, or a less tendentious one, and that more of reality would peep through the screen. In retrospectively reviewing these criticisms (with which I remain in many ways in sympathy) I want to argue that breaking the spell which held so many millions spellbound is not a matter of conforming the television construction to reality but of questioning that reality and what can be made to appear in that reality. Or, better, it is a matter not of questioning the 'construction' and the 'reality' separately (the former thus inevitably emerging as a distortion of the latter) but together. [...]

If we attempt to construct 'football' as an object of representation we find it to be a game played with a ball and with the feet, usually on a

161

marked-out grassy pitch but also in playgrounds, gymnasiums, back-streets and so on: we find a continuum from kickabouts engaged in by small children who do not know the rules let alone stick to them, to organised matches, watched by thousands, between professional teams supervised by referees who penalise every infringement that catches their eye. We find also that 'football' exists way outside the context of actual play; it exists in the activities of club directors and sports-gear manufacturers, newspaper correspondents and television advertisers, in the training undergone by players, amateur as well as professional, in brawls and riots occasionally leading to international incidents; and above all it exists as the object of a constant and repetitive discussion which the apparatus feeds. It is a mistake to think of the football spectator's week (any more than the player's) as limited to about two and a half hours on a Saturday afternoon, beginning with an expectant arrival in the stadium and ending with an elated or dejected departure to the car park or bus stop. Although the match (or, more precisely, the final whistle) is clearly pivotal, what pivots around it is no less important — reports of other games listened to on the radio on the way home, the same again on television on arrival, Jimmy Hill on television later that night, the Sunday papers, television again on Sunday afternoon, then the Monday papers, discussion among friends and workmates not just about the match but about the various reports, then the mid-week gossip about team changes and transfers, and so on through to the build-up for next Saturday's match. And since next Saturday's match will probably be an away game, our hypothetical spectator will this time (unless an avid supporter) live only for the reports, the television presentation (if any) and the discussion, without having had direct sight of the match itself.

Football then, for the average adult spectator, lives largely in representation and recall. To the process that had already taken shape in the first part of the century television has in the first instance merely added an intervening stage, midway between direct sight and reading about it. Television football shares in both those aspects. At one extreme there is live coverage of an entire game, which is more or less a substitute for direct sight; and at the other extreme are highlights from a match already reported on, possibly already directly seen. Screened 'highlights', moreover, share with reporting the qualities of being selective and judgemental. The memorable incident is recalled — the goal, the near miss, the spectacular foul — and judgement is passed on it. What British television has recently added to the process is the air of infallibility. Better than the spectator on the terraces or the reporter in the press box, the television camera *sees* the truth — and Jimmy Hill confirms. No longer the (un)pleasure of uncertainty. The spectator as self-appointed arbiter is dispossessed; judgement is returned to the camera and the confirming voice: 'I think we can now see that the player was definitely not offside.'

What this affects is an essential part of the imaginary structure of the game — partisanship. [. . .] As a spectator sport (and discounting the pools), football — unlike racing, boxing or even baseball — is a purely partisan affair. It excites loyalty which can often be lifelong, and certainly in the vast majority of cases extends beyond the duration of a single game. Regular supporters often prefer to sit or stand at the ends of a ground, not just because it is cheaper but because being at the end puts the spectator in the firing line: your position is that of your team, coming forward or being driven back. The same partisanship infects the reading of reports: the local paper can be relied on to report your side ('City unlucky again'); other papers are suspect, probably biased against you — like the ref.

Into this structure television intervenes by reaffirming impartiality. Broadcasting indifferently to supporters of both sides and of neither, television adjudicates from the half-way line, using the end cameras mostly for replays. Also, by using camera positions down one side of the ground, television preserves 'flow' according to the classic rules inherited from cinema, in particular the 180° rule.* The impartial and voiceless flow of images is enough to contain and neutralise any effect of interruption produced by the pauses for replays — which are in any case interruptions sanctioned by the voice from elsewhere, that of the unseen but all seeing commentator. Images and commentary thus collude to produce a position which is both neutral and authoritative and which derives its authority, in part at least, from the commentator's claim to preserve the neutrality immanent in the image.

In exchange for the loss of team identification, television tends to offer a focus on individuals. The principal merit of the mid-way position — the position of the TV camera master shot and of the 'best' seats — is that it affords a view of the match as a whole, and in particular of tactical moves. British television, however, sacrifices the global view to a succession of partial views, cutting in frequent close shots with a long-focal lens which voyeuristically single out individual confrontation, the display of ball control, the involuntary expressivity of pleasure and pain. [See Buscombe (ed.), 1975, pp.48-9.] The effect can be seen as one of humanising the spectacle, but it is not exactly that — despite the occasional obvious pitch for the moment of pathos, often involving a shot of a distraught or contemplative manager on the bench. More often the effect is best described as fragmentation-within-flow: the scene is parcelled out, displacing the individual body or bodies from the team context in order to make them a part-object or object of a component-desire, with 'wholeness' restored to the view only by the flow of images

* The 180° rule 'dictates that if two people are placed opposite each other and the camera is showing them from one side, the director may not cut to a shot showing the characters from the opposite side' (Buscombe (ed.), 1975, p.32). [Eds.]

into new objects linked by the movement of the ball.

For the true fan this is very inadequate compensation for the loss of the team-identified position; but for the millions whose closest contact with football is *The Big Match* or *Match of the Day* the loss is not felt, and the pleasure of television, as a spectacle in itself, comes into operation in its own right. Although there is a 'hard' argument that television is preferred because it can be enjoyed so comfortably at home, it is also the case that the pleasure it offers is not just a comfortable surrogate, but is actually different, calling different attitudes and emotions into play. For many fans, certainly, television is mainly there to be part of the process of repetitive recall; it is also required for the rest of the audience to be alive in a simulated present. To the audience which does not 'follow' the game, television presentation has a life of its own; identifications are made *ad hoc*, with the movement of play. There is no reason to see in the adoption of such a position any loss of authenticity; deprived of the posture of partisanship and occasionally subjected to the voice of callow impartial authority, the televiewer is not for that reason removed from the 'real thing'.

There remains a further aspect of the question of team-identification to be considered, which is the political. It is a well-known fact that many clubs, particularly in big cities, carry with them traces of ethnic or religious division. Hearts and Hibs in Edinburgh, Rangers and Celtic in Glasgow, City and United in Manchester, Liverpool and Everton on Merseyside are traditionally distinguished by being respectively Protestant and Catholic (i.e. Irish). There are also clubs with a strong tradition of local Jewish support, and there is an increasing distinction emerging between clubs which employ black players and those which seem hesitant to do so.

Now it is often argued that the relation is one of cause and effect, with 'real' social divisions at the level of religion or race being reflected or expressed at the level of football. While this may contain an aspect of contingent truth in some cases, as a general formulation it is inadequate. It would be better to say that football is *available* for a whole variety of political or quasi-political identifications, but that these identifications are also transferable and may indeed be transferred from football onto something else. [. . .] If one looks at the history of the game one finds, in addition to cases of clubs founded around pre-existing divisions, cases of clubs founded to produce an identity — say between a works and its works team — and a constant slippage of this identity, so that a works team becomes a local team and from there a national representative and from there perhaps simply a representative of football. Or a football identity (and its attendant identifications) may displace itself onto politics. (This last would appear to be the case with some London football supporters and the National Front, where clearly it is not a matter of fascism displacing itself onto football, but, if anything, the other way round.)

To argue this is not to argue for the primacy of a silly ball-game over more 'serious' questions, but for a certain degree of conjuncturally determined autonomy in the movement of identifications, an 'arbitrariness of the sign' in terms of what football-as-signifier can be made to represent. This arbitrariness is not total, and is held in check by a variety of factors of undoubted materiality. But there is no easily assigned primacy of one factor over another, nor of external factors over those internal to football. Nor, and this is crucial, is any identity either total or inviolable. As Argentina shows.

THE WORLD

By any standards the map of the 'World' Cup is bizarre. [. . .] All countries of the world are theoretically permitted to compete, and the game is playable and indeed played in all of them. But in practice the Cup is dominated by the nations of two continents — Europe and South America. There are a few political exclusions (People's China has only just been recognised by FIFA, the world governing body of the sport) and the system of qualifying rounds limits the number of peripheral countries that can take part in the finals. But it is rare for any African, Asian or even Central American team to progress beyond the first stage of the final rounds. [. . .] The Cup is held roughly alternately in Europe and in South America and has usually been won by teams playing on their home continent.

While the structure may seem to conspire to perpetuate the existing pattern of dominance, it is also worth stopping for a moment to consider the history out of which this structure emerged. The game started in Britain and spread outwards from there with industrial and commercial expansion, but not with settler-colonialism. Football went where the flag didn't. It spread to West, Central and Eastern Europe and to Latin America, helped a bit by British works managers and by local Anglophile bourgeoisies, but after a while autonomously; via France it went to the countries of French Africa; and since decolonisation it has spread further throughout the Third World. But to most areas of the Empire the British exported other sports — hockey, cricket and (for whites only) rugby. North America developed its own mass of popular sports and even established its own 'baseball zone' in countries particularly vulnerable to US hegemony — Cuba, South Korea, Japan. The United States did actually have a World Cup soccer team in the 1930s — based, interestingly enough, on a works team from Bethlehem Steel — and doubtless it will have one again; but for the moment it is conspicuous by its absence.

The momentum turning football into a whole-world (largely Third-World) game is an interesting phenomenon in its own right: the oil boom

165

has brought in the Arab countries; Cuba (despite Fidel Castro's penchant for baseball) is developing football as a game at which to compete with its Latin neighbours; People's China is emerging as a football power. All this will have its effect in due course. But more significant in the present is the effect on political representation of the absence of the United States. This absence, coupled with the relative weakness of the Soviet Union as a football power, means that there is no representation within World Cup football of the Super-power contest which so dominates, for example, the Olympic Games. In general East-West conflict is weakly represented. The two Germanies may be drawn against each other in the qualifying rounds, and generally there are two or three East European countries involved in the finals. But the division between 'East' and 'West' as it affects Europe and as it overlaps with the division 'socialism'/'capitalism' has little place on the signifying map of the World Cup. Its place is taken by a division along another axis, that of 'North' and 'South', bringing a different set of political significations into play.

Schematically, the signifying map of the World Cup is one which on the one hand opposes Europe to South America and on the other hand associates one half of Europe (the Southern half) with the majority of countries of South America. The division within Europe can be described as Nordic versus Latin, while that within South America opposes the Spanish-speaking nations of the continent (which in Northern European eyes represent an intensified degree of Latinity) to Portuguese-speaking and multi-racial Brazil. The motivating signifiers of these divisions are hair and skin colour, onto which are overlaid imputed differences of national 'temperament' and style of play. Thus, on a crude example, 'Latin' is associated with 'fiery', while 'Nordic' is supposedly 'cool'. But the 'cool' of the Nordic fair-haired Dutch, expressed in their controlled possession-play, is shared by the 'tropical' Brazilians (often of African or Amerindian descent), in implicit contrast to the hot-headed Italians or Argentinians. Meanwhile these visible or imputed distinctions 'correspond' to a set of facts extracted from other discourses. Of the countries competing in the 1978 finals, the most Nordic — Sweden, Holland — are also those in which there is least poverty (except among dark-skinned immigrants); the most dark-skinned countries — Tunisia, Iran, Brazil — are those in which there is the most; and the Latin (Italo-Hispanic) countries are somewhere in between.

Which 'correspondences' are going to be signified is clearly open to variation: suppose, for example, that 'Latin' Bulgaria rather than 'Nordic' Poland had been the 'Socialist' team in competition. And *how* the correspondences and signifying distinctions are going to be taken up will vary as well, since there are different standpoints from which they can be taken up and different codes governing their application. [. . .]

Football is about winning, and the question posed in Buenos Aires in June 1978 was whether a European team would win the Cup on South American soil for the first time. Then, following from that, there was the question of which European team could do it — might it be Scotland? — and which South American team — Argentina or Brazil? — was most likely to stop them. Then, functioning as an urgent over-determination, there was the political question: what did it mean that the Cup was being staged in Argentina, and that Argentina might well win the Cup on its home ground? In the event Argentina did win. So what meaning should we attribute to that?

An early reaction among some European leftists to the realisation that the country where the Cup was to be held was now a vicious military dictatorship was to call for a boycott. [. . .] It was also suggested — again in Europe — that the Argentine left might take steps to sabotage the cup. These childishly punitive proposals were vigorously repudiated by both the marxist and the Peronist left in Argentina, on the obvious grounds that little harm would be done to the regime but a lot of popular anger would be aroused which would be turned against the opposition. From a European perspective too it soon became clear that simply opposing the Cup was an action that could only rebound against its initiators.

Given that the Cup would — and did — take place unimpeded, the question then arose in more general terms of what sort of political representation was already implicit in its staging and how this representation could be affected so that the 'Argentina' of the Cup could be seen also to be the Argentina of political repression. It was to this demand that the *Time Out* feature addressed itself, as did various articles by journalists in the regular press, such as Hugh McIlvanney in *The Observer*. Against the chorus of fatuous references to the 'British connection' in Argentina or to the rapturous reception the Scots could expect there, a counterpoint emerged documenting the tortures, murders and 'disappearances' perpetrated by agents of the present Argentinian regime and hinting, occasionally, at the collusion of certain imperialisms, North American but also British, in protecting it.

The limitation of this approach, as adopted, was that it never addressed the question of how the two forms of representation — the football and the politics — were related. It was assumed — at least for the most part — that the football representation was intrinsically apolitical, or political only in a state of latency, and that politics could somehow be introduced parallel to it and then, by a crossing of the threads, inserted into it. To a certain extent this assumption was verified in the way the Cup was televised — set within a closed arena, with alternating shots of the competing players and of the spectators boxed inside the stadium — and in the approach taken by the Argentine authorities, which insisted on the 'normality' of the Cup as an international event. Indeed the most immediately striking feature of the Cup as televised was its political indifferentism. The picture was shot by a West German-trained Argentinian production team and differed very little from the picture produced by the Germans for the 1974 Cup, held in Germany. The sound track was provided, for Britain, by the usual British commentators and presenters, and also differed very little from 1974. On both sound and picture Argentina was represented as a perfectly normal country. On the one hand there was none of the celebratory iconography by which a country or a regime can mark its political specificity — red flags, swastikas, Statues of Liberty and the like: no-one could have done a Leni Riefenstahl with the 1978 World Cup. But on the other hand there was little that could be taken to refer to the conditions of life of the people or to any set of social relations outside of those of football. There were teams, there were crowds, there was a man in an overcoat who was designated as General Videla and with whom (according to some later reports) the Argentine team did not shake hands. But that was all.

In another way, however, Argentina — a certain concept 'Argentina' — was a real presence on the television screen, a way that is so obvious that it is amazing that it should pass unremarked. [. . .] This presence was marked, in the first instance, simply in the form of a colour, blue, which was that of a national flag, a national team and of all the banners that filled the stadium on any occasion on which Argentina was playing, but most conspicuously on the day of the final itself. Had the dark blue and white of Argentina been opposed to another symbolising blue, say that of Italy, the signifying pattern might have been different, but as it was the opposing side happened to be Holland — a country whose signified identity was singularly weak, since its team colour (orange) was not the colour of its flag (red, white and blue), while even its name (*Nederland*, Holland, *Pays-Bas*) and that of its people (*Nederlands*, Dutch, *Hollandais*) is uncertainly attributed by speakers of other languages. Against the weak presence of the Dutch (with their tiny handful of supporters), the omnipresence of the blue declared an identity, that of an Argentinian nationhood axed around football and from which any other Argentina (the Argentina of Borges, of Evita, of Welsh settlers in Patagonia, or whatever) was for the time being evacuated. And to this Argentina, as with those models of molecules featured on science programmes, all sorts of meanings could then attach.

Present in the 'Argentina' created by World Cup television was the effect of certain images, to which camera and commentary constantly returned. Above all the featuring of individuals — the saturnine Luque, the mercurial Kempes, the sylph-like Ardiles, the melancholic team-manager Menotti chain smoking on the sidelines. The figure of Menotti, with his name connoting Italian extraction and his watery eyes, was particularly interesting. Like his Brazilian counterpart Coutinho,

168

Menotti was reputed to have 'modernised' the South American game and to have made it more European — a phrase which can have at least two meanings, one related to football and one more general. Related to football (and as spoken by a British commentator) it meant an end to the 'clogger' image with which Argentinian football is traditionally credited (cf. Alf Ramsey's remarks about 'animals' at the time of the 1966 Cup); more generally (and no doubt a lot less consciously) it carried connotations of the 'modernisation' in whose euphemistic name apologists of American and British imperialism justify support for reactionary regimes in (specifically) Brazil and Iran — but it also suggested a *rapprochement* between us and them, a relaxation of the 'dago' stereotype. Meanwhile, as the Cup proceeded, it was becoming clearer and clearer that this modernised Argentina was up for sale, and that just as Brazil now produces engines for Fiat so Argentina would produce midfield engine-power for Valencia and Spurs.

What is important to note about this representation is that, however obliquely, certain discourses are spoken through it which give Argentina a collocation neither as an undifferentiated 'Third-World' country nor (the way the left would have it) as a fascist regime. This in itself is not a cause for complaint. A national concept is always both overdetermined in its production and polyvalent in its availability and its effects, and, of the various ways a country can be conceptualised, those which define it either by its regime or by some generic placement in a geo-political camp are not necessarily the most constructive (though on occasion they may be). The parallel case of Brazil is instructive here. Brazil won the World Cup in Chile in 1962 under a parliamentary regime; performed badly in England in 1966 under a military government; and won the Cup again in Mexico in 1970 after a second coup had brought in a new, harsher, military dictatorship. But throughout the period Brazilian football remained unchanged, unavailable to governmental exploitation, but significantly available to a racial and third-worldist reading which has already had its effects throughout the world and is having further effects in England now as young black players emerge to take their place in the game. By these standards the example of Argentina is far less progressive — not so much because the military escaped relatively unscathed in the reporting of the Cup as because the representation of Argentina proved to be finally containable with the limits of imperialist discourse. The effects on the way football is played and spoken of in Britain will probably be progressive — though more because of Scotland's débâcle than because of what was to be learnt, positively, from the ways others played the game, or even because of the importation of Ardiles, Villa or Tarantini. But a Dutch victory would have been progressive too, in strict footballing terms; and in wider terms the 'Argentina' that won the Cup was too much (though all too accurately) constructed in a client relationship to Europe for there to be much of a rupture in the complex of ideological representation. In television terms, finally, although I would not argue for the filming of football in long shot on grounds of realism, the relatively laid-back style of the World Cup coverage (by British standards) did produce a sense of the game being played by teams, and by teams which knew how to use space. [. . .]

(First published in *Screen*, vol. 19, no. 4, winter 1978/79.)

Reference

Buscombe, E. (1975), *Football on Television*, London: British Film Institute.

Science on TV: A Critique

The differences between the dramatically changing role of science and the way that it is represented on TV needs to be examined with a view towards generating a much more critical approach — one which has the effect of opening up issues for public debate, rather than, as at present, leading to closure. Science, technology and medicine and their respective modes of discourse are an increasingly important component of the social formation in advanced capitalist countries. After school, for the overwhelming majority of people in Britain, science (which we will use as a generic term for science, technology and medicine) is experienced almost wholly through the film and broadcast media. For most of the general population 'science' is constructed through TV science programmes, both 'serious' and fictional. In the commonly understood meaning of science, it makes little sense to talk of a discrete body of knowledge and set of practices, apart from this representation. TV, then, is the principal bearer of the social meaning of 'science', and it is our contention that such a meaning has real material effects within our society. TV's construction is a lot more than a simple mirroring of scientific endeavour, an innocent transmission of scientific achievement into the public domain.

As part of a larger project, it is our intention in this article to interrogate the view of science as presented by TV, because it plays an important role in impeding the possibility of social and political intervention to change the course of science, technology and medicine. The current ideology of science on TV is a material force in reinforcing current priorities and practices in society.

Any adequate analysis of TV's view of science would have to deal with the following issues:

1) The already existing ideologies and conceptions of science which TV 'feeds off' and its practitioners appropriate and propagate in the course of programme elaboration; for example, empiricism, positivism, and the current philosophies of science as represented in the work of Karl Popper and Thomas Kuhn, and those who debate about their positions.

2) The social and cultural formation of TV's practitioners, their view of the television process and their role within it, including their class, education and training, as well as the subculture of media and cultural theory within which they move.

3) The specific labour process of television, the division of labour within TV practice and the institutionalisation of science's own division of labour within TV departments, including the separation of content from the requirements of production and the barriers between writers, presenters, researchers, directors, etc.

4) The various televisual styles and techniques usually regarded inside television as 'common sense', 'natural', and 'transparent'. TV's meanings are constructed through these devices and, in the case of science, are crucial in the maintenance of the status of scientific knowledge.

5) Directly economic determinations, particularly the increasing requirements of co-production deals with the United States.

Because of the state of our own research at the time of writing, this article will concern itself principally with (1) and (4), while touching the other questions where appropriate. This does not mean that we consider those questions primary. It is simply the case that we thought it worthwhile to take stock of our work in progress. We draw our examples from the following series: *Horizon, Tomorrow's World, Don't Just Sit There, The Voyage of Charles Darwin, The Body in Question, Oppenheimer*, and various 'one-off' documentaries. We will not be concerned here with the fictional representation of science in the context of drama and children's TV — *Doctor Who, Quatermass, Blake's Seven, Star Trek*, etc. — or science as treated in several recent popular feature films, such as *Alien, Close Encounters of the Third Kind, The Empire Strikes Back*, etc., some of which have already appeared on television. This ought to be attempted in any wider study, and the interaction and overlap between the various genres thoroughly analysed. Nor will it be possible, except in passing, to examine the way that science enters into and is elaborated by various news and current affairs series not primarily designated as 'scientific'.

As this article is addressed primarily to questions of TV representation and programme-making strategies, we would like to finish with some suggestions as to how TV might deal with them — alternatives at the level of TV styles, conventions and representational devices. How would one do a TV programme about a particular subject — to signify which meanings for which audiences — is a question which must be continually posed. TV science practitioners constantly defend their work with the unchallengeable rebuff 'Oh, we did that in a programme in September 1977 . . .' (rather like the US tourist rampaging through Europe — 'We've *done* Rome and we've *done* Paris', etc.). *How* precisely they did it, how it was treated, what were the dominant meanings, ought to be the principal questions at issue. But it should be borne in mind that alternative programme-making strategies could best be elaborated in the process of production. This is a process in which we have become involved since our research began, and our participant observations about it will be presented in our larger study.

How science is presented on television is not merely a matter of aesthetic nuance. It is a cliché that science, technology and medicine are impinging more and more directly and pervasively on people's lives — a true cliché. They are not merely impinging (a model drawn from the erroneous 'internal-external' dichotomy between science and society). They are reconstituting work and consumption. Television proclaims these changes and occasionally plays an impressive role in agenda-setting. For example, the *Horizon* programme 'Now the Chips are Down' had an important part in waking up the government and the public to the importance of microprocessors, while *The Mighty Micro*, despite its numerous weaknesses, spelled out some of the likely effects of chips.

But the *impact* of the new technology on work, employment, leisure and consumption are not the only aspects. The dramatic increases in the real subordination in the labour process have hardly been mentioned: monitoring, pacing, surveillance, the scientific management (or Taylorisation) of white collar work. The ways in which such programmes are presented separates the substance of knowledge and technology from the process of origination and prioritisation which would make explicit the values involved. These topics are precluded by the breathless form of presentation which operates at an expository pace and conveys a sense of inevitability rather than one of social choice. The means of production, the setting of research and development agendas, and the social relations of production and application of scientific knowledge all embody particular positions about the development of society, yet these are rarely examined. Looking at the issue at a more exclusively economic level, as Frank Webster and Kevin Robins have shown in their article 'Mass Communication and "Information Technology" ' (1979) the entire domain of information and communication has merged into those of social control in all spheres of life and is increasingly directed by multinational corporations (Mattelart, 1979, p.9).

Equally dramatic changes are afoot in medicine: in artificial fertilisation and implantation, cryogenesis, foetal diagnosis, choice of infant sex, host mothers, transplant surgery, cerebrally-implanted electrodes, mood control, control of immune responses, treatment of viral diseases and cancer. The public is slowly being made aware of some of the consequences of biotechnology for the food, drug and chemical industries, and the significance of genetic engineering and cloning is becoming apparent. It is not yet widely appreciated, however, that biotechnological and medical changes are likely to affect our lives, jobs and economy even more than microprocessors and to raise problems which we have not yet begun to know how to debate or to resolve. Whose baby is it, for example, when the egg which comes from one person, with the sperm from AID, is then gestated and given birth to by another person? What does it mean to change living forms virtually at will by means of genetic engineering? How will the different spheres of life be maintained when home terminals for clerical and executive work, as well as for leisure and shopping, eliminate the current bases for distinguishing the roles of houseworker, home worker and consumer? What will become of labour-intensive agricultural societies when a single machine in a single traverse of a field can do the work currently requiring intensive cultivation and up to eight machines and twelve energy passes per crop? We choose these questions from a large number of pertinent ones in order to convey a sense of the sorts of social and political questions which the current modes of presentation of science do not seem inclined or equipped to consider.

We have on the one hand a firmly-established and highly-regarded set of conventions for the presentation of science — conventions which are expository, narrative and fundamentally celebratory, purveying culture to an audience of passive consumers who regard a spectacle. On the other hand, we have developments in science which are fundamentally reconstituting aspects of life, including conception, birth, behavioural control, work, education, sexuality, leisure, consumption, bodily repair, senescence, death and the recycling of human organs. There is an alarming inconsistency between the mode of presentation and the significance of these issues. We want to argue that it is an urgent priority for television to alter its approach to these matters in fundamental ways:
— to move from science as cultural consumption to science as critique;
— from the content of science as progress to an analysis of the constitution of science, technology and medicine, of their labour processes and of their articulations with other practices;
— from the 'impact' of science to the process of constitution of its research programme, opening up to public scrutiny and prioritisation the origination of issues, facts and artifacts.

In order to see the point of recasting the approach to science, it is necessary to undermine the prevailing distinction between science and society — two domains which are treated as interacting, with the interaction more or less (usually less) spelled out. We want, instead, to propose a conception of science as constituted by and constitutive of social relations just as others have treated technology and medicine as social relations (see David Dickson, 1974, Webster and Robins, 1979, Figlio, 1978 and 1979 and Young, 1977).

As things now stand, the eyes of programme-makers are firmly fixed on the content of knowledge and the process of discovery. There is, in addition, another topic which tends to be considered separately from the substance of knowledge (in itself regarded as 'neutral'): its social impact. The result is that discovery and substance are presented as internal to science, while social impact is seen as an interacting variable. Science is one thing, context another. We think this approach has produced a systematic blinkering, a tunnel vision with separate programmes and

174

separate series concerned with aspects of a single totality which should be seen as a whole. The social relations and social processes of science should be conceived of as integral to its substance. It is worth mentioning that this is by now a commonplace in radical studies of other aspects of culture. The privileged treatment of science in these respects is curious, to say the least. Literature, drama, plastic and graphic arts, cinema, and television itself are currently studied according to models which attempt to relate the context, presentation, content and impact into a single coherent account of meanings. This is also a commonplace in the treatment of science from periods other than our own. Historians of ancient, medieval, Arab, Renaissance, seventeenth, eighteenth and nineteenth-century science go to considerable lengths to show how the science is constituted by the historical forces of the period, including frames of reference, major theoretical concepts and even specific research topics. All bear the stamp of their times and places. One only has to think of Foucault's emphasis on the preoccupation with classification across a wide range of disciplines in the eighteenth century, as well as his historical accounts of psychiatry and clinical medicine (see Foucault, 1970, 1971 and 1973).

Yet the origins, process, substance and impact of current science are still parcelled out into different niches. The BBC, in particular, actually institutionalises these divisions in its programme-making departments. *Horizon* does a programme on 'The Real Bionic Man'; *Man Alive* another on the ethical, compassionate and legal problems of obtaining organs for transplant ('Wanted: Human Spare Parts'); *Horizon* does a programme on adipose brown tissue whose metabolism may explain fatness and thinness; *Man Alive* does a programme on fat as a feminist issue of body image. None of these programmes gives any hint of how its explanations might conceivably articulate with other theories. *Brass Tacks* does a programme 'Fit to be Born' on the questions surrounding Mongolism, Spina Bifida, and Tay Sachs disease, in which we are told nothing about the state of scientific knowledge of the origins and natures of these defects beyond their being genetic.

Horizon increasingly attempts to address questions which go beyond the exposition of the content of science but does so in an uncritical fashion. In a programme about sugar production in Brazil we are told (three times) that 'Brazil has plenty of cheap labour', which is roughly equivalent to saying that Pakistan has lots of thin people. In a programme on Mexican oil *Horizon* manages to state in conclusion that 'Nobody wants the oil to distort the Mexican economy or the happier aspects of the Mexican way of life' and cuts to olé singers with guitars and sombreros. These examples are drawn from a large collection to indicate just how careless of other aspects of its context science programmes can be. The division of labour operates here as in other spheres so that it precludes access to the totality of relations which make up any whole. *Horizon* does science alternating with environment; *Tomorrow's World* does new technologies in a 'gee whiz' way; *The Risk Business* does a combination of 'gee whiz' technology and retooling in the 'national interest'; *Man Alive* tells 'stories of folk' on the receiving end — the sociological and human interest aspects; *The Money Programme* deals with the economics of it all; *Open Secret* catches out individuals and companies who have abused (otherwise neutral?) science and technology.

Another obstacle to a wider and deeper approach to the representation of science is the over-reliance on the image of scientific endeavour which scientists hold and propagate when considering their work in public contexts. It is our impression, backed up by discussions and interviews with people taking part in the making of science programmes, that belief in the relative autonomy of knowledge is being uncritically propagated on television. The boundary between the academy and the market-place is being constantly defended on the box, in Presidential Addresses, (e.g. to the Royal Society) and perhaps in secondary education. As far as we can tell, this is principally a matter of public relations, since it certainly isn't a view propagated by scientists at work. In other settings, the socio-economic constitution of science, technology and medicine is a commonplace, not excluding the offices, coffee rooms, conferences and granting bodies of scientists, technologists and medical workers. Of course, there are mediations between capital and the state on the one hand and individual researchers on the other, but the research councils, university grants committees and private foundations are themselves increasingly calling for research which meets the needs of industry, while a shrinking public purse makes hustling for direct grants from industry more and more necessary. Whole labs and institutions are dependent on short-term grants for specific projects. Similarly, there is a growing field of research within large industries — IBM, ICI, Dupont. The drug industry depends on such labs. Bell Laboratories is the largest private research facility and exists within the world's largest corporation. On a smaller scale the burgeoning fields of microprocessors and biotechnology make little or no distinction between pure and commercial research. The PhDs they employ and the Nobel Laureates they retain as consultants accept that funding from Standard Oil and National Distillers means that commercial criteria dictate what research they do and when/what to share with colleagues and when to publish. It makes little difference whether one is working in the university or in the new commercial firms in California, Switzerland or Britain.

This is not the place to give an exhaustive history of the diminishing mediations between science and industry. Our point is that the blinkered presentation of science on TV depends on an historically outmoded conception of academic freedom and pure research. What matters in social terms is the interrelations and mutual determinations among the

176

socio-economic and intellectual forces which evoke an area of inquiry and its potential and real relations within the wider community. This should occur before it's all sewn up. Instead of perpetuating a false and idealised conception of the scientists, television could play an important role in the critical evaluation of the issues raised by science. This means opening up the process of origination of new knowledge and scrutinising the goals and purposes built in to research areas, machines, products and procedures. Science and technology (literally) embody choices and priorities selected from the manifold ways of ordering and using natural processes. In that sense, agenda-setting and research policy determine what knowledge and priorities will be pursued. Television is extremely important in this process since it has become the principal agenda-setting medium in our society as far as the general public is concerned. The more apparent it becomes that science, technology and medicine are reconstituting our lives and work, the more important it becomes to open up these manifestations of fixed capital and decide what social relations we want embodied by and in them, before they become dead labour which it is nearly impossible to revive. This concludes our sketch of the critical perspective from which we approach current science on TV.

WHITE COAT, TEST TUBES AND A 'TALKING HEAD'

We turn now to what we consider to be the characteristic televisual styles and techniques for presenting science. The usual mode of presentation of a topic in science is narrative, linear, expository and didactic. The course of the programme alternates between voice-over and 'talking head'. A talking head is television's way of saying 'this is brought directly to you without distortion or mediation'. In the case of science programmes this form of presentation is usually reinforced by racks of test tubes or an impressive piece of apparatus directly behind the talking head, a white lab coat or other apparel, and the knowledge that we are being addressed by 'the top man (sic) in the field' or the 'rising star'. The talking head is either directly addressing the camera or speaking across camera to an unseen interviewer whose questions have been edited out. This is in striking contrast with interviews on programmes where it is accepted that the issue is controversial and open, to some minimal degree at least, to public scrutiny, doubt, debate, etc; for example *Panorama, Weekend World*. In those programmes we see and hear the interviewer and cut back and forth from interviewer to various protagonists, speaking directly to one another, being challenged and arguing on camera. When scientists disagree on television, one talking head is followed by another, and they are almost never in direct conversation, much less in debate; e.g., *Horizon, Open Secret*. Similarly, the telling of the story does not convey direct conflict but rather the solving of a mystery, the fitting together of pieces of a puzzle. Stark disagreement is an interruption in

177

the plot line. Science and its telling are synonymous with progress and convey a sense of authority and the advancing edge of objectivity. By these devices and conventions, among others, a special status for scientific knowledge is assured. It is positivist in that it privileges scientific knowledge above other forms of inquiry and in that it separates facts from their contexts of meaning and represents them as above the battle of competing interest groups and classes.

When voice-over is employed, the characteristic tone is moderate, assured, reasoned. It is appropriate to a 'community' which is presented as neutral, objective, normally harmonious, disinterested and working for the good of humankind. Humour, irony, paradox and rhetorical questioning are rare, as are invitations to the viewer to dissent, criticise or respond. This mode of presentation, of audience positioning, is epitomised in the voice of Paul Vaughan, *Horizon*'s usual narrator: even, dignified cultural celebration; familiar, evoking trust. *Horizon* is almost the Wimbledon of science on TV, and Paul Vaughan is its Dan Maskell. This tone is common to series across the arts and sciences. It is hegemonic in the precise sense that it induces deference and organises consent by eliciting willingness to be the passive recipient of versions of history organised and presented for our edification. Patient, restrained, conveying in some cases real enthusiasm, but never shrill: Lord Clark, Alistair Cooke, Jacob Bronowski, David Attenborough, James Burke, Brian Magee, Jonathan Miller. It recalls the styles of presentation of Sir Isaiah Berlin and Lord Annan in the arts and Sir Peter Medawar, Lord Ashby and Stephen J. Gould in science-writing. It is in sharp contrast to the hectoring 'Must-I-go-through-this-again' tone of explanation to a wilfully slow pupil which characterises some politicians, e.g. Mrs Thatcher and MM Callaghan and Healey. In the domain of science Patrick Moore and Magnus Pyke are atavistic exceptions to highlight the norm. They harken back to a thirties and forties film caricature of the eccentric absent-minded professor.

Scientific and technological interviewees are rarely pressed as others are by a (Sir!) Robin Day, Brian Widlake or Brian Walden ('Let me put this to you, Minister . . .'). Indeed, since the questions are usually edited out, the talking head has a clear, undisputed run. The technique used in science interviewing is television's most permissive one, known as 'open-elicit'. The interviewer simply asks a leading question and lets the tape run while the interviewee gives his/her version of events. The interviewee's status and credibility are enhanced by being allowed to construct the story and present it directly to camera, without interruption or apparent mediation.

In short, the conventions of television's presentation of science are those of the informative lecture. The viewer is expected to be interested but unsophisticated. This is made very obvious in the blockbuster programmes celebrating Einstein's centenary. In both cases, the figure representing 'everyman', standing in for the audience, was (male and) portrayed as a comical *Dummkopf* — Peter Ustinov in Nigel Calder's BBC epic and Dudley Moore in another BBC special covering similar ground. The assumption (intention?) seems to be that the audience are not expected to become more sophisticated as viewers of science, technology and medicine. The audience is itself constructed as a group of simpletons to be 'better informed', which is not the same thing as being challenged by subtle and demanding ways of presenting issues. Still less does the prevailing mode of presentation invite genuine engagement or comment on the part of the watching millions.

All this is in contrast with the growing assumption that viewers can deal with great variation in modes of presentation in films, drama series, spy stories, westerns, cop shows: a degree of unexplained cutting, lack of resolution, paradox, irony, comedy, etc. Admittedly, in radical representational terms, these don't go far, but it is worth pondering that the makers of *Kojak*, and *The Sweeney*, *Dallas*, and *Soap*, not to mention ostensibly up-market offerings such as *Pennies from Heaven* and *Tinker, Tailor, Soldier, Spy*, assume their audiences have a greater visual and plot sophistication than the supposedly elite viewers of *Horizon*. In making this comparison we do not want to imply that fictional programmes do not convey dominant meanings, but the principal difference at work here is that between 'factual' and 'fictional' TV. The latter does not pretend to offer facts and can therefore allow the viewer more 'freedom' within a complex of conventions and styles. 'Non-fiction' TV, of which science programmes are the paradigm, claims to represent the facts. Therefore, any ambiguity in the representation is seen as a failure of exposition. Science, of course, is defined by the attempt to eliminate ambiguity. However, if the boundary between the substance, context and social relations of science was relaxed, the camera could invite us to draw our own conclusions and make observations on individuals and debates in the same way that it does in other controversial areas. The existing conventions in science programmes treat implicit or explicit ambiguities as a simple failure of exposition. We would argue that by virtue of their adherence to the positivist notion of the 'fact' and the notion of value-free objective activity, science programmes must demand a much more rigid system of closure than do other TV genres. These assumptions do not leave questions open to debate or to critical scrutiny of terms of reference.

Thus, science broadcasting is 'educating' viewers in one sense — the nature of scientific 'progress' — while firmly keeping them in the role of school children in relation to visual and critical sophistication. It is also worth briefly considering the other genres of 'factual' television. In sharp contrast to science broadcasting which is only concerned with the complexities of finding, London Weekend Television, for example, has made it a policy to upgrade their viewers' understanding of current events by representing controversies *as such,* laying bare the complexities of issues in opposition to TV's 'bias against understanding'. An attempt is made to avoid premature closure, even though in the hands of producer David Cox and presenter Brian Walden this technique has become threadbare. Indeed, a pioneer of this approach, Peter Jay, claimed that this was one of the main aims in the planned programming of the new franchise holder for breakfast television, TV-AM. Other programmes often clearly take sides in areas of controversy, despite all kinds of journalistic ideologies to the contrary. For example, Granada's *World in Action,* ATV's *Vodka-Cola,* and some of Yorkshire TV's documentaries are powerfully partisan. Science broadcasting is unique in remaining totally expository, 'neutral', above the battle and determinedly wary of developments in visual presentation. Indeed, *Horizon*'s Editor is quite candid in avowing the extremely important role of talking heads and 'visual wallpaper' in the series' format — 'When in doubt, cut to a centrifuge or an analagous piece of scientific equipment'.

FROM 'HORIZON', THE CULTURAL FLAGSHIP, TO TV POP SCIENCE

In the light of the above framework and critique, we want to look more closely at certain programmes and series. *Horizon* has been for many years the flagship of the BBC's fleet of science programmes. It came out of the Science and Features Department, founded in 1963, neatly pre-empting the 'white heat' of Harold Wilson's technological revolution. Science and Features also produces *The Risk Business, Medical Express, Young Scientist of the Year, The Great Egg Race, Tomorrow's World, Open Secret,* and *The Royal Institution Christmas Lectures,* in addition to the major series — Calder, Bronowski, Leakey, Miller, Attenborough — and various one-off documentaries.

Most of the general remarks we have made above have had *Horizon* as their primary reference point. The programme has been enormously influential, has been the training ground of many producers of science programmes and is closely imitated by the American programme *Nova,* where many of its refugees have gone to work. Since its foundation in 1964, it has produced up to forty fifty-minute programmes per year. That's a lot of miles of tape and film not to have broadened their horizons with. (It should be added that in the 1980-81 *Horizon* series, their range of topics has widened but that their approach remains the same.)

This is not to say, of course, that the programme isn't excellent within its own terms of reference. If one accepts those parameters, it is nonpareil, as its offerings on endorphins, the Jupiter space mission, Earth's magnetism and 'The Cancer Detectives of Lin Xian' have shown. Indeed, the last of these transcended *Horizon*'s normal brief by giving full weight to the social origins, labour process and relations of research. It's just a pity that this radical approach was negated in the programme's concluding statement. Instead of recognising the Chinese method of socio-medical research as an implicit critique of Western medicine's dependence on prophylactic solutions, the final contention was of an equivalence between them — a sort of medical corollary of détente.

On the other hand, the series epitomises the existing approach in the bulk of its production. Most of its producers exhibit a very deferential attitude towards the self-conceptions of mandarin scientists. Within the department there is a surprisingly naive enthusiasm for having access to the 'top man in the field', a source any Kuhnian would suggest should at least be complemented by reference to dissenters from the reigning paradigm. Similarly, reliance on the Scientific Consultative Committee ensures that, with rare exceptions, only established approaches need apply. More significantly, the question of how programme topics get chosen leads us back to a startlingly complacent source. We are told by *Horizon's* Editor that they select themselves: 'There they are, staring up at you in the literature' — *Nature* and *New Scientist* are the favourite sources of ideas. This puts them in close touch with a consensus and with the latest developments but can hardly be said to take them beneath established views.

In a recent Open University TV programme on how *Horizon* is made, members of the production team displayed a remarkably facile and complacent view of their approach:

Chris Pollitt: 'Despite difficulties, television producers do strive for a particular conception of objectivity. At viewings like this one they aim to improve accuracy, clarity and — a favourite television word this — "balance". To achieve these aims *Horizon* itself needs to master its subject matter. You don't carry in-house expertise, I mean neither you, for example, nor Chris, would be . . . ?'
Simon Campbell Jones: 'No. We have a fair amount of background knowledge. I have made a nuclear programme of my own. Many other producers have made programmes in this area, and a lot of discussion goes on in the club and in the canteen and sort of up and down the corridors about what everybody is doing. And one can lean on other people and get clues and ideas. It's basically getting contacts. And once you've got into the sort of circuit, of scientists and people within a topic area, you then find that you can more or less complete that circuit. By the time you've gone right round it, you know that you've got everybody in that field.'

Here we have a repetition of the clichés of television objectivity coupled with a description of research methodology which falls a long way short of aggressively seeking out non-establishment views.

Significantly, the *Horizon* team are very preoccupied with retaining the good will of the scientific community and don't often go in for hard hitting analyses unless the topic is already an established scandal. Even there, in the case of the IQ controversy, they are preoccupied with whether or not it's 'good science', where the real point at issue in this case is the ideological power of a particularly influential form of scientism which legitimates social and racial hierarchies by 'scientific' means. We asked a *Horizon* researcher about their relations with the growing community of people who think, do research and make critical stands on the history, philosophy and social relations of science as well as the new disciplines such as science policy, 'science, technology and society', bioethics, technology assessment. He replied, 'We have no regard for that community.' When taxed about this, he made it very clear that it was the scientific community, not the people who think *about* science, to which *Horizon* directs its attention. Nor do they give much credence to the explicitly critical perspectives of political pressure groups who are concerned with science. They may present issues raised by media-orientated Friends of the Earth, but not by the British Society for Social Responsibility in Science and associated groups such as Health and Safety, Politics of Health, *Radical Science Journal,* Socialist Environment and Resources Association, Network for Alternative Technology and Technology Assessment. Born in the wake of the Pilkington Committee's recommendations that science should be more prominent on television (1961), *Horizon* epitomises the existing approach and influences its 2-5 million audience week after week.

Two science programmes aimed at a 'mass audience' are placed in strategic slots. *Tomorrow's World,* founded in 1967, falls between *Nationwide* and *Top of the Pops,* with the result that it has 8-10 million viewers. Its presenters are very clean and wholesome. Originally Raymond Baxter, and now the current team of Michael Rodd, Judith Hann and Kieran Prendiville, represent the best of their respective generations. Baxter was a Spitfire pilot who savoured the Merlin engine in a retrospective, nostalgic programme on Rolls Royce, while the new team convey the achievements and enthusiasm of a keen grammar school meritocracy. The programme's pace and tone are no accident. The originator of the series, Aubrey Singer, who went on to become Controller of BBC 2 and then BBC radio, is reported to have said that the response he desired was an awed 'Gee Whiz!' from the viewer after every item. Dazzle them with the glossy, shiny end-products of science, wrapped up in a wholesome, pastel-coloured package, but ensure that they don't have to think much about what they're marvelling at. The emphasis is on progress, and questioning and criticism are rare.

There isn't much difference either between Raymond Baxter's nostalgic patriotism and the new format and team of presenters. When *Tomorrow's World* wanted to underline the importance of engineering in the wake of the Finniston Report, they didn't wheel out any of the entrepreneurs of the new NEB-sponsored microchip firms or the winner of the Nobel Prize for inventing the body scanner. We were treated instead to Michael Rodd reverentially interviewing HRH The Prince of Wales who professed to know little about it, though he was sure it was important, and was glad to be Hon. something or other to the relevant society and to encourage young people to take up engineering as a career, since creativity, invention and enterprise are essential to Britain's future prosperity. The facelift which *Tomorrow's World* underwent when Raymond Baxter departed has left it with a visage which is shallow and flashy. It is offering a very straight version of the meritocratic dream to young people awaiting *Top of the Pops* — a sort of technological version of Pan's People or Legs & Co. In the current economic climate this borders on the socially obscene.

There is no regular ITV equivalent, but for thirteen weeks in the summer, slotted between *Crossroads* and *Coronation Street,* Yorkshire TV brings us *Don't Just Sit There,* a programme which represents a significant and — at least in its intentions — in some ways laudable negotiation of the relationship between science and the 'public'. In 1974 the IBA said that they wanted more factual programmes to go out before 9pm. Most of the ITV companies were stumped, but the Controller of Yorkshire TV complied and came up with *Don't Ask Me,* which had the unusual feature that viewers were invited to send in questions. The programme makers were seeking outside stimuli; Austin Mitchell was the compere; Rob Buckman and Magnus Pyke were the experts who gave the answers. The model was the Victorian science lecture, and although the format worked in TV terms, it still left a polarisation of us v. them. They spent two more years developing a different format, and David Bellamy came up with a model more like the Victorian scientific society, with the studio and viewing audiences taking a much more active part. Where *Horizon* provides elitist cultural celebration without apparent mediation between 'top men' and the consumer, and *Tomorrow's World* issues an invitation to help re-tool Britain for the glossy, meritocratic future, *Don't Just Sit There* is avowedly mundane and populist. Its presenters are all shameless hams: Rob Buckman or Miriam Stoppard (medical), David Bellamy (botanical/zoological) and Magnus Pyke (physical), though these demarcations are not strictly followed. The pace is manic, often zany, driven by Pyke's delivery, with props and hearty fun reminiscent of *It's a Knockout.* For all its hucksterism, it has two great merits. First, it invites the viewers and studio audiences to raise questions, suggest research projects and propose and work on their own answers — though not to raise issues or debate problems. The format doesn't invite topics which can't be handled snappily, and an undisguised facticity pervades the whole spectacle. Second, it makes a serious effort to demystify expert knowledge in general and specific ways, particularly through analogy. The knock-about atmosphere is attractively irreverent, in contrast to

Horizon where the theme music and tone invite one into the cathedral of science. Its explanations are, on the whole, accessible.

The programme does, however, display the contradictions of populism. On the one hand, the invitation to participate is genuine, and people are drawn in: 'We want you, the viewer, to actively help us understand the science of everyday things and make them more interesting'. The viewers propose topics and supply their own ingenious answers as well as data for the nationwide surveys, e.g. on rainfall, geographical distribution of types of cats or rats, outrageous kinds of wines, home-made synthetic rubber, ways of drying lettuce, problems with heart pacemakers, what makes a hula hoop return when skidded across the floor, cures for babies who won't sleep, ways of identifying the contents of unlabelled cans without opening them. The format precludes controversial social, industrial and educational issues and concentrates heavily on the domestic sphere. On the other hand, the resident experts act as judges in the contests and as explainers of just what scientific principles are being illustrated. Us v. them is less in the foreground compared with the earlier format of the series, but the current one remains patronising. The presenters tend to give with one hand and take back with the other as they cut short the participants' exposition and announce what the medical or physical law or symptom is. It is almost as though they cannot refrain from protesting that the programme's format is in danger of upstaging their own expertise (David Bellamy suffered least from this anxiety). One is reminded of Socrates in the *Platonic Dialogues*, speaking at great length and then asking the rhetorical question, as when he proves to the slave boy in 'The Meno' that he already knows the Pythagorean Theorem. The audience is, in the end, in the hands of the 'experts', even though the interaction is less pompous and authoritarian than in other science programmes. In the last analysis the 'participation' seen here is *ersatz*, a carefully manufactured glimpse of more democratic possibilities.

Indeed, the production staff told us that the presenters' expertise was itself only a PR role, since it could lead to difficulties if, say, Pyke and Stoppard pitted their knowledge against what the producers wanted them to say. Their role is that of actors but with expert qualifications to lend legitimacy to their performances.

THE DRAMATIC CONSTRUCTION OF 'GENIUS'

The other series we want to consider at length is the impressive and lavishly produced *The Voyage of Charles Darwin*. We were, like everyone else, enthralled and impressed by the photography, the acting, the attention to period detail, and above all the attempt to portray an intellectual odyssey in dramatic terms. The trick was done, however, at a high price. Both the socio-economic and the intellectual contexts were simply edited out, and we were left with a dramatically successful but historically simplistic opposition between Captain Fitzroy's biblical literalism about the Divine creation of species and Darwin's putative inductivism leading to the theory of evolution by natural selection. Fossil facts discovered on the voyage, species differences encountered in the Galapagos islands — these, we are told, led the humble naturalist to his discovery. This nice young man comes across as the quintessence of English empiricism.

What, then, were the questions which were unasked? Why, for example, was *The Beagle* charting the coast of South America with such great care in the first place? Why did Britain want to know so much? What were the economic, geopolitical and cartographic desiderata which created the expedition? What was the intellectual context within which Darwin conducted his studies? We get no hint that Darwin learned Lamarck's theory of evolution while still a student at Edinburgh and little indication that his own grandfather had published a much-discussed evolutionary theory in 1794. We see Darwin given Volume I of Lyell's *Principles of Geology,* but we are not told of its crucial bearing on the question of the origin of species. We do not see Volume II reach him in Montevideo, with its early chapters reviewing the issue of evolution with great care. Darwin had a working library on *The Beagle,* but there is no sign of it. Instead of these important indicators of his intellectual milieu, we see him tramping about, puzzling over myriad findings. This is, of course, half the story — but only half. Similarly, after his return to England, we learn nothing of the contemporary debate over evolutionism. In the year when Darwin wrote out the first extended version of his theory, the evolutionism in Robert Chambers' *Vestiges of the Natural History of Creation* (1844) was a *cause célèbre,* but we hear nothing of it. Similarly, in Darwin's own musings the theories of scarcity and of the interactions between people and nature loom very large. The ideas of Malthus on the relationship between nature's resources and population growth were central to both the socio-economic context and the scientific one. They were the basis of the 1834 Poor Law and a key influence on Darwin's thinking in the weeks of 1838 when he first focused on the mechanism of natural selection.

We sketch these matters in some detail to highlight the contrast between two sorts of verisimilitude in the making of the series. There were maritime and historical advisers. The maritime adviser's injunctions were deferred to, down to the finest detail. The historical adviser, on the other hand, was listened to with care when he pointed out that the script presented a version of events which was in no way true to history, not even to Darwin's own *Autobiography,* which the production team claimed to be following. Their main source was a personal reminiscence, written from memory for his grandchildren years later and never intended for publication. The adviser argued that a much more interesting story could be told which took greater account of the intellectual and other contexts. The episodes were even re-written, but in the end he was overruled. The historical adviser was given the option of removing his name from the credits. The reason given was that 'dramatic criteria' called for a more stark, simpler version, which was supplied by re-writes from the producer and director, Christopher Ralling and Martin Friend. Dramatic criteria (and the requirements of US co-producers) had also led them to bring forward the maritime aspect, stress the suicide of the previous captain of *The Beagle* and build up Fitzroy's part far beyond his role in Darwin's later life. This was done to keep up the opposition between them throughout the series. It is our opinion that the deference to appearances (a strictly empiricist notion of authenticity) and the tradition of tele-dramas based on life at sea in the Victorian era led to the deference to the maritime adviser. One is reminded of *The Onedin Line* which was also directed by Martin Friend, whose experience in that series and knowledge of Spanish were important advantages. The tradition of valuing dramatic qualities above scientific ones (a function of the pecking order within the hierarchy of British culture and of TV in particular) and failing to increase the sophistication of viewers about the complexities of science, made it possible (and perfectly permissable) to play fast and loose with the scientific, socio-economic and intellectual aspects. We end up with a dramatically successful, ideologically loaded portrayal of the lone genius pitted against the forces of ignorance and superstition, which no student of science or history could take seriously. An important opportunity was missed, and a version of science and its social relations which is of no critical use in our culture was propagated. The naive inductivism and empiricism attributed to Darwin are truly embarrassing. The series resurrects a feature of dominant ideology which even its conservative proponents (e.g. Sir Karl Popper) have transcended. It is true that Darwin once said that he proceeded according to true Baconian principles, collecting facts with no theory in mind. But he also said that everyone knows that a fact has to count for or against some theory or other to have any meaning. Once again, we only get half the story.

The producer of the series, Christopher Ralling, went on to become Head of BBC Documentaries. In a lecture that he gave at the American Film Institute inaugurating a season under the title 'Salute to the BBC', he gave this breathtakingly banal version of his ground rules: '1. Never invent a major scene which did not actually take place. 2. Always use the actual words if they are available. 3. Whenever possible use the actual geographical locations' (*Listener*, 10 January 1980, p.43). Once again, it is undeniable that these principles have produced very effective television within the bounds of TV naturalism, which is itself a version of empiricism, unable to go beyond surface appearances. This was especially true in the location filming and in the expression of actual words in a 'natural' way. But which words? Which locations? Which scenes? The list is deceptively straightforward, ignoring the ways in which historians select events and construct their meanings. History remains unproblematically transparent. The list is also too short. It ignores wider historical forces, intellectual and ideological movements. It is, in short, a positivistic account, treating facts as though they were separable from the network of meanings which give them life and historical efficacy. Similarly, the metaphysical and theological issues are reduced to a conflict between 'science' and 'religion' which recent scholarship on the period has set aside. The upshot is a half admirable attempt to present an intellectual odyssey dramatically. It did this only by traducing the very richness which gave Darwinism meaning in nineteenth century history. It reduces the complex determinations of his life, works and milieu to a decontextualised individualist inductivism and presents these within the conventions of narrative naturalism. The American co-producers could insist that something very dramatic happen before the American viewer could change channels; the maritime adviser could call for changes in uniform or rigging; the historical adviser was simply overruled and ignored. How can this — the finest rendition of science on TV — do for us what culture should: help us to discriminate more subtly and sensitively among the facts and values which make up our lives?

How might a radical science programme-making strategy approach the life and work of Charles Darwin? One essential starting-point would be the necessary break with the ideological division between 'factual' and 'fictional' television within the time-honoured but nonsensical distinction between drama and documentary. *All* TV is a selected, constructed process of representation, as is all investigation of nature. We cannot, of course, elaborate a total strategy here, but the foregoing critique obviously delineates the sorts of things we would not do, the devices we would not adopt. What follows is more an approach than a set of programme directions.

It would be absolutely essential to break with the chronological, naturalistic narrative which Ralling adopted in taking us through Darwin's intellectual odyssey. Such a form is completely incapable of dealing with a complex set of historical determinations and almost automatically sites historical causality within the confines of one heroic individual. Any understanding of Darwin as a historical product in the nineteenth century and as a historical subject today has to set aside Ralling's absolutist view of Darwin's own texts as having some kind of immanent meaning, apart from their appropriation by his reviewers, protagonists, antagonists and a whole series of socio-political, intellectual and cultural discourses in his own period and in our own. One could start with his texts, possibly his notebooks in late 1838, when he was beginning to formulate clearly the theory of natural selection. However, even starting from such texts, one would constantly move backwards and forwards, referring continually to his precursors and antecedents, attempting to build up the complexity of the social/economic/ intellectual/political network of articulations in which he found himself and which constructed him. It would be important to make clear that the meaning of what he wrote was a synthetic appropriation of the debates into which he intervened.

We disagree fundamentally with Ralling's chosen approach to Darwin, which is to privilege Darwin's own retrospective account of himself and to move all the way from Darwin's texts to a naturalised, dramatic reconstruction which then obscures their relative nature, their own historicity. We would wish to highlight and literally display the texts within the production, in a way which sets them against contemporary and current discourses. A powerful model for our chosen form of historical film making is provided by Film and History Project's *Song of the Shirt*, which we recommend to readers and to TV science and history documentarists alike and which through its inter-discursive, dynamic representation of women garment workers in the 1840s, outside the usual naturalistic framework, succeeds in pointing up the relative, ideologically circumscribed positions of the tellers of history. There is no loss, and many would argue considerable gain, in dramatic effectiveness.

Similar problems arise with respect to the BBC series *Oppenheimer*, written by Peter Prince and directed by Barry Davies (see Gardner, 1980). This dramatised account of the fortunes of the 'father of the atom bomb' employed the same narrative strategies as *The Voyage of Charles Darwin* to broadly similar effect. It worked through a process of identification with Oppenheimer, 'the man' at the centre of the story. All the enormous social, economic and political questions surrounding the invention of the bomb had consequently to be subsumed and explained through personalised 'dramatic' incidents involving Oppenheimer himself. The producer is quite candid about this approach: 'Drama allows you to explore what it was like to be Oppenheimer'. The writer had one rule of thumb in selecting which incidents to dramatise: 'If it concerns Oppenheimer it's more important than if it has general importance but doesn't concern Oppenheimer directly'. This guideline led to some strange omissions and compressions of history. Pearl Harbour, the first nuclear reaction in Fermi's pile, Einstein's personal intervention with Roosevelt are all missing moments in the drama. Perhaps more importantly, the context in which the twenty-year span of the drama takes place is subsumed and almost completely unexplained. In particular there is no accounting for the generalised attraction of intellectuals to the Communist Party in the 1930s (for very good reasons) and the anti-communist hysteria of McCarthyism in the late 1950s. These are not incidental details which can be taken for granted as part of a current audience's knowledge of the period. But a dramatised, personalised account, such as this, cannot halt or digress for such prosaic niceties.

Taking Oppenheimer as its centre, then, historical and political conflict on a large scale are necessarily (give the chosen form) worked out through a series of confrontations — with his wife Kitty, with Edward Teller, Jane Tatlock, General Groves, various security personnel, McCarthy's henchmen. This is an extremely limited attempt to humanise history and relies for its effect on the employment of a well-known typography of almost stereotypical dramatic characters. For instance, one has the bitchy wife, the suicidal, neurotic mistress, the bullying, authoritarian military man, the humiliated adjutant who seeks revenge, the loyal retainers, the lawyer of integrity, etc. All these are portrayed as almost essential human types who ricochet around the fully-rounded Oppenheimer at the centre of events.

Such an approach as this precludes the vitally important materialistic view of history as the resolution of forces. History becomes, instead, one man's moral dilemma, a position in which the audience is inscribed and forced to adopt. In the whole process of the invention of the bomb there are a host of social, political and economic forces at work which this personal conflict and drama can come nowhere near suggesting. The birth of the bomb was achieved through the most extraordinary harnessing of financial and scientific power on an international scale. Competition between key institutions was temporarily halted and collaboration imposed. Financial provision was limitless. Huge industrial and research complexes, including Los Alamos, were built at breakneck speed. Over 250,000 people were eventually mobilised to wipe out 152,000 at Hiroshima and Nagasaki. Perhaps only US capital at its most dynamic and ebullient could have achieved this in the time-span available. Yet these enormous processes, this gigantic scale of co-operation and effort, simply cannot be conveyed within the scenario of personal drama surrounding a single individual, important as he was. Such a preferred narrative approach as this cannot help but imply — wrongly — that individuals are the central agents of history. History, as Marx said, is made by individuals but not under conditions of their own choosing. Its portrayal cannot be reduced to the small change of domestic and workplace tittle-tattle.

One is consequently forced to ask, as with the Darwin series, what could one have done instead? Within the broad framework of selected personal and dramatised sequences, one would want to adopt a broadly inter-discursive approach which mixes genres and attempts to portray the changing of historical forces through a range of televisual devices. For example, at certain points within the dramatic narrative, one could break off to use more orthodox documentary devices and sequences of exposition. One could continually shift the point of view within which the audience is positioned so that they are able to *explore* the various aspects of this historical dilemma. One could get the audience to examine in Brechtian fashion, as opposed to being forced to identify with the central persona of Oppenheimer and his own restricted perspective and network of personal relationships. One can see that while politically such a method is eminently more desirable, suggesting a genuinely materialistic dramaturgy, it would demand a break with the shibboleths of orthodox TV drama. Among the most important of these are the maintenance of narrative unity and tension, involvement and identification with the characters, immersion in the plot and suspension of disbelief. However, one can see from this brief analysis how such devices, so beloved of TV, are not simply neutral and useful means of telling a good story. They are, on the contrary, ideological techniques which actually preclude the representation of the full range of proximate and distant determinations which make up a materialist history.

CONCLUSION: A MODEL

We would like to see the domain of science opened up in at least three ways. First, sources: what forces evoke and constitute the kind of questions, frameworks and specific priorities of science? How do we come to frame the manifold of nature in the ways that we do? This topic goes as wide as asking why biology is currently framed in terms of information, communication, coding and control and as narrow as looking into how foundations and research councils prioritise their grant giving. Here is a list of research areas which were initially funded on a large scale for military purposes and are currently being employed in ways which produce real subordination in the sphere of production: nuclear power, computing, transistors, microprocessors, numerical control of machines, containerised transport, rocketry, electronic voice recognition. It would be enlightening to see the origins, development and applications in a single framework.

Second, the labour process: what are the relations of production of science, technology and medicine? The materials of labour or raw materials, the means of labour or means of production, the human labour or purposive human activity — these are the elements of any labour process, and science should also be closely examined in these terms. The social process of the production of knowledge, research and development of new technologies and products, the process of experimentation and testing of new drugs and medical procedures are in need of closer analysis. The division of labour in the lab, who does what in which social arrangements, the career structure — all these are part of the understanding of the social relations of science. It is, if you like, the bringing of anthropology to the workplace of scientific production. This is a process which has been begun in Bruno Latour and Steve Woolgar's *Laboratory Life: The Social Construction of Scientific Facts* (1979). The social study of factory work and life has been subjected to close scrutiny in this way. Why not science?

Third, articulations: how do the results connect up with the rest of society? A *Horizon* programme called 'The Fight to be Male' appears without any consideration of the relationship between its arguments about a 'sex centre' in the brain and the issues raised about sex and gender by the feminist and gay movements. To be sure, the social or environmentalist explanations were mentioned, but only as alternatives, bordering on straw men. The 'impact' of chips or transplant surgery should not be separated from the description of the hardware and techniques. Matters internal to science are not separable from their social relations. When Jonathan Miller placed himself in sensory isolation in *The Body in Question*, he only spoke of its relationship with the senses and bodily well-being. He made no reference to the development and use of sensory deprivation — largely in military and security forces interrogation — even though it was a matter of contemporary news. Similarly, when he spoke of blood transfusions as part of an anthropological 'gift relationship', he made no mention of the common sale of blood for sustenance by the poor, alcoholics or drug addicts. Only the body, as a discrete entity, was in question, not the social relations of the body of medical knowledge, much less the mode of production into which bodies are inserted. It could, of course, be argued that we have had an orgy of articulations in James Burke's series *Connections*. There is some truth in that, but his frenetic accounts tend to be *merely* connections. He celebrates the association of ideas in an idiosyncratic manner, unrelated to the forces and contradictions which evoke research and the resolutions of forces which research projects embody.

We advocate an approach which keeps all three themes in relation to each other: sources or constitution, labour processes or social relations of production, articulations or contextual relations. Our purpose in advocating a different approach to science on TV is to open up the process of origination of new facts, artifacts and procedures to public scrutiny and debate. As things now stand, we are faced with them at the point of impact when they are so highly developed and/or capitalised that it is difficult to believe that a real democratic process is possible.

Glancing, in conclusion, at the labour process of television itself, one side effect of our approach would be to undermine the existing division of labour in broadcasting and to reconstitute the totality of relations which make up science, technology, medicine and their representation to the general public. If these are as important as we have argued them to be, the ways in which they are treated by television become a central question of society and culture, and the alteration of current modes of representation becomes an important project for those who wish to change the structure of society.

(First published in this volume.)

References

Dickson, D. (1974), *Alternative Technology and the Politics of Technical Change*, London: Fontana.

Dunn, R. G. (1979), 'Science, Technology and Bureaucratic Domination: Television and the Ideology of Scientism', *Media, Culture and Society*, no. 1.

Figlio, K. (1978), 'Chlorosis and Chronic Disease in Nineteenth-century Britain: the Social Constitution of Somatic Illness in a Capitalist Society', *Social History*, no. 3.

Figlio, K. (1979), 'Sinister Medicine? A Critique of Left Approaches to Medicine', *Radical Science Journal*, no. 9.

Foucault, M. (1970), *The Order of Things: An Archaeology of the Human Sciences*, London: Tavistock.

Foucault, M. (1971), *Madness and Civilisation: A History of Insanity in the Age of Reason*, London: Tavistock.

Foucault, M. (1973), *The Birth of the Clinic: An Archaeology of Medical Perception*, London: Tavistock.

Gardner, C. (1978), 'Blinding with Science', *Time Out*, 20-26 October 1978.

Gardner, C. (ed.) (1979), *Media, Politics and Culture: A Socialist View*, London: Macmillan.

Gardner, C. (1980), 'One Man's Bomb', *Time Out*, 24-30 October 1980.

Jones, G., Connell, I., Meadows, J. (1977), *The Presentation of Science by the Media*, University of Leicester Primary Communications Research Centre.

Kellner, D. (1979), 'TV, Ideology and Emancipatory Popular Culture', *Socialist Review*, no. 45, May/June 1979.

Kuhn, T. (1971), *The Structure of Scientific Revolutions*, 2nd ed., Chicago: University of Chicago Press.

Latour, B. and Woolgar, S. (1979), *Laboratory Life: The Social Construction of Scientific Facts*, New York: Russell Sage.

Mattelart, A. (1979), *Multinational Corporations and the Control of Culture: The Ideological Apparatuses of Imperialism*, Hassocks: Harvester Press.

Popper, K. (1963), *Conjectures and Refutations: The Growth of Scientific Knowledge*, London: Routledge & Kegan Paul.

Ralling, C. (1980), 'What Is Television Doing to History?', *Listener*, 10 January 1980.

Webster, F. and Robins, K. (1979), 'Mass Communications and "Information Technology" ', in Miliband, R. and Saville, J. (eds.), *The Socialist Register*, London: Merlin.

Young, R. (1973), 'The Historiographic and Ideological Contexts of the Nineteenth-century Debate on Man's Place in Nature', in Teich, M. and Young, R. (eds.), *Changing Perspectives in the History of Science: Essays in Honour of Joseph Needham*, London: Heinemann.

Young, R. (1977), 'Science *is* Social Relations', *Radical Science Journal*, no. 5.

Young, R. (1979a), 'Science is a Labour Process', *Science for People*, nos. 43/44.

Young, R. (1979b), 'Science as Culture', *Quarto*, December 1979.

Checklist of Films and Television Programmes

The Body in Question (BBC) November 1978.
The Clone Affair (BBC) May 1979.

192

Connections (BBC) October 1978.

Einstein's Universe (BBC) March 1979.

Horizon (BBC): 'Sweet Solutions' March 1979.

'The Real Bionic Man' April 1979.

'The Fight to be Male' May 1979.

'The Mexican Oil Dance' September 1979.

'The Fat in the Fire' December 1979.

'The Cancer Detectives of Lin Xian' February 1980.

Man Alive (BBC): 'Fats and Figures' January 1980.

Oppenheimer (BBC) October 1980.

Screening Nuclear Hazard (OU/BBC) June 1980.

The Voyage of Charles Darwin (BBC) October 1978.

The Song of the Shirt (Film and History Project), dir. Sue Clayton and Jonathan Curling, distributed by The Other Cinema.

PART III
POPULAR FILM AND PLEASURE

Introduction

This section attempts to explore the very difficult questions relating to the area of pleasure. It is concerned with the seemingly endless questions of why and how we enjoy particular cultural forms and of what are the fundamental cognitive processes at work in popular film. Of course, it is not only popular film which raises these questions, but it is in this context that they are posed most urgently. What is the nature of pleasure? Is it, as many commentators and 'common sense' suggest, *beyond* analysis?

Recently this and related questions have become central problems for cultural analysis. Once you have analysed a given text in terms of its communicative or ideological aspects, what is left over? Do those forms of analysis exhaust what can be said about texts? If so, then what can we say about the apparently simple *fact* of pleasure? There have been various answers to this from psychologists, behaviourists and sociologists, but in the realm of film attempts to answer the question are only just beginning to emerge. These forms of analysis are beginning to ask questions about the ways in which we admire or identify with certain types of heroes; how we indulge in the 'pleasure' of sexual stereotypes or of the portrayal of violence; how we find some forms of pleasure in identifying the 'truth' via certain forms of 'knowledge' and 'realism' or, in some cases, the pleasure located in anti-realism. What seems to be clear is that the answers cannot come from a single level of analysis; they are partly political, partly social, partly psychological and partly personal. From the readings which follow we will see that there is no general and universal form of pleasure valid for all human beings in all social contexts. There are specific, albeit overlapping, forms of pleasure in particular historical and institutional contexts. The readings here deal with only one of those — popular film. This is only a start for the analysis of pleasure; it is by no means all that can, or will, be said about it.

Stephen Heath's analysis of the immensely popular film *Jaws* attempts to come to terms with what the author calls the 'pleasure-meaning-commodity complex' signalled by such a film. Film as *meaning*, as a communicative system; film as *commodity*, produced and marketed by a specific industry; *film as pleasure,* as entertainment and enjoyment. To understand how these three aspects are held together we need to understand film as a 'specific signifying practice'; that is, as a complex form of language speaking to us from particular sites and which we freely consent, and pay, to listen to and see. Film deploys certain strategies and processes to involve us, to make us enjoy: certain shots, images, sounds, music which produce moments of secrecy and revelation, tension and resolution, loss and jubilation. Heath argues that these, in turn, are structured around themes to do with politics, sexuality, 'manly achievement', pride and so on, producing an entity which is simultaneously profitable, meaningful and pleasurable.

The dimension of sexuality is taken up by Laura Mulvey. Here the emphasis is upon the *visual* pleasure obtained through certain ways of seeing and looking. One of the dominant pleasure-forms in narrative (conventional) cinema, Mulvey argues, is that inscribed in the location of women in an eminently visible though subordinate position. Women, in the majority of films, are there to be *seen*. Men are there to *act*. Also conceiving of film as a 'signifying practice', Mulvey argues that this 'dominant look' is itself part of the structure of cinema; it is a structured 'way of seeing' deeply embedded within the cinematic code and informed by certain ideological conceptions in society as a whole. In her analysis Mulvey attempts to link certain psychological processes ('voyeurism', 'scopophilia') to more general sexual structures (male dominance or 'patriarchy'), and suggests that this is one dominant form of pleasure and fascination in our culture.

Another, related form of pleasure is that located in the desire for 'knowledge' and 'truth'. In its most immediate form this is the process at work in countless detective stories in literature and in film. The narrative structure 'pulls us in' to the text, involves us in the intrigues and suspense, allows us to know something the participants do not know, provides clues and ultimate revelations. Colin MacCabe argues that a more sophisticated version of this is at work within the texts of the dominant 'realist' tradition. MacCabe uses the notion of a 'hierarchy of discourses' to describe the ways in which the 'classic realist text' discreetly posits a central 'truth' in the hidden voice of the narrators. This provides a form of knowledge about what is going on and a hierarchy within which all available discourses can be measured against the central 'truth' — a principle of constancy and of reality.

The never-ending flow of publications on Marilyn Monroe, the suicides following the death of Rudolf Valentino, are a testament to the centrality of 'stars' in our culture. They are certainly a dominant form of pleasure. Richard Dyer begins to ask why this might be so by treating stars themselves as signs. They have a meaning, they signify something in relation to other cultural, political and ideological forms. The ways in which they do this around themes of human interest, identification, sexuality and pure fascination are the subject of this reading. It, like the other readings, takes on the question of pleasure by breaking it down into particular forms and resisting any notion that pleasure is 'neutral'.

From a different theoretical perspective, the article by Thomas Elsaesser, 'Narrative Cinema and Audience-Oriented Aesthetics', considers, in very detailed terms, the precise mechanisms at work in narrative cinema which relate it to society and to individual consciousness. Focusing on particular aesthetic processes, Elsaesser locates the question of pleasure in the complexity of the viewing situation itself. Unlike reading a book, or watching the television, cinema must of necessity establish and reproduce in very intense ways what Elsaesser calls a 'psychic matrix', which operates through a process of transformation of elements of narrative, image and action into consistent and cogent meanings. Two of these 'transformational processes' are the focus of the article — plot and *mise en scène* — and the author attempts to show how, in the dominant narrative tradition of Hollywood cinema, these are the basis of its aesthetic mode of production and its particular pleasures.

Jaws, Ideology and Film Theory

Every review of the film *Jaws* begins with some reference to its status as *the* film, not so much super-production as super-product, the box-office record-breaker expected to gross more than a quarter of a billion dollars. But the product also *means* (part of its meaning, of course, is to be 'the most profitable movie in history'), and means as *entertainment*, a moving and pleasurable experience marketed and bought.

Analysis must grasp this pleasure-meaning-commodity complex, and recent developments in film theory have been concerned to pose precisely the problems which arise from such an emphasis. [. . .] Epitome of 'cinema', *Jaws* can perhaps provide a focus for discussion that will allow something of these problems to be understood.

At one level, the ideology of *Jaws* is clear enough, the province of a traditional 'content analysis'. *Jaws* is a Watergate film: Mayor Larry Vaughan of Amity, Long Island, serves his electors ('Amity needs summer dollars') by hushing up a shark attack ('I was acting in the town's best interest'); the white male middle class — not a single black and, very quickly, not a single woman in the film — in the person of police chief Martin Brody will recognize its complicity (a literal slap in the face from the mother of a boy who dies when the beaches stay open) and pull the town through with an ordinary-guy brand of heroism born of fear-and-decency.

Order is fragile but possible, mistakes are made (Vaughan is simply weak, caught out serving his town, and Brody with him; the evil is something else, call it a shark) but you — Brody — can redeem them (kill the shark), and better than any screwball romantic myth (Quint, a vague memory of *Moby Dick,* of which *Jaws* is the middle-class re-make) or any expert (Hooper, the whizz-kid with all the equipment finally defeated by the shark).

Other elements extend out from this core with a symptomatic rightness: as for example, the story Quint tells of the sinking of the *Indianapolis* in shark-infested waters after transporting the Hiroshima bomb ('1,100 men went into the water, 360 men came out, anyway we delivered the bomb'). The story functions to motivate Quint's character as determined shark-killer, but does so excessively, placing — in the play between Quint, Hooper and Brody, as they wait out at sea in the summer of America's final year in Vietnam — destruction and conscience and manliness and menace and just doing-the-job (the scene ends with the three men joining in a song — 'Show me the way to go home' — interrupted by the shark outside trying to rip into their world).

This clear ideology, the *narrative image* of the film, is made up of such elements held in a loose coherence round the central core, and working in the space of the film. It is the 'working-space' that is important; to remain at the level of a content analysis in these terms is to fail to engage with the ideological *operation* of the film, its production, as also — the two running together as a set of relations — with the pleasure derived from this film about a shark and its pursuers. In short, it is to fail to engage with the fact of *film*.

The fact of film has been the concern of film theory in its attempts to define film as a specific object of study, and it is in this context that one can grasp the initial role of structuralism and the early 'structuralist' semiology.

Semiological description brought consideration of the ways in which meanings are articulated in film. In particular, attention was given to the codes of the image (the construction of iconic signs, problems of denotation and connotation) and to the codes of the arrangement of film in sequences (the definition of syntagmatic units, the structures of film narrative).

This last was a part of the work of the French theoretician Christian Metz whose *Language and Cinema*, published in 1971, was a rigorous investigation of the nature of cinema as language, a mapping out of the difficulties involved in that linguistic analogy, in order to give precision to the use of the term 'language' in respect of film.

Language and Cinema rests firmly (and finely) within the limits of 'structuralist' semiological description, focused on the object cinema, as opposed to the operation cinema. Its effect, nevertheless, taken in conjunction with surrounding theoretical developments — the encounter of Marxism and psychoanalysis on the terrain of semiotics — was to allow the problem to be henceforth understood as that of the study of film as *specific signifying practice*.

Signifying indicates the recognition of film as system or series of systems of meaning, film as articulation. *Practice* stresses the process of this articulation, which it thus refuses to hold under the assumption of notions such as 'representation' and 'expression'; it takes film as a work of production of meanings and in so doing brings into the analysis the question of the positioning of the subject within that work, its relations of the subject, what kind of 'reader' and 'author' the film projects.

Specific represents the need for analysis to understand film in the particularity of the work it engages, the differences it sustains with other signifying practices. This does not, however, entail pulling film towards some aesthetic idea of a pure cinematicity (on a line with the idea of 'literarity' derived in literary criticism from Russian formalism, which has often become a way of avoiding crucial issues of production and ideology in its precise appeal to a technicist 'structuralist poetics').

Specificity here is semiotic, and a semiotic analysis of film — of film as signifying practice — is the analysis of a heterogeneity, a range of codes and systems at work in film over and across its five matters of expression (moving photographic image, recorded phonetic sound, recorded noise, recorded musical sound, and writing; the latter as, for example, in the prominent 'Amity welcomes you' hoarding in *Jaws*).

Specificity is thus both those codes particular to cinema (codes of articulation of dialogue and image, codes of scale of shot, certain codes of narrative organization, etc.) and the heterogeneity in its particular effects, its particular inscriptions of subject, and meaning and ideology. Directed in this way, the study of film is of neither 'contents' nor 'forms' but, breaking the deadlock of that opposition, of *operations*, of the process of film and the relations of subjectivity in that process.

Such a direction can further be seen as holding in a fundamental intersection three component areas: the conditions of film production and distribution, the individual film, and the general apparatus of cinema. As was said earlier, the film industry manufactures film products, but these products mean, and sell on meaning and pleasure; between *industry* and *text*, we also need a category like *machine*.

This category is cinema itself, understood in its stock of constraints and definitions, its possibilities and points of determination, with respect to which film can be distinguished as specific signifying practice and a particular film seized dialectically in its operation. Each of the three areas can bring with it its own set of tasks and study procedures, but attention to their intersection is *constantly* important.

In the light of these propositions, let us come back to *Jaws*, to this particular film. Space will not permit detailed analysis of the movement of its filmic system; one or two fragmentary indications must serve to suggest the terms of that movement, and lead on to some consideration of machine and industry, indications that will be developed from the opening shots of the film.

The first shot has the camera underwater veering rapidly forward through the sea-bed forest to the accompaniment of ominous rhythmic music. Cut to a group of young people at a night-time beach party; the cut is heavily marked by changes in colour, from the coldish underwater tones to the rich orange-yellow reflections of a fire, in music, a youth is playing a harmonica, and in rhythm, the camera now tracks smoothly right along the group — faces kissing, smoking, drinking — until it stops on a young man cooking off-frame.

Eyeline cut to the girl who is revealed as the object of his gaze, followed by a cut to a high angle shot down onto the party establishing its overall space. Then comes a run down to the sea, the girl shedding her clothes as the boy stumbles drunkenly after; as she swims out, the boy collapses; an underwater shot, now moving up to the surface between the girl's legs, precedes the shark's attack; the next morning the boy wakes, sits up into frame as we look out with him on the empty ocean.

For the narrative, this sequence is precisely and simply the beginning, the initial premise: the arrival of the shark. At the same time, however, it sets off a number of other series which knot together as figures over the film.

Thus, for example, the presence of the shark is given in the very first shot with its violent underwater movement tied to no human point of view, and the underwater shot is then used in the first part of the film to signify the imminence of attack: we are placed *as* the shark as it rises to the girl and, later, to the little boy on the float.

Once systematized, it can be used to cheat: it occurs to confirm the second day-time beach attack, but this is only two boys with an imitation fin. More importantly, the shot binds up with an immediate marking out, in the sequence, of a danger of sexuality and the displacement of the latter onto the shark: the girl leads the boy on; as she strips, he follows with 'I'm coming, I'm definitely coming'; when she is attacked, he lies on the beach moaning again 'I'm coming, I'm coming' (the novel has the report of the attack held up while the duty patrolman finishes reading a story about a woman who castrates an assailant with a knife secreted in her hair).

One inexorable movement of the film is then to get rid of women; in an exact rhyming inversion of the girl's provocative run down to the sea, where the shark is ready, Brody's wife runs — with a similar following shot, now from left to right — away from the sea, out of Quint's shark-hung lair ('Here's to swimming with bow-legged women!'), out of the film, as the men set off to deal with the evil, the boat seen moving off in long shot through a trophy pair of shark's jaws.

The stress on dismemberment — after the girl, all the victims are male and the focus is on losing legs — finds its resonance in this context, as too does the scene where Quint and Hooper compare shark wounds (and drink to their legs!), as again does the apparently gratuitous image of the old man in the bathing cap with hanging breasts, who comes to taunt Brody with his fear of the water.

This excess over the narrative in the opening sequence disturbs the coherence of the end. In the former we look out with the boy over the menacing sea (a shot elsewhere repeated from Brody's point of view); in the latter we look with Brody and Hooper from the sea back to the land, the menace destroyed, Brody's fear overcome ('I used to hate the water, I can't imagine why'); a closing — rhymingly inverted — high-angle shot establishes the beach again, empty and clean. But what cannot be resolved is the whole shark displacement, the elements of the first sequence are left hanging and no woman comes back — here too *Jaws* is a white male film.

Such indications begin to show something of the multiple series working over the narrative in a film text, series that combine across the different matters of expression and codes in rhymes, repetitions, turns. In fact, film is potentially a veritable flux of affects, a plurality of intensities, and narrative functions to contain that affectivity, which is thus 're-released' as 'excess', 'disturbance', 'figure' — symptomatic demonstrations of the *work* of containment.

This engages the intersection with cinema the machine. Narrative is not essential to cinema, but historically the latter has been developed and exploited as a narrative form: *against* dispersion, *for* representation, where representation is less immediately a matter of 'what is represented' than of positioning; narrative in cinema is first and foremost the organization of a point of view through the image-flow, the laying out of an intelligibility, the conversion of seen into scene as the direction of the viewing subject.

The grounding of vision in the subject as the perspective of intelligibility is crucial. Cinema is implicated in a founding ideology of vision as truth (Lumière aims 'to reproduce life itself') but film, in its flux, can also produce discontinuities, disruptions, 'shocks'. Hence, from the start, there is a need to reconstruct that truth of vision, to establish ways for holding a film's relations as the coherence of the subject-eye — continuity techniques, matches, 30 degree and 180 degree rules, codes of framing, and so on.

Indeed, the drama of vision becomes a constant reflexive fascination in films. Hitchcock's *Rear Window* is a supreme example, but *Jaws* is also reflexive with its play on the unseen and unforeseeable, the hidden shark and the moments of violent irruption — the corpse in the boat-hull, the shark rearing from the water close behind Brody as he shovels chum.

Jaws, moreover, has the whole film summarized in the images flickeringly reflected on Brody's glasses as he skims through the pages of the books about sharks, occasionally fixing a corresponding image — the whole film except, precisely, for Brody, the vision to come, the film's 'resolution'.

Film is the constant process of a phasing in of vision, the pleasure of that process — movement and fixity and movement again, from fragment (actually thematized in *Jaws* as dismemberment) to totality (the jubilation of the final image). Genres are different balances of the process, shifting regulations of the subject, particular closures of desire.

But genres are also necessities of the industry, the optimal exploitation of the production apparatus requiring the containment of creative work within established frameworks. This double determination brings us back once more to the complex of intersection: films are industrial products, and they mean, and they sell not simply on the particular meaning but equally on the pleasure of cinema, this yielding the return

204

that allows the perpetuation of the industry (which is why part of the meaning of *Jaws* is to be the most profitable movie); a film is not reducible to its 'ideology' but is also the working over of that ideology in cinema, with the industry dependent on the pleasure of the operation. The problems for film theory today are those of approaching an understanding of the fact of film in these terms.

Jaws has placed the focus here on the dominant American cinema. But it must be stressed that such an understanding is a point of development in certain areas of avant-garde film, seeking to pose the material conditions of film in the interests of alternative practices, other cinema.

Film theory has continually to learn from those practices which must indeed provide its very edge; as it has too, dialectically, to turn back into them, a moment of their advance in the transformation of the relations of subject and meaning in film. The study of Hollywood film (*Jaws* included), its strategies, its frictions, its pleasure, can have an importance in this context — if only that study be directed, critically and specifically, to Hollywood film itself as signifying *practice*.

(First published in *The Times Higher Education Supplement,* 26 March 1976.)

Visual Pleasure and Narrative Cinema

[...]

DESTRUCTION OF PLEASURE AS A RADICAL WEAPON

As an advanced representation system, the cinema poses questions of the ways the unconscious (formed by the dominant order) structures ways of seeing and pleasure in looking. Cinema has changed over the last few decades. It is no longer the monolithic system based on large capital investment exemplified at its best by Hollywood in the 1930s, 1940s and 1950s. Technological advances (16mm., etc) have changed the economic conditions of cinematic production, which can now be artisanal as well as capitalist. Thus it has been possible for an alternative cinema to develop. However self-conscious and ironic Hollywood managed to be, it always restricted itself to a formal *mise en scène* reflecting the dominant ideological concept of the cinema. The alternative cinema provides a space for a cinema to be born which is radical in both a political and an aesthetic sense and challenges the basic assumptions of the mainstream film. This is not to reject the latter moralistically, but to highlight the ways in which its formal preoccupations reflect the psychical obsessions of the society which produced it, and, further, to stress that the alternative cinema must start specifically by reacting against these obsessions and assumptions. A politically and aesthetically avant-garde cinema is now possible, but it can still only exist as a counterpoint.

The magic of the Hollywood style at its best (and of all the cinema which fell within its sphere of influence) arose, not exclusively, but in one important aspect, from its skilled and satisfying manipulation of visual pleasure. Unchallenged, mainstream film coded the erotic into the language of the dominant patriarchal order. In the highly developed Hollywood cinema it was only through these codes that the alienated subject [...] came near to finding a glimpse of satisfaction: through its formal beauty and its play on his own formative obsessions. This article will discuss the interweaving of that erotic pleasure in film, its meaning, and in particular the central place of the image of woman. It is said that analysing pleasure, or beauty, destroys it. That is the intention of this article. The satisfaction and reinforcement of the ego that represent the high point of film history hitherto must be attacked. Not in favour of a reconstructed new pleasure, which cannot exist in the abstract, nor of intellectualised unpleasure, but to make way for a total negation of the ease and plenitude of the narrative fiction film. The alternative is the thrill that comes from leaving the past behind without rejecting it, transcending outworn or oppressive forms, or daring to break with normal pleasurable expectations in order to conceive a new language of desire.

PLEASURE IN LOOKING/FASCINATION WITH THE HUMAN FORM

The cinema offers a number of possible pleasures. One is scopophilia. There are circumstances in which looking itself is a source of pleasure, just as, in the reverse formation, there is pleasure in being looked at. Originally, in his *Three Essays on Sexuality*, Freud isolated scopophilia as one of the component instincts of sexuality which exist as drives quite independently of the erotogenic zones. At this point he associated scopophilia with taking other people as objects, subjecting them to a controlling and curious gaze. His particular examples centre around the voyeuristic activities of children, their desire to see and make sure of the private and the forbidden (curiosity about other people's genital and bodily functions, about the presence or absence of the penis and, retrospectively, about the primal scene). In this analysis scopophilia is essentially active. [. . .] Although the instinct is modified by other factors, in particular the constitution of the ego, it continues to exist as the erotic basis for pleasure in looking at another person as object. At the extreme, it can become fixated into a perversion, producing obsessive voyeurs and Peeping Toms, whose only sexual satisfaction can come from watching, in an active controlling sense, an objectified other.

At first glance, the cinema would seem to be remote from the undercover world of the surreptitious observation of an unknowing and unwilling victim. What is seen on the screen is so manifestly shown. But the mass of mainstream film, and the conventions within which it has consciously evolved, portray a hermetically sealed world which unwinds magically, indifferent to the presence of the audience, producing for them a sense of separation and playing on their voyeuristic phantasy. Moreover, the extreme contrast between the darkness in the auditorium (which also isolates the spectators from one another) and the brilliance of the shifting patterns of light and shade on the screen helps to promote the illusion of voyeuristic separation. Although the film is really being shown, is there to be seen, conditions of screening and narrative conventions give the spectator an illusion of looking in on a private world. Among other things, the position of the spectators in the cinema is blatantly one of repression of their exhibitionism and projection of the repressed desire on to the performer.

The cinema satisfies a primordial wish for pleasurable looking, but it also goes further, developing scopophilia in its narcissistic aspect. The conventions of mainstream film focus attention on the human form.

Scale, space, stories are all anthropomorphic. Here, curiosity and the wish to look intermingle with a fascination with likeness and recognition: the human face, the human body, the relationship between the human form and its surroundings, the visible presence of the person in the world. [The French psychoanalyst] Jacques Lacan has described how the moment when a child recognises its own image in the mirror is crucial for the constitution of the ego. Several aspects of this analysis are relevant here. The mirror phase occurs at a time when the child's physical ambitions outstrip his motor capacity, with the result that his recognition of himself is joyous in that he imagines his mirror image to be more complete, more perfect than he experiences his own body. Recognition is thus overlaid with mis-recognition: the image recognised is conceived as the reflected body of the self, but its misrecognition as superior projects this body outside itself as an ideal ego, the alienated subject, which, re-introjected as an ego ideal, gives rise to the future generation of identification with others [the entry into the social symbolic 'order']. This mirror-moment predates language for the child.

Important for this article is the fact that it is an image that constitutes the matrix of the imaginary, of recognition/mis-recognition and identification, and hence of the first articulation of the 'I', of subjectivity. This is a moment when an older fascination with looking (at the mother's face, for an obvious example) collides with the initial inklings of self-awareness. Hence it is the birth of the long love affair/despair between image and self-image which has found such intensity of expression in film and such joyous recognition in the cinema audience. Quite apart from the extraneous similarities between screen and mirror (the framing of the human form in its surroundings, for instance), the cinema has structures of fascination strong enough to allow temporary loss of ego while simultaneously reinforcing the ego. The sense of forgetting the world as the ego has subsequently come to perceive it (I forgot who I am and where I was) is nostalgically reminiscent of that pre-subjective moment of image recognition. At the same time the cinema has distinguished itself in the production of ego ideals as expressed in particular in the star system, the stars centring both screen presence and screen story as they act out a complex process of likeness and difference (the glamorous impersonates the ordinary).

[Above we] have set out two contradictory aspects of the pleasurable structures of looking in the conventional cinematic situation. The first, scopophilic, arises from pleasure in using another person as an object of sexual stimulation through sight. The second, developed through narcissism and the constitution of the ego, comes from identification with the image seen. Thus, in film terms, one implies a separation of the erotic identity of the subject from the object on the screen (active scopophilia), the other demands identification of the ego with the object

208

on the screen through the spectator's fascination with and recognition of his like. The first is a function of the sexual instincts, the second of ego libido. This dichotomy was crucial for Freud. Although he saw the two as interacting and overlaying each other, the tension between instinctual drives and self-preservation continues to be a dramatic polarisation in terms of pleasure. Both are formative structures, mechanisms not meaning. In themselves they have no signification, they have to be attached to an idealisation. Both pursue aims in indifference to perceptual reality, creating the imaginised, eroticised concept of the world that forms the perception of the subject and makes a mockery of empirical objectivity.

During its history, the cinema seems to have evolved a particular illusion of reality in which this contradiction between libido and ego has found a beautifully complementary phantasy world. [. . .] The look, pleasurable in form, can be threatening in content, and it is woman as representation/image that crystallises this paradox.

WOMAN AS IMAGE, MAN AS BEARER OF THE LOOK

In a world ordered by sexual imbalance, pleasure in looking has been split between active/male and passive/female. The determining male gaze projects its phantasy on to the female figure which is styled accordingly. In their traditional exhibitionist role women are simultaneously looked at and displayed, with their appearance coded for strong visual and erotic impact so that they can be said to connote *to-be-looked-at-ness*. Woman displayed as sexual object is the leit-motif of erotic spectacle: from pin-ups to strip-tease, from Ziegfeld to Busby Berkeley, she holds the look, plays to and signifies male desire. Mainstream film neatly combined spectacle and narrative. [. . .] The presence of woman is an indispensable element of spectacle in normal narrative film, yet her visual presence tends to work against the development of a story line, to freeze the flow of action in moments of erotic contemplation. This alien presence then has to be integrated into cohesion with the narrative. As Budd Boetticher has put it:

> What counts is what the heroine provokes, or rather what she represents. She is the one, or rather the love or fear she inspires in the hero, or else the concern he feels for her, who makes him act the way he does. In herself the woman has not the slightest importance.

(A recent tendency in narrative film has been to dispense with this problem altogether; hence the development of what Molly Haskell has called the 'buddy movie' [for example *Butch Cassidy and the Sundance Kid*], in which the active homosexual eroticism of the central male figures can carry the story without distraction). Traditionally, the woman displayed has functioned on two levels: as erotic object for the characters within the screen story, and as erotic object for the spectator within the auditorium, with a shifting tension between the looks on either side of the screen. For instance, the device of the show-girl allows the two looks to be unified technically without any apparent break in the diegesis.* A woman performs within the narrative, the gaze of the spectator and that of the male characters in the film are neatly combined without breaking narrative verisimilitude. For a moment the sexual impact of the performing woman takes the film into a no-man's-land outside its own time and space. [. . .] Similarly, conventional close-ups of legs (Dietrich, for instance) or a face (Garbo) integrate into the narrative a different mode of eroticism. One part of a fragmented body destroys Renaissance perspective, the illusion of depth demanded by the narrative, it gives flatness, the quality of a cut-out or icon rather than verisimilitude to the screen.

An active/passive heterosexual division of labour has similarly controlled narrative structure. According to the principles of the ruling ideology and the psychical structures that back it up, the male figure cannot bear the burden of sexual objectification. Man is reluctant to gaze at his exhibitionist like. Hence the split between spectacle and narrative supports the man's role as the active one of forwarding the story, making things happen. The man controls the film phantasy and also emerges as the representative of power in a further sense: as the bearer of the look of the spectator. [. . .] This is made possible through the processes set in motion by structuring the film around a main controlling figure with whom the spectator can identify. As the spectator identifies with the main male† protagonist, he projects his look on to that of his like, his screen surrogate, so that the power of the male protagonist as he controls events coincides with the active power of the erotic look, both giving a satisfying sense of omnipotence. A male movie star's glamorous characteristics are thus not those of the erotic object of the gaze, but those of the more perfect, more complete, more powerful ideal ego conceived in the original moment of recognition in front of the mirror. The character in the story can make things happen and control events better than the subject/spectator, just as the image in the mirror was more in control of motor co-ordination. [. . .] He is a figure in a landscape. Here the function of film is to reproduce as accurately as possible the so-called natural conditions of human perception. Camera technology (as exemplified by deep focus in particular) and camera

* [The term 'diegesis' refers to the unified fictional world of the film's narrative.]

† There are films with a woman as main protagonist, of course. To analyse this phenomenon seriously here would take me too far afield. Pam Cook and Claire Johnston's study of *The Revolt of Mamie Stover* in Phil Hardy, ed: *Raoul Walsh*, Edinburgh 1974, shows in a striking case how the strength of this female protagonist is more apparent than real.

movements (determined by the action of the protagonist), combined with invisible editing (demanded by realism) all tend to blur the limits of screen space. The male protagonist is free to command the stage, a stage of spatial illusion in which he articulates the look and creates the action.

[Above we] have set out a tension between a mode of representation of woman in film and conventions surrounding the diegesis. Each is associated with a look: that of the spectator in direct scopophilic contact with the female form displayed for his enjoyment (connoting male phantasy) and that of the spectator fascinated with the image of his like set in an illusion of natural space, and through him gaining control and possession of the woman within the diegesis. (This tension and the shift from one pole to the other can structure a single text. Thus both in *Only Angels Have Wings* and in *To Have and Have Not*, the film opens with the woman as object of the combined gaze of spectator and all the male protagonists in the film. She is isolated, glamorous, on display, sexualised. But as the narrative progresses she falls in love with the main male protagonist and becomes his property, losing her outward glamorous characteristics, her generalised sexuality, her show-girl connotations; her eroticism is subjected to the male star alone. By means of identification with him, through participation in his power, the spectator can indirectly possess her too.) [. . .]

[This] can be illustrated more simply by using works by Hitchcock and [Josef von] Sternberg, both of whom take the look almost as the content or subject matter of many of their films. Hitchcock is the more complex, as he uses both mechanisms. Sternberg's work, on the other hand, provides many pure examples of fetishistic scopophilia.

It is well known that Sternberg once said he would welcome his films being projected upside down so that story and character involvement would not interfere with the spectator's undiluted appreciation of the screen image. This statement is revealing but ingenuous. Ingenuous in that his films do demand that the figure of the woman (Dietrich, in the cycle of films with her, as the ultimate example) should be identifiable. But revealing in that it emphasises the fact that for him the pictorial space enclosed by the frame is paramount rather than narrative or identification processes. While Hitchcock goes into the investigative side of voyeurism, Sternberg produces the ultimate fetish, taking it to the point where the powerful look of the male protagonist (characteristic of traditional narrative film) is broken in favour of the image in direct erotic rapport with the spectator. The beauty of the woman as object and the screen space coalesce; she is no longer the bearer of guilt but a perfect product, whose body, stylised and fragmented by close-ups, is the content of the film and the direct recipient of the spectator's look. Sternberg plays down the illusion of screen depth; his screen tends to be

211

one-dimensional, as light and shade, lace, steam, foliage, net, streamers, etc, reduce the visual field. There is little or no mediation of the look through the eyes of the main male protagonist. On the contrary, shadowy presences like La Bessière in *Morocco* act as surrogates for the director, detached as they are from audience identification. Despite Sternberg's insistence that his stories are irrelevant, it is significant that they are concerned with situation, not suspense, and cyclical rather than linear time, while plot complications revolve around misunderstanding rather than conflict. The most important absence is that of the controlling male gaze within the screen scene. The high point of emotional drama in the most typical Dietrich films, her supreme moments of erotic meaning, take place in the absence of the man she loves in the fiction. There are other witnesses, other spectators watching her on the screen, their gaze is one with, not standing in for, that of the audience. At the end of *Morocco*, Tom Brown has already disappeared into the desert when Amy Jolly kicks off her gold sandals and walks after him. At the end of *Dishonoured*, Kranau is indifferent to the fate of Magda. In both cases, the erotic impact, sanctified by death, is displayed as a spectacle for the audience. The male hero misunderstands and, above all, does not see.

In Hitchcock, by contrast, the male hero does see precisely what the audience sees. However, in the films I shall discuss here, he takes fascination with an image through scopophilic eroticism as the subject of the film. Moreover, in these cases the hero portrays the contradictions and tensions experienced by the spectator. In *Vertigo* in particular, but also in *Marnie* and *Rear Window*, the look is central to the plot, oscillating between voyeurism and fetishistic fascination. As a twist, a further manipulation of the normal viewing process which in some sense reveals it, Hitchcock uses the process of identification normally associated with ideological correctness and the recognition of established morality and shows up its perverted side. Hitchcock has never concealed his interest in voyeurism, cinematic and non-cinematic. His heroes are exemplary of the symbolic order and the law — a policeman *(Vertigo)*, a dominant male possessing money and power *(Marnie)* — but their erotic drives lead them into compromised situations. The power to subject another person to the will sadistically or to the gaze voyeuristically is turned on to the woman as the object of both. Power is backed by a certainty of legal right and the established guilt of the woman (evoking castration, psychoanalytically speaking). True perversion is barely concealed under a shallow mask of ideological correctness — the man is on the right side of the law, the woman on the wrong. Hitchcock's skilful use of identification processes and liberal use of subjective camera from the point of view of the male protagonist draw the spectators deeply into his position, making them share his uneasy gaze. The audience is absorbed into a voyeuristic situation within the screen scene and diegesis which

212

parodies his own in the cinema. [. . .]

In *Vertigo,* subjective camera predominates. [. . .] The audience follows the growth of [the character Scottie's] erotic obsession and subsequent despair precisely from his point of view. Scottie's voyeurism is blatant: he falls in love with a woman he follows and spies on without speaking to. Its sadistic side is equally blatant: he has chosen (and freely chosen, for he had been a successful lawyer) to be a policeman, with all the attendant possibilities of pursuit and investigation. As a result, he follows, watches and falls in love with a perfect image of female beauty and mystery. Once he actually confronts her, his erotic drive is to break her down and force her to tell by persistent cross-questioning. Then, in the second part of the film, he re-enacts his obsessive involvement with the image he loved to watch secretly. He reconstructs Judy as Madeleine, forces her to conform in every detail to the actual physical appearance of his fetish. Her exhibitionism, her masochism, make her an ideal passive counterpart to Scottie's active sadistic voyeurism. She knows her part is to perform, and only by playing it through and then replaying it can she keep Scottie's erotic interest. But in the repetition he does break her down and succeeds in exposing her guilt. His curiosity wins through and she is punished. In *Vertigo,* erotic involvement with the look is disorientating: the spectator's fascination is turned against him as the narrative carries him through and entwines him with the processes that he is himself exercising. The Hitchcock hero here is firmly placed within the symbolic order, in narrative terms. He has all the attributes of the patriarchal super-ego. Hence the spectator, lulled into a false sense of security by the apparent legality of his surrogate, sees through his look and finds himself exposed as complicit, caught in the moral ambiguity of looking. Far from being simply an aside on the perversion of the police, *Vertigo* focuses on the implications of the active/looking, passive/looked-at split in terms of sexual difference and the power of the male symbolic encapsulated in the hero. [. . .]

SUMMARY

The psychoanalytic background that has been discussed in this article is relevant to the pleasure and unpleasure offered by traditional narrative film. The scopophilic instinct (pleasure in looking at another person as an erotic object), and, in contradistinction, ego libido (forming identification processes) act as formations, mechanisms, which this cinema has played on. The image of woman as (passive) raw material for the (active) gaze of man takes the argument a step further into the structure of representation, adding a further layer demanded by the ideology of the patriarchal order as it is worked out in its favourite cinematic form — illusionistic narrative film. The argument returns again to the psychoanalytic background in that woman as representation signifies castration, inducing voyeuristic or fetishistic mechanisms to circumvent her threat. None of these interacting layers is intrinsic to film, but it is only in the film form that they can reach a perfect and beautiful contradiction, thanks to the possibility in the cinema of shifting the emphasis of the look. It is the place of the look that defines cinema, the possibility of varying it and exposing it. This is what makes cinema quite different in its voyeuristic potential from, say, striptease, theatre, shows, etc. Going far beyond highlighting a woman's to-be-looked-at-ness, cinema builds the way she is to be looked at into the spectacle itself. Playing on the tension between film as controlling the dimension of time (editing, narrative) and film as controlling the dimension of space (changes in distance, editing), cinematic codes create a gaze, a world, and an object, thereby producing an illusion cut to the measure of desire. It is these cinematic codes and their relationship to formative external structures that must be broken down before mainstream film and the pleasure it provides can be challenged.

To begin with (as an ending), the voyeuristic-scopophilic look that is a crucial part of traditional filmic pleasure can itself be broken down. There are three different looks associated with cinema: that of the camera as it records the pro-filmic event,* that of the audience as it watches the final product, and that of the characters at each other within the screen illusion. The conventions of narrative film deny the first two and subordinate them to the third, the conscious aim being always to eliminate intrusive camera presence and prevent a distancing awareness in the audience. Without these two absences (the material existence of the recording process, the critical reading of the spectator), fictional drama cannot achieve reality, obviousness and truth. Nevertheless, as this article has argued, the structure of looking in narrative fiction film contains a contradiction in its own premises: the female image as a castration threat constantly endangers the unity of the diegesis and bursts through the world of illusion as an intrusive, static, one-dimensional fetish. Thus the two looks materially present in time and space are obsessively subordinated to the neurotic needs of the male ego. The camera becomes the mechanism for producing an illusion of Renaissance space, flowing movements compatible with the human eye, an ideology of representation that revolves around the perception of the subject; the camera's look is disavowed in order to create a convincing world in which the spectator's surrogate can perform with ver-isimilitude. Simultaneously, the look of the audience is denied an intrinsic force: as soon as fetishistic representation of the female image threatens to break the spell of illusion, and the erotic image on the screen appears directly (without mediation) to the spectator, the fact of fetishisation, concealing as it does castration fear, freezes the look, fixates the spectator and prevents him from achieving any distance from the

* [i.e. that which is arranged in front of the camera.]

image in front of him.

This complex interaction of looks is specific to film. The first blow against the monolithic accumulation of traditional film conventions (already undertaken by radical film-makers) is to free the look of the camera into its materiality in time and space and the look of the audience into dialectics, passionate detachment. There is no doubt that this destroys the satisfaction, pleasure and privilege of the 'invisible guest', and highlights how film has depended on voyeuristic active/passive mechanisms. Women, whose image has continually been stolen and used for this end, cannot view the decline of the traditional film form with anything much more than sentimental regret.

(First published in *Screen*, vol. 16, no. 3, Autumn 1975.)

Realism and the Cinema: Notes on some Brechtian Theses

Throughout his life Brecht conducted, together with a continually experimenting artistic practice, a sustained theoretical reflection on his own and other's work. In the early thirties drawing up a project for a new critical review Brecht wrote:

> Amongst other things the review understands the word 'criticism' in its double sense — transforming *dialectically* the totality of subjects into a *permanent crisis* and thus conceiving the epoch as a critical period in both meanings of the term. And this point of view necessarily entails a rehabilitation of *theory* in its productive rights. [Brecht, 1970, p.93.]

The importance of theory and its productive effects in the aesthetic domain persists as a central concern throughout Brecht's writings. Two areas in which Brecht felt the need for theory to be particularly pressing were the debate on realism in which Lukács' positions achieved dominance in the early thirties and the relatively new cultural area of the cinema. His reflections on these topics were published in 1967 under the titles *Über den Realismus* and *Über Film* and these sections have since been totally translated into French and sections of them have recently been published in English. The aim of this article is to elaborate some of the positions advanced in those two works. It is not an attempt to extract a coherent theory from Brecht's theoretical writings (and still less to offer a coherent account of the relation of this theory to his artistic practice) but rather a set of digressions which take as their starting point some Brechtian theses.

THE CLASSIC REALIST TEXT

Criticism, at least Marxist criticism, must proceed methodically and concretely in each case, in short scientifically. Loose talk is of no help here, whatever its vocabulary. In no circumstances can the necessary guide-lines for a practical definition of realism be derived from literary works alone. (Be like Tolstoy — but without his weaknesses! Be like

Balzac — only up-to-date!) Realism is an issue not only for literature: it is a major political, philosophical and practical issue and must be handled and explained as such — as a matter of general human interest. [Brecht, 1974, p.45.]

One of the difficulties of any discussion about realism is the lack of any really effective vocabulary with which to discuss the topic. Most discussions turn on the problems of the production of discourse which will fully adequate the real. This notion of adequacy is accepted both by the realists and indeed by the anti-realists whose main argument is that no discourse can ever be adequate to the multifarious nature of the real. This notion of the real is, however, I wish to suggest, a notion which is tied to a particular type of literary production — the nineteenth century realist novel. The dominance of this novel form is such that people still tend to confuse the general question of realism with the particular forms of the nineteenth century realist novel. In order to make the discussion clearer I want therefore to attempt to define the structure which typifies the nineteenth century realist novel and to show how that structure can also be used to describe a great number of films. The detour through literature is necessary because, in many ways, the structure is much more obvious there and also because of the historical dominance of the classic realist novel over much film production. What to a large extent will be lacking in this article is the specific nature of the film form but this does not seem to me to invalidate the setting up of certain essential categories from which further discussion must progress. The structure I will attempt to disengage I shall call the classic realist text and I shall apply it to novels and films.

A classic realist text may be defined as one in which there is a hierarchy amongst the discourses which compose the text and this hierarchy is defined in terms of an empirical notion of truth. Perhaps the easiest way to understand this is through a reflection on the use of inverted commas within the classic realist novel. While those sections in the text which are contained in inverted commas may cause a certain difficulty for the reader — a certain confusion vis-à-vis what really is the case — this difficulty is abolished by the unspoken (or more accurately the unwritten) prose that surrounds them. In the classical realist novel the narrative prose functions as a metalanguage that can state all the truths in the object language — those words held in inverted commas — and can also explain the relation of this object language to the real. The metalanguage can thereby explain the relation of this object language to the world and the strange methods by which the object languages attempt to express truths which are straightforwardly conveyed in the metalanguage. What I have called an unwritten prose (or a metalanguage) is exactly that language which, while placing other languages between inverted commas and regarding them as certain material expressions which express certain meanings, regards those same meanings as finding transparent expression within the metalanguage itself. Transparent in the sense that the metalanguage is not regarded as material; it is dematerialised to achieve perfect representation — to let the identity of things shine through the window of words. For insofar as the metalanguage is treated itself as material — it, too, can be reinterpreted; new meanings can be found for it in a further metalanguage. The problem is the problem that has troubled western thought since the pre-Socratics recognised the separation between what was said and the act of saying. This separation must be thought both as time and space — as the space, which in the distance from page to eye or mouth to ear allows the possibility of misunderstanding — as the time taken to traverse the page or listen to an utterance which ensures the deferred interpretation of words which are always only defined by what follows. The problem is that in the moment that we say a sentence the meaning (what is said) seems fixed and evident but what is said does not exist solely for the moment and is open to further interpretations. Even in this formulation of the problem I have presupposed an original moment when there is strict contemporaneity between the saying and what is said, but the difficulty is more radical for there is no such original moment. The separation is always already there as we cannot locate the presence of what is said — distributed as it is through space — nor the present of what is said — distributed as it is through time.

This separation bears witness to the real as articulated. The thing represented does not appear in a moment of pure identity as it tears itself out of the world and presents itself, but rather is caught in an articulation in which each object is defined in a set of differences and oppositions.

It is this separation that the unwritten text attempts to *anneal*, to make whole, through denying its own status as writing — as marks of material difference distributed through time and space. Whereas other discourses within the text are considered as material which are open to reinterpretation, the narrative discourse simply allows reality to appear and denies its own status as articulation. This relationship between discourses can be clearly seen in the work of such a writer as George Eliot. In the scene in *Middlemarch* where Mr Brooke goes to visit the Dagleys' farm we read two different languages. One is the educated, well-meaning, but not very intelligent discourse of Mr Brooke and the other is the uneducated, violent and very nearly unintelligible discourse of the drunken Dagley. But the whole dialogue is surrounded by a metalanguage, which being unspoken is also unwritten, and which places these discourses in inverted commas and can thus discuss these discourses' relation to truth — a truth which is illuminatingly revealed in the metalanguage. The metalanguage reduces the object languages into a simple division between form and content and extracts the meaningful content from the useless form. One can see this process at work in the following passage which ends the scene:

> He [Mr Brooke] had never been insulted on his own land before, and had been inclined to regard himself as a general favourite (we are all apt to do so, when we think of our own amiability more than what other people are likely to want of us). When he had quarrelled with Caleb Garth twelve years before he had thought that the tenants would be pleased at the landlord's taking everything into his own hands.
>
> Some who follow the narrative of this experience may wonder at the midnight darkness of Mr Dagley; but nothing was easier in those times than for a hereditary farmer of his grade to be ignorant, in spite somehow of having a rector in the twin parish who was a gentleman to the backbone, a curate nearer at hand who preached more learnedly than the rector, a landlord who had gone into everything, especially fine art and social improvement, and all the lights of Middlemarch only three miles off. [Eliot, 1967, pp.432-3.]

This passage provides the necessary interpretations for the discourses that we have read earlier in the chapter. Both the discourses of Dagley and Mr Brooke are revealed as springing from two types of ignorance which the metalanguage can expose and reveal. So we have Mr Brooke's attitude to what his tenants thought of him contrasted with the reality which is available through the narrative prose. No discourse is allowed to speak for itself but rather it must be placed in a context which will reduce it to a simple explicable content. And in the claim that the narrative prose has direct access to a final reality we can find the claim of the classic realist novel to present us with the truths of human nature. The ability to reveal the truth about Mr Brooke is the ability that guarantees the generalisations of human nature.

Thus then a first definition of the classic realist text — but does this definition carry over into films, where it is certainly less evident where to locate the dominant discourse? It seems to me that it does and in the following fashion. The narrative prose achieves its position of dominance because it is in the position of knowledge and this function of knowledge is taken up in the cinema by the narration of events. Through the knowledge we gain from the narrative we can split the discourses of the various characters from their situation and compare what is said in these discourses with what has been revealed to us through narration. The camera shows us what happens — it tells the truth against which we can measure the discourses. A good example of this classical realist structure is to be found in Pakula's film *Klute*. This film is of particular interest because it was widely praised for its realism on its release. Perhaps even more significantly it tended to be praised for its realistic presentation of the leading woman, Bree (played by Jane Fonda).

In *Klute* the relationship of dominance between discourses is peculiarly accentuated by the fact that the film is interspersed with fragments of Bree talking to her psychiatrist. This subjective discourse can be exactly measured against the reality provided by the unfolding of the story. Thus all her talk of independence is portrayed as finally an illusion as we discover, to no great surprise but to our immense relief, what she really wants is to settle down in the mid-West with John Klute (the detective played by Donald Sutherland) and have a family. The final sequence of the film is particularly telling in this respect. While Klute and Bree pack their bags to leave, the soundtrack records Bree at her last meeting with her psychiatrist. Her own estimation of the situation is that it most probably won't work but the reality of the image ensures us that this is the way it will really be. Indeed Bree's monologue is even more interesting — for in relation to the reality of the image it marks a definite advance on her previous statements. She has gained insight through the plot development and like many good heroines of classic realist texts her discourse is more nearly adequate to the truth at the end of the film than at the beginning. But if a progression towards knowledge is what marks Bree, it is possession of knowledge which marks the narrative, the reader of the film and John Klute himself. For Klute is privileged by the narrative as the one character whose discourse is also a discourse of knowledge. Not only is Klute a detective and thus can solve the problem of his friend's disappearance — he is also a man, and a man who because he has not come into contact with the city has not had his virility undermined. And it is as a full-blooded man that he can know not only the truth of the mystery of the murders but also the truth of the woman Bree. Far from being a film which goes any way to portraying a woman liberated from male definition (a common critical response), *Klute* exactly guarantees that the real essence of woman can only be discovered and defined by a man.

The analysis sketched here is obviously very schematic but what, hopefully, it does show is that the structure of the classic realist text can be found in film as well. That narrative of events — the knowledge which the film provides of how things really are — is the metalanguage in which we can talk of the various characters in the film. What would still remain to be done in the elaboration of the structure of the classic realist text in cinema is a more detailed account of the actual mechanisms by which the narrative is privileged (and the way in which one or more of the characters within the narrative can be equally privileged) and also a history of the development of this dominant narrative. On the synchronic level it would be necessary to attempt an analysis of the relationship between the various types of shot and their combination into sequences — are there for example certain types of shot which are coded as subjective and therefore subordinate to others which are guaranteed as objective? In addition how does music work as the guarantee or otherwise of truth? On the diachronic level it would be necessary to study how this form was produced — what relationship obtains between the classic realist text and technical advances such as the development of the talkie? What ideological factors were at work in the production and dominance of the classic realist text?

To return, however, to the narrative discourse. It is necessary to attempt to understand the type of relations that this dominant discourse produces. The narrative discourse cannot be mistaken in its identifications because the narrative discourse is not present as discourse — as articulation. The unquestioned nature of the narrative discourse entails that the only problem that reality poses is to go and look and see what *Things* there *are*. The relationship between the reading subject and the real is placed as one of pure specularity. The real is not articulated — it is. These features imply two essential features of the classic realist text:

1. The classic realist text cannot deal with the real as contradictory.
2. In a reciprocal movement the classic realist text ensures the position of the subject in a relation of dominant specularity.

THE CLASSIC REALIST TEXT AS PROGRESSIVE ART

In general, do not be content with providing an insight into the literature of the country in question, but follow the details of literary life itself. Consider literary phenomena as events and as social events. [Brecht, 1970, p.77.]

It may be objected that the account that I have given of the classic literary text is deficient in the following extremely important fashion. It ignores what is the usual criterion for realism, that is to say subject matter. The category of the classic realist text lumps together in book and film *The Grapes of Wrath* and *The Sound of Music, L'Assommoir* and *Toad of Toad Hall*. In order to find a criterion with which to make distinctions within the area of the classic realist text it is necessary to reflect on contradiction. I have stated that the classic realist text cannot deal with the real in its contradiction because of the unquestioned status of the representation at the level of the dominant discourse. In order to understand how contradiction can be dealt with it is necessary to investigate the workings of an operation that is often opposed to representation, namely montage.

In his essay on 'Word and Image' in *The Film Sense,* Eisenstein* defines montage. Amongst numerous examples of montage he quotes the following from Ambrose Bierce's *Fantastic Fables*:

A Woman in widow's weeds was weeping upon a grave. 'Console

---

* [Sergei Eisenstein, perhaps the most influential early Soviet film maker.]

yourself, madam,' said a Sympathetic Stranger. 'Heaven's mercies are infinite. There is another man somewhere, beside your husband, with whom you can still be happy.'

'There was,' she sobbed — 'there was, but this is his grave.' [Eisenstein, 1968, pp.14-15.]

Eisenstein explains the effect of this fable in terms of an interaction between the visual representations in the story. The woman is a representation and so is the mourning dress — they are, in Eisenstein's terms, objectively representable — but the juxtaposition of these representations gives rise to a new image that is not representable — namely that the woman is a widow. It is the expectation created by the juxtaposition which is undercut by the final line uttered by the woman. For the moment we shall only notice the following points:

1. that Eisenstein, concerned very largely with a simple definition of representation, fails to recognise that widow is just as objective a representation as woman or mourning dress, and

2. that montage involves both an interaction between representations and a shock.

[...] Eisenstein thinks of the world as being composed of basic objects available to sight which are then linked together in various ways by the perceiving subject with the aid of his past experiences. [...] He takes the example of Vronsky looking at his watch, after Anna Karenina has told him that she is pregnant, and being so shocked that he sees the position of the hands but not the time. Thus the position of the hands is the primitive object in the world and the time is what the human subject creates through his linking of this object with other items of his experience. Montage is thus, for Eisenstein, in this passage (which must not be confused with Eisenstein's cinematic practice), the manipulation of definite representations to produce images in the mind of the spectator. But now it can be seen that this definition of montage does not contradict representation at all. If we understand by representation the rendering of identities in the world then Eisenstein's account of montage is not opposed to representation but is simply a secondary process which comes after representation. Eisenstein would have montage linking onto representation but not in any sense challenging it. The representation starts from an identity in the world which it re-presents, the montage starts from representations, identities, and combines them to form an image.

Eisenstein's acceptance of representation can be seen in those passages where representation is contrasted with montage. For Eisenstein the opposite to montage is 'affadavit-exposition' which he defines as *'in film terms, representations shot from a single set-up'* [ibid., p.37]. Thus montage is the showing of the same representation from different points

222

of view. And it is from this point that we can begin to challenge Eisenstein's conception of montage. A point of view suggests two things. Firstly a view — something that is seen — and secondly a location from which the view may be had, the sight may be seen. Thus the suggestion is that there are different locations from which we can see. But in all cases the sight remains the same — the activity of representation is not the determining factor in the sight seen but simply the place from where it is seen. The inevitable result of this is that there is something the same which we all see but which appears differently because of our position. But if there is identity; if there is something over and above the views which can be received at different points then this identity must be discernable from some other 'point of view'. And this neutral point of view is exactly the 'representations shot from a single set-up'.

What is at work in Eisenstein's argument is the idea that there is some fixed reality which is available to us from an objective point of view (the single set-up). Montage is simply putting these fixed elements together in such a way that the subject brings forth other elements in his experience — but without any change in the identities, the elements that are being rendered. It is essential to realise that this account leaves both subject and object unchallenged and that montage becomes a kind of super-representation which is more effective at demonstrating the real qualities of the object through the links it can form within the subject. Thus Eisenstein would analyse the Bierce story as the representation of a given set of elements which are first organised in one way then in another. There is, however, no such set of fixed elements in the Bierce story. It is not that there is a set of elements which the reader composes 'in his mind' but rather that these elements are already determined by the method of representation. What Eisenstein ignores is that the method of representation (the language: verbal or cinematic) determines in its structural activity (the oppositions which can be articulated) both the places where the object 'appears' and the 'point' from which the object is seen. It is this point which is exactly the place allotted to the reading subject.

A careful analysis of the Bierce story may enable us to discover how montage operates and why that operation is difficult to grasp. We can read three different discourses at work in the Bierce story (a discourse being defined as a set of significant oppositions). The narrative discourse, the discourse of the Sympathetic Stranger and the discourse of the Woman. The question is whether, as Eisenstein holds, the narrative discourse represents simply a woman and a mourning dress. But 'woman' is not some simple identity as Eisenstein would have us believe. Whereas the Sympathetic Stranger identifies woman in terms of religion and state — thus our relationships are determined in heaven and are institutionalised by the state on earth — the Woman determines her own identity as 'woman' in terms of desire and transgression — relationships are formed through the transgressing of the state's institutions and this transgression is linked with a certain sexuality; for relationships between a man and a woman outside the bond of holy matrimony are explicitly sexual. We can now understand that the montage works through a contest between the identities offered by the different discourses. In the Bierce story, the woman's statement jars with what has gone before so that we re-read it — the identifications that we made (that were made for us) are undermined by new ones. What is thrown into doubt is exactly the identity (the nature) of woman and this doubt is achieved through the 'shock' of the woman's statement as the identity already proferred is subverted. It is also clear from this analysis that there is no neutral place from which we can see the view and where all the points are located. There is no possible language of 'affadavit-exposition' that would show the scene 'as it really is'. For how we see the scene will be determined by the way in which we identify 'woman' — and this determination is a feature of the available discourses; the discourses in which 'woman' can figure.

We are still, however, left with the problem of how we can mistake this effect of montage, as I have suggested Eisenstein has done, and the answer to this question can be found in the apparent similarity of the discourses in the Bierce story. For the three discourses are so similar that we can be persuaded to read them as one. All that is missing from the first and second is provided by the third. The third discourse can be read as 'closing' the text. For with the information thus given to us we can read the previous discourses in a 'final' — that is to say *once and for all* — manner. We can fill in the gaps in the first two discourses — see the real identities which are mistaken. But this is to ignore the fact that what are at question in the story are different discourses. Different discourses can be defined as discourses in which different oppositions are possible. Although at one level — the level of the legal relationship to the body and the grave — both discourses coincide (she *is* or *is not* the wife), at another level there are a set of oppositions of an emotional nature (she *does* or *does not* mourn some man) which the stranger cannot articulate outside the oppositions determined by the legal relationship. Bierce's story, through the coincidences between the discourses on one level, suggests to Eisenstein a set of identities in the world. But the identities rest in the discourses. Thus opposed to Eisenstein's concept of montage resting on the juxtapositions of identities already rendered, we could talk of montage as the effect generated by a conflict of discourse in which the oppositions available in the juxtaposed discourses are contradictory and in conflict.

All this by way of explaining that the classic realist text (a heavily 'closed' discourse) cannot deal with the real in its contradictions and that in the same movement it fixes the subject in a point of view from which everything becomes obvious. There is, however, a level of contradiction into which the classic realist text can enter. This is the contradiction between the dominant discourse of the text and the dominant ideological discourses of the time. Thus a classic realist text in which a strike is represented as a just struggle in which oppressed workers attempt to gain some of their rightful wealth would be in contradiction with certain contemporary ideological discourses and as such might be classified as progressive. It is here that subject matter enters into the argument and where we can find the justification for Marx and Engels' praise of Balzac and Lenin's texts on the revolutionary force of Tolstoy's texts which ushered the Russian peasant onto the stage of history. Within contemporary films one could think of the films of Costa-Gavras or such television documentaries as *Cathy Come Home*. What is, however, still impossible for the classic realist text is to offer any perspectives for struggle due to its inability to investigate contradiction. It is thus not surprising that these films tend either to be linked to a social-democratic conception of progress — if we reveal injustices then they will go away — or certain *ouvrieriste* tendencies which tend to see the working class, outside any dialectical movement, as the simple posses-sors of truth. It is at this point that Brecht's demand that literary and artistic productions be regarded as social events gains its force. The contradictions between the dominant discourse in a classic realist text and the dominant ideological discourses at work in a society are what provide the criteria for discriminating within the classic realist text. And these criteria will often resolve themselves into questions of subject-matter. That this tends to leave open any question about the eternal values of art is not something that should worry us. As Brecht remarks:

> To be frank, I do not set such an excessively high value on the concept of endurance. How can we foresee whether future generations will wish to preserve the memory of these figures [figures created by Balzac or Tolstoy]? (Balzac and Tolstoy will scarcely be in a position to oblige them to do so, however ingenious the methods with which they set their plots in motion.) I suspect it will depend on whether it will be a socially relevant statement if someone says: 'That' (and 'that' will refer to a contemporary) 'is a Père Goriot character'. Perhaps such characters will not survive? Perhaps they precisely arose in a cramping web of relations of a type which will no longer exist. [Brecht, 1974, p.46.]

MOMENTS OF SUBVERSION AND STRATEGIES OF SUBVERSION

The practical methods of the revolution are not revolutionary, they are dictated by the class struggle. It is for this reason that great writers find themselves ill at ease in the class struggle, they behave as though the struggle was already finished, and they deal with the new situation, conceived as collectivist, which is the aim of the revolution. The revolution of the great writers is permanent. [Brecht, 1970, p.25.]

In [1974] *Screen* published Franco Fortini's text on 'The Writer's Mandate' which took the position that art is that area which deals with the irreconcilable contradictions of life over and beyond the particular contradictions of the class struggle and of their successful resolution in the revolution. It was suggested in the Editorial that, in order to avoid a fall into romantic and ultra-left positions, these irreconcilable differences had to be theorised within the scientific concepts offered to us by psychoanalysis. Freud's theory is a theory of the construction of the subject: the entry of the small infant into language and society and the methods by which it learns what positions, as subject, it can take up. This entry into the symbolic (the whole cultural space which is structured, like language, through a set of differences and oppositions) is most easily traced in the analytic situation through that entry which is finally determining for the infant — the problem of sexual difference. Freud's insight is that the unproblematic taking up of the position of the subject entails the repression of the whole mechanism of the subject's construction. The subject is seen as the founding source of meanings — unproblematically standing outside an articulation in which it is, in fact, defined. This view of the subject as founding source is philosophically encapsulated in Descartes' *cogito*: I think, therefore I am — the I in simple evidence to itself provides a moment of pure presence which can found the enterprise of analysing the world. Jacques Lacan, the French psychoanalyst, has read Freud as reformulating the Cartesian *cogito* and destroying the subject as source and foundation — Lacan rewrites the *cogito*, in the light of Freud's discoveries as: I think where I am not and I am where I do not think. We can understand this formulation as the indicating of the fundamental misunderstanding (*méconnaissance*) which is involved in the successful use of language (or any other area of the symbolic which is similarly structured) in which the subject is continually ignored as being caught up in a process of articulation to be taken as a fixed place founding the discourse. The unconscious is that effect of language which escapes the conscious subject in the distance between the act of signification in which the subject passes from signifier to signifier and what is signified in which the subject finds himself in place as, for example, the pronoun 'I'. The importance of phenomena like verbal slips is that they testify to the existence of the unconscious through the distance between what was said and what the conscious subject intended to say. They thus testify to the distance between the subject of the act of signification and the conscious subject (the ego). In this distance there is opened a gap which is the area of desire. What is essential to all of those psychic productions which Freud uses in the analytic interpretation is that they bear witness to the lack of control of the conscious subject over his discourses. The mechanisms of the unconscious can indeed be seen as the mechanisms of language. Condensation is the work of metaphor which brings together two signifieds under one signifier and displacement is the constant process along the signifying chain. The ego is constantly caught in this fundamental misunderstanding (*méconnaissance*) about language in which from an illusory present it attempts to read only one signified as present in the metaphor and attempts to bring the signifying chain to an end in a perpetually deferred present.

The relationship between the unconscious and desire, the subject and language is concisely summarised by Lacan in the following passage:

> There is not *an* unconscious because then there would be an unconscious desire which was obtuse, heavy, caliban like, even animal like, an unconscious desire lifted up from the depths which would be primitive and would have to educate itself to the superior level of consciousness. Completely on the contrary there is desire because there is unconsciousness (*de l'inconscient*) — that's to say language which escapes the subject in its structure and in its effects and there is always at the level of language something which is beyond consciousness and it is there that one can situate the function of desire. [Lacan, cited in Wahl, 1968.]

It is clear that the classic realist text, as defined above, guarantees the position of the subject exactly outside any articulation — the whole text works on the concealing of the dominant discourse as articulation — instead the dominant discourse presents itself exactly as the presentation of objects to the reading subject. But within the classic realist text the dominant discourse can be subverted, brought into question — the position of the subject may be rendered problematic. If we return to our original example of George Eliot we can see this process of subversion at work in *Daniel Deronda*. Within the text there is a discourse, the writings of Mordecai in Hebrew which are unmastered by the dominant discourse. The text tells us that they are untranslatable and thus that there is an area outside the text's control. This area is exactly the area of the mother-tongue (Daniel's mother is Jewish) and this mother-tongue subverts the assured positions of both the characters in the text and the reading subject. My business here is not to give a full analysis of George Eliot's work but rather to indicate the possibility of *moments* within a classical realist text which subvert it and its evident status for subject and object. [. . .] These *moments* are those elements which escape the control of the dominant discourse in the same way as a neurotic symptom or a verbal slip attest to the lack of control of the conscious subject. They open up another area than that of representation — of subject and object caught in an eternal paralysed fixity — in order to investigate the very movement of articulation and difference — the movement of desire. [. . .] Over and above these *moments* of subversion, however, there are what one might call *strategies* of subversion. Instead of a dominant discourse which is transgressed at various crucial moments we can find a systematic refusal of any such dominant discourse. One of the best examples of a cinema which practices certain strategies of subversion are the films of Roberto Rossellini. In *Germany Year Zero,* for example, we can locate a multitude of ways in which the reading subject finds himself without a position from which the film can be regarded. Firstly, and most importantly, the fact that the narrative is not privileged in any way with regard to the characters' discourses. The narrative does not produce for us the knowledge with which we can then judge the truth of those discourses. Rather than the narrative providing us with knowledge — it provides us with various settings. Just as in Brecht the 'fable' serves simply as a procedure to produce the various *gests,* so in Rossellini the story simply provides a framework for various scenes which then constitute the picture of Germany in year zero. [. . .] Secondly, Rossellini's narrative introduces many elements which are not in any sense resolved and which deny the possibility of regarding the film as integrated through a dominant discourse. The Allied soldiers, the street kids, the landlord, the Teacher's house — all these provide elements which stretch outside the narrative of the film and deny its dominance. [. . .]

It may be objected that it is deliberately perverse to tear Rossellini away from realism with which he has been firmly connected both through his own statements and through critical reception. The realist element in Rossellini is not simply located in the subject matter, the traditional criterion of realism, for I have already argued that the subject matter is a secondary condition for realism. What typifies the classic realist text is the way the subject matter is ordered and articulated rather than its origins. To deal with the facts of the world is, in itself, not only a realist but also a materialist viewpoint. The materialist, however, must regard these materials as ordered within a certain mode of production, within which they find their definition. And it is here that one could begin to isolate that element of realist ideology which does figure in Rossellini's films as a certain block. If the reading subject is not offered any certain mode of entry into what is presented on the screen, he is offered a certain mode of entry to the screen itself. For the facts presented by the camera, if they are not ordered in fixed and final fashion amongst themselves, *are* ordered in themselves. The camera, in Rossellini's films, is not articulated as part of the productive process of the film. What it shows is in some sense beyond argument and it is here that Rossellini's films show the traditional realist weakness of being unable to deal with contradiction. In *Viva l'Italia* the glaring omission of the film is the absence of Cavour. It is wrong to attack this omission on purely political grounds for it is an inevitable result of a certain lack of questioning of the camera itself. Garibaldi can be contrasted with Francisco II of Naples because their different conceptions of the world are so specifically tied to different historical eras that the camera can cope with their contradictions within an historical perspective. Here is the way the world is now — there is the way the world was then. But to introduce Cavour would involve a simultaneous contradiction — a class contradiction. At this point the camera itself, as a neutral agent, would become impossible. For it would have to offer two present contradictory articulations of the world and thus reveal its own presence. This cannot happen within a Rossellini film where if we are continually aware of our presence in the cinema (particularly in his historical films) — that presence itself is not questioned in any way. We are not allowed any particular position to read the film but we are allowed the position of a reader — an unproblematic viewer — an eternally human nature working on the material provided by the camera.

A possible way of advancing on Rossellini's practice (there are no obvious films which have marked such an advance although some of Godard's early films might be so considered) would be to develop the possibility of articulating contradiction. Much in the way that James Joyce in *Ulysses* and *Finnegans Wake* investigated the contradictory ways of articulating reality through an investigation of the different forms of language, one could imagine a more radical strategy of subversion than that practised by Rossellini in which the possibilities of the camera would be brought more clearly into play. What would mark such a cinema and indeed any cinema of subversion would be that feature quoted by Brecht at the beginning of this section — the fact that it would be ill at ease in the class struggle, always concerned with an area of contradiction beyond the necessity of the present revolution — the ineliminable contradictions of the sexes, the eternal struggle between Desire and Law, between articulation and position.

A POSSIBLE CATEGORY: THE REVOLUTIONARY TEXT

Socialist emulation forms individuals in a different way and produces different individuals. Then there is the further question whether it is anyway as individuating a process as the capitalist competitive struggle. [Brecht, 1974, p.47.]

It is precisely this sharp opposition between work and leisure, which is peculiar to the capitalist mode of production, that separates all intellectual activity into those activities which serve work and those activities which serve leisure. And those that serve leisure are organised into a system for the reproduction of the labour force. Distractions must not contain anything which is contained in work.

229

Distractions, in the interest of production, are committed to non-production. Naturally, it is not thus that one can create a style of life which forms a unique and coherent whole. And this cannot be put down to the fact that art is dragged into the productive process, but to the fact that it is incompletely involved in the productive process and that it must create an island of 'non-production'. The man who buys a ticket transforms himself in front of the screen into an idler and an exploiter (*Ausbeuter*). Since booty (*Beute*) is placed within him here he is as it were victim of im-ploitation (*Einbeutung*). [Brecht, 1970a, pp.178-9.]

In ['Diderot, Brecht, Eisenstein'] Roland Barthes suggests that revolutionary artists such as Eisenstein and Brecht must, of necessity, remain within the world of representation. Barthes throughout his article uses the structure of fetishism as his model for the structure of representation. Stephen Heath's ['Lessons from Brecht'] investigates this comparison at length but it might be useful to indicate briefly the importance of the concept of fetishism. The fetish is that object which places the subject in a position of security outside of that terrifying area of difference opened up by the perception of the mother's non-possession of the phallus. Although most popular accounts of fetishism concentrate on the fetishised objects, it is exemplary for Barthes as a structure which holds both subject and object in place — it is the fetish above all that holds the subject in position. What is essential to Barthes' argument is the idea that the subject must always be the same — caught in the same position *vis-à-vis* the world. Within this view a revolutionary work of art can do no more than provide a correct representation (provided by the Party) of the world. It may be helpful to attain this goal to subvert the position of the subject so that his acceptance of the new representation is facilitated but finally the revolutionary artist is committed (condemned) to the world of representation.

Within the framework I have constructed in this article one could say that the revolutionary artist may practice certain strategies of subversion but must finally content himself with the production of a progressive realist text. The question I want to raise here, and it must be emphasised that it can only be raised, is the possibility of *another* activity which rather than the simple subversion of the subject or the representation of different (and *correct*) identities, would consist of the displacement of the subject within ideology — a different constitution of the subject. It has been accepted, particularly over the last ten years in France, that the subject is the crucial concept for a Marxist theory of ideology — a theory which would attempt to explain the non-coercive ways in which the capitalist mode of production ensures the reproduction of labour power and would also attempt to furnish guidelines for the practical tasks in the question of changing ideology — the whole problem of the cultural revolution. One of the difficulties of using the subject as such a key term is that it is an ideological notion which is willy-nilly transformed into a descriptive scientific concept. The sub-ject — that which under-lies experience — is a production, very largely, of modern European philosophy from Descartes to its most sophisticated articulation in the philosophers of German Idealism.

The main problem facing anyone wishing to articulate a theory of film within a Marxist theory of ideology is that by and large no such Marxist theory exists. Marx never really returned to the subject after 1846 and none of the other great Marxist theoreticians (with the possible exception of Gramsci) has found the time to devote themselves to the problem. In many ways the starting point of any such investigation must be Louis Althusser's essay on the topic entitled 'Ideology and Ideological State Apparatuses (Notes towards an Investigation)' [Althusser, 1971]. In this essay Althusser puts forward and defends the thesis that ideology has no history. By this he does not mean that specific ideologies do not have a history involving both internal and external factors but that the very form of ideology is always the same. Althusser argues that the central and unvarying feature of ideology is that it represents the imaginary relationship of individuals to their real conditions of existence. Ideology is always 'imaginary' because these representations place the subject in position in his society. In other words ideology always has a place for a founding source outside the real articulations.

Before discussing this thesis there are two preliminary points that must be made, which while they do not touch directly on the thesis need to be borne in mind when discussing it. The first, which I have already touched on, is that the subject is an ideological notion. Moreover, it is an ideological notion which is tied very closely to the rise of the bourgeoisie. It would be outside the scope of this article and beyond the author's competence to trace the evolution of this notion with any precision. Suffice to say that Cartesian philosophy, Newtonian physics and the grammar of Port-Royal* all involve very precisely that notion of a unified subject of experience and that the birth of this notion in the seventeenth century suggests very important links with the growing economic and political domination of the European bourgeoisie — the works of Locke provide perhaps the most obvious example of the need for this category of subject in the justification both of the new science and the new civil order. All this simply by way of a warning of the difficulties of dealing with the notion of the subject.

Secondly it is necessary to realise what an important break Althusser's thesis marks with certain methods of Hegelianising Marx. For Althusser is concerned to attack that view which, seeing ideology as 'merely' illusory, holds out the promise that the victorious conclusion to the class

* [Port-Royal: the centre of Jansenism in seventeenth-century France. See Goldmann, 1964.]

struggle will result in the arrival of the new and true ideology which will correspond to the real. This view merely incarnates the Hegelian vision that being and consciousness will finally coincide within a simple view of the end of class struggle. It is the proletariat that will realise the beautiful dream of the real becoming rational and the rational becoming real. Whatever reservations one may have about Althusser's thesis, it is important that they do not involve a slipping back into such a Hegelian model with all the lack of contradiction and struggle that it implies.

To return, however, directly to Althusser's thesis. It seems an inevitable result of this thesis that art can be allotted no specific field of action other than its effects on the content of ideology. As such art remains firmly within the realm of ideology, being simply one of a number of internal factors within the evolution of ideologies. This is, of course, quite compatible with classical Marxist positions on art, but traditional Marxist thought has often felt itself embarrassed by this simple lumping of art into ideology — one of the most famous examples of such an embarrassment is Marx's own attempt to deal with the problem of Greek art. [See Marx, 1973, pp.110-11.] There is, however, another way in which this problem can be approached and it is suggested by Brecht's remark on the position of the spectator in the cinema (quoted at the beginning of this section) and by much of Brecht's theory and practice. Here one would have to deny both Althusser's (and Marx's) thesis that ideology has no history and at the same time delimit a special area of activity which is neither that of science nor that of ideology. This activity might be characterised by its ability actually to work on and transform the very form of ideology — to change the position of the subject within ideology.

What Brecht suggests in his comments on the spectator in the cinema is that the very position offered to the spectator is one that guarantees the necessary re-production of labour power. It is the cinema's ability to place the spectator in the position of a unified subject that ensures the contradiction between his working activity which is productive and the leisure activity in which he is constantly placed as consumer. Althusser makes the very important point in his essay that ideology is not a question of ideas circulating in people's heads but is inscribed in certain material practices. The reactionary practice of the cinema is that which involves this petrification of the spectator in a position of pseudo-dominance offered by the metalanguage. This metalanguage, resolving as it does all contradictions, places the spectator outside the realm of contradiction and of action — outside of production.

Two films which suggest a way of combating this dominance of the metalanguage, without falling into an agnostic position *vis-à-vis* all discourses (which would be the extreme of a subversive cinema — intent merely on disrupting any position of the subject) are *Kuhle Wampe* (the film in which Brecht participated) and Godard-Gorin's *Tout va bien*. In both films the narrative is in no way privileged as against the characters. Rather the narrative serves simply as the method by which various situations can be articulated together. The emphasis is on the particular scenes and the knowledge that can be gained from them rather than the providing of a knowledge which requires no further activity — which just is there on the screen. Indeed the presentation of the individual's discourses is never stripped away from the character's actions but is involved in them. Whether it is a question of the petit-bourgeois and the workers discussing the waste of coffee in the S-Bahn or the various monologues in *Tout va bien* — it is not a question of the discourses being presented as pure truth content which can be measured against the truth provided by the film. Rather the discourses are caught up in certain modes of life which are linked to the place of the agent in the productive process. The unemployed workers know that waste is an inevitable part of the capitalist process because they experience it every day in their search for work. Equally the workers in the meat factory know that the class struggle is not finished for they experience the exploitation of their labour in such concrete details as the time that is allowed them to go to the toilet. The film does not provide this knowledge ready-made in a dominant discourse but in the contradictions offered, the reader has to produce a meaning for the film (it is quite obvious in films of this sort that the meaning produced will depend on the class-positions of the reader). It is this emphasis on the reader as producer (more obvious in *Tout va bien* which is in many ways more Brechtian than *Kuhle Wampe*) which suggests that these films do not just offer a different representation for the subject but a different set of relations to both the fictional material and 'reality'.

Very briefly this change could be characterised as the introduction of time (history) into the very area of representation so that it is included within it. It is no accident that both films end with this same emphasis on time and its concomitant change. 'But who will change the world' (*Kuhle Wampe*) — 'We must learn to live historically' (*Tout va bien*) — this emphasis on time and change embodied both within the film and in the position offered to the reader suggests that a revolutionary socialist ideology might be different in form as well as content. It also throws into doubt Barthes' thesis that revolutionary art is finally caught in the same space of representation that has persisted for 2,000 years in the West. The monolithic conception of representation ignores the fact that post-Einsteinian physics offers a conception of representation in which both subject and object are no longer caught in fixed positions but caught up in time.

It might be thought that this possibility of change, of transformation — in short, of production — built into the subject-object relation (which could no longer be characterised in this simple fashion) simply reduplicates the Hegelian error of final reconciliation between the orders

233

of being and consciousness. But this is not so in so far as this possibility of change built into the relation does not imply the inevitable unfolding of a specific series of changes but simply the possibility of change — an area of possible transformations contained within the relation.

It seems that some such account must be offered if one wishes to allow the possibility of a revolutionary art. Otherwise it seems inevitable that art can simply be progressive or subversive and Brecht's whole practice would be a marriage of the two, in which subversive effects were mechanically used simply to aid the acceptance of the progressive content of his work.

A DEFINITE CATEGORY: REACTIONARY ART

It is our metaphysicians of the press, our partisans of 'art' who would like more emphasis on 'fate' in human processes. For a long time now fate, which was once a sublime notion, has been nothing more than a mediocre received idea: by reconciling himself to his condition, man arrives at that much longed for 'transfiguration' and 'interiorisation'. It is equally a pure notion of the class struggle: one class 'determines' the fate of the other. [Brecht, 1970a p.179.]

One fashionable way of receiving and recuperating Brecht, which has been at work since the beginning of the Cold War, is to see him as a satirist ridiculing his contemporary society and the excesses of capitalism and fascism. This approach negates the productive element in Brecht's work and turns the techniques for the production of alienation effects into pure narcissistic signals of an 'intellectual' work of 'art'. A very typical example of this vulgarisation and de-politicisation of Brecht can be seen in Lindsay Anderson's *O Lucky Man!* An explicitly Brechtian film — the loosely connected scenes are counter-pointed by the Alan Price songs — the film pretends to offer a tableau of England in 1973 much as *Tout va bien* attempts to offer a tableaux of France in 1972. But whereas in the French film the tableaux are used to reflect the contradictions within the society — the different articulations of reality — in the English film tableaux are all used to express a stereotyped reality of England which the spectator is invited to enjoy from his superior position. The scenes may seem to be dominant over the reality revealed by the narrative but as the film progresses along its endless development it becomes obvious that the narrative simply confirms the evident truths which are offered to us on the screen. And these truths turn out to be that endless message of the reactionary petit-bourgeois intellectual — that we can do nothing against the relentless and evil progress of society (run as it is by a bunch of omnipotent capitalists with the morality of gangsters) except note our superiority to it. A longer analysis of the film might well be in order were it not for the fact that

Walter Benjamin had already written the definitive critique of this particularly impoverished artistic strategy. It is perhaps a testament to the paucity of petit-bourgeois imagination in the era of monopoly capitalism that what Benjamin wrote forty years ago about the satirical poet Erich Kästner can be applied word for word to *O Lucky Man!* It is for this reason that the Benjamin article is included in this issue on Brecht.

(First published in *Screen,* vol. 15, no. 2.)

References

Althusser, L. (1971), 'Ideology and Ideological State Apparatuses (Notes Towards an Investigation)' in *Lenin and Philosophy, and Other Essays,* London: New Left Books.

Barthes, R. (1974), 'Diderot, Brecht, Eisenstein', *Screen,* vol. 15, no.2, Summer 1974.

Brecht, B. (1970), *Sur le Réalisme,* Paris: l'Arche.

Brecht, B. (1970a), *Sur le Cinéma,* Paris: l'Arche.

Brecht, B. (1974), 'Against Georg Lukács', *New Left Review,* no. 84, 1974.

Eisenstein, S, (1968), *The Film Sense,* London: Dobson.

Eliot, G. (1967), *Middlemarch,* London.

Fortini, F. (1974), 'The Writer's Mandate', *Screen,* vol. 15, no.1, Spring, 1974.

Goldmann, L. (1974), *The Hidden God,* London: Routledge and Kegan Paul.

Heath, S. (1974), 'Lessons from Brecht', *Screen,* vol. 15, no.2, Summer 1974.

Marx, K. (1973), *Grundrisse: Introduction to the Critique of Political Economy,* Harmondworth: Penguin.

Wahl, F. (ed.) (1968), *Qu' est-ce que le structuralisme?,* Paris.

Stars as Signs

Stars as images are constructed in all kinds of media texts other than films, but nonetheless, films remain [. . .] privileged instances of the star's image. [Here accordingly we are concerned with the question as to how stars function in films themselves. We approach this question initially, principally from the point of view of character.] It is assumed that one can conceptualise a star's total image as distinct from the particular character that she or he plays in a given film. [In order to examine the] relationship between these two entities, [therefore, it is necessary, first, to consider] the notion of character itself. [. . .]

STARS AND 'CHARACTER'

In films, stars play characters, that is, constructed representations of persons. To understand how stars 'are' in films, we need to understand what is meant by character in film and how it is achieved.

This understanding is made peculiarly difficult by the fact that, in so far as there has been any theoretical consideration of character in fiction (in any medium), it has primarily been directed to exposing its fallacious aspects — having demonstrated that characters are not real people, that they are an effect of the text, constructions, critics and theorists have not proceeded to an examination of how this effect, so widely known and understood, is achieved, what the rules of construction are. [. . .]

I have throughout this section used the word 'character' to refer to the constructed personnages of films and the word 'personality' to refer to the set of traits and characteristics with which the film endows them.

To discuss character we need to discuss the *notion* of character and the *construction* of character, and the relation of stars to both.

THE NOTION OF CHARACTER

In the most general sense, all fictions have characters, that is, fictional beings, whether human, animal or fantastic, who carry the story, who do things and/or have things done to them. However, how these beings are conceptualised has altered in the history of fiction. This has been most clearly shown by Ian Watt in his *The Rise of the Novel,* a very useful reference here in that it both reveals the historical and cultural boundedness of notions of character and opens up the particular notion of character that dominates in our particular socio-cultural period. This

236

section is accordingly organised around a discussion of these two themes, followed by a brief discussion of attempts to move beyond the dominant conceptions of character operative in our time. The relevance to stars will be examined as we go along.

The cultural-historical specificity of notions of character

In *The Rise of the Novel*, Ian Watt argues that the novel form arose in the period it did in accord with changes in Western thought. He takes each of the major formal characteristics of narrative fiction — plot, characterisation, the representation of time and space, prose style — and shows how in each of these respects the novel marks a radical break with previous modes. In terms of characterisation, the most significant feature is the 'particularisation' of characters, that is, fiction is no longer dealing with 'general human types' embodying broadly moral or intellectual concepts, but with 'particular people in particular circumstances'. This is signalled by, among other things:

> the way the novelist typically indicates his [sic] intention of presenting a character as a particular individual by naming him [sic] in exactly the same way as particular individuals are named in ordinary life. [Watt, 1963, p.19.]

In previous literature, characters were given either historical or type names:

> In either case, the names set the characters in the context of a large body of expectations primarily formed from past literature, rather than from the context of contemporary life. (ibid.)

Other aspects of novel form — the representation of time and of space — also relate to the novelistic notion of character. In the novel, time and space were particularised, thus reinforcing the sense of the characters' particularity. The awareness of time, and of change over time, was accompanied by the novel interesting itself 'more than any other literary form in the development of its characters in the course of time'. (p.23.) The attention to the particularity of space also allows for the novel's examination of the interaction between an individual and her/his environment (although this concern develops somewhat later in the novel's history than the other elements just discussed).

That the novel, in general and in its promotion of a particular notion of character, is a product of bourgeois society has become a truism of literary history. [. . .] The novel may be taken as the bourgeois narrative form par excellence, but its general features have also been aimed at by other forms. [. . .]

Before turning to an examination of the characteristics of this novelistic conception of character, we need to consider the extent to which star images and film characters belong to this conception.

Stars. It is worth noting that stars are themselves a peculiarly characteristic feature of bourgeois theatre (and only subsequently cinema). The emergence of stars in the theatre is usually dated from the eighteenth century with such actors as Garrick, Peg Woffington, Sarah Siddons, Edmund Kean, Schröder and Rachel. This relates to the emergence of the theatre as both a viable economic enterprise and a respectable profession (neither dependent on patronage nor itinerants regarded as little better than rogues and vagabonds). Along with this went a change in the conception of what theatres and actors were. In earlier theatre, the actors either were recognised to be playing prescribed roles which were more important than themselves or, in early professional companies such as the *commedia dell'arte* troupes, were completely identified with their roles. [. . .]

There is a sense in which the history of stars in the cinema reprises the history of the change in concepts of character and the individual as defined by Watt, *et al*. The conventional wisdom concerning the history of stars in the cinema is that there has been a shift from stars as ideas, gods and goddesses, to stars as representations of ordinary life, mortals, just like you and me. This is a shift similar to that from characters as embodiments of moral or intellectual principles to characters as 'particular people in particular places' (although only the early stars were believed to *be* absolute qualities). [. . .]

Characters in the cinema. It has also been argued that there is a parallel history in the changes in predominant conceptions of character in the cinema (in cinematic traditions that use stars and in those that do not). Thus from a cinema focused principally on heroic or emblematic characters, who represent, respectively, ideals or ideas, there has been a shift to a cinema that deals with individual characters. The kind of evidence that is adduced for this view is the changing nature of the cowboy in Westerns — the cowboy of the early silent Western is either chivalric or a figure of (recent) myth, and the polarisation of values in characters is fairly complete, [. . .] (down to the clothes they wore, black for villains, white for heroes). With the various innovations in the genre's development — history (e.g. *The Iron Horse*), psychology (e.g. *The Left-Handed Gun*), naturalism (e.g. *Will Penny*) — the characters have become more individuated and less easily labelled good or bad. [. . .] Where in the 1930s-40s, films in both Hollywood and Europe subordinated character to the working out of a plot, films since the early 1960s have concentrated more and more on 'character'. (Braudy's (1976) examples include the image and roles of stars such as James Dean and Marlon Brando and directors such as Truffaut and Altman.) This can be seen as a logical progression of the novel's concern with particular characters in particular situations, a progression that the novel itself has taken. That is, whereas the early novels/films were still using character to illustrate aspects of the overall design of the plot, later novels/films, it is argued, use the plot to illuminate aspects of character. If this is broadly true, then, since at the level of 'high art' and criticism this emphasis on character was brought to a head by — and largely went out with — Joyce, Woolf and Proust, among others, in the earlier part of this century, we have the remarkable (but actually very common) phenomenon of the most modern of the arts lagging several decades behind its seniors. A particularly important aspect of this model is whether it in fact applies only to half the characters/stars in films, i.e. only to men. In her discussion of stereotyping in the cinema, Claire Johnston extends [the] discussion of iconography in the early cinema:

> Iconography as a specific kind of sign or cluster of signs based on certain conventions within the Hollywood genres has been partly responsible for the stereotyping of women within the commercial cinema in general, but the fact that there is a far greater differentiation of men's roles than of women's roles in the history of the cinema relates to sexist ideology itself, and the basic opposition which places man inside history, and women as ahistoric and eternal. As the cinema developed, the stereotyping of man was increasingly interpreted as contravening the realisation of the notion of 'character'; in the case of woman, this was not the case; the dominant ideology presented her as eternal and unchanging, except for modifications in terms of fashion, etc. [Johnston, 1973, pp. 24-5.]

There are arguable (and hotly debated) exceptions to Johnston's rule: the woman's film, Howard Hawks, [. . .] recent 'character studies' such as *Klute, Alice Doesn't Live Here Any More* and *Julia* — but all these are undoubtedly *exceptional*, thus suggesting the broad truth of the rule. What makes them exceptional is that these all feature women as central characters. This immediately involves the films in reconciling the stereotyping of women in general and the individual requirements of protagonists. (In general, secondary characters of either sex are types, for reasons of economy as much as anything else — it takes longer and requires more detail to establish and develop an individual character.) Whether the female *star's* image also conforms to Johnston's rule is less clear — it is hard to see that Davis, Garbo, Monroe or Fonda are less individuated, or more type based, than Wayne, Brando and Redford.

The novelistic conception of character
The following qualities may be taken to constitute an abstract of the novelistic conception of (or prescription for) character:

239

i)   particularity
ii)   interest
iii)   autonomy
iv)   roundness
v)   development
vi)   interiority
vii)   motivation
viii) discrete identity
ix)   consistency

i) particularity
This has already been discussed as the defining characteristic of novelistic conceptions of character. A more frequent, and extreme, term for this is 'uniqueness' of character.

ii) interest
[It has been] argued that the emphasis on particularity rests on the 'liberal' humanism of the novel, that is, 'an acknowledgement of the plenitude, diversity and individuality of human beings in society, together with the belief that such characteristics are good as ends in themselves. It delights in the multiplicity of existence and allows for a plurality of beliefs and values . . .' [Harvey, 1965, p. 24.] This means that the novelist 'must accept his [sic] characters as asserting their human individuality and uniqueness in the face of all ideology (including his own limited point of view) . . .' (ibid., p. 25.) As a result, Harvey suggests that it is impossible to reconcile novelistic character with 'monistic' commitments, such as Christianity and Marxism.

iii) autonomy
It is assumed that characters should have, or appear to have, 'a life of their own'. Precisely because they are no longer representatives of ideals or ideas, they must not appear to be merely a part of the design of the text, whether that be a thematic structure or simply a plot. We are not to see a character's construction, nor her or his function in the text's structure. We should have the illusion of 'life' in front of us. [. . .]

iv) roundness
The notion of 'round' as opposed to 'flat' characters is most familiar from E. M. Forster's *Aspects of the Novel*. Forster is not claiming a rigid distinction between the two nor denying the usefulness of 'flat' characters, but roundness is clearly for him what novels 'are about'. Roundness means that characters cannot be understood in terms of one particular trait but rather in terms of a multiplicity that fuses into a complex whole. Round characters have the capacity to surprise the reader by the revelation of unexpected layers of character. Round

characters are neither good nor bad, but a complex mixture of both.

v) development
At a minimum, characters in novels should change. The fact that the novel can show 'life by time' (Forster) means that it can — and should — show a character's movement through time and how s/he changes. [...]

vi) interiority
It is in the capacity of the novel to reveal what is in the heart and mind of a character directly, that is, without necessary recourse to inferences from what she or he says aloud, does or looks like, that the novel's special greatness is held to lie. Thus Paris claims that the novel:

> gives us an immediate knowledge of how the world is experienced by the individual consciousness and an understanding of the inner life in its own terms. [Paris, 1974, p. 23.]

Devices such as authorial comment and internal monologue are held to give the reader access to a character's 'interiority' in a way closed to theatre, film and other forms of narrative fiction. [. . .]

vii) motivation
The actions of characters should be motivated. This requirement involves both particularity and interiority, since what is understood by motivation is 'psychological' reasons for doing things. As Jeremy Hawthorn, in an attack on this aspect of characterisation, puts it:

> Anything the character . . . does . . . is . . . explained in terms of that character alone in abstraction from his [sic] situation, and never in the particular, concrete context which called out some potentialities rather than others into the realm of action. [Hawthorn, 1973, p. 60.]

viii) discrete identity
By this is meant the sense of characters having an existence and an identity independent of what they say and what they do — a self as well as roles. This is a problem for any narrative form, in that character logically only exists in the detail of the medium, in 'the words on the page'. [. . .]

ix) consistency
The notion of a character's consistency is somewhat tricky. The fact that a character is discrete involves the assumption that, while character may be round, may change, surprise or reveal unexpected qualities, all this takes place within broad parameters of personality, the existence of which is guaranteed by the character's discrete identity. Harvey

241

discusses this problem in terms of 'the idea of a stable ego':

> one aspect of our notion of identity lies in our sense that the self is discrete, isolate, unique; to this we may add the common assumption that it is a constant, stable thing. (op. cit., p. 119.)

[...] The persistence of the notion of coherence/consistency in relation to character is clear in the following quotation from Cleanth Brooks and Robert Penn Warren, taken from a frequently reprinted, widely used, basic text book on literary criticism. The use of 'obvious' in the first sentence is a good indication of how unchallenged this idea of character feels itself to be.

> An obvious test of fiction . . . is that the motives and actions of its characters are rendered coherent. It is the glory of fiction that the great artists have been able to render coherent so many strange and out-of-the-way, often apparently self-contradictory, examples of human nature. [Brooks and Warren, 1959, p.173.]

It should be stressed that while it is appropriate to call these aspects 'bourgeois', this is not because any category of the individual is necessarily bourgeois. [...] The peculiarities of the bourgeois conception of the individual/character are, first, that the stress on particularity and uniqueness tends to bar, or render inferior, representation of either collectivity and the masses or the typical person/character (types being relegated to a merely functional role in promoting the central character): and second, that the concern with interior motivation reinforces a model of history and social process in which explanation is rooted in the individual conscience and capacity rather than in collective and/or structural aspects of social life. [. . .]

IDENTIFICATION

The bourgeois conception of character intends to produce characters that are unique and individuated. Yet, clearly, not *so* unique and individuated as to be beyond comprehension or representativeness. For all their individuation, Hamlet, Elizabeth Bennett, the narrator of *Remembrance of Things Past* and Martha Quest are figures of identification, figures with whom the reader can, and is almost required to, empathise or at least feel some sense of familiarity. While the psychology of identification has been little explored, [. . .] it is clear that, as Joan Rockwell argues in *Fact from Fiction*, identification depends upon a fit between the traits of the character and those traits known about, understood, delineated by, available to the wider culture.

In the context of the bourgeois conception of character, we can discern two kinds of ideological work that identification is made to do:

a) that identified by Rockwell as a general aspect of identification within all ideological systems, namely the reinforcement of norms:

> Fiction not only legitimates emotions and aspirations, it also . . . particularly since the appearance of the novel with its devotion to the minutiae of personal relationships, gives models and patterns of acceptable and unacceptable behaviour . . . if the reader or watcher of drama can recognise enough of himself [sic] in a fictional character to make identification possible, identification with a literary character may be quite decisive in transmitting norms and influencing personal behaviour. [Rockwell, 1974, pp. 80-1.]

b) the specific emphasis of bourgeois characterisation on the individual serves to mask the ideological role of character. By feeling that we are identifying with a unique person, we ignore the fact that we are identifying with a normative figure. It needs only to be added that ideology works better when we cannot see it working. [. . .]

Star images and character
Star images are constructed personages in media texts. [. . .] [They can be seen] as types, yet they also bear many of the hallmarks of novelistic character. This is not as surprising as it may look. As the process of identification demonstrates, it is in fact perfectly possible, and indeed fundamentally inherent in the form, for a fictional character in the novelistic mode to be both normative with respect to social types and individuated with respect to the specific realisation of those types in a given character. The individuation of types is even taken to be the mark of 'greatness' in literature. [. . .]

From this point of view, star images do in many respects correspond to novelistic notions of character. They are particular and interesting. (The aspect of particularisation that Watt discusses most fully is the use of proper names to replace emblematic ones. However, a residue of the emblematic remains in the names of characters in the most 'realist' fiction and this element is probably even stronger with stars – hence John Wayne rather than Marion Morrison, Marilyn Monroe rather than Norma Jean Baker. The fact that Fonda and Redford have retained their real names may relate to the cinema's becoming increasingly 'character-oriented'.) They are autonomous, although the notion of 'manipulation' is fairly widespread and this tends to undercut the illusion of the star's autonomous existence. Their existence in the real world is a guarantee of their independent identity.

Other aspects are more of a problem. That is, with regard to roundness, development, interiority, motivation and consistency star images aspire to the condition of novelistic characterisation in a medium not altogether developed to this end. Roundness, development and consistency may be taken together here, since all involve the nature of *change* in a star's image. Certainly there is no requirement that a star image should change, and a star's apparent changelessness over a long period of time can be a source of charisma. Apart from growing older, the image of Cary Grant or Bette Davis has not really 'deepened' since the period in which they were established as stars. Equally, attempts by a star to change may meet with box-office failure – Ingrid Bergman is the locus classicus. (Her popularity with American audiences was killed stone dead – for a few years – by her decision to make films with Roberto Rossellini and have their child without marrying him.) Some star image's careers do change – Joan Crawford, Jane Fonda – or at any rate 'deepen': John Wayne, Marilyn Monroe. All these work within the notion of consistency – there must at least be traces of Crawford's flapper in her working women, of Fonda's sex-pot in her radical portraits – and the careers of Wayne and Monroe can be seen as disquisitions on the West and sex, respectively. With most stars this emphasis on consistency (or *apparent* consistency, since on investigation most images can be seen to condense conflicting values) may in fact go further than suggested in the abstract of the novelistic concept of character above, so that *sameness* becomes the over-riding feature.

This is probably best explained by considering stars' appearances as serials. Just as Charles Dickens found in publishing his novels in serial form, and as contemporary soap opera also finds, changes in character are hard to handle in this form since they and milieu, rather than plot, are the form's anchors. Because stars are always appearing in different stories and settings, *they* must stay broadly the same in order to permit recognition and identification. [. . .]

Where interiority is concerned access to the inner thoughts of stars is also problematic, especially as they are always appearing in different roles. However, interviews and articles about or by them ('ghosted' or otherwise) may be read as granting such access, and the belief in the transparency of the face as a window to the soul is also widespread. What these elements lack is the precision and detail available to the novel, and the authority of the author's 'voice' to tell us the 'truth' about the character. [. . .]

What is abundantly clear is that stars are supremely figures of identification [. . .] and this identification is achieved principally through the star's relation to social types (and hence norms) as discussed [earlier]. What are the forms of the relationship between the star's uniqueness and her or his social normativeness?

a) as a general rule, the star's uniqueness, seen as the only true locus of lived life, is a guarantee of the ideological truth of the type to which s/he belongs.
b) one of the types that stars embody is the type of 'the individual' itself;

244

they embody that particular conception of what it is to be human that characterises our culture.

c) the specific relation of a star to her/his type may be conceptualised in the following ways:

Transcendence. By this it is assumed that the 'great' stars transcend the type to which they belong and become 'utterly' individual. That this is how many stars are experienced and that it is a condition to which the whole apparatus of the star system aspires are crucial aspects of the system's particular ideological flavour. However, the notion of a pure individuality, untainted by common social characteristics, is unsound both as a theory of personality (cf. Burns, 1972) and as a theory of characterisation, since an utterly unique personality/character/star in a film would be indecipherable (since decipherment/comprehension of any meaning/affect depends on shared, and therefore to some degree generalisable, signs).

Maximisation. [It has been suggested that stars are] 'maximised types':

> In the movies we are faced with figures that embody in terms of contemporary references maximum states of age, beauty, strength, revenge or whatever. [Alloway, 1971, p.12.]

Alloway instances Burt Lancaster as 'an ex-convict but a loyal friend with a code of honour' and Kirk Douglas as 'socially acceptable but faithless and currupt' in *I Walk Alone*:

> The two men are maximized symbols, one, as Agee pointed out, for old-fashioned entrepreneurial elan (Lancaster as good bootlegger), and one for modern executive skills (Douglas as corrupt behind a corporate shield). Both attitudes to business (i.e. life) are appropriate in the 'capitalistic' United States. (ibid.)

Alloway deliberately talks here of the stars and the characters they play as one, and it is not clear whether he regards the stars as maximised types or just characters in Hollywood movies. The notion of maximised types would seem to tell us something about a star like John Wayne, who can be read as the Westerner par excellence, the man of the West taken to his logical conclusion. However, this perhaps only tells us about a tendency of stars' images – even Wayne has weaknesses and complexities that counteract this maximising tendency, and equally a star as profoundly contradictory as Monroe was also at the same time the 'ultimate' dumb blonde.

Inflection. Here the star is seen to be within a distinct type mould and yet to be sufficiently different from it to be experienced as an individual variation on it. The most obvious examples are the line of cowboys from

William S. Hart to John Wayne, or Draculas from Max Schreck to Christopher Lee. The variation may be little other than adding a few superficial idiosyncrasies to the type, but it may also exaggerate or foreground aspects of the type to such an extent that the type itself changes. (E.g. the gradual emphasis on the *attractiveness* of the vampire, explicit in the literary sources but initially repressed in the cinematic versions until Christopher Lee, since when it is a stock feature of the type.) This introduction of new elements may, on examination, be seen to put the type at risk, either by introducing a contradictory element (e.g. Garbo/Christina's erotic attachment to her maid-in-waiting in *Queen Christina*, whereas the type traditionally either poses female royal rule as a choice between asexuality and heterosexuality – Davis as Elizabeth I – or else conflates female power with heterosexual manipulation – Dietrich as Catherine the Great); or by revealing the contradictoriness of the type (e.g. the male fascist, isolate pitch to which Clint Eastwood has taken the tough guy image) or, as in the Lee example, by bringing out a repressed element of the type.

Resistance. In some cases the star's image's career has been centrally about attempts to overthrow the type to which he or she belongs. This has usually been done in the name of individuality, and the star's struggle to assert individualism in the face of typicality then becomes central to their image. [. . .] However, such resistance may also act to expose the oppressiveness of the type. Although 'individualism' can be seen in the contradictory development of Marilyn Monroe in relation to the dumb blonde sex symbol type to which she belonged, this development can be read in terms of suggesting how demeaning this type is.

[. . .]

Alternative conceptions of character
Types. As noted above, type characters are acknowledged to have a place in novelistic fiction, but only to enable the proper elaboration of the central, individuated character(s). In this respect, no star could be just a type, since all stars play central characters. (It may even be a rule that where the central character in a film is constructed by all other means as just a type, then the 'individuality' of the star masks this just as it does her/his image's typicality.)

Types have been used deliberately in the cinema in two ways. First, in the various notions of *typage,* stemming from the theories of Eisenstein, Kuleshov, Vertov.* Here, performers were selected for roles on the basis

* [Russian film makers and theorists active primarily in the early experimental years following the Russian Revolution in 1917.]

of the appropriateness of their physical bearing to a particular, socially defined category of persons. (This 'appropriateness' is a matter of correspondence between a given performer and the tradition of representing the given social category, although Eisenstein for one tended to overlook this point and see the correspondence as between the performer and the social category, in reality.) Types in this tradition are often inflected to express the category's relative political desirability: e.g. the rough-but-noble face of the peasant, the over-sophisticated appearance of the bureaucrat, although this does not generally mean that the types are endowed with psychological traits. Second, types may be exaggerated, reversed or otherwise foregrounded in order, in Claire Johnston's words, 'to provide a critique' of the 'ideological tradition' to which the types belong. [. . .] I am bound to say that my experience of teaching this line of argument, to which I felt broadly committed, has raised considerable doubts as to its validity. Very few students, even when acknowledging the thesis in principle, have felt they could see it at work in the supposed instances of it, e.g. the work of Arzner and Rothman. Whilst this does not wholly undermine the thesis, it does make it harder to sustain. The relation to stars renders the issue even more complex. [. . .]

Deconstruction. Much of the argument against 'character' in literary criticism has come from a formalist position. This has moved from the obviously correct position that characters are not real people and only exist in their construction in the text to a position that suggests the only interest of literature is in the formal qualities of the text and its structuring. The radical variant of this position in relation to character suggests that texts should cease to construct the illusion of lived life in the use of characters and show how characters are simply devices that are part of a wider design. [. . .] Stars are of course wholly incompatible with this since they always bring with them the illusion of lived life, and indeed are often used to achieve this with films that are in other ways, admirably or not, schematic in their use of character. (E.g. in the case of Lang, Edward G. Robinson in *Woman in the Window*, Gloria Grahame in *The Big Heat* or Joan Fontaine in *Beyond a Reasonable Doubt* threaten, at any rate, to inform their role with the reverberations of their image, just by being in them; similarly Marlene Dietrich outlives von Sternberg's calligraphic use of her.)

Brecht. Brecht's views on character have often been wrongly collapsed both into types and into deconstruction. Brecht's aim was not anti-realist, but rather to reinvent realism according to historical-materialist principles. In terms of character this included:

1) a rejection of casting actors because they 'looked right' (the very basis of typage):

It is pure folly to allot parts according to physical characteristics. 'He has a kingly figure'. Do all kings have to look like Edward VII? 'But he lacks a commanding presence'. Are there so few ways of commanding? 'She seems too respectable for Mother Courage'. Have a look at the fishwives. [Brecht, 1964, p.243.]

2) a rejection of psychological, rounded character construction in favour of characters seen as, in John Willett's words:

an inconsistent bundle of conflicting motives and interests, as inconsistent as himself [Brecht], or as the world in which we all live. Such characters are never 'rounded': they have to be presented as a jagged mass of broken facets, clear and hard and often transparent, offering many irrelevancies and distortions to the eye. [Willett, 1959, p.55.]

... the actor ... has to be able to show his [sic] character's coherence despite, or rather by means of, interruptions and jumps. [Brecht, 1964, p.55.]

It is too great a simplification if we make the actions fit the character and the character fit the actions: the inconsistencies which are to be found in the actions and characters of real people cannot be shown like this. (ibid., p.195.)

3) An emphasis on 'showing' or 'presenting' a character rather than embodying it, so that the actor sometimes steps out of character, comments on it, plays it a different way, etc. It is this last that has been interpreted as a mode of 'deconstruction', which to a certain extent it is. However, Brecht does not advocate the destruction of character through deconstruction, but rather the restructuring of character according to the principles outlined in the previous paragraph. The stepping out of character is not intended to destroy the reality of the character, but rather to give the performer/audience the opportunity of seeing the character in a new light, discovering a new contradiction, analysing the character's social, historical or political significance, etc. This breaks novelistic realism, but does not throw the baby of character out with the bathwater of psychologism and individualism.

The possibility of using stars in a Brechtian fashion resides in the star's embodiment of given social values which, if s/he performed with 'interruptions and jumps' and if the fit between her/his image and the character in the film was suitably manipulated, could break down the psychologistic, individuated assumptions of the star's image's character. In this way, various latent aspects of star images could be foregrounded: the contradictions they mask and condense, the anti-individualism aspects of typicality, the problem of interiority, and the knowledge of manipulation. This would not mean that the star as an entity ceased to exist, but that the nature of her/him as an entity would be radically altered, becoming 'an inconsistent bundle'. Examples of this that might be worth following up include comedians of various kinds – the Marx Brothers, Gracie Allen, Jerry Lewis – and Godard's use of Marina Vlady in *Two or Three Things I Know About Her* and of Jane Fonda and Yves Montand in *Tout va bien*. [. . .]

THE CONSTRUCTION OF CHARACTER

A character's personality in a film is seldom something given in a single shot. Rather it has to be built up, by film-makers and audience alike, across the whole film. A character is a construct from the very many different signs deployed by a film (within the context of cinema). (Cf. the discussion of character and the 'semic' code in Barthes, 1974.) The overall principle of construction is the conception of character outlined above, but within that we have to ask A) what signs are used in the construction of character, and how; and B) what specific problems of character construction film poses.

Signs of character
In this section, I shall write principally from the point of view of the audience/reader/decoder of films. In other words, the question posed is, what are the signs that we as viewers latch on to in constructing characters? (I do not assume thereby a complete reciprocity, in terms of film-makers/audience, encoder/decoder understandings of the medium, but nor do I assume complete disjunction either.) In detailing these, I have also indicated what seem to me the largely unproblematic and immediate inferences that we draw from these signs, although the more difficult issues of inference I leave for later.)

The signs of character in film include:

   i)   audience foreknowledge
   ii)   name
   iii)   appearance
   iv)   objective correlatives
   v)   speech of character
   vi)   speech of others
   vii)   gesture
   viii) action
   ix)   structure

(It will be clear that we have different orders of signs here, i) and viii) in particular referring to much larger sign-clusters than the rest. And even with the rest, we shall only be concerned with the sign's articulation at an

249

already fairly high degree of complexity; for example, I shall take it that discussion of speech will not involve us in discussion of phonetics.)

i) *audience foreknowledge*
We may come to the cinema with certain preconceptions about a character. These may be derived from:

a) familiarity with the story. Many films are based on pre-existing books, often best-sellers or classics, plays, TV series, or else on traditional stories. There will thus be members of the audience with expectations about the character derived from their knowledge of the film's source. (The most famous example is probably Rhett Butler in *Gone With the Wind*.) [. . .]

b) familiar characters. Certain characters exist across a span of films, or of films and other media, and may be incarnated by different stars; e.g. Sherlock Holmes, Tarzan, Dracula. (Are there any female examples?) Characters may also be biographical; e.g. Fanny Brice in *Rose of Washington Square*, *The Great Ziegfeld*, *Funny Girl*, *Funny Lady*.

c) promotion. Advertising, posters, publicity, etc. may set up certain expectations about character. (E.g. what sort-of-person would we expect Monroe and Brando to be playing on the evidence of the posters for *Niagara* and *Reflections in a Golden Eye*? Figs. 3.1 and 3.2)

d) star/genre expectations. We expect John Wayne to play a certain kind of character, and we expect anyone playing the male lead in a Western to fit broad parameters of cowboy characterisation. This may be less (but seldom more) clear-cut with other stars/genres.

e) criticism. Accounts of films – and the characterisation in films – by critics and reviewers may also lead us to try to read a character in a certain way.

Fig. 3.1: *Poster for* Niagara, *1952*.

Fig. 3.2: *Poster for* Reflections in a Golden Eye, *1967.*

N.B. All of these forms of foreknowledge are expectations which may or may not be fulfilled. They do not have the prescriptive rigidity that holds for traditional character/stories in so-called 'traditional' societies. [. . .]

ii) name

The character's name both particularises her/him and also suggests personality traits. Although names in films seldom have the effect of 'fixing' a character clearly from the word go, as in the classic 'charactonym' of morality plays and comedy (see Van Laan, 1970, p.76), they do usually imply quite a lot about character. This may be material — the class and ethnic backgrounds of Stanley Kowalski and Blanche Dubois* — or 'psychological' — the harsh consonants of Kowalski and the open vowels of Dubois, the connotations of Blanche (French = 'sophisticated'; denotes white, meaningful in the context of her background in the South, and also in the traditional opposition of white/pale skin = feminine; dark/brown skin = masculine). Names can be foregrounded in relation to identity. Thus the Monroe character in *Bus Stop* has chosen the name Cherie for its charming connotations, just as the Don Murray character mispronounces it Cherry for his lubricious view of her. [. . .]

A star's own name can be similarly analysed, as suggested above, and it is very common for people to speak of a character in a film as having the star's name. This may be because names are harder to establish in films

* [The characters played by Marlon Brando and Vivien Leigh in the film version of Tennessee Williams' *A Streetcar Named Desire*, directed by Elia Kazan, 1951.]

than in the novel or even, courtesy of the programme, the theatre, since it depends upon characters saying them repeatedly.

iii) *appearance*

What a character looks like indicates their personality, with varying degrees of precision. (When it is misleading — as in Mary Astor's superb plausibility in *The Maltese Falcon* — this becomes an issue in the narrative.) Appearance may be divided into:

a) physiognomy. We are able to place people's physiognomy according to such broad cultural oppositions as masculine:feminine (applied to both sexes), old:young, handsome:ugly, sensitive:crude, generous: mean, nice:nasty, etc., as well as to ethnic types. There are also types of face and build thought to be characteristic of groups such as mothers, businessmen, lesbians, cowards, intellectuals and the nobility.

b) dress. Clothes and aspects of dress such as hair-style and accessories are obviously culturally coded and widely assumed to be indicative of personality. [. . .] Dress is usually taken to point both to the social order in general and to the temperament of the individual concerned. Thus Robert Redford's clothes in *The Way We Were* place him in terms of period, age-group, class, occupation, etc., at the same time indicating certain personality traits, both stereotypic (the all-American boy) and relatively personalised (clean, warm-looking clothes, comfortable-but-not-sloppy). (Fig. 3.3) This 'dual' articulation of dress can be used in films to raise the issue of 'identity': e.g. the play on dress, both Chance's and Feathers', in *Rio Bravo; Now Voyager,* with its protagonist's 'progression' through different dress styles/self definitions, imposed by her mother (shapeless 'spinster's dresses'), her sister (glamour), her lover (camellias), and, perhaps, herself (an amalgam of all three styles). (Figs. 3.4-3.6) [. . .]

Fig. 3.3: *Robert Redford in* The Way We Were, *1973.*

Fig. 3.4   Fig. 3.5

Fig. 3.6

Figs. 3.4–3.6: *Bette Davis as Charlotte Vale in* Now, Voyager, *1942; from 'dowdy spinster' (3.4) through 'woman of fashion' (3.5) to a 'whole person' (3.6). Note how the pattern of the first is integrated with the stylishness of the second in the final synthesis.*

253

iv) *objective correlatives*

[It has been argued that Flaubert used] 'physical correlatives to symbolize mental states' [Scholes and Kellogg, 1966]. This may be considerably extended in film through:

a) decor and setting. A character's environment — whether a home or a general landscape — may be felt to express her or him. (E.g. Bree's [the Jane Fonda character] room in *Klute*.) [. . .]

b) montage. As in the classic example of Kerensky and the peacock in *October*, montage may, by association of images, indicate aspects of character.*

Fig. 3.7: *Norman Bates/Anthony Perkins in* Psycho, *1960*.

c) symbolism. A character may be associated with a particular object, or an animal. (b and c would seem to be rare in Hollywood cinema — but consider Hitchcock's use of birds of prey in relation to Norman/Anthony Perkins in *Psycho* (Fig. 3.7) and caged birds in relation to Tippi Hedren in *The Birds* (Fig. 3.8).) [. . .]

* [Alexander Kerensky led the short-lived provisional government in Russia from February to October 1917. He was the butt of ridicule from many quarters; Eisenstein's film comparison of him with a peacock is possibly the most memorable.]

Fig. 3.8: *Melanie/Tippi Hedren in* The Birds, *1963.*

v) *speech of character*

What a character says and how he/she says it indicate personality both directly (what a character says about her/himself) and indirectly (what a character betrays about her/himself). Importantly, we are more inclined to trust our perception of the latter than the former. [. . .] A special case of the former is voice-over, whether in the role of narrator or just as a device for the expression of inner thoughts. These we are more inclined to believe, since the former is grounded in the convention of the (more or less) omniscient narrator and the latter in a belief in the truth of the 'private'.

vi) *speech of others*

What other characters say of a character, and how they say it, may indicate a personality trait of that character and/or of the characters speaking. Again, the question of who we believe and why is problematic. N.B. v) and vi) include dialogue, that is, speech between characters and not just isolated statements.

vii) *gesture*

The vocabulary of gesture may be read according to formal (that is, recognised to be governed by social rules) and informal (or involuntary) codes. Both may be taken as indicative of personality and temperament, although only the former recognises the social dimension of personality.

255

For this reason, the latter are often taken as giving particularly privileged access to a character's 'true' self. (E.g. one could examine the obvious 'tough' stance assumed by Bree in her first meeting with Klute and the way it is 'betrayed' by slight nervous facial grimaces and finger movements.) This will be discussed in the section on performance.

viii) *action*

Action is not always easy to distinguish in practice from gesture. It refers to what a character does in the plot. A rule of thumb might be that an action furthers the narrative in some way and points towards plot, whereas a gesture does not further the narrative and points towards character. (In an intimate narrative situation, a raised eyebrow may constitute an action, since, for example, it furthers the development of a relationship.) In terms of Bree in the scene discussed in the previous paragraph, the action is that she does not let Klute in.

ix) *structure*

The notion of action already points towards the question of plot, one of the most familiar kinds of structure that film may have. The role of structure in character may, however, extend beyond plot. This involves us in a brief discussion of different concepts of structure in relation to character, and consequently this sub-section is considerably longer than those above.

a) *sequence: structure*. The notion of the structure of a narrative fiction involves a crucial assumption about the way we read such fictions, namely, that we are able, at the end of reading, to construct what the structure(s) of the text is (are). Narrative is linear, one thing follows another, and we therefore read it sequentially; but we can also grasp its overall shape, after we have read it. [. . .] Roland Barthes, in *S/Z*, has inflected this in terms of two reading codes, the hermeneutic and the proairetic. The former is sequential; it is the questions the narrative poses, and the reader poses of the narrative, as it/he/she goes along. The latter is the overall shape of the narrative as one understands it at the point at which one stops reading (which may or may not be before the end of the story). The relationship or tension between these codes is as important as the codes themselves; it is not the either-or that the sequence/space opposition tends to pose.

The important problem posed by this distinction is how far one accepts an emphasis on structure as something that corresponds to the actual practice of reading (and not just to critical ingenuity). On one's answer to that depends one's assessment of what structure can tell one about character and the importance of structure *vis-à-vis* other signs of character.

b) *function*. The notion of function in relation to character and structure revolves around an issue that has been debated since Aristotle, but with special insistence since the emphasis on character in the nineteenth century novel. Baldly, this issue is whether characters are to be seen as functions of the structure, their personality determined by the requirements of the plot (or other structural principle) or whether, on the contrary, structure is to be seen as emanating from character, the plot in particular expressing the personality of the characters. [. . .]

This issue invokes wider debates. Within a Marxist frame of reference, two polemical positions can be outlined. A polemic in favour of structure over character sees the reverse as expressing bourgeois individualism (the discrete self seen as the motive of both individual action and the course of human history) and, in a modernist inflection of the polemic, sees undue emphasis on character disguising the facticity of structure that is an inescapable element of any work of fiction. The polemic in favour of character over structure identifies an emphasis on structure with myth, fatalism or crude determinism, and rejects the notion that a fiction's facticity must necessarily be foregrounded in order for audiences to know that they are watching a fabrication. However, it seems to me that the emphasis on character can also be an emphasis not only on the individual but also on human activity, while the emphasis on structure can also be an emphasis on the determinations that act on a human life. This suggests that some way of articulating the relation between structure and character, determinations and human activity, may lead out of the reactionary implications of adhering too exclusively to either side of the dialectic.

With this in mind, further issues arise:

1) How does one identify where the emphasis lies in terms of structure or character (and their functional relationship)? At present, we shall have to rely on intuition and plausible arguments, since as far as I know no theorisation of this has been undertaken.

2) The fit between a character's personality and the demands of plot/thematic structure, etc., or between the shape of the plot and the personality traits it is required to express, may be more or less good. Fitting the star image to this adds a further complication. [. . .] The important point here is to be aware of the *problem* of fit, and, to fulfill the sacred requirement of coherence, of the film's necessary apparent resolution of that problem.

3) This question of fit, and of emphases on character and structure, can lead to some interesting articulations of the problem of the individual and the determinations that act upon her or him. It may be a way of coming to grips with the idea of a star's 'transcending' their material. [. . .] Whether in the final analysis one decides structure or character dominates depends on how you read the film; and perhaps precisely the

point of the film is that it is about the tension between the two, that is, between determinations and human action.

c) *concepts of structure*. Most critics who have devoted attention to structure have tended to regard character as a function of it. Their difference lies in the ways in which structure is conceptualised.

Some critics treat the structure of a given fiction as particular to it. However, most critics of structure have seen a given work's structure as an instance of more generalised structures, whether across particular genres or bodies of works [. . .] or across narrativity in general. Two broad differences of conceptualisation may be discerned: *linear* structures and *relational* structures. *Linear* structures are for our purposes plots (although in principle they could be logical patterns such as syllogisms or musical ones such as sonata form), that is, a progression of events, one following another in an ordered sequence. [. . .] Such structures constitute the basic patterns upon which a host of seemingly different stories are built. [. . .] *Relational* structures are identified not in a linear sequence but in certain root relationships or oppositions. The most popular version of this has been that of binary oppositions. [. . .] Whether using linear or relational concepts of structure, most critics have been content to locate characters as functions of those structures.

[. . .]

Problems of character construction in film

Placing. Nearly all forms of narrative fiction attempt to 'place' the reader/audience in relation to the characters, in terms both of the understanding we are to have of a character and our judgement of or feeling for him/her.

This involves the notion of coherence. Out of the mass of details about personality that we may be given about a character, we construct a coherent character and attitude towards him or her. We decide that certain aspects are 'true' and correspondingly likeable, approvable or otherwise, and use these aspects to comprehend and judge the other aspects. It seems that this is a tendency of both texts and readers, but it should be pointed out that 1) what the text tries to get the reader to construct may not in fact be what s/he constructs; and 2) it may be our job as students of film to construct the totality of traits, in all their complexity and contradiction, and attempt to work out which of these is signalled as the 'true' and 'positive' aspect(s) of the character without ourselves reducing the polysemy of traits to that (those) anchoring trait(s).

Much placing depends upon the way a film associates a character with cultural/ideological values and attitudes. Such cultural assumptions are partly to do with stereotypical views of the social group to which a character belongs. That is to say, we judge a character to a certain extent on how s/he fits with our previous assumptions of what members of that group are like. This judgement in turn differs according to whether, first, we take our assumptions as unalterable and therefore take those traits of the characters that conform to our assumptions as the essential and defining ones against which to place all the others; *or* second, we may tend to consider cases where characters seem to break with stereotypes as traits thereby more individuated and hence more 'real'. [. . .]

Cultural assumptions may also be of a different order, concerned with the circumstances under which 'transparency', 'sincerity', 'authenticity' and hence 'the true person' are to be found. These have been mentioned in passing above, and seem in our culture to cluster around notions of the private and the uncontrolled. That is, when people are not in public, and especially in circumstances defined as intimate (the family, bed), they are held to be more 'real' than otherwise; and when people 'let themselves go', pour forth their thoughts and feelings in an untrammelled flow, then they are being their 'true selves'. (The latter also relates to popular psychoanalysis, the notion of the Id, or that which is repressed, always threatening to burst forth and somehow, by its very force and intensity, being thought of as more 'real' than the super ego that controls it.)

These cultural assumptions 'get into' films via iconography of social personality types and conventions of *mise en scène*, montage, performance, etc. Let me briefly exemplify all this from *All About Eve*. Margo/Bette Davis has an ambitious admirer in Eve/Anne Baxter, who acts as her devoted slave while secretly desiring to usurp her star status. Equally, Margo is torn between her devotion to the theatre and her desire for a permanent heterosexual relationship. The film tries to place us in relation to this tension such that we acknowledge and feel it as a real and legitimate tension, and yet ultimately feel the second should have supremacy over the first. Two scenes illustrate how this is achieved. The first occurs when Margo arrives late for the audition of Miss Caswell (Marilyn Monroe) for a small part in a play she, Margo, is currently starring in. She meets Miss Caswell in the foyer, and the latter explains to her that Eve has stood in for her, knew her lines perfectly and was 'wonderful'. Margo goes into the auditorium and pretends not to know what has happened. She goes onto the stage as if to start the audition and then feigns surprise, followed by anger, when she is told that Eve had taken her place. By having Margo delay her anger and then 'deliver' it on a stage in a display of histrionics (a brilliantly witty speech, delivered with expert timing and thrust), the film effectively undercuts the legitimacy and authenticity of her anger. This has been achieved by the refusal through *mise en scène* of the private (it is on a stage) and through performance of the uncontrolled (it is superbly 'played'). In a later scene, Margo has been in the country with a couple who, because they also like Eve, fix their car so that they run out of petrol when running

Margo to the station in time for a performance; hence Eve, her understudy, has to go on for her. The man leaves the car to find petrol, and Margo talks to the woman about being an actress and how, if you haven't got a man, no matter how famous you are, you are not really fulfilled as a woman. Whereas the scene discussed above undercuts what Margo says through *mise en scène* and performance, this scene uses these features to substantiate what she says. Thus the fact that the man leaves turns the situation into a private conversation between women friends (itself a paradigm of an occasion for authenticity, unburdening one's heart, and also in this film clearly within the tradition of the protagonist and the confidante, to whom the former always speaks her heart and mind), while the long held close-up bespeaks a rhetoric of truth already discussed. In this scene, the 'truth' of the tension — that in the end for a woman marriage is more important than career — is asserted, assisted, it need hardly be added, by the massive resonance of that 'truth' in partriarchal culture. Further complexity is added to this if one places Margo and Eve iconographically. The former is 'monstrous', tough, bitchy, in her first scene shown with her face plastered in cold cream and her eyes moving about neurotically. The latter on the other hand is a 'sweet girl' with a soft voice, pretty features and modest appearance (she wears a mac in the first scene, and afterwards very simple dresses). This iconographic contrast is also clear in the party scene in the middle of the film. The film however, in its course, cheats these iconographic implications. Eve is revealed as hard as nails underneath, and as having only her career at stake; while Margo is revealed as easily hurt, vulnerable, ultimately wanting to settle down with a man. This iconographic reversal is a departure from stereotypes and thus may be read as 'realism'. Equally the fact that it meshes so powerfully with the ideology of a woman's place also secures it the label of 'realism' (i.e. conforming to prevailing norms). The fact that Bette Davis plays Margo allows the tension to appear to be 'authentic' (i.e. not decided in advance in favour of one term over the other), in that she was someone who put her career before her private life while at the same time insisting that beneath it all she was just a woman in need of a man. (However, her autobiography, *The Lonely Life*, which echoes some of Margo's sentiments in the car scene, was published eleven years after the release of *All About Eve*.) [. . .]

Star identification. The phenomenon of audience-star identification may yet be the crucial aspect of the placing of the audience in relation to a character. The 'truth' about a character's personality and the feelings which it evokes may be determined by what the reader takes to be the truth about the person of the star playing the part.

In a discussion of *Last Tango in Paris*, E. Ann Kaplan (1974) suggests that the intention of the film, as evidenced by *mise en scène* and the character of Tom (Jean-Pierre Léaud), is to act as a critique both of two dominant film styles (1950s American and French New Wave)*, including the appropriate acting style, and of the ideological values that go with them (broadly categorisable as, respectively, Hemingway-tough male dominance and anguish, and chic and 'modern' irresponsibility and permissiveness). The film's method involves putting a distance on the characters in order to be able to see their cinematic/ideological representativeness — and this includes the Brando character, Paul. However, argues Kaplan, because it is Brando and because he employs an acting style which 'has the effect of drawing the audience in close to the character', the film's aim of placing us at a critical distance to him does not come off. Instead Brando/Paul's view (and Kaplan suggests they are almost identical in this instance) comes to dominate the film and thus seems to be legitimated. For all the subtle undercutting and irony that Bertolucci [the director] deploys and that Kaplan draws attention to, Brando — as image (the reverberations of *Streetcar Named Desire* and *On the Waterfront* still remaining) and as performer [...] — is so powerful that 'it was logical for people to take Brando's consciousness for the consciousness of the film'. Since Brando's view — a hatred of 'the false middle-class way of being' which is taken out on women — becomes identified as the truth about the character and the film, the seemingly anti-sexist intentions of the latter are overturned by the (very complexly) sexist attitudes of the former. It would be wrong to deduce from this example that it is always the case that the star image is the ultimate locus of truth about character. Partly the search for one truth about character (on our part) may do violence to the contradictoriness and polysemy of character, partly each case needs to be argued as carefully as Kaplan argues hers. [...]

STARS AS CHARACTERS IN FILMS

What then is involved in studying a film in terms of a star and the character she or he plays?

We may note first of all the points at which the star is effective in the construction of character. These can be considered from two points of view: the fact of a star being in the film, and their performance in it. [...] As regards the fact that a given star is in the film, audience foreknowledge, the star's name and her/his appearance (including the sound of his/her voice and dress styles associated with her/him) all already signify that condensation of attitudes and values which is the star's image. Perhaps this is most blatantly demonstrated by Marlene Dietrich's appearances in *Around the World in Eighty Days* (1956) and *Touch of Evil* (1958). The former is, with its string of cameo appearances by stars,

*[A journalistic form designating a new group of French directors who made their first feature films after 1958–9.]

testimony enough to how much a star's mere presence in a film can signal character. When Dietrich tells Quinlan/Orson Welles his sombre fortune, towards the end of *Touch of Evil*, it is enough that it is her telling it for it to take on a mysterious and faintly erotic authority. The Dietrich example is particularly interesting, in that the enigmatic-exotic-erotic complex which her image signifies and which is irresistibly read into her appearances is sustained principally by vague memories of the Sternberg films, glamour photographs and her cabaret act, and not by the substance of her films or interviews. Her face, her name even, carries the 'mystique', no matter what films she makes or what she says.

The star image is used in the construction of a character in a film in three different ways:

Selective Use
The film may, through its deployment of the other signs of character and the rhetoric of film, bring out certain features of the star's image and ignore others. In other words, from the structured polysemy of the star's

Fig. 3.9: *Mia Farrow and Robert Redford in* The Great Gatsby, *1974, both equally glamorously lit.*

262

image certain meanings are selected in accord with the overriding conception of the character in the film.

This selective use of a star's image is problematic for a film, in that it cannot guarantee that the particular aspects of a star's image it selects will be those that interest the audience. To attempt to ensure this, a film must use the various signifying elements of the cinema to foreground and minimise the image's traits appropriately. For us it is not enough simply to say that such-and-such a film uses such-and-such an aspect of a star's image: we have to show *how*. Let me take a conveniently narrow example, the use of one signifying element, lighting, in relation to Robert Redford. We might begin by considering the way he is lit in *The Way We Were* and *Butch Cassidy and the Sundance Kid* as compared to in *All the President's Men*. In the first named, Redford is primarily the film's erotic/romantic focus and he is accordingly glamorously lit, with light from behind that both creates the warm glow of classic Hollywood glamour photography and also makes his already fair, all-American hair still more golden (Fig. 3.9).

More surprisingly, perhaps, this lighting is also used on him as Sundance, and not only in the scenes with Katharine Ross (Fig. 3.10). This suggests that the interest of Redford as Sundance is still in his erotic/romantic aspect. [. . .] Effectively both films also minimise Redford's 'political' side. [. . .] *All the President's Men* on the other hand is entirely concerned with his political side and accordingly not at all with the erotic/romantic. He is lit in standard 'high-key' lighting. [. . .] As Bob Woodward, Redford is not filmed in any mock *cinéma vérité* lighting; he is still the 'attractively modelled' classic film hero (Fig. 3.11), but without the glamorous, erotic/romantic emphases of *The Way We Were* and *Butch Cassidy and the Sundance Kid*. [. . .]

Perfect Fit

In certain cases, all the aspects of a star's image fit with all the traits of a character. That is, all the various signs of character, including those achieved through the use of stars, accord. (Probably some aspects of the star's image will not be especially important, but they will not be incompatible either.) There are cases of this working with already known characters — Clark Gable as Rhett Butler in *Gone With the Wind*. [. . .] — and one would expect it to be the case with films not based on previous material but written and developed expressly for a given star.

For example, John Wayne. While most Wayne films simply use, and celebrate, his relaxed, masculine, Westerner/leader qualities, certain have also brought in his awkwardness with women and his 'authoritarian self-sufficiency' [. . .]: *Red River, Rio Bravo, The Searchers, The Man Who Shot Liberty Valance*. Equally a film like *The Sands of Iwo Jima*, by eliminating women from the scene and setting the narrative within an accepted authoritarian social structure, capitalises on the Wayne image

Fig. 3.10: *Robert Redford in* Butch Cassidy and the Sundance Kid, *1969 — glamour lighting, including halo effect, for his role as love interest.*

without having to criticise it. As Lawrence Alloway observes:

> His authority, physically massive, more at ease with men than women on the screen, makes him a natural for action pictures with teaching situations. [Alloway, 1971, p.37.]

(such as *The Sands of Iwo Jima*). 'A natural' here indicates the perfect fit between image and character. [. . .]

Problematic Fit

Although good cases can certainly be made for both a selective use of a star image and perfect fits between star images and film characters, it

264

Fig. 3.11: *Robert Redford in* All The President's Men, *1976 — plain, high key lighting for his role as the serious, questing journalist.*

seems to me that the powerfully, inescapably present, always-already-signifying nature of star images more often than not creates problems in the construction of character. [. . .] The contradictory and polysemic nature of the images makes it hard either to delimit a few aspects or to fully articulate the whole thing with the character as constructed by the other signs in the film. [. . .] In certain cases, the contradiction may be at all points, such that one can conceptualise the problem in terms of a

265

clash between two complex sign clusters, the star as image and the character as otherwise constructed. A prime example of this, in my view, is Monroe as Lorelei in *Gentlemen Prefer Blondes*. Everything about Anita Loos' character (in best-selling novel and smash hit Broadway musical and in Carol Channing's widely seen and known about interpretation of her in the latter) as well as the script of the film (e.g. what Jane Russell/Dorothy says about Lorelei), other performances and casting (e.g. the obvious manipulability of 'wet' Gus/Tommy Noonan and 'dirty old man' Piggy/Charles Coburn, the suspicion of 'straight man' Malone/Elliott Reid) and the structure of the film (Dorothy and Lorelei as polar opposites, in name, hair colour, interests in men and money; the basic hermeneutic of the Lorelei plot being whether or not Gus will realise Lorelei's true intentions); all of this constructs Lorelei as a cynical gold-digger, who fully understands how to use her sex appeal to trap rich men and is motivated above all by cupidity. Her dialogue as written is self-aware and witty, signalling (to us and to herself) amusement at what she is doing even while she is playing the *fausse-naive*. The weight of the Monroe image on the other hand is on innocence. She is certainly aware of her sexuality, but she is guiltless about it and it is moreover presented primarily in terms of narcissism — i.e. sexuality for herself rather than for men. At this stage in her image's development, her motivations were taken to be 'spiritual', either in the magic, 'little-girl' aspirations to be a movie star or in the 'pretentious' interests in Acting and Art. There is thus a quite massive disjunction between Monroe-as-image and Lorelei-as-character. They only touch at three points: the extraordinary impact of their physicality, a certain infantile manner and a habit of uttering witticisms. Yet even these points need to be qualified. Lorelei is quite definitely in control of her physicality whereas Monroe (at this stage in her image) was equally clearly not; Lorelei pretends to be infantile, Monroe was by and large taken to be so; Lorelei's wit expresses an intelligent but cynical appraisal of the situation, whereas Monroe's remarks to the press (known as Monroeisms) were regarded far more, at this point, as wisdom on a par with that 'out of the mouths of babes and sucklings' (i.e. wise by chance rather than by design). As a result of this disjunction (and one would need to demonstrate through close analysis the full complexity of the two image clusters we are talking of, Monroe's and Lorelei's), the character of Monroe-as-Lorelei becomes contradictory to the point of incoherence. This is not a question of Lorelei/Monroe being one thing one moment and another the next, but of her being simultaneously polar opposites. Thus, for instance, when Lorelei/Monroe says to Piggy that she had expected him to be older, him 'being a diamond miner and all', the lines as written and situated (in particular by Russell/Dorothy, straight-woman and confidante, thus in some measure privileged with respect to the truth of narrative and characters) indicate her manipulative propensities, but, because they emanate from

Monroe's mouth, they also at the same time indicate innocent pleasure in being sexy. [. . .]

[We could also consider the case of Charlton Heston. According to Michel Mourlet:]

> Charlton Heston is an axiom. By himself alone he constitutes a tragedy, and his presence in any films whatsoever suffices to create beauty. The contained violence expressed by the sombre phosphorescence of his eyes, his eagle's profile, the haughty arch of his eyebrows, his prominent cheek-bones, the bitter and hard curve of his mouth, the fabulous power of his torso: this is what he possesses and what not even the worst director can degrade. It is in this sense that one can say that Charlton Heston, by his existence alone, gives a more accurate definition of the cinema than films like *Hiroshima mon amour* or *Citizen Kane,* whose aesthetic either ignores or impugns Charlton Heston. (Quoted by Colin McArthur, 1967, in 'The Real Presence'.)

What analysis is concerned to do is both to discover the nature of the fit between star image and character, and, where the fit is not perfect or selective, to work out where the contradictions are articulated (at what level(s) of signification of character) and to attempt to see what possible sources of 'masking' or 'pseudo-unification' the film offers (such as the irresistible unifying force of a star image). [. . .]

CONCLUSION

I'd like to make four concluding remarks, which should be taken not as a summing up, much less as drawing things to a point of closure, but rather as suggestions of priorities or emphases for future work.

First of all, there is the question of the audience. Throughout, [. . .] the audience has been conspicuous by its absence. In talking of manipulation, consumption, ideological work, subversion, identification, reading, placing and elsewhere, a concept of the audience is clearly crucial, and yet in every case I have had to gesture towards this gap in our knowledge and then proceed as if this were *merely* a gap. But how one conceptualises the audience — and the empirical adequacy of one's conceptualisations — is fundamental to every assumption one can make about how stars, and films, work. We do not know enough about the production of media texts, and little empirical work has been done in the light of recent, more sophisticated theories of cultural production. Equally, the status as knowledge of the various formal or interpretative approaches to media texts has to remain problematic. Yet these weaknesses are as nothing compared to our ignorance, theoretical and empirical, of how films work for, on, with audiences — and which preposition you plump for is crucial. There are signs, however, that this absence is beginning to be made up by new theoretical developments and research projects. In addition, there is still quite a lot of data in much of the old empirical audience research work of which to make new sense.

One of the ways in which the question of the audience has been approached in recent years is through the notion of people as 'subjects'. Briefly, at its broadest, this approach is concerned with the way that ideology works not just as a set of ideas and representations that people use but as a process which also constructs people (as 'subjects'). What is decisive about this approach is that it refuses once and for all any notion of people as 'essences' existing outside of, over against ideology. What this approach puts in crisis consequently [. . .] is the sense of freedom, creativity, continuity, optimism and enterprise that founded the concept of the person in bourgeois society, and has informed much Marxist thought as well. This sense of crisis as to what a person is seems to me to be central also to the star phenomenon. It can be seen to lie behind star charisma as a generalised phenomenon, in that stars speak centrally to this crisis and seem to embody it or to condense it within themselves. How they speak to, embody or condense it may be predominantly in terms of reaffirming the reality of people as individuals or subjects over against ideology and history, or else in terms of exposing precisely the uncertainty and anxiety concerning the definition of what a person is. Whether affirming or exposing, or moving between the two, stars articulate this crisis always through the cultural and historical specificities of class, gender, race, sexuality, religion, sub-cultural formations, etc. Yet all stars seem to me to work also at the more general level — itself culturally and historically specific — of defining what a person is. I have suggested at various points how stars can be seen variously to handle opposed, or uneasily related, notions such as:

    star-as-person : star-as-image
    star-as-image : star-as-character
    star-as-auteur : star-as-text
    star-as-star : star-as-actor
    star-as-self : star-as-role
and now
    star-as-essence : star-as-subject

A fruitful way of studying the stars then would seem to be charting the ways that this crisis is articulated in, through and by them.

(Extracted from Richard Dyer, *Stars*, London: British Film Institute, 1979.)

References

Alloway, L. (1971), *Violent America*, New York: Museum of Modern Art.

Barthes, R. (1974), *S/Z*, New York: Hill and Wang.

Braudy, L. (1976), *The World in a Frame*, Garden City, New York: Anchor Press/Doubleday.

Brecht, B. (1964), *Brecht on Theatre* (ed. J. Willett), London: Methuen.

Brooks, C. and Warren, R. (1959), *Understanding Fiction*, New York: Appleton-Century-Crofts.

Burns, E. (1972), *Theatricality*, London: Longman.

Harvey, W. (1965), *Character and the Novel*, London: Chatto and Windus.

Hawthorn, J. (1973), *Identity and Relationship*, London: Lawrence and Wishart.

Johnston, C. (1973), *Notes on Women's Cinema*, London: Society for Education in Film and Television.

Kaplan, E. (1974), 'The Importance and Ultimate Failure of *Last Tango in Paris*', *Jump Cut*, no. 4, Nov.-Dec. 1974.

McArthur, C. (1967), 'The Real Presence', *Sight and Sound*, vol. 36, no. 3, Summer 1967.

Paris, B. (1974), *A Psychological Approach to Fiction*, Bloomington: Indiana University Press.

Rockwell, J. (1974), *Fact From Fiction*, London: Routledge & Kegan Paul.

Scholes, R. and Kellogg, R. (1966), *The Nature of Narrative*, New York: Oxford University Press.

Van Laan, T. (1970), *The Idiom of Drama*, Ithaca: Cornell University Press.

Watt, I. (1963), *The Rise of the Novel*, Harmondsworth: Penguin.

Willett, J. (1959), *The Theatre of Bertolt Brecht*, London: Methuen.

Narrative Cinema and Audience-Oriented Aesthetics

Theoretical interest in the cinema has recently tended to focus on notions such as 'distanciation', 'anti-illusionism', 'audience-participation'. The feeling is that the cinema ought to raise the consciousness of the spectator, demystify and instruct him about (political) reality and the ideological function of the cinema itself. In one sense, this is a discussion about the cinema as an institution within a certain society. But it also involves another one — and both are important — about how art, and in particular, the cinema relates to society and individual consciousness via the aesthetic processes themselves. How closely, in other words, are aesthetic developments tied to social ones, how do their structures interact with and determine each other, and more specifically, in what way — if any — can or should aesthetic processes serve non-aesthetic ends? One of the Marxists of this century who thought a good deal about these problems was Walter Benjamin. He came to the somewhat melancholy conclusion that art which fails aesthetically can be of no use politically (melancholy for Benjamin insofar as Dr Goebbels thought the same), and that to politicise art (as opposed to aestheticising politics, which is how Benjamin characterised art under fascism) was a difficult and complex undertaking: if change, so Benjamin argued, is the result of the interplay of dynamic forces at all levels in society, then the way that art can contribute to change (and this included social change) is by the 'production' of aesthetic forms, by creating ways of realising and releasing the inner dynamics of artistic activity, and by engaging in the dialectics of form and content, 'material' and mode of articulation. In effect, the only way art can be revolutionary according to Benjamin is by being 'auf der Höhe der Zeit' — abreast with the times. This may be a modest, and perhaps disappointingly unrevolutionary conclusion, but it poses a useful question — what are the specifically aesthetic modes of production in, for instance, the cinema, and what is its material and what its mode of articulation. [. . .]

The experience of watching a movie immerses the spectator in a temporal sequence. The cinema, despite the importance it gives to spatial organisation and visual iconography, is an art which depends for its articulation on time: a segment, usually between 1½ and 2 hours, is marked off by a very strong caesura at either end (lights down — projection of film — lights up) giving the spectator a sense of closure and enclosure more radical than either watching television, a play or listening to a concert or the radio is able to produce, not to mention the infinitely weaker sense of closure noticeable when picking up or putting down a book, or the virtually 'open' time experience of looking at a picture or a sculpture. It would therefore appear that in the cinema we are subjected to a particularly intense organisation of time, experienced within a formal structure which is closed, but in a sense also circular: we are 'captured' in order to be 'released', willingly undergoing a fixed term of imprisonment. However, this means that while we are watching a film — any film — a pressure (of anticipation, of oppression?) is generated which by its very nature has a strong psychic component and which would seem to demand some form of manipulation and cathexis, by way of projection, transformation and discharge. At the same time, it is easy to see that this pressure is artificial, 'fictional', an 'illusion' in terms of the intellect, because it is induced at will, every time we buy a ticket at the box-office, and therefore repeatable like a laboratory experiment, and thus quite unlike the emotions and psychic pressures encountered in 'real life'.

The question is whether such an energy or pressure inherent in the film event and apparently existing logically prior to any particular film, does not necessarily impinge on the actual film, regardless of whether this film sets out to accommodate and manipulate this energy in its visual-dramatic articulation or not. Perhaps one would here find a clue to why the popularity of films is such a (from an aesthetic point of view) erratic affair, for what it suggests is a reciprocal relationship between film and audience: a film not only immerses and absorbs an audience into *its* world, there is also a countercurrent where the spectator immerses the film into *his* (psychic) world, brought to the threshold of consciousness by the energy emanating from the viewing situation itself. The consequences are significant: communication between film and audience may depend vitally on the way this field of force establishes itself, and it may be that no communication is possible if the energy-flow from the spectator finds no appropriate channel. If, in Roman Jakobson's terminology, the 'phatic'* aspect of the communication process is blocked by a form of psychic resistance, could it be that, whatever its message, a film simply does not 'work'? If it is therefore true that this phatic element is more psychological in the cinema than in any other artistic medium and an integral part of the cinematic process of

---

* [According to the linguist Roman Jakobson, the 'phatic' dimension refers to those elements of the communication process whose aim is simply to establish *contact* and ensure that channels are open. Its most obvious form is in expressions like 'Good morning', 'How are you?', where the aim is not to solicit or provide information, but simply to establish linguistic contact.]

communication, one would expect to find it a determining factor of the code, and the possibility arises that the material conditions of the cinema as segmented time experienced in an enclosure will be reflected in its specific mode of 'producing' meaning. What are the mental and emotional predispositions which the tightly organised time experience engenders? First of all, it would seem to intensify the need for orientation, direction, causal sequence and 'rhythm'. Being enclosed in a darkened room, cut off visually from the surroundings and exposed to a state of isolation, the spectator looks for a focus — and finds it in the rectangle lit by the projector, the screen, which thereby functions visually as a point of orientation and psychologically as a kind of escape or safety-valve for the insecurity, aggression, anxiety mobilised by the viewing situation. Whether he intends it or not, the spectator cannot but project emotional energies onto the images on the screen. There is no possibility for Brecht's cigar-smoking sports-fan or Benjamin's 'distracted examiner' in the cinema.

Secondly, one is watching movies not at the pace one chooses, and in the random order one normally observes the 'world outside', but in a sequence selected and combined by someone else. This increases the spectator's unfreedom, just as montage and action, controlled by the director, and the irreversibility of the film-strip running through the projector impose an artificial rhythm. If this visual rhythm can in itself be very disorienting, especially when markedly at variance with one's perception of motion (e.g., speed-up or slow-motion), it is neutralised by the spectator's ability to construct for himself a time-space continuum as a perceptual hypothesis, which reduces the degree of anxiety caused by the sense of unfreedom and dependence, the passivity and state of receptivity to which he is exposed. Such a paralysis of visual and bodily motor-forces, however, produces in adults heavy defences, of an emotional, ideological and intellectual kind. In other words, the fact that the spectator is pinned to his seat and only has the screen to look at, causes impulses to arise which demand to be compensated, transferred and managed, and it is on this level that style, ideational content, causality, narrative sequence, plot, themes, point of view, identification, emotional participation enter into the viewing situation: whatever else they are, they are also ways in which the film manipulates, controls and directs the defences and impulses mobilised by motor-paralysis.

Thus, the essentially psychological handling of time in the cinema enters into the formal articulation of the filmic material in a variety of ways, and it may not be altogether an exaggeration to say that the primary material of the cinema is not celluloid or the ideological consciousness of the spectator, nor even a particular theme, story or subject, but the viewing situation itself, and that its typical 'mode of production' is the transformation of this situation into 'meanings' by aesthetic processes and rhetorical devices.

On the face of it, the situation as I have described it makes a very strong case for a certain type of cinema — the narrative cinema, working with fictional, spectacular, dramatic or 'illusionist' means and embodying a very conscious manipulation of audience responses. But before arguing this more fully (and also its limitations), the existence of what I would call a 'psychic matrix' can be proven negatively. Whenever for some reason or other the energy and the defensive mechanisms of the viewing situation are not managed by a film, or where tension is not 'objectified' in terms of conflict, suspense etc. the audience often produces 'fall-out' reactions, such as restlessness, aggressiveness (irritation, protective laughter, verbal comment) or a feeling of boredom, claustrophobia. To watch a 'bad' film can be a disproportionately depressing experience. This suggests that such a film is at odds with the psychic matrix and therefore fails to make phatic contact with its audience. No film therefore encounters a 'neutral' audience, but a tissue of expectations and potential stimuli-responses.

Phrased like this, the psychological model of the function of narrative is not without crudity and over-generalisation. But it does suggest one rather important speculation. For instance, it seems possible to argue that on the vexing question of 'realism' it offers some insight. One need not reflect very long to realise that the only element which is mimetic in even the most realistic film is the physical movement of the characters, and the Hollywood behavioural realistic code makes no exception. But rather than interpreting the emphasis on body-movement and gesture, the observance of rough and ready canons of verisimilitude and consistency as 'realism' and relating it to the ideational or referential part of the 'message', it seems to make more sense to see them contributing primarily to the establishment and maintenance of phatic contact, and that consequently 'representation' in the cinema has little to do with either literary realism or illusionist representation in the visual arts, because it belongs to a different function of the communication process. This would mean that the 'modernist' arguments against 'illusionism', or talk about the monocular 'castration' of the camera are misconceived — at least in the form in which they are generally propounded, since it seems likely that the function of mimesis in the narrative cinema is of a primarily psychological kind and only to a secondary degree belongs to the sphere of perception at all. As E. H. Gombrich has shown, psychologically speaking realism is determined by function and use (the stick that serves as a hobby-horse) and that 'illusion' is not a one-to-one matching, but a complex process of 'consistent' or 'purposive' reading, in view of some particular function or end. Realism in this sense is entirely in the eye of the beholder. Such an interpretation would account for the fact that one can tolerate in effect a good deal of motivational improbability in the characters, lack of plausibility in the situations, elliptical narrative and other discontinuities, provided that the phatic contact is maintained and that there are other elements which do provide for the possibility of 'consistent reading' on another level of articulation, or manage to make the apparent discontinuities function consistently within different (often symbolic) orders of coherence and systematisation.

If what I have asserted about the existence of a psychic matrix is correct, and it does constitute a primary, albeit perhaps 'negative' level of articulation in a film, it needs arguing that it does not only significantly influence a film's possibilities of communicating with an audience, but also plays a role in the visual articulation itself, and consequently in the process of generating meaning and aesthetic value. A film is the transformation of discontinuous particles (images) into a perceptual continuum which at the same time regulates and structures an artificially closed, psychologically active time experience in the spectator. This 'model' — the accumulation and management of discontinuities and their sequential articulation through transformation (which we find on the semantic level of a narrative film) — corresponds to a similar model — the accumulation and management of energy impulses and their transformation into dynamic patterns — in the primary relation of spectator to film. Their interpenetration constitutes the aesthetic dimension of the cinema, its specificity as a code, and it also defines the relationship of the film-maker to his material, by indicating the scope within which he can generate meaning and communicate it. Perhaps it is therefore useful to approach a film as an aesthetic object by imagining it to be the result of a series of transformational processes: transformation of psychic impulses into segments of action, of action into emotional response, of emotional responses into 'consistent readings', of consistent readings into plot-elements or larger, symbolic structural units, and of plot into continuous phatic contact as well as ideational, poetic, ideological, etc. 'meaning'. Evidently, this is not a hierarchical progression, but an interpenetration and coalescence of simultaneous processes. From the point of view of film aesthetics, whenever transformational processes of this kind can be shown to be present in a systematic form, one can speak of a film as having aesthetic coherence and one can identify different 'levels of discourse'.

In what way does this illuminate the study of narrative films and of the classical Hollywood narrative in particular? I shall in the following deal only with two aspects, the function of 'plot' and of 'mise en scène' as two distinctive transformational processes.

It is well known that the narrative tradition developed by Hollywood is based on strongly profiled, 'typical' plots: geometrical in shape (linear, though occasionally circular or tangential), consecutive, generated by an alternating rhythm of conflict, climax, resolution. Western and gangster films almost invariably embody plots of pursuits, quests, treks, and themes centred on the ambition to arrive, make it, get to the top, or

274

to avenge, control. Even in psychological films and melodramas one finds similar plot-dynamics and thematic conjunctions: to expiate, to control the self, to adapt by purging or successively working out anti-social impulses and forces, overcoming internal and external obstacles. Regularly the spectator is introduced to one or several protagonists placed in a certain situation or a set of circumstances, usually containing elements of tension, friction, mystery or contradiction. The subsequent action follows out in what amounts to roughly chronological order either the genesis of this situation (via a flash-back structure) or the progressive implications and final resolution of the protagonists having to confront each other within the situation. These dramatic configurations engineered through plot and protagonists are evidently important structural constants in the American cinema. On the one hand, they strongly reflect the dynamics of the psychic matrix: precisely because of the high degree of schematisation the plots provide a possible way of regulating psychic pressure, and on this level, they could be seen as the primary vector of energy, a macro-structure of cathexis, projecting and objectifying libidinal and aggressive drives. This would help to account for the inordinate emphasis of the Hollywood tradition on action, violence, eroticism, the predominance of energy-intensive heroes, the graphs of maximum investment of vitality, phallic models of identity and self-assertion, instinctual drive-patterns, the accentuation of voyeuristic and fantasising tendencies and projections, as well as the value placed on the spectacular, the exotic, the adventurous. Being quite possibly subliminal ways of charting a course of energy expenditure/ management, these plots compensate very directly, and from a psychological point of view very efficiently, motor inhibitions and allow for massive discharges of anxiety feelings through the arousal of less primary but dramatically or intellectually validated tensions and 'suspense' which is then managed by the plots and the action.

On the other hand, because of the dynamic nature of these plots, they are capable of intensive and almost infinite 'thematisation', so that they not only take on all manner of secondary, tertiary meanings (moral, social, intellectual, etc.) but also absorb a great variety of ideational substances — about American society, the American family, alienation, the national character, the national past (cf. the melodrama of the 50s, the topical or sociological significance of Capra's movies, of the Warner pictures about the depression, the socially progressive prison movies of the late 40s, etc.).

Another aspect of how the strongly articulated plots reflect the viewing situation is the way they accelerate chronology into causality, in accordance with the principle 'post hoc ergo propter hoc', making sequence suggest a cause-and-effect relation, thus emphasising the irreversibility of the film experience, in itself dramatised and thematised especially in the thriller and the film noir: time is always running out on the gangster, and an aura of fatality, doom and inescapable annihilation accompanies the action. The viewing situation here parallels a social and cultural metaphysics, which evolved in conjunction with the fast action montage of the B-picture that couldn't afford proper sets, and which suggested extreme psychological repression in the gritty stoicism of the flamboyantly anti-social criminal. But if we bear in mind the relation of these patterns to the viewing situation, it would seem likely that, for instance, the central protagonist, defined as he generally is in dynamic terms as the focus of perpetual agitation and motion, reflects and catalyses not necessarily the frustrations and desires engendered in everyday life and under capitalism, but more specifically the pressures and constraints which the psychic matrix mobilises in the spectator. [. . .]

However, it would be unfair to say that the plot only serves to establish phatic contact with an audience and to produce a form of energy cathexis. Just as other cinematic traditions have evolved ways in which phatic contact and cathexis can be maintained without strongly dramatic, linear plots, so the strong plot in American cinema can have a more directly aesthetic function. Because of its dynamic nature, it plays a vital part in the processes of transformation mentioned above: by energising the narrative articulation, it provides a way in which the accumulation of discontinuities can fuse into patterns, suggesting totalities and contexts of meaning which are effective precisely because they are only suggested. Intellectual structures of meaning, for instance, seem to become aesthetically important in the cinema only when they are communicated dynamically, that is as 'rhythm', which means that discontinuities in articulation and sequence (what is 'left out') become a major source of narrative energy, the discontinuities acting as the release-mechanisms for 'switches' between various levels of discourse. [. . .]

If we therefore look at the history of Hollywood, we can see that the strongly articulated plot has been the basis for some of the most sophisticated and elaborate codes of transformation, and that the aesthetic significance of these films lies precisely in the 'production' of levels of meaning through the transformational relay, of establishing a distance and perspective if you like, between the ideational 'content' and its sequential structure in the actual film. This process, of course, is generally known as *mise en scène*, and auteur criticism has made this its domain.* In a sense, all *mise en scène* is transformation, and all

---

* [*Auteur* theory (from the French word for 'author') is a method of film criticism formulated by French writers in the 1950s which was probably the first to allow any serious consideration of Hollywood directors such as Hitchcock, Hawks, Minnelli, Preminger. In its simplest form, it claims that the work of any film-maker should be analysed in terms of its thematic consistency and development through a number of films.]

276

transformation is 'distanciation', the more so as the *mise en scène* supplies a whole range of systematic ways by which 'story-material' is 'managed' as forms of narrative discourse. In this tradition of film-making, not only the viewing situation itself is part of the filmic material, but the primary transformation of the viewing situation (i.e. cathexis achieved by means of conventional and stereotyped plots and schematic plot-structures) makes up the material basis, and is therefore subject to further transformation in the articulated film. Thus, the work of directors like Hitchcock, Lang, Sirk, Cukor, Minnelli, Ray, Losey, is proof that the relationship of 'plot' to 'meaning' has always been far from simple, for these directors, among others, have evolved quite specific modes of transformation which allow them to handle their material in ways designed to produce out of the common viewing-situation and often conventional plots highly individualised levels of discourse.

In some respects, the best 'plot' oriented cinema stands in the literary tradition of Flaubert. With *Madame Bovary*, Flaubert set out to write a 'realist' novel which not only described the phenomenological surface and the inner dynamism of a given society in a cool and detached way, but also the kind of consciousness and fantasies which this society produces. It is the society and the individuals who inhabit it that constitute his 'material', and the mind of his heroine made up the limits of what he could communicate directly. Faced with the problem of presenting essentially banal events and characters in a literary form which depicted them and their motivations 'from inside' while at the same time 'placing' them critically, Flaubert evolved a style not unlike that of the modern narrative *mise en scène* in the way it blends the 'invisible' narrator, and a mode of presentation where the objective surface description merges with the emanations of a subjective consciousness. In the cinema, this 'classical' style of the invisible camera and the single visual articulation is associated with 'neo-realism'. [. . .]

In the context of our present discussion, therefore, the 'phenomenological' element in the classical narrative style might be better defined as the integration of the subjective perception — of the spectator or of a character — with an objective presentation inside the same narrative movement and the single visual articulation. That which in the cinematic image appears as unmediated, direct representation, always in a tense one might call the 'present continuous', could be used to yield an additional 'level of discourse' for the objective 'placing' (historically, ideologically, stylistically) of the characters and events thus represented. It meant that the 'description' of an external world at the same time functioned as the metaphoric code for a subjective awareness, reacting to, and being conditioned by that external world. 'There is', Flaubert wrote, 'not a single isolated description in my book that could be called gratuitous, all serve my characters or have a direct or indirect rapport with the action.'

It is a statement which could have been made by any of the directors we now think of as 'classical': from Ford to Preminger and Lang, from Welles to Renoir or Mizoguchi, for it expresses one of the most important acquisitions of cinematic *mise en scène*: the neutralisation of phatic contact, by a transformation of spectator-projection, into 'subjective' vision within the action itself, and the transformation of that subjective vision into a critical discourse which 'places' and 'relates' things and people as it 'shows' them. [. . .] In the American cinema the transformation of representation into subjective extension and materialisation of an inner world has given rise to the theme of the vision itself as the subject of the 'discourse', notably in the films of Lang and Hitchcock, but also through a genre like the musical, as the dramatic embodiment of the relation between the emotional desire for self-projection (which 'absorbs' the phatic energy of the viewing situation) and its voyeuristic compensation in the visual spectacle of the 'show', whose mechanisms the films of Donen, Minnelli or Cukor render explicit. [. . .]

If the double 'aspect' of the image as representation of an action or segment of an action and emanation of a participating consciousness is undoubtedly one of the fundamental ways in which the narrative as story transforms itself into discourse, it is by no means the only one. Any study of the work of the major directors in the narrative tradition will show that the transformational processes employed constitute systems of exchange (open to Freudian as well as Marxist interpretations). Operated by such 'poetic' devices as symbolisation, metaphoric condensation or metonymic displacement, ellipsis, iconographic overdetermination, visual 'rhymes' or the parodying of genre situations and visual cliches, the narrative can 'save' plot, 'invest' meaning in objects, 'substitute' causal relations in a way that suggests analogies with the 'saving' of psychic energy in dream work and jokes, the 'investment' and accumulation of capital, or the substitution processes known as reification and fetishism: at the same time, they refer us back to the viewing situation and the need for energy- and defence-management through formal articulation and the production of ideational intellectual meaning.

In their function as stylistic devices, these systems are not only capable of producing these meanings, they are also able to place them in a critical perspective: they allow the film-maker to establish a dialectical relationship between 'material' and its formal articulation. Again, these are not the only 'modes of production' available to a film-maker. We must add the more general means of structuring the narrative through repetition, parallels, contrasts, juxtapositions, spatial organisation, foregrounding of non-diegetic elements, de-phasing of dramatic climaxes, use of visual or aural leitmotifs, and the possibilities of the sound-track in general. And we should include the pictorial elaboration of the image and sequence itself, by means of camera-angle, visual composition, colour, lighting, placing of characters, framing and other principles of selection, together with the various principles on the axis of combination, i.e. which shot follows which, how long a shot is held, whether the camera follows a character's movement or not and so on. [. . .]

In the narrative cinema, therefore, the relation of 'device' to 'motivation' is a varied and fluid one, and in the Hollywood tradition, for example, an individual director's style can often be defined by the extent to which he lets the discourse dominate the story or is prepared to embed it in the plot as a 'stylistic' amplification. [. . .]

On this level, these are rough typological distinctions and they do not seem to yield any evaluative criteria, but simply serve to indicate that an immense variety of types of discourse can articulate itself within a comparatively restricted range of basic story- and plot-material, whereby the relation of narrative as story to narrative as discourse can be a dialectical one. [. . .]

The cinema as an act of communication involves two complementary processes: recognition and 'surprise' — information can only be communicated by a high level of redundancy, and the element of recognition corresponds to the level of redundancy carried by any system of communication. What I have called the phatic aspect of 'identification' is therefore complemented by the processes of recognition and surprise (or frustrated recognition) — the latter acting as a stimulus towards renewed projection and increased participation.

Recognition in the cinema, however, can take a variety of forms: recognition of stereotypes, clichés, genre-conventions, iconography; recognition of plot-situations or typical drive-patterns; recognition of the actors and stars; recognition of other movies; recognition of a director's style and themes — all of which in their different ways and on different levels of intellectual sophistication create a matrix of expectations and anticipatory projections coexisting and fusing with the more primary matrix of the viewing situation itself. Like the latter, the matrix of expectations can be frustrated [. . .] or it can be manipulated, either by 'managing' it through gratification (amplification, orchestration, dynamisation) or — in order to shift the level of participation from the emotional to the intellectual level — through postponed gratification by means of distanciation, irony, reversal, counterpoint, or stylistic elaboration.

None of these forms of recognition, on the other hand, seem to involve or produce the illusion that what is being represented is mistaken for 'real' in the way one might be mistaken about a person's anger or affection being 'real' or merely simulated: one of the functions of imaginative literature and fictional narrative in the cinema is precisely to shift this problem to another plane — namely where we know what we read or see is 'real' on the level of articulation, and 'unreal' on the level of the referent. For fictional realism, however we define it, is not concerned with the mimesis of substances, but based on an analogy of functions, i.e., it furnishes a system of symbolic representations. Thus, for instance, the cinematic image produces representation for symbolic use, and this primarily by virtue of being able to imitate or represent motion: any kind of imaginative participation takes place only under dynamic conditions, and in the cinema this first-level dynamism is furnished by the movements of the characters and the camera. The fictional framework therefore allows us to construe all movement as symbolic of functions, i.e. as potentially significant, by interpreting it as purposive and motivated. In this context it is of less importance whether we think of the 'motivational' impulses as intellectual ones emanating from the locus of intentionality we normally call the director or as behavioural-psychological ones presented through the characters. Regardless, in other words, of where we locate the motivation or how we construe the purpose, it is the endeavour towards 'consistent readings' within the fictional framework (an endeavour heavily relying on recognition) that provides the basis for stimulating active participation, and thereby for understanding, communication, cognition, 'raising of consciousness', etc.

If the endeavour is consistently and instantly gratified, the level of participation will be correspondingly low, because the elements of redundancy are predominant in relation to the informational message. The spectator will be bored, and he will feel the pressure of the psychic matrix, unable to project itself through participation onto the screen. If this endeavour is partially frustrated, it produces an energy which the film-maker can use in order to re-orient the spectator towards another level of discourse: the frustration acts once more as a transformational relay in the communication process. If on the other hand it is consistently frustrated, the energy will regress — into irritation, aggressiveness and boredom. This is a continuous spectrum of responses, because the regressive effect can also occur if the effort towards re-orientation is too difficult or obscure for the audience, although a more experienced spectator will be able to derive increased participation from having been able to tolerate a high degree of frustration without regression and arriving at the recognition of the new level of discourse, i.e. of having his phatic energy temporarily blocked and frustrated, and subsequently accommodated and managed in a more sublimated, possibly intellectualised form by the narrative articulation. There is thus a close relationship between the motor-inhibition of the viewing situation, the need for projection, the presence of movement on the screen, the stimulation of emotional participation, the temporary frustration of participation through discontinuity, ellipsis and other forms of narrative transformation which in turn maintain the efforts towards consistent reading, plotting of meaning, confirmation of meaning, emotional assent, 'raising of consciousness', etc.

At the same time, plot-situations, whether strongly articulated or merely conjectured through attempts at consistent reading, produce states of tension, contradiction, conflict — and this emotionally as well as intellectually. Every new term in the sequential development, every alteration of the narrative configuration will modify these states and call into being other forces. This again relates the spectator in a highly dynamic way to the unfolding sequence or action, if he is given the opportunity to manage and tolerate these tensions, rather than having to suppress or reject them. This level of tolerance is generally regulated by the fictional nature of the narrative, what we know as 'suspension of disbelief' — a process only inadequately described by the notions of empathy and identification, because as I have tried to indicate, the actual process in the cinema at least is less passive or indeed simple than what these notions commonly suggest.

Recognition, for example, in a fictional framework, opens the possibility for the spectator to relax his defensive mechanisms active in real life and to entertain feelings, states of being, fantasies, desires normally repressed or heavily censored. Narrative films in particular foster a state of consciousness with a low ego-object definition (as indicated above in the fusion of subjective/objective *mise en scène*) associated in psychology with oral fantasy material and yielding a high degree of pleasure. On one level this represents a 'liberation', because it sets free impulses associated with early stages of human development and permits them to manifest themselves in a non-repressive way: in this sense, the tensions communicated through the plot do have their analogy on a more fundamental psychic level, where they arouse and structure dynamically the spectator's own fantasies. [. . .]

The particular achievement of the best Hollywood tradition has been to transform — partly because maintaining a very active phatic contact with its audience — fantasy material and popular mythology into secondary discourse, often about these fantasies and the nature of the cinematic communication in a given social context. These discourses were themselves gratifying, because productive of meaning.

To sum up: there exists in the narrative cinema a continuous spectrum of transformational processes: from seeing the hero act out gratification of drives experienced vicariously to the most complex and aesthetically demanding manipulations of emotional responses and management of fantasy material through stylistic elaboration; from the transformation of energy cathexis into intellectual curiosity to the handling of a-priori expectations in a manner that produces both recognition and 'problem-solving' behaviour. The narrative cinema can (depending on the fantasy material and the disposition of the spectator) produce a plethora of meanings and forms of discourse, while at the same time interacting with more primary psychological patterns inherent in the cinema as an institution and a physical/physiological time-experience. So long as the cinematic experience as well as its ability to signify is defined by such an interaction of limiting conditions, the narrative form appears to be the most complex and difficult mode of signification: it enables the spectator to make contact with his 'total' or submerged self by stimulating access to levels of fantasy material normally closed; it manages, shapes and articulates these fantasies either within the plot itself, by the way patterns of tension and conflict are established within the story through interplay of different characters' responses to each other (all of whom can be 'objects' of spectator-projections), or formally by stylisation or distancing devices (irony, 'placing') and other systematisations (elaborating 'meanings' and patterns, shaping the plot into symbolic action). All this contributes directly to the communication process made up of recognition and surprise: for instance, the discovery of formal patterns, of esoteric meanings, of stylisation is as much part of an identification process as the more elementary identification with, say, drive-oriented heroes or the dynamics of the strongly articulated plot. From the point of view of audience-oriented aesthetics, distanciation techniques are simply additional forms of ensuring participation, necessary where a more 'dangerous' or heavily repressed fantasy requires more complicated forms of management. An intellectual spectator, for example, might find the fantasies of the American popular cinema only acceptable in forms which are 'overmanaged' through stylisation and distanciation. Where he cannot find these defences in the articulation itself, such a spectator might well try and 'overmanage' them himself, via 'cultism' or 'camp'. On the other hand, the function of the *mise en scène* in this context of the popular cinema is to produce a kind of 'surplus' meaning, available to the perceptive audience (or registering in the ordinary spectator in an unconscious fashion) for regulative or pleasurable management.

This, then, is one way of seeing the specifically aesthetic work of the director on the cinematic material, his mode of production — and it characterises the method of the best narrative cinema as dialectical and its approach as materialist. That in the case of Hollywood, the directors have often been not only restricted in their choice of ideational codes, but even limited in the fantasy projections by economic and ideological reasons, does not seem to invalidate their aesthetic procedures, but rather underlines the enormous productivity of cinematic forms which the narrative cinema is capable of under its limiting conditions.

(Originally delivered as a paper to a seminar organised by the Educational Advisory Service of the British Film Institute in March 1969.)

PART IV
HISTORY, POLITICS AND CLASSICAL NARRATIVE

Introduction

History in various guises is a staple of television programming. For many people television is the only medium through which they are exposed to history after schooling. The spectrum of tele-history ranges from costume drama (*The Six Wives of Henry VIII, Edward and Mrs Simpson, Testament of Youth*) through various kinds of personalised documentary (*The Ascent of Man*, Alistair Cooke's *America*) and dramatised reconstructions of historical events (*Culloden, Three Days in Szczecin*) to programmes constructed wholly or in part out of film archive footage (*The World at War, The Troubles*). These series and one-off plays with historical settings are among the most prestigious output of British television; they sell well internationally, win large audiences at home, and nowadays often attract co-finance from abroad.

While the broadcasting institutions would strictly demarcate within tele-history between documentary series and drama, this distinction has recently been blurred by various hybrids of drama-documentary, which lay claim to greater historical accuracy because the sequence of events depicted (and, in some cases, the dialogue spoken) is in some fashion authenticated by archive sources. Nevertheless, the scope for fictionalisation in the very shooting and editing of such reconstructions of actuality is enormous, as notorious examples like *Death of a Princess* have made plain.

Moreover the factual sanctity of straight documentary series has been problematised, either by historians who differ on matters of interpretation (for example, the advisers on the two television histories of Ireland transmitted in 1980, *The Troubles* (Thames) and *Ireland: A Television History* (BBC)), or, more fundamentally, by students of the media who point out that these various series collectively offer a very partial construction of 'acceptable' history.

According to this view, television history is fabricated to serve the needs of the present. As Keith Tribe puts it in one of the readings collected in this Part: 'The "lessons of history" are not inscribed in the simple existence of a past; they are the product of the construction of a history which can be deployed in contemporary arguments.' The issue becomes *how* history is deployed. Most conventional tele-history promotes an idealised construction of the British heritage: sagas of royal families, accounts of voyages of exploration, of military campaigns and wartime experiences. Certain topics are noticeable by their comparative absence from the subject matter of acceptable tele-history: the history of imperialism (as opposed to colonial history) or the history of the labour movement, for example. Until *Shoulder to Shoulder*, feminist history had also received scant attention. Even historical dramas with little commitment to historical accuracy — the royal soap operas in particular — carry a particular construction of British history pivotting around the personalities and activities of monarchs.

A seminal critique of orthodox tele-history was made by Colin McArthur in 1978, in a British Film Institute monograph called *Television and History*, extracts from which are reprinted in this Part. McArthur's analysis centres on the cosy symmetry between conventional traditions of British historiography, the dominance of history of a bourgeois stamp, and the presentation of the past on television. One manifestation of this is the preponderance of Great Men on television, deriving from a liberal historiography which foregrounds the actions and thoughts of individuals, particularly in the serialised biographies of figures as diverse as Charles Darwin and Lord Mountbatten. McArthur also finds the aesthetic categories of bourgeois history epitomised in the nostalgic return to Victorian and Edwardian milieux characteristic of many drama series (*Upstairs, Downstairs*; *The Duchess of Duke Street*), as well as of adaptations of literary classics (*The Forsyte Saga*). After analysing an episode of *Upstairs, Downstairs* set during the General Strike of 1926, in which he finds turns of phrase reminiscent of the 1973 miners' strike, McArthur goes on to elaborate what an alternative tele-history might look like.

One of the forms of television historical drama which McArthur holds up as a model in this respect is the series *Days of Hope*. Our second reading is a selection from a debate that was conducted in relation to this series in the pages of *Screen* between 1975 and 1978. McArthur's adversaries maintained that it was impossible simply to recover radical history by pouring a politically progressive content (history from a working-class point of view) into a bourgeois form (the realist drama), as they allege was the case with *Days of Hope*. In particular, Colin MacCabe, extending his criticism of the 'classic realist text' (see Part III of this Reader), argued that realistic representations of the past are inherently self-confirming, unable to produce a contradiction which, remaining unresolved, would oblige the viewer to think for her or himself. Attempts at progressive history such as *Days of Hope* or *Culloden*, according to this view, are doomed to be recuperated by their commitment to the idea of a single unified 'truth' and an image which can only confirm it.

In 1980 John Caughie, writing again in *Screen*, picked up the debate about progressivism, this time through the concept of documentary drama. He traces the roots of this hybrid form back to naturalism in the novel and the theatre, and analyses its two kinds of 'look': the rhetoric of dramatic fiction, and the social space of a document to be looked at. 'My argument against the documentary drama as it has been formulated has

286

been that, though it is struggling on the right side, it produces itself within a self-confirming integration, and produces a spectator who is also confirmed in an already determined position.' While returning to *Screen*'s initial criticism of *Days of Hope*, Caughie also insists that, given institutional constraints on production, and the political forces current at the time of screening, a film may be progressive television if, by merely extending the range of representation to previously 'invisible' social groups, a repressed history is thereby recovered. Unfortunately, such instances of progressive history on television remain a handful among a cornucopia of costume drama and potted histories serving other ideological concerns of the present.

Historical Drama

Elderly people in our culture are frequently oriented towards the past, the time of their vigour and power, and resist the future as a threat. It is probable that a whole culture in an advanced state of loss of relative power and disintegration may thus have a dominant orientation towards a lost golden age while life is lived sluggishly along in the present. (R. S. Lynd)

[. . .] In many respects the archetype of nostalgia for an earlier period is *Upstairs, Downstairs* (LWT), certainly one of the most successful, in commercial and critical terms, both in the UK and abroad (for example, it won an 'Emmy' — the US television drama award). Clearly, the series' excellence in terms of the norms of bourgeois drama — the writing, the playing, the production values — are important elements in its success, but the argument of this monograph is that all television (including drama) fulfils an ideological function and that there will be a relationship between the popularity of a programme and the extent to which it reinforces the ideological position of the majority audience.

To be speculative, it seems reasonable to suppose that a society going through a period of historical transition and finding it immensely painful and disorienting will therefore tend to recreate, in some at least of its art, images of more (apparently) settled times, especially times in which the self-image of the society as a whole was buoyant and optimistic. For post-war Britain, faced as it is with adjustment to being a post-colonial power, a mediocre economic performer, a multi-racial society and a society in which the consensus of acceptable social and political behaviour is fragmenting (all, of course, factors which are intimately inter-related), what better ideological choice, in its art, than to return to the period of the zenith of bourgeois and imperial power or to immediately succeeding periods in which the façade of that power appeared convincing.

[. . .] No matter what period history-writing or historical drama is ostensibly dealing with, in reality it is providing for the ideological needs of the present. Thus, one of the projects of programmes such as *Upstairs, Downstairs* is the feeding of a dangerous contemporary nostalgia for more settled times but it is doubtful if a project of such generality would sustain the series over the lengthy period of its run. One would expect to find, therefore, that — just like *Edward the Seventh* — *Upstairs, Downstairs* will offer more concrete ideological guidance to the 'problems' of today. Unlike *Edward the Seventh*, it does not deal regularly with historical personages (although this or that historical figure will appear in a particular episode). It operates ideologically, therefore, by what could be called a process of cannibalising history, by taking particular historical events and offering ideological guidance by refracting them through the on-going, well-signified, and well-understood value-system of the series.

This value-system is well-known. The series deals with a particular household through the late Victorian, Edwardian and early Georgian periods. With an unerring ideological accuracy which presents the curious mixture of the aristocratic and the *haut bourgeois* lying at the heart of the British system of class power, the series has the (original) wife coming from an aristocratic family and the husband (the absolutely key ideological force in the series) as an upper middle-class Tory Member of Parliament. The mix of the aristocratic and the bourgeois is skilfully retained, after the death of the first wife on the Titanic, by ennobling the husband and having him marry a bourgeois woman.

It is the *household* which the series deals with. We come to know the husband and wife, their children, relations and friends *and* the domestic staff — as hierarchical in their way as the family above stairs — with the butler and cook functioning as the analogues of the husband and wife. (This analogue was made explicit at the end of the series by the marriage of the butler and the cook.)

We see the family and the servants in their own lives and in their inter-relationships and despite the sometimes quite extreme dramatic situations – bereavement, suicide, unwanted pregnancy, etc. — and despite the fact that both classes are seen 'warts and all' — the overall mood of the series is one of celebration of the relatively cosy stability of a society in which everyone (certainly the regular 'characters') knows his/her place, accepts it and is treated with 'dignity' and 'kindness' within it.

Within the range of 'characters' the audience has come to know (and, dare one say it, 'love') expectations are created as to what their responses will be to any situation or event. Thus, the aristocratic wife, though kind and charming, is a little 'old-fashioned'; the somewhat feckless son is liable to opt for apocalyptic solutions to problems (he eventually blows his brains out); the Scottish butler effectively conceals his basic humanity under a sharp sense of class proprieties further stiffened with Calvinism; and the spinsterish lady's maid, though loyal and plucky, does not pretend to understand the complexities of society. Standing like a rock at the centre of the series — the ideological rock, that is, not the dramatic rock, a role which oscillates between the Scottish butler and the lady's maid — is the father of the house. It is invariably he who finds the 'sensible' solution to crises where solutions are possible: it is he who is our ideological guide through history and, by extension, through the problems of the present.

This, then, is the ongoing framework through which history is mediated. It is useful, therefore, to consider in some detail how a particular historical event (the General Strike) is refracted through *Upstairs, Downstairs.*

The title of the episode within which the General Strike figures — 'The Nine Day Wonder' — is in itself ideologically interesting and gives some indication of where the programme's sympathies will eventually lie. The question is broached very early on in the episode between Hudson (the Scottish butler) and James (the feckless son of the house). Their attitudes would be recognised as characteristic by the audience:

> *James:* Coal fires in May. Miners out on strike and the rest of the country all jumping on the bandwagon. What a mess!
>
> *Hudson:* I gather there's still hope of a settlement, sir. The trade union leaders are at Downing Street at this very moment. It's just been announced on the wireless.
>
> *James:* But it shouldn't have been allowed to come to this. A General Strike is a direct affront to the government. An insult to democracy. It should be forbidden. By law.
>
> *Hudson:* I agree with you, sir. I feel deeply ashamed of my fellow working man.
>
> *James:* You, Hudson? You've got nothing to be ashamed about. Not your fault. It's men like Cook and Thomas and Bevin . . . so called leaders . . . having the nerve to hold the country to ransom . . . and threaten the liberty of ordinary, decent people . . .

The phrase used by James 'hold the country to ransom' was a key media phrase during the miners' strike of 1973/74 which led to the fall of the then Conservative government. The use of this phrase signals to us that the central ideological project of the programme has to do with attitudes not to the General Strike *per se,* but to working class militancy in our society here and now.

The other figures in the household talk and act in character: Frederick, an ambitious footman and wartime batman to James, talks with relish about the armed forces getting ready for the fight to come (he and James 'scab' on the buses); Hudson, claiming Winston Churchill as authority, asserts that 'all miners are reds' to which Ruby, the kitchen-maid, retorts that her uncle is a miner and he's not a red. Lady Prudence, a close family friend, having remarked on the lack of consideration of the strikers, throws her home open to Oxbridge students 'scabbing' on the trains; and Georgina (the father's ward), while censorious of James' pomposity, nevertheless organises deliveries of the British Gazette.

Against such blinkered responses, Richard (the father) enters and begins to fulfil his ongoing ideological role of mediator and compromiser, of incarnating Social Democracy. Asked what had happened to the last-minute talks between the TUC leaders and the Government, Richard replies:

> Ended in confusion. Apparently some *Daily Mail* printers refused to print an article which condemned the strike. Baldwin got to hear about it and sent Thomas and company home. Far too hasty in my opinion. Nobody wants this wretched strike. They were looking to Baldwin to help them save face.

Significantly, Richard's first condemnation is not of the strikers, but of the government and when James talks of the masses as about to do a Russia 1917 job, he replies:

> I don't go as far as James, but there's certainly a strong feeling of solidarity in the working classes, rather like the early days of the war.

This construction by Richard of the British working-class as decent, human and patriotic will be taken up and developed when Ruby's uncle, already referred to, comes to the house with a fellow-miner, both of them having come from the north of England on a miners' delegation. However, at the same time as Richard is fulfilling his *ideological* role of mediator and spokesman for Social Democracy against blind reaction, he nevertheless fulfils his *class* role of complimenting everyone, family and servants alike, on the measures they are taking to keep things going — 'we must all pull together, do what we can' — and his last act before leaving for the House ('to see what I can contribute') is to give Hudson permission to enlist as a special constable. The point at which Richard's *class* role and his *ideological* role fuse — or, more accurately, where the contradictions lie uneasily together — is when he addresses the servants collectively about the strike and sounds most like a social democratic politician:

> Now I don't want to go into all the issues . . . who's right and who's wrong in this dispute. I'm sure you realise very clearly that for the future life and prosperity of this country the strike must not be allowed to succeed. Nor, on the other hand, must it develop into a violent and bitter struggle between the classes. A solution will be found. In the meantime, we must all show restraint, patience, good humour . . .

The scene in which this speech occurs is reminiscent of those in English war films when the commanding officer gives a morale-boosting talk to the 'other ranks'. Richard even compliments Ruby (standing in as cook for the absent Mrs Bridges) on the quality of last night's apple dumplings. It is a mark of the ongoing power of the series — of the 'human' capital accumulated by the characters in previous episodes —

that this scene can be played straight with no hint of the programme-makers being distanced from the event they are portraying.

All episodes of *Upstairs, Downstairs* function centrally in terms of personal crises or sharp inter-personal animosities. The General Strike acts as a catalyst for the tensions adumbrated in the series as a whole. Thus James and Georgina clash over his blood-curdling views on the outcome of the strike and the class-collaborative figures of Hudson and Frederick clash with others such as Edward the chauffeur and Ruby the kitchen-maid (significantly, the less intelligent characters as presented in the series) who have a sharper sense of class solidarity.

Despite the overall project of nostalgically presenting a society which is relatively cosy and stable, *Upstairs, Downstairs* does have a 'then' and 'now' view of class. It is part of a wider feature of bourgeois historical drama as a whole [...] that the past is re-read from the point of view and with all the knowledge of the present. This is in evidence when Frederick, having had explained to him why working men want other working men like himself to support the strike, replies, 'That's daft, that is. I mean . . . we got no grievances . . . have we?' and, more obviously, when Edward begins to get uneasy about his non-participation:

> . . . you see all these people standin' round in groups, bus drivers, engine drivers and that, all out of work, stickin' up for the miners . . . well it's started me thinkin' maybe we should be out there with 'em . . .

However, he is brought into line by Rose's angry appeal to his sense of loyalty to His Lordship, the evidence of 'clever people . . . on the wireless . . . sayin' it's wicked and causin' misery', and her invocation of Mr Hudson's name.

The programme's presentation of Ruby's Uncle Len and his friend Arnold is absolutely central in terms of its ideological project of valorising Social Democracy. The two are introduced at a key dramatic moment (i.e., just prior to the commercial break) and their presentation connects with the working out of the same project through the figure of Richard:

> *Arnold:* We're not fightin' constitution. We're fighting for bread. We're makin' no demands. We're not chasin' moon.
> *Len:* Just a simple livin' wage.
> *Rose:* But I thought it was the miners started it.
> *Arnold:* Nay . . . it were forced on us . . . when owners locked us out and government supported them.
> *Len:* But church says we're right. Archbishop of Canterbury himself . . .
> *Arnold:* Aye . . . and BBC won't broadcast what he says. Government won't let 'im. Call ourselves a Christian country!

The programme presents the miners (in terms of the writing, casting and playing) as human, dignified, a-political and, by implication, Christian. They explicitly deny that they are communists and when a row follows the appearance of Hudson on the scene, the audience is left with the distinct feeling that the miners emerge with greater credit and dignity than Hudson. When they return to the house towards the end of the programme and learn that the strike has been called off they leave vowing not to accept the decision, thereby signalling the actuality of the sequel, the miners' six-month struggle at the end of which starvation drove them back to work.

Richard's interventions during the rest of the programme show him working for the compromise which will 'preserve the dignity' of all concerned (and preserve the social status quo), his eulogies on strong trade unions and civil liberties and, finally, his epilogue on the strike:

It was a fair trial of strength. Both sides kept their heads. There was loyalty, self-sacrifice, very little anger. I think the whole nation can be proud . . .

It is interesting that a programme such as *Upstairs, Downstairs,* using the mechanisms which it has carefully constructed since its inception, should refract history so as to land on exactly the same ideological spot as a series, *Edward the Seventh,* which is more directly concerned with history. However, to revert to the ongoing argument of this monograph, they both represent superstructural activity in contemporary Britain and, as such, will necessarily show ideological similarities. The humanisation of the British monarchy and the valorisation of Social Democracy constitute the best available terrain on which to fight for the maintenance of the socio-economic status quo.

I have tried to demonstrate the process of ideological intervention in the here and now primarily by discussion of historical drama since this (like all the other 'entertainment' areas of television) is the area where we are most off our guard. The case could, of course, have been argued with equal detail in relation to tele-history programmes. I am aware of no tele-history programme in which a Marxist historian has been invited to make a substantial contribution and the inflated, internationally co-produced 'personal' histories have all been by figures, conservative like Clark or reformist like Galbraith, who rest easily within the parameters of Social Democracy. [. . .]

Ideological struggle is not like other forms of struggle. The only method to be used in this struggle is that of painstaking reason and not of crude coercion. (Mao Tse-Tung)

[I] have sought to demonstrate that the dominant practices of history-writing and television production (both individually and in mutually reinforcing ways) allow free passage to philosophical categories and aesthetic structures congenial to the maintenance of the system of social relations of advanced capitalism. In so doing, these dominant practices suppress, push to the margins, allow only limited currency to, alternative philosophical categories and aesthetic structures which are uncongenial to that system.

[I want now] to indicate the extent to which alternatives to the dominant practices have been allowed currency in the juncture between television and history in Britain, what such alternatives look like and where further examples of alternative practices might be sought.

Inherent in the characteristic bourgeois separation between art and social life is the view that so long as the media-worker is clearly seen to be producing fiction, then what he/she does is of little political consequence. The moment, however, that the forms he/she uses cease to be unambiguously 'fictional' and begin to look like the 'factual' production of the media, then he/she is seen to pose a political threat.

It should come as no surprise, therefore, that — as has been indicated earlier — radical historians have been rigorously excluded from participation in 'factual' programmes about history and that the broaching of alternative views of history has come from workers in the area of television drama seeking to extend and render politically relevant the constraining forms of bourgeois television drama. In the examples discussed below, therefore, the emphasis will be upon the extent to which it is necessary to transgress the dominant *aesthetic* forms of television in order to transgress the dominant bourgeois conception of history.

An early example of active reflection on the ways of rendering history on television is provided by *Culloden* (BBC), transmitted in 1965. One of the premises on which *Culloden* is constructed is the supposition: what if the resources and techniques of television had been available in 1746? However, it does not present itself as a simplistic 'window on the world' of 1746: it is a programme with a clear position on the events it describes, as the rubric following the title indicates:

An account of one of the most mishandled and brutal battles ever fought in Britain.
An account of its tragic aftermath.
An account of the men responsible for it.
An account of the men, women and children who suffered because of it.

There follows a dramatic reconstruction of the battle and its aftermath with the techniques of documentary, *vox pop* and *vérité* television much in evidence, e.g., interviews with participants, a commentator on-camera (interestingly an eighteenth century figure — the biographer of Cumberland, the English commander — rather than a figure translated from another historical period) and an 'invisible' off-camera narrator whose narration (as well as carrying the pro-Highland, anti-English statement of the piece) provides 'hard' information about the precise times of the various phases of the battle, the precise weaponry and tactics used, and the precise clans and regiments involved and their casualties.

The features transgressive of bourgeois television drama operate alongside extensive retentions of many of its features: linear narrative; 'classical' composition and *mise en scène*; the careful orchestration of dramatic *crescendi*; and the central role accorded *individuals*. This mix proved both a critical and a popular success, *Culloden*'s originality lying in its deployment of well understood television procedures in a new context rather than in the creating of a new relationship between the events on the screen and the viewer.

The impulse of *Culloden* was an extremely generous and progressive one, the reminding of British audiences of events not far short of genocide which occurred barely two hundred years ago in this country. This, the rendering immediate of history, and the information it gives to a wide and diverse audience of other aspects of British history, are the strengths of the programme. The latter point is well illustrated by the early scene in which — in the most characteristic motif of this and others of Peter Watkins' works — the camera lingers on *faces*, in this case the faces of the clansmen, and the narration proceeds:

> . . . Angus Macdonald, servant of a sub-tenant. He owns nothing. Lowest in the clan structure, he is called a 'cotter'. This man is totally dependent on the men above him in the clan system. They, in their turn, on the tacks men. They, in their turn, on *this* one man: the man who has brought them all onto the moor. Alexander Macdonald . . . Chief of the Macdonalds of Keppoch, the owner of all his tenants' land. The rent he has charged them is to fight with him as clan warriors whenever he decrees. This is the system of the highland clan — human rent.

As a statement, in a dramatic programme aimed at a wide audience, of the social relations of feudalism, this is more than adequate. What, then, might be the limitations of *Culloden* as an alternative to the dominant practices in television- and history-writing? These have to do with its central impulse [. . .] to give viewers the sense of actually being there at Culloden and its aftermath; its consequent impulse to make viewers *feel* rather than *think* history; and its encapsulation of itself strictly within the period and chronology of the events it deals with. On this latter point, it has been remarked above that in designating a participant as on-camera reporter of the battle, the programme opted for the contemporary figure of Cumberland's biographer — thus retaining the period as conceptually distinct from the twentieth century — rather than injecting a modern figure with all the knowledge and historical perspective of his own time.

One has the feeling that the makers of the programme would have regarded the latter course of action as an *unacceptable* transgression of television's 'laws', even though such a transgression is present, albeit invisibly, in the off-camera interviewer of Prince Charlie and the other figures at Culloden.

The voice-over narration compounds this limitation. Immensely flexible (in terms of handling concepts) as narration may be, the narration of *Culloden* makes little attempt to locate the meaning of *Culloden* within the historico-political forces of the modern world. To be sure, the narration locates the battle in a context wider than itself:

> Thus has ended the last battle to be fought in Britain and the last armed attempt to overthrow its king. The establishment has been saved, peace restored, church, crown, trade and commerce safeguarded.

However, the key concepts of which the programme is virtually innocent are *mode of production, uneven development, colonialism* and *imperialism*. Although, as indicated above, the programme refers to the clan system and how it operates, there is no sense that the clash at Culloden is meaningful within the struggle between feudalism and nascent capitalism spread over several centuries in Europe and that the 'vigorous police action' of Cumberland's troops after Culloden, leading to the near-extirpation of Gaelic culture, is meaningful in the context of Europe's relationship with the Third World over the same centuries.

The key point to be noted is that for the programme to have foregrounded these historico-political concepts, it would have had substantially to recast its aesthetic strategies.

Perhaps the most controversial alternative project involving television and history was the BBC's 1975 transmission of *Days of Hope*, a series of four ninety-minute plays dealing with the decade 1916–1926, a period chosen by the makers (who included writer Jim Allen, producer Tony Garnett and director Ken Loach) on account of its centrality in working-class history. Among the important constituents of this period were the aftermath of the Russian Revolution, the First World War and what working-class attitudes to it were, the Irish rebellion, and the General Strike of 1926. The debate which the makers hoped would ensue from the transmission of the films was that about *reformism* or *revolutionism* as the means to working-class power. In the event, the quite sharp public debate which followed the transmission centred on issues of factual accuracy ranging from whether soldiers in 1916 wore their equipment this way or that to whether particular senior figures in the Labour administration and Trades Union Congress conspired with rightist forces against working people; and on the issue of whether such an obviously 'political' work should have been transmitted at all. In the latter context William Deedes, the editor of the right-wing *Daily Telegraph*, in a discussion on the BBC's *Tonight* immediately after the last programme in the series, advanced the argument referred to above: that *Days of Hope* was confusing as to whether it was 'art' or history and that such ambiguity ought not to be permitted. Needless to say, no such argument was advanced against, say, *Edward the Seventh* nor did any public debate follow its transmission. The lesson to be learned, of course, is that programmes which support the dominant ideology are regarded as natural and the few which do not are regarded as political.

The transmitting of *Days of Hope* (as of all the work of Allen, Loach and Garnett) was an extremely important event which has not received, particularly on the left, the analysis it deserves, an analysis which would have to include the specific aesthetic strategies of *Days of Hope*, the extent to which it is similar to the bourgeois television drama which surrounds it and the ways in which it is significantly different. Some sense of what this kind of analysis might look like is provided by Raymond Williams in his remarks on another Allen/Garnett/Loach play, *The Big Flame* (BBC), in his article 'A Lecture on Realism', a quietly polemical piece which, as Williams puts it, seeks:

> to take the discussion of realism beyond what I think it has been in some danger of becoming — a description in terms of a negation of realism as single method, of realism as an evasion of the nature of drama, and the tendency towards a purely formalist analysis — to show how the methods and intentions are highly variable and have always to be taken to specific historical and social analysis . . . [Williams, 1977.]

Clearly, one of the perspectives Williams has reservations about is that of the journal *Screen*. [. . .] Williams' warnings notwithstanding, certain elements of realist practice and, within this, of *Days of Hope*, remain highly problematic. As Colin MacCabe writes:

> In order to fracture this unity (whereby knowledge of the truth is guaranteed) it would be necessary to pose the problem of the conditions of representation; it would be necessary to interrogate the reality of the constitutional tradition which allows films like *Days of Hope* to be shown on television. To pose these problems would also and immediately pose the problems of the lessons of what happened then for the situation today — the transparent immediacy of the film would be broken by analysis. Only thus could the position of the viewer be fractured and with no obvious assigned position, he or she would have to work on the material. It could be objected, at once, that such a film would have a much smaller audience than *Days of Hope* managed to attract. But this raises the question (which does not seem to have been

posed by the makers) of who the play is addressed to. In so far as this question is not posed then the film falls within a bourgeois conception of history in which the past is understood as having a fixed and immutable existence rather than being the site of a constant struggle in the present. And it is this conception of history which places *Days of Hope* firmly within the most typical of the BBC's varieties of artistic production: the costume drama. Another feature of this lack of analysis is the context of the knowledge that Ben (one of the main characters) and the viewer have gained by the end of the film. Given the fact that this knowledge is final, which is a necessity imposed by the form, and given that the General Strike was a failure, a necessity imposed by history, the only knowledge that the text can produce (which will have the necessary finality and leave history as it is) is that of betrayal. Given that we can see that the working class were honest, straightforward and committed to socialism, their defeat must be the work of leaders who betray them. And this, of course, raises the question of the film-makers' political sympathies and affiliations. [MacCabe, 1976; see also section 4, Part IV of this volume.]

Among the substantial issues raised by MacCabe about *Days of Hope*, the concession appears to be made that the kind of text MacCabe is canvassing in his critique of the classic realist text, the kind of text which provides the necessary space for the operation of a conceptual apparatus, must of necessity attract a smaller audience than works such as *Days of Hope*. That conclusion is premature on the evidence of what is, in many respects, the most interesting attempt thus far to unite television and radical historiography in a dramatic mode which promotes both pleasure and analysis — the television adaptation of the 7:84 Theatre Company's play *The Cheviot, The Stag and the Black, Black Oil* (BBC).

It is evident, even from the sequences surrounding the programme's opening titles, that it is transgressive of one of the dominant features of both bourgeois historiography and bourgeois drama — encapsulation within a single historical period. There is, surrounding the main titles, a montage of shots: a truck on a building site; a highlander being chased through the heather by redcoats; an oil explosion at sea; an oil rig; sheep grazing; a gentleman (wearing shooting gear of an indeterminate period of the last hundred years) shooting deer; and a worker shooting a Verey pistol to ignite a gas jet on an oil rig. This montage poses a conceptual relationship, which the programme will develop, linking: the Highland Clearances of the first half of the nineteenth century whereby crofters were moved out to make room for the more economically productive Cheviot sheep; the development of Highland game parks in the second half of the nineteenth century; and the exploitation of the Highlands in the off-shore 'oil boom' of the 1970s.

The sequences surrounding the main titles signal something else which is crucially important: something which also complicates the

298

temporality of the programme and at the same time signals that it is not simply a television adaptation of the play but an artefact which joins television adaptation with a *specific* performance before an audience of highlanders in Dornie in the western highlands. The interaction between the events happening on the stage (and by imaginative extension the events presented in more traditionally televisual terms) and the specific audience is a key element in the force of the piece.

Another dominant feature both of bourgeois historiography and bourgeois drama which is transgressed is the autonomy and continuity of the individual consciousness. In *The Cheviot, the Stag and the Black, Black Oil* this takes the form of the abandonment of the practice whereby particular actors or actresses are encapsulated within a particular 'character' with the consequent focus of interest being the development of that character and the performance of the actor/actress, and its replacement with a practice which has more to do with the demotic forms of circus and music hall whereby actors and actresses assume a variety of roles within the space of the work according to the requirements of the sub-scene. Thus, in the course of *The Cheviot, The Stag and the Black, Black Oil*, a particular player may fulfil the roles of narrator, singer, scene-shifter, nineteenth century land speculator, twentieth century property speculator, and Texas oil man. Crucially, the processes of giving direct pleasure to the spectators (largely through songs and sketches) and the requirements of political reflection take precedence over the display of actorial virtuosity which is such a central impulse in the bourgeois (particularly British) theatre, cinema and television.

An important feature of dominant television practice, voice-over narration from which the political stance of the piece is adumbrated and reinforced, is retained but its content is rendered progressive and analytic. The discussion of *Culloden* above pointed to the lack of certain key concepts such as *mode of production, uneven development, colonialism* and *imperialism* in its handling of the events of Culloden and its aftermath. These concepts are strikingly present in *The Cheviot, the Stag and the Black, Black Oil*, in the songs, the humorous sketches, the historical reconstructions and, pre-eminently, in the narration which never loses sight of the relationship of the Clearances, the Game Parks and the 'oil boom' to each other and to historical forces and phenomena outside Britain itself. Thus, a narration, which shifts from player to player (underlining the demotic, ensemble-based practice of the company), goes on:

> . . . the Clearances gathered momentum. Hundreds of thousands of people were driven from their homes all over the north of Scotland. There is no doubt that a change had to come to the highlands. The population was growing too fast. The old methods of agriculture couldn't keep anyone fed. Even before the Clearances, emigration had been the only way out for some. But this coincided with something

else. English, and Scottish, capital was growing powerful and needed to expand. Already huge profits were being made as a result of the Industrial Revolution and improved methods of agriculture and this accumulated wealth had to be used to make more profits because this is the law of capitalism and it expanded all over the globe. And just as it saw in China, the Middle East, Africa, the West Indies, Canada, ways of increasing itself, so here, in the highlands of Scotland, it saw the same opportunity. The technological innovation was there — the Cheviot, a breed of sheep that could withstand the highland winter and produce fine wool — and the money was there. Unfortunately, the people were there too . . .

and

Between 1810 and 1880 the landlords and speculators stocked the hills with sheep . . . somebody, somewhere had a safe return on investment. But the people had to go. They went to the appalling slums of Victorian Glasgow, on cholera-ridden boats to Canada, America, Australia, South Africa and they themselves drove out and subjugated other peoples for their land. The highland exploitation chain-reacted round the world . . . in Australia the aborigines were hunted like animals, in Tasmania not one was left alive; in America the plains were emptied of men and buffaloes and the seeds of America's imperial power were firmly planted . . .

There is a tendency among those seeking alternatives to the dominant bourgeois forms and practices to reject out of hand the whole catalogue of techniques and effects of bourgeois art and pose radical alternatives on a one-to-one basis. As an example of this, the central reliance of bourgeois art on dramatic climaxes and *crescendi* is felt to require, on the part of some radical practitioners, a commitment to severely cerebral structures and to forms of de-dramatisation. This, of course, is a matter to be decided within the overall strategy of particular works, but an across-the-board rejection of dramatic pacing and climax should be viewed with great caution. The cerebral dimensions of *The Cheviot, the Stag and the Black, Black Oil* has already been demonstrated, primarily by reference to its montage, actorial and narrational strategies. *Within that particular mix* its use of very traditional dramatic forms is telling, as in the sequence, a historical reconstruction on film, in which the Duke of Sutherland exhorts his tenants to enlist in his own regiment for service in the Crimean War. The sequence is structured round dramatic reversals; the confident address by the Duke; the sullen silence of his tenants; the Duke's desperate offer of six golden sovereigns to every man who enlists; the continued sullen silence; the Duke's vicious attack on their 'cowardice'; and the carefully controlled pacing within which an elderly and dignified tenant rises to address the Duke, culminating with the words:

> It is the opinion of this country that if the Czar of Russia should occupy Dunrobin Castle we could not expect worse at his hands than we have experienced at the hands of your family in the past fifty years. We have no country to fight for. You robbed us of our country and gave it to the sheep. Therefore, since you prefer sheep to men, let the sheep defend you.

It is difficult to resist the conviction that, *in an appropriate mix of methods and techniques designed to foreground conceptual issues and provoke reflection,* traditional strategies executed with the force of the sequence referred to above must retain a place.

(Extracted from Colin McArthur, *Television and History*, London: British Film Institute, 1978.)

References

MacCabe, C. (1976), '*Days of Hope* — A Response to Colin McArthur', *Screen*, vol. 17, no. 1, Spring 1976.
Williams, R. (1977), 'A Lecture on Realism', *Screen*, vol. 18, no. 1, Spring 1977.

2

The *Days of Hope* Debate: Introduction

Since its first transmission in 1975, *Days of Hope* has been a focus of debate, both at a popular and at a more theoretical level, about the presentation of history on television.

Days of Hope is a series of four filmed plays based round the experience of an English working-class family during the period from the imposition of conscription in 1916 until the General Strike in 1926. The three principal characters are Ben and Sarah, a Yorkshire brother and sister, and Sarah's husband Philip, who in the first episode is a conscientious objector in hiding from the police, and later becomes a Labour MP. Ben, on the other hand, begins by enlisting in the Army, is sent first to Ireland and then to Durham to put down the miners' strike, and by the fourth episode is working with his sister as a communist organiser during the General Strike. Although actual politicians and trade union leaders are impersonated throughout the series, the emphasis is on how this crucial decade in British history divided families and changed political loyalties and aspirations.

Days of Hope was made by a team which had often collaborated on naturalistic drama for television: producer Tony Garnett, director Ken Loach, and writer Jim Allen. They wanted to produce an 'historical novel' of the inter-war years. Interviewed by the *Radio Times* for a feature to inaugurate the first transmission in September 1975, they explained their project:

> *Tony Garnett:* 'Our motive for going into the past is not to escape the present; we go into the past to draw lessons from it. History is contemporary.'
> *Ken Loach:* 'The traditional view is that England has always been a peaceful and stable society where violence is a teenage aberration: we wanted to show that England is founded on a violent past which involves the forceful suppression of dissent. We wanted to take the lives of individual characters and show how they fitted into the larger canvas of events. History isn't dust after all, it's real people . . . We want anybody who feels themselves to be suffering from crises today, people who are caught by price rises, inflation and wage restraint, to watch the films and realise that all this happened before. And we hope they will learn some lessons from the opportunities that were lost in

2

1926 and the defeats inflicted on the working class that time. We haven't given any solutions, though the judgment we make is clear, I think, at the end and is stated for the record.'

Jim Allen: 'The General Strike offered the opportunity for the creation of a workers' state in Britain. This opportunity was lost by the sell-out of the TUC, the Labour Party and the Communist Party. The message is: don't let it happen again.'

Days of Hope drew a torrent of letters to the *Radio Times* and to newspaper editors, objecting to either minor points of inaccuracy (the wrong cap badge on a uniform) or major ones (*were* conscientious objectors staked out in No Man's Land?), or lambasting the BBC for transmitting left-wing propaganda. For many correspondents, the naturalistic style of the series produced a danger of confusing historical fact and dramatic fiction. Thus, a writer to the *Daily Telegraph*:

> We expect the BBC to provide entertainment and information; when a programme seeks to combine both it is important that the information be a balanced view of the truth as far as possible, and not politically biased as this series undoubtedly is. (1 October, 1975.)

A reviewer in *The Times* argued that naturalism made for shapeless drama:

> Naturalism which has such splendid results, which really makes the viewer feel he is a fly on the wall of history, also loads a production with problems: it militates against form, for instance. It tends to preclude a writer rounding off a scene as neatly, making a point as concisely, constructing his drama with as much craft, as he would if he were writing a conventional 'play'. (4 October, 1975.)

For a few other critics, the portions where the conditions of dramatised documentary were observed (for example, in the General Strike episode, the dialogue was based on actual speeches) were more effective than the scenes deriving from conventions of family romance. In the aftermath of *Days of Hope*, the debate about drama-documentary, particularly its use in presenting recent history, was to dominate popular discussion of television.

The writers of *Screen*, on the other hand, had long maintained that realist narrative, of which naturalism was a degraded form, was incompatible with radical conceptions of history and politics. Colin McArthur opened the debate on *Days of Hope* by criticising *Screen* for remaining aloof from the popular discussion of political drama. In the next issue of the journal, Colin MacCabe answered the charge that the formalist concerns of his position on the classic realist text (for further elaboration, see Part III of this reader) precluded conjunctural considerations and the study of the audience.

But the following year, the Edinburgh Film Festival took up the issue of Popular Memory, and a shift in MacCabe's position is apparent in the third reading, from the *Edinburgh 77 Magazine*. Although he still finds the series guilty of an empiricist attitude to knowledge, he argues it differs from the majority of ideologically conventional films in that it poses a collective subject: Ben and Sarah are meant to stand for their whole class.

Finally, in 'History and the Production of Memories', Keith Tribe compares *Days of Hope* to films on French history and questions the legitimacy of harnessing the conventions of costume drama to the engine of contemporary political concerns. This issue, as we've seen, lay at the heart of much of the popular criticism of the series.

Days of Hope

When I was asked to contribute a piece on *Days of Hope* to the Film Culture section of *Screen*, my initial impulse was to produce something which concentrated almost exclusively on the limitations of *Days of Hope* on account of its commitment to realist/naturalist forms; on an examination of the BBC's conception and presentation of *Days of Hope*; and on an examination of the kind of public discussion which has surrounded it — all of these critiques mounted from what could broadly be called the *Screen* perspective. These critiques are very necessary and I shall duly proceed to them, but a piece which ended there would confer on my particular application of 'the *Screen* perspective' a certainty which I am very far from feeling. I really want to write an altogether more tentative piece which, as well as posing *Days of Hope* as problematic, poses *Screen*, the nature and style of the interventions it makes and, in particular, its position on realism/naturalism, as equally problematic.

The BBC was in something of a cleft stick over *Days of Hope*. On the one hand, it sought public praise for its 'liberalism' in putting it on, but on the other hand, it did not want to draw too much attention to it as a special political event. The BBC's strategy, therefore, was to present the programmes as mutedly as their objective importance would allow, and at the same time to insist that this was Art and not Politics. The *Radio Times* of September 6-12, the week the four-part *Days of Hope* began, carried a four-page book spread of text and pictures (the kind of coverage an important new series would get) but significantly (and unlike its coverage of the near-concurrent series *The Explorers*) did not feature *Days of Hope* on its cover, which was given over to pictures of a new current-affairs 'personality'.

The *Radio Times* comment on *Days of Hope*, stressing, as it did, history as simply 'the setting for a series of four new dramatic films' and captioning photographs of two of the three major characters in terms relating to the individual psychology of these characters, was at odds with the way Tony Garnett, Ken Loach and Jim Allen discussed the series in the accompanying interview (e.g., 'Our motive for going to the past is not to escape the present: we go into the past to draw lessons from it. History is contemporary'). The *Radio Times* interviewer was himself at some pains to de-politicise (in his terms) *Days of Hope*, most notably in the anecdote with which he concludes his piece. Having recorded Jim Allen's comments on the treachery of the TUC, the Labour Party and the Communist Party during the General Strike, the interviewer quotes the view of Karl Radek ('one of the leading Bolsheviks who opposed Stalin') to the effect that the General Strike was not a revolutionary movement, but a wage dispute.

The BBC's insistence on the separation of Art and Politics (a separation adamantly maintained by many TV critics in the public discussion following the screenings) reached its apotheosis in the remarks of Shaun Sutton, Head of BBC Drama, on the *Tonight* programme of October 3 when he indicated that of the last eight hundred plays the BBC had transmitted, only ten were 'political', in Sutton's terms: i.e. their subject-matter was politics and history.

The quality of the public discussion following *Days of Hope* cannot have been pleasing for Garnett, Loach and Allen. Setting aside the charges of propaganda and 'lack of objectivity' — charges made, of course, only against programmes which challenge the dominant ideologies in our society — a disproportionate amount of comment was on two themes: one, that *Days of Hope*, whatever its political position, was 'great art'; and, two, that the lovingly created background detail was, in one or other respect, inaccurate. It is here that the limitations of *Days of Hope*'s commitment to realist/naturalist forms becomes manifest, for by deploying certain strategies: classical narrative, individuated characters, and, most particularly, the great stress on the accuracy of costume, set decoration and the other inert elements of the profilmic event, *Days of Hope* creates the space for the kind of tangential criticism which dominated public response. Its authors' refusal to countenance auto-reflexive devices, i.e. devices which directly create an awareness of the process of production, guaranteed that much critical response would take the irrelevant lines it did. To be assertive for a moment, it is reasonable to expect an allegedly radical film to tell us something about the problems of making films for a large broadcasting institution within a dominant artistic discourse as well as about the 'reality' it signifies. One is bound to be suspicious, at the very least, of the anti-intellectualism and mystification suggested by Tony Garnett's remarks when questioned about work methods — 'I think it's counterproductive to define the way we work because once you've done it we might not be able to do it any more . . . I don't think people want to know all these details: what they're interested in is the way the films look and what they're saying.' I have drawn attention above to the kind of public discussion which followed *Days of Hope* and it is here that I would like to begin to air the reservations I have about *Screen*, the nature and style of its interventions into British film and television culture, and the degree of certainty with which it presents its position.

The public debate following *Days of Hope* was characterised by double-think and intellectual poverty, but it was, nevertheless, a considerably public and general debate to which *Screen* might have brought a good deal of sense and intellectual sophistication regarding the relationships among politics/history/aesthetics had it produced an *issue* coinciding with the appearance of, and devoted to, *Days of Hope* rather than print my own couple of thousand words. Behind this particular example is the suggestion that *Screen* might usefully become deeply involved in, bring its particular perspective to bear on, areas which the film and television culture at large regards as important (e.g., the dominance of American capital in the British film industry and the aesthetic as well as economic consequences of this; the debate within ACTT on the issue of nationalisation and the lack of an aesthetic dimension to that debate: the Annan Commission and the future of television). To engage with such areas would begin the process of demonstrating *Screen's* relevance to many people seriously interested in film and television who — to judge by the remarks I hear in diverse film cultural contexts up and down the country — are presently unable to gauge *Screen's* relevance.

It is in this context that I want to look at *Days of Hope* in relation to a characteristic *Screen* text on realism, Colin MacCabe's 'Realism and the Cinema: Notes on some Brechtian Theses'. [See Part III of this volume.]

MacCabe purports to reveal a structure which he calls 'the classic realist text' which he suggests might be applicable both (primarily) to the nineteenth century novel and to the standard narrative fiction film. Interestingly, the 'classic realist text' is not defined — as popular belief would have it — in terms primarily of its subject matter, but as a formal structure 'in which there is a hierarchy amongst the discourses which compose the text'. This hierarchy is defined in terms of a dominant point of view, the narrator's, which is never revealed as *constructed* but is presented as *transparent* and *natural*, possessing knowledge and truth regarding the other discourses in the text and the world at large. 'Whereas other discourses within the text are considered as material which is open to re-interpretation, the narrative discourse simply allows reality to appear and denies its own status as articulation.' MacCabe's suggestion and his literary example from *Middlemarch* are extremely convincing, as indeed is his filmic example from *Klute*. MacCabe attempts to relate his model of the classic realist text to the cinema, concedes that it is much less easy than in literature to identify the dominant discourse, but suggests that it is to be found in the cinema in the narration of events. Thus, in terms of *Klute*, 'if a progression towards knowledge is what marks Bree, it is possession of knowledge which marks the narrative, the reader of the film and John Klute himself.'

I can follow the applicability of MacCabe's model to *Klute*; what worries me is its *general* applicability and, in particular, its applicability to *Days of Hope*. Certainly, from what we know of *Days of Hope* and from the published utterances of its makers, the process of narration itself is rendered transparent. What is not clear to me is that this confers *knowledge* and *truth*, of the order of a narrator in literature, on the organisation of the narrative. Nor am I certain that Philip, Ben or Sarah — the three principal 'characters' of *Days of Hope* — are privileged bearers of knowledge of the same order as John Klute.

A key suggestion in MacCabe's piece is that 'the classic realist text (a heavily "closed" discourse) cannot deal with the real in its contradictions and that in the same movement it fixes the subject in a point of view from which everything becomes obvious'. This is followed by a passage which must command a great deal of assent and which might stand as a rubric for *Days of Hope*:

> There is, however, a level of contradiction into which the classic realist text can enter. This is the contradiction between the dominant discourse of the text and the dominant ideological discourses of the time. Thus a classic realist text in which a strike is represented as a just struggle in which oppressed workers attempt to gain some of their rightful wealth would be in contradiction with certain contemporary ideological discourses and as such might be classified as progressive. It is here that subject matter enters into the argument and where we can find the justification for Marx and Engels' praise of Balzac and Lenin's texts on the revolutionary force of Tolstoy's texts which ushered the Russian peasant onto the stage of history. Within contemporary films one can think of the films of Costa-Gavras or such television documentaries as *Cathy Come Home*. What is, however, still impossible for the classic realist text is to offer any perspectives for struggle due to its inability to investigate contradiction. It is thus not surprising that these films tend either to be linked to a social-democratic conception of progress — if we reveal injustices then they will go away — or certain *ouvrieriste* tendencies which tend to see the working class, outside any dialectical movement, as the simple possessors of truth.

What seems problematic about this passage is MacCabe's assertion that the classic realist text is incapable of handling contradiction. In *Days of Hope*, there is a scene in which Pritchard, the gentlemanly Northern coal owner, lectures Ben and the three arrested Durham miners on the excellence of the British tradition of peaceful, gradual and constitutional reform while, in the background, the soldiers brought in to suppress dissent in the coalfield indulge in bayonet practice. I am not clear how such a scene fails to handle contradiction in MacCabe's terms. Such a strategy is not uncommon in *Days of Hope* (the framing of a credulous populace with sheep; the intercutting of a quaker pacifist meeting with a jingoistic recruiting meeting, etc). What is certainly true is that contradiction is broached primarily at the most *obviously* structured moments of *Days of Hope*, at the points where it most *obviously* sheds its naturalist trappings.

At one point MacCabe mentions that 'the category of the classic realist text lumps together in book and film *The Grapes of Wrath* and *The Sound of Music*, *L'Assommoir* and *Toad of Toad Hall*'. My worry is that a category which does just that may be functioning at such a level of generality as to cast doubt on its operational usefulness. My hunch is that we must think in terms of Realisms and that a particular Realism will be progressive or conservative/reactionary not only to the extent to which its subject-matter is in contradiction with the dominant ideologies in that society, but to the extent to which its formal strategies mark a departure from the dominant film or television discourses of that society.

I find both *Days of Hope* and the *Screen* position on Realism problematic in this respect. *Days of Hope*'s realism involves the shedding of certain classical (primarily Hollywoodian) mechanisms and strategies, most notably the star and the dramaturgical device (most evident in the melodrama) of the climax. In almost every other respect *Days of Hope* retains the mechanisms and strategies of classical Hollywoodian narrative: e.g., linear construction; positioning of actors (in relation to the camera) to reveal mood and motivation; 'sculptural' lighting; heavy reliance on set decoration and costume. It is this massive retention of classical features which render it accessible and open it up the charges of 'recuperation' (meaning something like 'absorption' or 'nullification', usually in a political context) which, I am sure, some of the writers in *Screen* would use to dismiss *Days of Hope* out of hand.

However, the fact is that *Days of Hope* (and previous Loach/Garnett work) does, by its shedding of certain features of classical realist narrative, set itself markedly apart from most other British film and television fiction, which arguably renders it *in some respects* progressive not only at the level of subject-matter but at the formal level too. That fact ought to have emerged in the public debate which followed the screening of *Days of Hope*, but did not owing to the lack of anything close to the *Screen* position being adumbrated and the incapacity of the major participants in that debate to articulate the problem.

This piece has emerged as even more tentative and uncertain than I would have liked. This is perhaps inevitable given my attempt to do many things: to mark the real intellectual strengths and advances of the *Screen* perspective; to point to what I see as defects in its practice and strategy; to resist posing *Days of Hope* as a chopping block for the (in my view) quite problematic *Screen* position on Realism; and to suggest (little more than implicitly) that the progressive realist text, such as *Days of Hope*, might be a more appropriate agitational weapon than the (utopian?) revolutionary text canvassed by *Screen*.

(First published in *Screen*, vol. 16, no. 4, Winter 1975/6.)

Days of Hope —
a Response to
Colin McArthur

Colin McArthur's article on *Days of Hope* raises a number of complicated questions. While I cannot hope to deal with them all satisfactorily, I wish to offer a provisional response to two of his points. Firstly McArthur claims that the analysis of realism offered by me in my 'Realism and the Cinema: Notes on Some Brechtian Theses', while attractive in certain respects, lacks the specificity to deal with a complex cultural phenomenon like *Days of Hope*. Secondly he suggests that this failure of specificity might be seen as symptomatic of a more general failure of *Screen*. While broadly sympathetic with *Screen*'s project of the elaboration of theoretical knowledge of film, McArthur considers that there is a lack of involvement on *Screen*'s part with the actual struggles in British film culture and that this lack crucially affects the particular theoretical positions produced and also the failure to win people to a realisation of the general necessity of theory.

The arguments that I put forward on realism can be summarised as follows. While traditional debates about realism have centred on content and the ability to reflect reality, classic realism should be considered as centrally defined by a certain formal organisation of discourses whereby the narrative discourse is placed in a situation of dominance with regard to the other discourses of the text. The narrative discourse does not just dispose the other discourses, it compares them with the truth or falsity transparently available through its own operations. The political question of such a realism is then whether this dominant discourse is in conflict with the predominant ideological discourses of the time. I argued further, however, that this formal organisation of discourses is fundamentally compromised by the relationship between reader and text on which it depends. The simple access to truth which is guaranteed by the meta-discourse depends on a repression of its own operations and this repression confers an imaginary unity of position on the reader from which the other discourses in the film can be read.

McArthur claims that if classic realism offers a discourse of knowledge in which the spectator is placed securely, it is difficult to locate such a discourse in *Days of Hope*. He argues that none of the characters in *Days of*

Hope enjoys the privileged position with regard to the narrative that, in the example I used, John Klute does in the film *Klute*. McArthur's problem stems I think from an error in the original article. In my eagerness to demonstrate the position of knowledge conferred by the narrative I neglected to emphasise the constitutive contradiction which makes the production of that position possible. This neglect was confirmed by my use of examples from *Klute*. For while the narrative always guarantees knowledge, it can never deliver all this knowledge in one fell swoop — there must always be the time of the telling which obscures the transparency of knowledge. It is this contradiction on which classic realism works: knowledge is guaranteed at the end of the story but the story is only possible on the condition of the lack of knowledge. Stephen Heath has characterised this situation as follows:

> The paradox of such a narrative is then this: aimed at containment, it restates heterogeneity as the constant term of its action — if there is symmetry, there is dissymmetry, if there is resolution, there is violence; it contains as one contains an enemy, holding in place but defensively, and the strategic point is the implacable disjunction of narrative and discourse, *énoncé* and *énonciation*, the impossibility of holding on the subject position of the one the subject process of the other. (Heath, 1975, pp.49–50.)

In *Klute* the basic contradiction is overlaid by another distinction, that between silence as knowledge and speech as ignorance. John Klute was heavily defined as silent and knowledgeable from the start of the film and my reading across these two separate features (the opposition of silence and speech and the progress towards knowledge) entailed that I ignore the process of narration in *Klute*. The point about the position of knowledge within classic realism is that it is produced through a disavowal — we know what is happening but we don't know what will happen, but we know that we will know what will happen. I can thus recast my argument to take account of McArthur's objection and claim that the production of a position of knowledge for the reader within a classical realist text is not dependent on a character who has constant access to the knowledge generated by the narrative. In fact in *Days of Hope* Ben's progress from an unthinking soldier to a committed revolutionary who has seen through the lies of the bosses, the unions and the Labour Party is a progress from ignorance to knowledge which is also the progress of the viewer. The important feature of this progress is that its end is guaranteed from its beginning and it is this certainty which enables the reader to place him or herself in a position of unity from which the material is dominated. And it is in the light of this clarification about the place of the discourse of knowledge that we can indicate the solution to McArthur's queries about contradiction. In my original article I claimed that the classic realist text could not deal with contradiction. McArthur holds that *Days of Hope*, despite fulfilling all my criteria for classic realism, can deal with contradiction. In evidence he cites the sequence in which the mine-owner speaks about the peaceful and constitutional British tradition while in the background the troops brought in to quell the miners indulge in bayonet practice. What McArthur here confuses is the narrative's ability to state a contradiction which it has already resolved, and the narrative's ability to produce a contradiction which remains unresolved and is thus left for the reader to resolve and act out. In other words while McArthur looks simply for contradiction in the text, we must look at how contradiction is produced in the audience. In the example McArthur cites there is a contradiction between what the mine-owner says and what the picture shows. But this is exactly the classic realist form which privileges the image against the word to reveal that what the mine-owner says is false. In this manner our position of knowledge is guaranteed — we may choose to disagree with what the narrative tells us but if it has already placed us in the position where we are sure we are right, it has not questioned the very construction of that position.

In order to fracture this unity it would be necessary to pose the problem of the conditions of representation; it would be necessary to interrogate the reality of the constitutional tradition which allows films like *Days of Hope* to be shown on television. To pose these problems would also and immediately pose the problems of the lessons of what happened then for the situation today — the transparent immediacy of the film would be broken by analysis. Only thus could the position of the viewer be fractured and with no obvious assigned position, he or she would have to work on the material. It could be objected, at once, that such a film would have a much smaller audience than *Days of Hope* managed to attract. But this raises the question (which does not seem to have been posed by the makers) of who the play is addressed to. In so far as this question is not posed then the film falls within a bourgeois conception of history in which the past is understood as having a fixed and immutable existence rather than being the site of a constant struggle in the present. And it is this conception of history which places *Days of Hope* firmly within the most typical of the BBC's varieties of artistic production: the costume drama. Another feature of this lack of analysis is the content of the knowledge that Ben and the viewer have gained by the end of the film. Given the fact that this knowledge is final, which is a necessity imposed by the form, and given that the General Strike was a failure, a necessity imposed by history, the only knowledge that the text can produce (which will both have the necessary finality and leave history as it is) is that of betrayal. Given that we can see that the working class were honest, straightforward and committed to socialism, their defeat must be the work of leaders who betray them. And this, of course, raises the question of the film-makers' political sympathies and affiliations.

But we have now advanced into the area of McArthur's other argument. In order to consider seriously the questions raised by *Days of Hope*, one would need the kind of thorough consideration of both television and the cultural and political situation which McArthur urges. McArthur's article indicates tasks to be undertaken and this reply merely attempts to show how past *Screen* work can provide a starting point from which to approach those tasks. If certain formalist tendencies can be discerned within an article such as my one on Brecht, it seems to me that a greater consideration of the place of the audience is necessary in order to correct that tendency. The work continues . . .

(First published in *Screen*, vol. 17, no. 1, Spring 1976.)

References

Heath, S. (1975), 'Films and System: Terms of Analysis', *Screen*, vol. 16, no. 1, 1975.

Memory, Phantasy, Identity: *Days of Hope* and the Politics of the Past

In the history of philosophy, discussions of memory have always been linked to problems of identity. For Plato, it was the faculty which allowed contact with our divine origin, removing us from the flux of phenomena to take us back to the security of the eternal soul and its ability to contemplate the unchanging forms. For Hume, and for the empiricist tradition, memory has always been the guarantee of identity; of that constancy which provokes the fictitious unit of the self.

The philosophical heritage which links memory so closely to notions of individual origin and personality should sound a caution to those who wish to talk of memory in relation to class. The empiricist tradition denies the term memory to any claim about the past which is not grounded in the individual's experience and this thesis emphasises the sense in which memory presupposes a unified ground for present and past: a subject of experience. To talk of a working-class or popular memory may all too easily lead to talking of class as a collective subject. A class, however, is not a subject, an identity, but rather the ever-changing configuration produced by the forces and relations of production. A set of economic, political and ideological forces constantly constitutes classes in struggle and classes can find no definition outside those struggles.

To slip into the use of a class subject will also deflect attention from the serious weakness of any empiricist theory of the past and its relation to consciousness. For if we look at some of the comments and asides of Marx and Freud we can quickly see that they pose a relation between present and past in memory which renders the very concept of subject incoherent. In his earliest writings on memory, Freud postulated memory traces as susceptible to re-articulation under the pressure of events in the present. For Freud the traces that composed memory were always open to a 're-inscription'. Such a re-inscription disturbs the unity and constancy on which the empiricist subject relies.

These problems, however, have received no attention from those

314

theorists on the left who have concerned themselves with popular memory. Rather than seeking to analyse or characterise that relation between past and present which is encapsulated in the term 'memory', those who consider the field have a tendency to content themselves with constantly stating and bemoaning the fact that since the First World War the working class's memory of its own struggles has grown weaker and weaker. This fading of the past is understood as almost irreversible in the face of an ever more absolute ruling-class control of the means of communication and information.

In response to this state of affairs a great deal of effort of intellectuals on the left has gone into preserving the memory of the people, a memory and memories that the people have consigned to oblivion. Such an effort has not been confined to left-wing academics or to the written word. Within the visual media one need think no further than the Loach-Garnett-Allen *Days of Hope* as recent evidence of a filmic effort to produce a different set of memory images to those usually summoned up in response to 'The Great War', 'The Twenties', 'The General Strike'. What I have to say about *Days of Hope* is specific but there are obvious consequences for a general attitude to the past and its representations.

Days of Hope covers the years 1916–1926 through the lives of three characters: Sarah Hargreaves, her husband Philip and her brother Ben Matthews. The first episode, set in 1916, shows Philip's treatment as a conscientious objector in the army and Ben's experience as a member of the British Army in Ireland at war with the IRA. The second episode portrays a miners' strike in 1921 and the behaviour of the ruling class and the army when vital interests are threatened. In this episode Ben deserts from the army which he had joined as a regular and allies himself with the miners. As a result of his desertion and his support for the miners he is sent to jail for three years. The third episode shows Ben coming out of jail to join the Communist Party and Philip becoming a Labour MP in the 1924 election. This episode turns around Philip's horrified discovery that the Labour Party has simply accepted secret Conservative plans to deal with a general strike. The fourth episode covers the period of the General Strike and cuts between the Council of Action in which Ben and Sarah are involved and the machinations within the TUC and Government which Philip observes from the sidelines. The series ends with the TUC's decision to call off the strike.

The films articulate a classic relation between narrative and vision in which what we see is true and this truth confirms what we see. This apparently tautologous statement is one that finds its reality in its distribution through the time of the narrative and across the space of shot and character. The reality of the character is guaranteed by the shot, and the reality of the shot is guaranteed by the character.

This coincidence of truth and vision which is achieved through narrative is accomplished in *Days of Hope* through the different

315

progressions of Ben and Philip. At the beginning of the four films, Ben is a young country lad without any political knowledge and unable to understand why Philip will not fight. Through his experiences with the army, the miners and prison he comes to understand the realities of class society and joins the Communist Party. By 1926, however, he is already beginning to have his doubts about the Party's subservience to Russia and Russia's subservience to Stalin. Ben acts as the major articulation between viewer and screen because what he sees and what we see are the same. Each stage of his political development is a response to what he has seen and what he has seen we have seen. Philip, on the other hand, starts out with a fully fledged commitment to pacifism and the Labour Party. The inadequacies of this position before the 'realities of the class struggle' are stated in the first film by a revolutionary who is only refusing to fight in a capitalist war and they are demonstrated in the third when we are shown the Labour Party's true relation to the capitalist state. Philip's refusal to abandon his political beliefs before the evidence of what he has seen leads him to become more cynical and apathetic about the abilities of the people. He ends up sneering at the popular enthusiasm in the Council of Action and supporting the union leaders' handling of the General Strike. Philip's politics are presented without any visual evidence to explain their origin or form. As such, and opposed to Ben's, they are simply *unrealistic*. The film emphasises Ben's position as true (co-incident with what we have seen) and Philip's as false (non-coincident) when, at the end of the film, Sarah sides with Ben against Philip and they declare 'We could have got what we wanted' and 'The Labour Party and the TUC are there to deliver the workers to the bosses.'

In this congruence of realms of truth and of vision, *Days of Hope* adopts an empiricist attitude to knowledge in which the process of the production of knowledge (a process which constitutes both subject and object) is elided into the instantaneous moment of sight. This sight places the subject outside any area of production or process and always already in the position of knowledge. Where *Days of Hope* differs from the majority of ideologically conventional films is that this subject is posed as collective. Our identification with Ben is marked primarily in terms of his class-membership; his truth (his view) is not individual but collective. *Days of Hope* positions a class as viewer, as subject. And it is as subject that the class is placed in relation to the past. The past is not submitted to re-articulation in terms of the present (for if it was, any subject would immediately become contradictory) but it is the constancy of the past that demonstrates identity in the present.

Marx understood the past as constantly confirming men in an imaginary relation to the present (e.g., *The 18th Brumaire of Louis Bonaparte*). In *Days of Hope* we can understand that the articulation between the *imaginary* and the *past* confirms not only Marx but also those

316

philosophers who could find no internal criteria for distinguishing between memory and phantasy. In both cases the subject finds itself in a relation of imaginary control. It is only the introduction of the present that can make those memories and phantasies any more than the constant confirmation of the subject's position. In analysis, for example, it is the work of interpretation and the resistances of the analysand which makes both memory and phantasy such a profitable ground of investigation. Similarly one can argue that the past is only interesting politically because of something which touches us in the present. Benjamin expressed this position acutely when he wrote: 'To articulate the past historically does not mean to recognise it "the way it really was" (Rank). It means to seize hold of a memory as it flashes up at a moment of danger. The danger affects both the content of the tradition and its receivers. The same danger hangs over both: that of becoming a tool of the ruling classes. In every era the attempt must be made anew to wrest tradition away from a conformism that is about to overpower it.' (Benjamin, 1970, p.257.)

Benjamin's attack on the reality of the past aligns itself with both Marx and Freud. Both the cure and the revolution have the aim of re-articulating the past out of any existence within the present at all. Marx writes: 'The tradition of all dead generations weighs like a nightmare on the brain of the living. And just when they seem engaged in revolutionising themselves and things, in creating something that has never yet existed, precisely in such periods of revolutionary crisis, they anxiously conjure up the spirits of the past to their service and borrow from them names, battle-cries and costumes in order to present the new scene of world history in this time-honoured disguise and this borrowed language.' (Marx, 1967, p.10.) In response to this threat from the past Marx calls for an active process of forgetting: 'The social revolution cannot draw its poetry from the past but only from the future. It cannot begin with itself before it has stripped off all superstition in regard to the past. Earlier revolutions required recollections of past world history in order to drug themselves concerning their own content. In order to arrive at its own content, the revolution of the nineteenth century must let the dead bury their dead. There the phrase went beyond the content; here the content goes beyond the phrase.' (ibid., pp.12-13.)

These considerations of Marx and Benjamin demand a relation to the past which attaches a primacy to the present. Only that which has an effectivity in the present is worth considering in terms of the past. What one might then focus on would be the very opposite of the mythical history of the working class which *Days of Hope* offers but rather a history of institutions. *Days of Hope* is concerned with the demonstration of the falseness of institutions (The TUC, The Labour Party) beside the truth of working-class experience. But that notion of class experience postulates a class subject and a class memory such that the features and positions of the working class are given for all time. Such a conception has nothing to do with political perspectives for revolutionary change. What revolutionary change does demand is a transformation of institutions and practices. To change institutions it may be necessary to understand them but simply to condemn them as false is to ignore their reality. In *Days of Hope* institutions have no reality over and above their ability to produce individuals who are betrayers. Instead of an analysis of the Labour Party or the TUC we are treated to the *sight* of the perfidy of a Wedgewood or a Thomas. Whereas in the first two episodes we are shown the reality of state power, the second two episodes concentrate on the individual betrayals involved in the accommodation of the institutions of the working class to that state power. There is thus no possibility of an explanation of the structure and history of those institutions which would make the behaviour of a Thomas or a Wedgewood possible. Such an investigation would, however, have to start not from the past but from the present and the introduction of the present would also subvert the primacy of the visual for the closure on which the guarantee of narrative is predicated would be broken.

It might be argued that to follow this up would be to produce programmes which would be turned down by television on the aesthetic grounds that they would be 'too difficult'. This may well be true but it raises the further question of whether the concept of 'audience' which is used for aesthetic judgements within television may render any political use of television fiction impossible.

All this is not intended as some condemnation of *Days of Hope*: there is much to admire in the first two episodes. But it is intended to indicate that the relationship between sight and story which produces the film is fundamentally inimical to the production of political knowledge. Further that this relation is complicit with an understanding of the working class's relation to its own past which reduces the working class to an identity.

(First published in *Edinburgh '77 Magazine*.)

References

Benjamin, W. (1970) *Illuminations: Essays and Reflections*, London: Jonathan Cape.
Marx, K. (1967), *The Eighteenth Brumaire of Louis Bonaparte*, Moscow: Progress Publishers.

History and the Production of Memories

In recent years the writing and re-writing of a new kind of history —
social history — has been taken up by radicals engaged with 'labour
history' in general, and perhaps more significantly by women who seek
to promote the development of a feminist consciousness through the
construction of a 'women's history'. These two threads are of course
interconnected; E. P. Thompson's *Making of the English Working Class*,
which was in many ways the turning point of British labour history in the
1960s, itself set the pattern for the women's history that was to follow.
Much of the importance of Thompson's work concerned the unearthing
of popular movements that had been previously ignored in traditional
histories, sometimes because on the one hand these dispersed and
anonymous insurrectionary groups left no records with which the
historians could work, while perhaps more often it was considered that
such subterranean movements did not warrant or repay close attention.
Thompson sought quite explicitly to 'give the people back their history'
— a history of their oppression and resistance to oppression.

Sheila Rowbotham, perhaps one of the foremost of contemporary
feminist historians, was herself a student of Thompson's, and has
produced a series of works which seek to demonstrate that women have
been systematically ignored in the male-dominated writings of historical
investigation. Thus the title of one of her books is *Hidden from History*, a
book in which she seeks to show that History has been constituted as a
narrative in which women are at most merely useful appendages to the
agents of history, men of the ruling and of the working class. By the
discovery of the activities of militant women of the past, she seeks to give
the contemporary women's movement a sense of the historicity of its
action, giving the struggles of women today a heritage which has been
suppressed and distorted in the history that is given to them.

Such work is of course politically very important in building an
articulate and militant progressive women's movement, but it is often
forgotten that this 'history' is itself only constituted as a response to the
histories that it opposes. While it is important to reveal the existence of
past struggles, such revelation provides no effects of itself. To ignore this
danger is to fall into the trap of endlessly discovering 'new' struggles, an
endless quest for the dead heroines of the past. But these female persons
are of course only heroic on the condition that their actions can 'teach us'

about our actions today; and consequently such actions are reworked in the image of contemporary concerns. [. . .] The 'lessons of history' are not inscribed in the simple existence of a past; they are the product of the construction of a history which can be deployed in contemporary arguments.

The Special Film Event at Edinburgh [in 1977] placed itself in the context of such debates, deploying as its title the words 'History/Production/Memory' to designate a series of issues around film, cinema and history. In particular, discussions and film showings centred around the debate on Popular Memory which had been printed in issues of *Cahiers du Cinéma*. This debate concerns itself with many of the problems that have been raised in the work of Thompson and Rowbotham, who can be taken as representatives of two currents of recent historical research. And of course in the case of women's history, with its problems and possibilities, the TV series *Shoulder to Shoulder* can be seen as an attempt to realise filmically the history of women's struggles.

The title of the event — 'History/Production/Memory' — might have been arrived at almost by accident, but it is in fact surprisingly appropriate as an index of the problems associated with the Popular Memory debate. For this series of terms embodies a theoretical problem, a transitivity that expresses two quite distinct conceptions of history and the status of historical argument. This title can be read as a double transformation, from history to memory, and from memory to history, both instances mediated by the presence of a work of production, the means of travelling from one term to the other and back again.

If we travel from left to right, as it were, a conception is exposed in which history is seen as a collection of past events, incidents, significations, persons and so on. By a work of production we move to the presence of a memory, the trace of this history in the present: a trace which is recorded in the utterances of persons and in the constitution of commemorative events. 'Production' here is primarily a work of recovery, the kind of activity that is associated popularly with women's history and radical labour history. But it must be noted that the conception of 'history' that we have here is a double one: it is at the same time the past, a collection of representations ascribed a prior existence, and also the process of its writing. 'History' thus denotes a nondiscursive past and a discursive present. This double form conspires to render these two elements mutually validating: the past informs and underwrites the validity of the present, and the writings on the past are guaranteed by their very involvement with the past. The past is history, and the writing of history is thus endowed with an autonomous effectivity. History not only exists, it is truth: the truth of past experience, and the truth of present historical accounts of it. To learn lessons from the past, it is necessary only to unlock this truth.

If on the other hand we travel from right to left in this title, a quite

320

different set of relationships appears. Beginning with memory, a work of production takes us to the past as history. This work of production is no longer a work of discovery, of revelation, but is rather a process in which specific materials are combined together and used to *fabricate* a history. This 'fabricated history' is not thereby false, nor erroneous; what is of importance is that its principles of validation have become disconnected from the simple existence of a prior chronology. Put simply, this conception is an anti-historicist one, denying that the past through its existence and transcription is a principle of validity in itself. The first position that was outlined assumes that History is something that is real and tangible, that can be effectively recapitulated, discovered, or of course distorted; but whatever the modality, it *is* and always will *be*. This fact of existence is the guardian of truth and the subverter of error. In the case of much women's history, traditional accounts are denounced for having omitted in a systematic manner female historical agents. The restoration of such agents into history is an act which restores the truth to historical discourse.

Anti-historicism abandons the past as a principle of validation which dominates all other concerns; it instead argues that 'history' is something perpetually constructed in a specific conjuncture, and that it is necessary to pose to historical discourse the question — what does it do? What arguments does it support, in what manner does it constitute its mode of proof, in what way is its evidence deployed? The conditions of production of history are not the acts of revelation of a past, but are determinate relations in a given conjuncture. A history must therefore be assessed according to the manner in which it is constituted. Such a position enables the question to be asked: why bother with history/the past? [. . .] As has been suggested, the object of the new working-class and women's history was above all a political one: to strengthen the movements within which they appeared by giving political demands a historical validity. The conditions for such work being effective are not however universal, and it cannot be supposed that to work on popular history is of itself politically progressive. In fact it can be argued that in certain cases such work could be at present diversionary. Anti-historicism does not attack history for the sake of it; it is a means of arguing that the political objectives of theoretical investigations have to be radically re-assessed. By arguing that the past is not an object of study it is possible to question the political validity of historical research which too often appears as its own guarantor.

These questions of 'history' are central to the idea of a cinematic modality called 'popular memory'. Distinct from the contemporary concern with the past, a concern which is associated with a nostalgic recovery of the past through a recreation of its paraphernalia, the notion of Popular Memory seeks to fix those films which use history in the construction of their narrative, drawing on the facticity of the past to assure the veracity of their statements. The term appeared first in 1974 when Foucault was interviewed by the editors of *Cahiers du Cinéma*, an interview which has appeared in *Radical Philosophy* and which is reprinted in the *Edinburgh '77 Magazine*. The films under discussion were principally *Lacombe Lucien*, *Night Porter*, and *The Sorrow and the Pity*, films which were seen by the *Cahiers* interviewers as the product of a specific political conjuncture in France, in which a new bourgeoisie sought to write its own history. This history seeks to deny the existence of popular struggle as an important factor in the national history. [but it could be argued that the *Cahiers* critics were led into an extreme position through their *over-valuation* of class politics in film . . .] *The Sorrow and the Pity* is indeed a powerful vehicle for the construction of histories. The popular memory of wartime France is demolished by a historical document which persuasively argued that little resistance took place and large sections of the population collaborated with the German occupation forces. This can be seen at work in Ophuls's film very clearly: interviews of persons today which describe their recollections of life under the occupation are contrasted with other accounts from wartime newspapers and German records of occupation which discredit their mode of recollection. Ophuls's use of the extended interview in combination with archive film permits a series of representations to be contrasted, and in so doing the 'evidence' offered by interview is severely questioned. Ophuls does not rewrite the history of wartime France, as Foucault suggests; what he does is rather question the use that is made of personal recollection. The subversive nature of Ophuls's film lies not in the 'new memory' but in the demonstration of the way that memory is subjected to reconstruction.

Ophuls's film is an instance of the *reorganisation*, rather than the *employment*, of a popular memory. The effect on French attitudes to the war is similar to the effect of Angus Calder's *The People's War*, a book which does much to reorganise the traditional views of Britain under the Blitz, and in particular emphasises the low credibility of Churchill at particular points in the war. Calder shows how for example the Battle of Alamein has become enshrined as a turning point in Britain's war not because of its actual military significance, but rather because it could be used to restore confidence in the existing political order headed by Churchill. It is perhaps ironic that Montgomery, the 'hero of Alamein', has become in the recent film *A Bridge Too Far* the 'villain of Arnhem', a central point of the film not noted by any of the film critics in their reviews. The problem however with Foucault's criticisms of Ophuls is that it is suggested that his film constitutes an act of theft: the real experience of the historical agents of resistance has been taken away from their heirs. The political consequences of Ophuls's film are seen as the triumph of the new bourgeoisie over a working class deprived of its heritage.

Other films of course seek to restore this heritage, and in the work of restoration promote the kind of historical work in the medium of film that was outlined at the beginning of this article. The Loach/Garnett television series *Days of Hope* represents such an attempt to use working-class history politically, deploying in a documentary play arguments about political organisation and the relation of leftist groupings to established political institutions. This series relies on conventions of realism to construct a historical drama which is located in the years 1916–1926. Central to the films as a mode of organisation is a family and its trials and tribulations, and in many ways this series depends on the genre of family romance to present its plot (much like the series *Poldark*, for instance). The comments that are made here will address themselves to problems that emerge in Episodes 1 and 3.

In the first episode we are introduced to a simple wartime country scene, a small family farm run by a father with his son Ben and his daughter Sarah. Ben is anxious to join the army, but is too young; his sister Sarah is married to a conscientious objector, Philip Hargreaves, contrasted with Ben imagistically not only as an opponent of the war but also as a town dweller unused to the heavy labour of the farm. Philip and Sarah have to leave, for the police are after Philip. The meal taken before they leave is effectively unscripted, full of hesitations and uncertain statements; one of the devices used in this series is to use actors without comprehensive scripts, so that conversation between them lacks the artificial coherence of scripted speech. This device becomes crucial in Episode 3, but in Episode 1 no particular person is privileged in this setting. Philip, arrested at an anti-war meeting, is forcibly drafted into the army, and after enduring brutal treatment in basic training is sent to the front with a lorry-load of other conscientious objectors, eventually to be tied to a post in no-man's land. He survives this experience to take part in later episodes.

Ben on the other hand joins the army, and revels in the uniform, visiting Sarah at the anti-war offices where she works and expressing his lack of understanding of the treatment that Philip is receiving. Instead of being drafted to France, Ben is instead sent with his unit to Ireland, to take part in the suppression of the countryside. We see him marching about the lanes with his unit, headed by an officer; they commandeer a house for the night, and then, the day after, one of the soldiers is led on to a mine by a small boy. Ben is detailed to catch the boy; he shoots at him in the woods, catches him, and the closing shot is of the soldiers marching along the lanes out of sight, the boy being dragged along with them. The soldier who had been killed was, we learn from a comment of Ben, a republican; he is in any case presented as one of the 'nicer' soldiers.

The plotting of this first episode does allow of a discrepancy between politics and persons. Philip takes up what can be seen to be an idealistic

(Christian socialist) position, but is shown to genuinely hold this position and be prepared to defend it under all circumstances. When he encounters a 'revolutionary' at the front, who talks to him of the need for violent struggle, the words of this revolutionary are not deployed as a denunciation of Philip, rather as the statement of conflicting socialist conceptions. Ben on the other hand is also given space to enjoy his induction into the army, and it is only through his experience in Ireland that he begins to question the role that he has adopted.

Clearly this plotting draws on 'history' for the mobilisation of a narrative. But this use of history goes further than the simple story that is presented, for it is the realism of the image that underwrites this narrative. It is notable that the letters that were printed in the *Radio Times* concerning the first episode concentrated on the veracity of the image: the clothes, the army buttons, whether the Army marched in threes or fours in 1916. The tonal quality of the pictures at the front, and certain of the sets, draw heavily on photographs that were taken at the time and which over the years have become recognised as images of the First World War. The slight fuzziness of the image in certain scenes, reminiscent of a Hovis or Ovaltine advertisement, further reinforces a visual quality of the past. British television is justly famed for its ability to create such plausible images of the past, down to the smallest detail, in marked contrast to American historical dramas where such realistic conventions are almost totally ignored.

The question that must be asked is however what function such careful reconstruction plays in the reconstruction of a past. It can be suggested that this veracity of the image is the vehicle for the veracity of the history that it constructs. This history is itself conceived as the truth of a past, a set of political events that we can draw lessons from. The project of *Days of Hope* is thus associated with the writing of a popular history along historicist lines. This history is however recognised as Truth by the viewer not by virtue of the 'facts' being correct, but because the image looks right. The recognition effect 'that's the way it was' is a product not of the historicity of the plot but of the manipulation of the image. As Colin MacCabe points out:

> The films articulate a classic relation between narrative and vision in which what we see is true and this truth confirms what we see. This apparently tautologous statement is one that finds its reality in its distribution through the time of the narrative and across the space of shot and character. The reality of the character is guaranteed by the shot, and the reality of the shot is guaranteed by the character. (MacCabe, 1977, p.14.)

The viewer of the programme is meant to learn from the experience that is presented in the same way that the character Ben learns from his experiences in Episodes 1 and 2 and, drawing conclusions from this experience, joins the Communist Party. The validity of the experience from which the character Ben draws his lessons is guaranteed by the fact that he as a subject is engaged directly with it. The validity of the lessons that the viewer is supposed to draw is guaranteed by the existence of a history which when properly represented can function as a pedagogic Truth. But this slide from character to viewer is only possible by the form of representation that is employed, and, as becomes increasingly clear in later episodes, there are certain real problems with the constitution and functioning of the history that is meant to instruct the viewer.

Episode 3 finds the Communist Ben living in the same house as the Labour MP Philip. The year is 1924, and Philip is again the idealist, this time the hard-working and possibly naïve believer in the viability of change through reform. Ben is the increasingly articulate voice of revolutionary change, and with his comrades confronts Philip with the difficulties of reformism. A notable sequence has Philip, again hesitating, uncertain (unscripted), defending the ability of the Labour Party to govern in the interests of working people. But this time, by cutting the scene on the unconvincing words of Philip, the position of the Labour Party and its policies is represented as unconvincing. The hesitations of a realist convention are deployed here to make Philip look a flabby but well-meaning politician. Authority is given to the declamations of Ben and his friends, and increasingly Truth comes to reside in the worker's accent, especially that of the Durham miners who arrive during the episode. The visit of these pit-men to a Soviet trade delegation in the Palace of Westminster is symbolic of the authenticity of these real workers: ignorant of the etiquette, unable to find their way around the corridors of power, they are portrayed as workers for whom this institution is irrelevant. The sympathetic portrayal of these miners, the status given to them in the image, represents the interests of the workers as divergent to the concerns of a Labour Government which is trapped in the illusions of the possibility of a Parliamentary road to social justice.

In many ways, the portrayal of militant workers in this episode is a gross insult to the movement which it purports to represent. For these real workers of 1924 are recognisable as such because they are cast in the image of contemporary workers, who in many ways are less articulate than their predecessors. The political configuration that is sketched out in Episode 3 is one that relates only to the present; in no way can it be seen as a 'faithful' representation of past organisations and militants. The veracity of the image thus conceals the 'ahistorical' nature of the politics that is represented.

This is not of course an argument for a real history: what is being suggested is that *Days of Hope* uses the image of a history to deploy contemporary political arguments. The objection is that it endows its Trotskyist conception of revolution and reform with a truth which is underwritten by a constructed history. The truth of the argument is thus conditional, not on the actual viability of the politics that set this history to work, but rather on the apparent truth of this history as an autonomous object. The work of a memory is thus duped into a particular political position, not through a historical discourse with its own principles of truth, but rather through the organisation of an image of the past which, through its 'verity', bestows its own truth. [. . .]

(First published in *Screen*, vol. 18, no. 4, Winter 1977/8.)

References

MacCabe, C. (1977), 'Memory, Phantasy, Identity: *Days of Hope* and the Politics of the Past', *Edinburgh '77 Magazine*.
Rowbotham, S. (1973), *Hidden from History*, London: Pluto Press.
Thompson, E. P. (1968), *The Making of the English Working Class*, Harmondsworth: Penguin.

Progressive Television and Documentary Drama

I want to return, here, to some of the questions which underlay an exchange between Colin McArthur and Colin MacCabe in *Screen* in 1976; a fairly brief exchange which hinged on the adequacy of Colin MacCabe's formulation of the 'classic realist text' to the television documentary drama, *Days of Hope*. On one level, what was at issue was simply the capacity of the realist form of *Days of Hope* to express or produce contradiction; at a more profound level, however, what was at stake was the way in which the notion of 'progressiveness' in television is to be conceived from the perspective of a journal such as *Screen*. 'I find both *Days of Hope* and the *Screen* position on Realism problematic', says McArthur, and he argues, from a position sympathetic to the journal, for a greater engagement in public and general debate (such as followed the first transmission of *Days of Hope* in 1975), and for a more clearly declared resistance to monolithic theoretical categories. In his reply, MacCabe acknowledges the need for 'the kind of thorough consideration of both television and the cultural and political situation which McArthur urges', and argues that *Screen*'s past work provides a starting point for an engagement with wider issues: 'The work continues.'

My interest in returning to this exchange after four years is less to arbitrate in the dispute, more to continue the work in a limited way on the more general point of documentary drama's place within television, and its relation to notions of 'progressive realism'. The work is largely that of digging over the ground. Some ghosts need to be laid, and others will rise to haunt the text. So be it: the work continues again . . .

In considering documentary drama's place within television it seems useful to situate it alongside some of the terms and assumptions which have been taken up by television and by television critics in thinking about drama; so the article begins with a couple of detours through notions of television drama, its relationship to theatre, and the pervasiveness of the term 'naturalism'. In these detours, my impressions have been informed by a reading of all issues of *The Radio Times* and *The Listener* during the 1960s, a period which seemed to be interesting both as a formative, 'post-primitive' stage, and as a period which has been widely constituted as some kind of 'Golden Age' of television drama. Clearly, neither journal can be expected to produce an advanced critical position: their function is rather that of an unguarded discourse, exposing the terms in which drama was thought, giving a sense of television's address. Clearly, also, there is a risk in generalising from a historically specific period: the generalisations, however, are those which the conservatism of television's theoretical and critical discourses permits. While television changes, there is a remarkable continuity in the way it talks about itself.

TELEVISION AND THE SINGLE PLAY

> It is not uncommon for the majority of viewers to see, regularly, as much as two or three hours of drama, of various kinds, every day. The implications of this have scarcely begun to be considered. [Williams, 1974.]

The importance of drama for television hardly needs restating. Not only, as Williams indicates, is it massively there, regularly, in its various kinds, but it is also, as a general characteristic of television, everywhere: 'the dramatic', spilling over the edges of programming categories, ordering the viewer's attention; the 'little dramas' which Stephen Heath and Gillian Skirrow expose and 'make strange' in their *World in Action* analysis [see Heath and Skirrow, 1977]. Given this importance, the lack of rigorous attention to television drama itself and to the television play is surprising. At a formal level, there are questions of the mechanisms of the look and of the subject of television drama which have barely begun to be asked; questions which are important not only for television itself, bringing to it work which has been done in film, but also for theory: television, in its different specificity, offers a resistance to universalised theories of representation, and to essentialisms of vision.

More centrally here, television drama raises difficult political questions. Part of the hesitancy in engaging with drama production may come from a reasonable suspicion of the way in which the cultural prestige of 'serious drama' is used by television and television reviewing. Or it may come from an assessment of the increasingly marginal place which theatre and theatrical forms occupy in present culture. Either way, what is clear is that the vast majority of politically engaged attention has been directed towards the forms of representation of actuality (current affairs, documentary, news), or to popular genres (soap opera, situation comedy, light entertainment). I want to offer here an argument for the importance of 'serious drama' within a political understanding of television.

Firstly, and somewhat tentatively, within certain areas of social and/or sexual unease, the single play or play series seems to function for television as some kind of cutting edge, working to extend television's social or sexual discourse. Drama tests, and occasionally extends, what it is possible not only to say, but also and more perilously, to show. It is possible for television to discuss homosexuality within the context of current affairs, but a play like *Coming Out* shows gay men in bed — albeit within a narrative which offers a liberal travesty of gay politics. The effect of *Cathy Come Home* was derived precisely from the *showing* of evidence which was already available as statistics for discussion. I register this point tentatively, and will come back to it in discussing notions of progressiveness, because the precise balance between 'progress' and 'regress', between progressive inclinations and the received conventions of narrative and dramatisation, seem to me problematic: more problematic, for television in its specific social circulation, than a theory of texts has allowed. For the moment, I am simply insisting on the necessary recognition that television's discourse is not static, but is under continual revision and extension, and I am suggesting that the single play or play series has a crucial functional role in that revision and extension. Given the social place which television occupies, any mechanism of change in its discourse seems important. At the same time, there are distinctions: there is change and there is change; there is 'progressiveness' and there is 'permissiveness'. My argument for the tentative and potential progressiveness of the extension of television's discourse is not the same as a campaign for liberalisation, for the extension of the easy liberal discourse which appropriates and consumes unease and contradiction. The discussion of television drama's progressiveness will ultimately have to involve some consideration of the form of its discourse as well as its content.

Secondly, and more assertively, drama's extension of the television discourse becomes politically important in a concrete way at the point at which it confronts censorship. It is precisely the extension of what can be said and shown that concerns the National Viewers' and Listeners' Association, and, more importantly, it is an uncertainty as to what can and cannot be shown which creates nervous reactions within institutional control. Explicit censorship is always a problem for broadcasting which claims public responsibility, since it exposes the tensions within that claim, opens up contradictions between broadcasting's declared principles and the determinations of its practice, and disturbs its view of itself: a confusion arises between the role of guardian and the role of public servant. Thus the censorship of current affairs programmes on Ireland throws into question again and again television's claim to be an independent, and hence objective, reporter. Clearly, broadcasting has developed a vocabulary to deal with such a confusion of roles, and, in suppressing current affairs material, can offer apparently clear criteria in terms of 'national security', 'civic responsibility', 'objectivity', or simple 'truth to fact', criteria, that is, which may throw a shadow over notions of 'independence' and 'the public's right to know', but which carry with them the appearance of reasonable authority which will seriously divide the audience only along already established political lines. The censorship of drama on the other hand, relies on a much less secure language: 'taste', 'public sensibility', 'the little gap between fact and fiction'; and it treads on a substantial area of the liberal consensus involving assumptions about the relationship of art and society, and about the creative artist's right to express him- or herself. Assumptions which broadcasting shares and supports in its insistence on the 'seriousness' of drama ('Drama is the most deeply penetrating way of knowing what it is to be human.' — *Radio Times,* 4 April, 1968) and on the necessary encouragement of creative freedom ('These twenty plays are the result of an invitation to authors of fame or promise to write for television without being subject to dictation on the kind of play required,' — *Radio Times,* 23 September, 1960). Within the context of its pronouncements, it is never comfortable for the institution to impose limits on what may be penetrated by 'serious drama', or to accept the role of curtailing the freedom of the artist.

Now, institutional discomfort is not in itself a cause for concern, and the contradictions it displays may be available only to an audience which is looking for them. A large part of the political importance of the censorship of drama lies less in its effects on public awareness, and more in the gap which it creates within the institutions between the 'creators' and the 'controllers'. Censorship in any form produces within television a certain kind of struggle which cannot simply be discounted because it tends to express itself within the terms of liberalism and freedom of expression, rather than in terms of the nature of the determinations which produce censorship. It is within the ideological and tactical groupings and regroupings of such struggles and tensions that programmes are made, some of which may escape the limits of what has been hitherto acceptable. Conflicts over censorship take different forms in different areas: in television journalism what is felt to be under attack is the journalist's professionalism, and the response is frequently professional guile and strategy. Historically, the dramatist has seemed less prepared for censorship, more surprised by it, relying on the assumed consensus that it is the artist's inalienable right to express the world the way he or she sees it. More recently, necessary shifts in response are appearing. But the general point I am making is that the political importance of television drama is tied up with the place which drama occupies in the movements of relationships within the institutions, and cannot be thought simply in terms of its form or its content, nor even exclusively in terms of the contact between the programme and its audience. Censorship, either public or internal, is important for the part it plays in these movements.

But, always accepting the importance of explicit censorship as an exposed point of contradiction, it is also necessary to insist on the political importance of the contradictions implicit in the discourses about 'serious drama' which circulate in the area between the campaigns

330

for liberalisation on the one hand and the actual, overt exercise of censorship on the other. The liberal aspects of the extension of social discourse have always been accepted within television drama, and while explicit censorship is an anathema on every side, 'provocativeness' is a positive value. This point is worth documenting. An unattributed *Radio Times* introduction to the 1966-67 season of the *Wednesday Play*:

> The aim of the *Wednesday Play* . . . is to provide one of those growing points — not only in television, but in the life of the nation — at which, the Pilkington Report suggested, 'the challenges to existing assumptions and beliefs are made, where the claims to new knowledge and new awareness are stated'. It is one of these key series in which broadcasting must be most willing to make mistakes; for if it does not it will make no discoveries. Mistakes draw criticism. Discoveries are uncomfortable. Both compel controversy. So on occasion does the *Wednesday Play*. It would be surprising — and disappointing — if it did not. (*Radio Times*, 2 November, 1966.)

Or Tony Garnett, introducing the 1965-66 season:

> To tell our stories, we shall have to break a lot of old rules about what is permissible in television drama; and although we shall not set out to offend people, we may be provocative — but out of a compassion that comes from a concern for human beings. (*Radio Times*, 7 October, 1965.)

'Provocativeness' and 'controversy' are recurrent terms in discussions of, or introductions to, the *Wednesday Play* series throughout the 1960s: terms which are celebrated by the drama producers, script editors and writers as indicating an engagement with the social problems of the day, and with the audience (the *Radio Times* continually holds out an invitation to the audience to participate in discussing the social problems which the series deals with).

The official discourse, as always, is more cautious, but it too has a certain Achilles heel in the notion of 'creative talent', and the right of the artist (never absolute, always liable to revision) to express his firmly held convictions. Thus, an official study, *Taste and Standards in BBC Programmes*, conducted by a BBC committee for its General Advisory Council in 1973, concludes:

> Outstanding programmes have come through an apparent defiance of accepted practice. *Culloden*, for instance, or *Till Death Us Do Part*, or some of the early *Wednesday Plays* all, to a greater or lesser extent, succeeded because their makers possessed the conviction and the talent to interpret in a new and challenging way the principle outlined

[in this paper]. Policy which stultified true capability would be no more worth defending than that which proved too slight to check the excess of the less talented people.

'Excess' is simply a question of lack of 'talent'. But if the liberal response within such a study is to give talent its head, the institutional response is to keep a firm grip on its safeguards: 'referral up'. The report ends with an unusually clear warning to the unwary, and to those whose 'talent' may be subject to question:

> The disadvantage in the system is the obvious one that arises from a producer's failure to realise that he has a problem which ought to be referred upwards. It may not always be a problem which will directly affect his programme, but it may have implications for his depart-ment or his output service of which his superiors ought to be informed. A producer's awareness of such consequential problems depends on the degree to which information is passed to him by his superiors about the wider affairs and interests of the BBC. It also depends on good management which can sense, even when the producer does not, that there is likely to be a problem of some magnitude.
>
> As Huw Wheldon, in the pamphlet *Control of Subject Matter in BBC Programmes*, expressed it: 'The wrath of the Corporation in its varied human manifestations is particularly reserved for those who fail to refer'.

This is the language of a paternal authority assuming control of its area of responsibility: 'the wrath of the Corporation', and the self-effacing joke surrounding it. But while the system it proposes gives a very clear indication of the ideal which it has in mind, the actual situation with which the authority has to deal is full of uncertainties which it itself invites: the lines between 'conviction' and 'excess', between the 'talented' and the 'less talented', between 'provocation' and 'offence'. It is along those lines that the skirmishes take place.

Circulating between these two discourses, then — the 'creative' and the 'official' — are the terms which are necessary to understand the aspiration, force and contradictions within which television drama is produced, an unstable system rather than a clearly determined control: the 'challenge to existing assumptions and beliefs'; 'uncomfortable discoveries'; 'conviction'; 'controversy'; 'offence'; 'mistakes'; 'the wider affairs and interests of the BBC'; 'the wrath of the Corporation in its varied human manifestations'; 'reference upwards'. Rather than relying on a model made up of sets of controls, determinations, and easy appropriations, or on an apparatus in which the dominant ideology simply dominates, this play of forces within the institutional discourse suggests a way of explaining how 'controversial' documentary dramas like *Days of Hope* or *Law and Order* can be commissioned, made, shown, celebrated and condemned, then withheld despite protest, then reshown in apparent deference to the protest.

The single play or play series is not essential to television. It has been virtually absent from American television for some time, and its expense and awkwardness within the schedules have made it perpetually precarious in Britain: bulletins on the ill health and imminent death of the single play were appearing in *The Radio Times* and *The Listener* in the early 1960s. It has been preserved on British television because it confers a certain cultural prestige, a 'seriousness', on television as a whole. But in order to function in this way, in order to be 'serious', drama occasionally has to appear to overstep limits, to show what has not been shown before. The tension surrounding this is politically important within the institutions, and is an important factor in determining the movements of forces within television. The nature of its political importance within the programme is more uncertain: I propose to come back to that uncertainty in its particular relationship to documentary drama.

TELEVISION AND THEATRE

Simply a note here, a marker to identify a field for consideration: the importance for the history of television of the relationship between television drama and theatre. If American television seems to be most readily identified by the physical, commercial and aesthetic links with Hollywood, British television has seemed to define many of its practices and aesthetics in relation to the theatre. Reviewing for *The Listener* in 1964, John Russell Taylor defined 'perfect television material' as:

> in theatrical terms the one-act play subject, built around a single incident or situation rather than a fully articulated plot. (*The Listener*, 9 January, 1964.)

Acting is mentioned in reviews in much the same way as it appears in theatre reviews, and indeed the cross-over of actors between theatre and television drama inevitably contributes to the definition of what a television performance should look like. Whereas American drama serials (*Washington: Behind Closed Doors, Holocaust*, the 'Best Sellers' series) feature actors who can be sold as stars because of their familiarity in cinema, the stars of British television drama have predominantly been created in the theatre, and do most of their work there. The relationship to theatre is part of what gives 'serious drama' its prestige within television. And at a basic level, the studio technology of the formative period in the 1950s and 1960s, with its continuous performance and its jealously rationed editing, encouraged theatre acting. It also encouraged an attention to acting at the expense of an attention to *mise en scène*. *Mise en scène* for studio drama tended to function (and still does) like theatre scenery (an appropriate background for the acting), rather than like the meticulously prepared, almost autonomous symbolic discourse of cinema. It is difficult to think of British television drama in terms of visual pleasure.

But the most marked feature which can be attributed to a respect for the theatrical mode of production is the privilege granted within single play drama to the writer and his or her creativity.

> What the television theatre needs most is new writers . . . In television the primacy of the word requires special emphasis because it is often denied by an electronic folklore of phrases like 'immediacy', 'visualisation', and worst of all 'personality'. (Frederick Laws, *The Listener*, 8 February, 1962.)

The position of the writer has clearly shifted over the last twenty years, and there is now much more evidence of the formation of 'teams' — Garnett/Loach/Allen, Trodd/Potter — but much of the prestige of drama is still accorded to and derived from its writers (think simply of the presentation of credits in *The Radio Times*). This defines a dominant attitude to television drama, albeit one which was already being contested in the 1960s by critics like Derek Hill and television writers like Troy Kennedy Martin, both of whom invoked the status of the director in the cinema.

What is most interesting about the privilege granted to the writer is the assumption it makes about the neutrality of television itself. Television is offered to writers as a passive instrument with which to work their creative will:

> Too many writers at first acquaintance with television tend to become over-awed by the mysteries of technique about which so much has been written. The producer should aim to liberate the writer from those entanglements — to encourage him to express his idea as he sees it and only at a later stage to begin to translate or reshape the work in terms of technical resources. (Michael Bakewell (formerly BBC Head of Plays), 'The Producer and the Television Play', *The Listener*, 7 July, 1966.)

And the theatre playwright David Rudkin, asked if he finds writing for television much different, says:

> Well, in the end, no, because I found that as soon as I forgot about the medium the writing was just as the writing always had been. I just

334

had to forget that the medium was there. (*Encore*, no 50, July-August, 1967, p.7.)

This is the utopia of an absent medium-meaning produced simply out of the idea. The producer is there merely to package the writer's sensibility, to give the word its appropriate shape. The idea of television itself as a producer of meanings is submerged in an instrumentalism which confers on writers the freedom to express themselves, with a little help with the technical bits: an instrumentalism, that is, which establishes the traditional division of labour between creativity and technique, the realm of the artist and the realm of the mere producer, and which perpetuates within discourse about television the fiction of the neutral relay [as Stuart Hall, 1976, has put it], offering unmediated access to a plurality of statements, positions, convictions. What this fiction within discourse does is discourage theoretical reflection on the medium, and it gives a secondary and quasi-autonomous status to questions of form: form comes after and is a separable issue. The privilege given to writers and their ideas goes some way towards explaining the astonishing formal conservatism of television drama over the past twenty-five years, a conservatism which has survived considerable technological change. Much of the relationship to theatre, then, was and is regressive. Based both on the cross-over of personnel between the two media, and on a respect for theatre's 'high cultural' standing, television has absorbed theatre's aesthetic of creativity, an aesthetic which carries along with it a resistance to theorisation, and a separation of idea and form. The conservatism of the theatrical connection has been attacked by television 'dissidents' from Troy Kennedy Martin to John McGrath [see Martin, 1964 and McGrath, 1977], but still largely defines the dominant assumptions about the television play.

But it is not enough simply to lay the attachment to theatre at the door of cultural snobbery, and leave it there. The relation of television to theatre may also help to explain the drama producer's anxiety that they should be seen to be controversial. What has to be preserved in the relationship is the memory of the key position which theatre occupied in the left-liberal cultural revolt in the period immediately after 1956, a year which was marked not only by Hungary, Suez, and the splits within the British Communist Party, but also by the Royal Court production of *Look Back in Anger* which initiated critical and popular discourses in which the renaissance of British theatre was associated with protest and 'Angry Young Men'. In the late 50s and early 60s, theatre was a pivotal site of culture and social dissension, informing other cultural practices (Lindsay Anderson and Free Cinema, the debate about 'commitment') with its attack on 'the Establishment'. However much the theatre of Osborne and Wesker now is to be criticised for its sentimentalism and its liberalism, for television drama, then, to identify itself with that theatre cannot be constructed as mere cultural snobbery but has to be seen as some kind of partisan shift.

That is to say, while at the formal and aesthetic level the relationship of television drama and theatre can be attacked for its conservatism, at the level of institutional positions, ideologies, and discourses it cannot simply be homogenised as a reactionary cultural attitude, but can be traced out in two contradictory 'traditions': one tradition which crudely can be identified with the Royal Court or with Joan Littlewood's theatre, and the other which can be identified with the persistence of an Edwardian theatre. Thus theatre can be identified with both the conservatives of television drama, and with the dissidents: it was in the magazine *Encore*, 'The Voice of Vital Theatre', that Troy Kennedy Martin delivered his assault on the naturalism of television drama.

BORING NATURALISM

> The ingredients were much as ever: the rooms, the squabbles, and so on. Boring naturalism was transcended by two things: spot-on dialogue and humour. (David Pryce-Jones, review in *The Listener*, 8 April, 1976.)

The idea of naturalism as nothing more than a negative — an absence of style, of craft, of 'spot-on dialogue and humour' — as a form which is either 'lapsed into' or 'transcended', is recurrent in critical discourses about television drama, and indeed the pressure on the term from all sides has produced a collapse in its meaning which may well be beyond rescue. Naturalism appears simply as bad realism.

On one level, exactly following a pattern established in the nineteenth century in critical and popular reactions to the work of Zola, naturalism is associated with sordidness, depression, the 'kitchen sink': 'the rooms, the squabbles, and so on'. The dismay of the critics is repeated in the complaints of the audience against depressing stories with inconclusive endings. A letter from 1961 is typical of a number of letters of its kind, and also serves to remind us of the social place which television once occupied:

> Once, the BBC Sunday play meant a gathering of the family round the set. It was a regular occasion and any visitors who dropped in were expected to join the circle. Now, however, everybody seems to find something better to do than to watch and listen to the morbid meanderings of neurotics and other unhappy people. The once-pleasant family hour is as dead as a Dodo. (*Radio Times*, 2 February, 1961.)

Not only are the plays about neurotics and unhappy people, but they

336

also meander: again, John Russell Taylor's single incident of situation rather than a fully articulated plot; again, more importantly, the nineteenth century Naturalists' privileging of description as against plot, of reporting on nature and on the environment as against a strong narrative and dramatic line with a fully elaborated resolution. Zola's statement of this in 'Naturalism on the Stage' is polemical, and no doubt over-stated in terms of his own novels, but it gives a clear indication of priorities:

> I have said that the naturalistic novel is simply an inquiry into nature, beings, and things. It no longer interests itself in the ingenuity of a well-invented story, developed according to certain rules. Imagination has no longer place, plot matters little to the novelist, who bothers himself with neither development, mystery, nor dénouement . . . You start from the point that nature is sufficient, that you must accept it as it is, without modification or pruning; it is grand enough, beautiful enough to supply its own beginning, its middle and its end .. . The work becomes a report, nothing more. [Zola, 1964, pp.123-4.]

The reaction against nineteenth-century naturalism has a long history: anathematised in the novel for its lack of form, and in the theatre for its lack of drama (Stanislavski regretted the occasional lapses into naturalism of the Moscow Art Theatre), it has come to be thought of as a mistake on the various routes to realism. The most articulate and most sustained critique is probably that of Lukács, who not only succeeds in differentiating naturalism from realism as a difference in method — the descriptive and the narrative — rather than as simply a failure of achievement, but also attempts to identify the political and ideological weakness of the 'descriptive method':

> The decisive ideological weakness of the writers of the descriptive method is in their passive capitulation to these consequences, to these phenomena of fully developed capitalism, and in their seeing the result but not the struggles of the opposing forces. And even when they apparently do describe a process — in the novel of disillusion — the final victory of capitalist inhumanity is always anticipated. [Lukács, 1970, p.146]

The popular complaint against the 'morbid meanderings' of the television play is repeated in Lukács' complaint against the ultimate political capitulation of the novel of disillusion.

For television, Troy Kennedy Martin traces television naturalism to its roots in the American television plays of Chayevsky, and to the influence of the Actor's Studio and the teachings of Strasberg and Stanislavski. [See Martin, 1964.] The defining features which he associates with this television naturalism are (a) a preoccupation with 'people's verbal relationships with each other', and a consequent privileging of dialogue at the expense of action, and (b) a strict observance of natural time, which meant that editing simply followed the characters rather than expressing a view of them. Both of these features Kennedy Martin associates with the regressive theatrical connection, and the 'new wave' which he proposes — 'The medium must be released so that a new generation of writers can use it' — is to develop new narrative styles exploiting the possibilities of cinematic montage and learning from the work of the French New Wave — interestingly it is to Resnais rather than to Godard that he refers. Kennedy Martin's article is important both as a polemic which continues to be influential, and as a 'denaturalisation' of theatrical naturalism for television drama, a refusal to accept the technological or aesthetic essentialisms in which naturalism and theatre produce the inevitable forms of television.

It is beyond the scope of this article to go much further, and the reader is referred to the considerably more elaborated account of television naturalism developed by Raymond Williams [see Williams, 1977a and 1977b], but two points of importance should be established from the above. Firstly, there is the historical association of naturalism with forms of political progressiveness and reformism. Zola's polemics for naturalism were also conducted as attacks against the politically reactionary forms of romanticism. For television, this is uncertain ground, a little minefield of 'formalisms' and 'reformisms'. Clearly the struggle to develop new forms is important: there is an urgent political need to resist the numbing conservatism of television drama and to open it up to less cosy representations, and if this struggle is to be conducted against something called 'naturalism', so be it. But naturalism in any kind of historical sense is something more than a form, a mere absence of style, or a looseness of narrative: it has served within a politics of radical humanism to introduce into the social discourses of theatre and literature, at certain points in their histories, an element (the working class, women, social justice) which had previously been excluded. The clear limitation of the 'reports' of naturalism as a form of social consciousness-raising is the ease with which they can be appropriated to levels of sympathy, charity, and an apolitical reformism: the 'new element' is introduced into discourse as if it had always been there, it is easily accommodated within existing forms, it simply adds to social discourse without changing the discourses which are already in play, extending conservative forms of representation without fundamentally troubling them. But for television, the historical association with an ideology of progressiveness at least has to be registered.

Secondly, and relatedly, there is a debate to be conducted, for television, about the specific history, forms and ideologies of naturalism: a debate which the ubiquity of the term in discussions of television drama simply eludes. The debate has concrete reference points in the writing of Lukács, Brecht, Williams, Zola. Here, I can only register a concern that the looseness and ahistorical formalism of the concepts of naturalism which circulate within writing and thinking about television allow an opposition to emerge which is equally formalist, equally loose, encouraging the approval and celebration of the mere appearance of style and stylisation: 'art television': an 'avant-garde' with Denis Potter at its head. What I think has to be considered for television — for its mode of circulating, for its institutional determinations, for its conservatism — is the possibility of a debate within naturalism as well as a struggle against it. It's in this light that I want to approach documentary drama.

DOCUMENTARY DRAMA

> Drama or documentary? — the 'Scotland Yard' programmes fall uneasily between. Basically these are documentary, each dealing with some different aspect of the extremely complex activities of Scotland Yard. Unfortunately it seems to have been felt, quite wrongly, that this would be insufficiently interesting in itself, so little shots of drama are injected and these give the impression, I am sure the quite unfair impression, that the police are incompetent or venal or both. (Hilary Corke, *The Listener*, 2nd June, 1960.)

Writing, apparently without irony, in 1960, Hilary Corke anticipates precisely the 'little gap between fact and fiction' which worried William Deedes (editor of the *Telegraph*) in the discussion which followed the transmission of *Days of Hope*, or dismays Lord Carrington over *Death of a Princess*: in a speech to the Anglo-Arab Middle East Association, he says, 'The new formula of mixing fact with fiction, dramatisation masquerading as documentary, can be dangerous and misleading'.

The formula is not, in fact, new, and forms of dramatised documentary have been occupying an uneasy place on television for more than twenty years. Before that, dramatic reconstructions of actuality have a history in cinema as old as cinema itself, beginning with Meliès' reconstructions of coronations and assassinations, and continuing with Soviet cinema's celebrations of the Revolution. For British television, the important cinematic antecedent could be found in the various ideologies and practices which were circulating in the documentary movement in the 1930s and 1940s — from *Fires Were Started* to Ralph Bond and the Co-operative Society films. In American theatre during the Depression, the Federal Theatre Project had developed the Living Newspaper to dramatise documentation about urban housing, farm-workers' struggles for unionisation, the power industry; and some of this was picked up by left-wing theatre groups in Britain, and subsequently developed by Joan Littlewood in the 1950s and 1960s. On radio, a crucial source of early television genres, dramatised documentaries were a commonplace, and had been given a certain left-wing inflection in the 'radio ballads' devised by Charles Parker and Ewan McColl (who was also associated with Joan Littlewood's theatre) which dramatised areas of working-class life and history. Far from being new, there are a number of histories and traditions which can be followed through from film, theatre, and radio into television.

Two ideas can be identified in this for an understanding of the development of television documentary drama: one, the 'documentary idea', can be associated with Grierson and Walter Lippman and the extension of democracy through social education and the presentation of information in its most accessible form; the other, to the left of this, attempts to recover lost histories and dramatise repressed documents. Television, in its dramatised documentaries of the 1950s and early 1960s, seems to have accepted the form fairly unproblematically within the terms of its social responsibility to inform and educate: there were dramatised documentaries on Scotland Yard, on bankruptcy, on the town vet, on regional symphony orchestras, on a doctor struck off the medical list, on the immigration service. Interestingly, in the light of the subsequent history of the form, these early programmes were as likely to be dismissed for their complicity, as regretted for their unease:

> I don't suppose the series will dare suggest an immigration officer can ever behave unreasonably, can abuse his alarming power, can ever become anything less than a sagacious and trustworthy protector of society. (Derek Hill, *The Listener*, 6 September, 1962.)

These information programmes appeared regularly on BBC until the end of 1962, and then disappeared as a clearly marked form. After 1962 there are isolated events of considerable importance — Peter Watkins' *Culloden* in 1964, the Loach/McTaggart *Up the Junction* in 1965, Peter Watkins' suppressed *The War Game* in 1966 — and the Loach/Garnett *Cathy Come Home* which appears at the end of 1966. It is the line which develops from *Cathy Come Home*, the line associated with the Loach/Garnett label — with the recovery of lost histories, with the exposure of social justice, with 'progressive realism' — that I am primarily concerned with here.

Something further should be added to separate this line from other forms of dramatised documentary which have become current. On one side of the line, there are American 'factions' like *Holocaust* or *Washington: Behind Closed Doors*; on the other side there are documentary reconstructions like *Three Days in Szczecin*, or *Invasion*. 'Factions' are constructed along firm dramatic, or melodramatic lines, their 'documentariness' coming from the actuality of their historical referent, rather than from any mixture of forms: there is in fact very little stylistic or narrative distinction between, say, *Holocaust* and the American television serialisation of *From Here to Eternity*. 'Dramadoc', on the other hand, is identified by Leslie Woodhead, producer of *Three Days in Szczecin* for Granada, as 'dramatised journalism':

> Our priorities, disciplines, sources and basic motivations are journalistic, and where there is a clash with dramatic values, journalism wins. We make bad plays — not a slogan, just a declaration of priorities. (*The Listener*, 23 September, 1976.)

This dramatised journalism is the aggressive development of the earlier innocuous information programmes, dramatising socially important events and documented facts which the cameras were not there to record at the time; the dramatic reconstruction is made necessary by television's need to show.

Each of these forms has its own interest and its own problems, and there is an obvious overlap within all forms of dramatised documentary, particularly between dramatised journalism and documentary drama, the one exploiting the visual rhetoric of the other. For the sake of particularity, however, I am interested here in the relation of documentary drama to drama, rather than its relation to journalism, and while the two forms share the possibility of a confusion between fact and fiction which gives them both an uneasy place within television, each has a formal and functional specificity which needs to be considered separately. Here I am concerned with the particular articulation of the dramatic and the documentary within fictional dramatic narrative, with the way in which the one functions for the other, and with the nature of the unease which the articulation seems to produce.

Within fictional dramatic narrative, it would clearly be a mistake to constitute documentary drama as a homogeneous category, and there are important shifts and developments between, say, *Cathy Come Home* or *The Big Flame* on the one hand, and *Days of Hope* and *Law and Order* on the other. Nor is it simply a process of evolutionary change: *The Spongers* probably has more in common with *Cathy Come Home* than it has with *Law and Order*. The variations — in narrative construction, in camera technique, in lighting, in acting — are important, but it seems more useful here to establish the consistencies: it is, in fact, one of the defining characteristics of documentary drama that it has a consistent televisual style, a visual appearance and a relationship to narrative space which is particular to it, which is recognisable, which circulates its own meanings. This consistency and specificity can be elaborated in terms of *mise en scène*, or more precisely in terms of the articulation of two looks — the look of the documentary, and the look of the dramatic fiction.

By the 'dramatic look' I mean the system of looks and glances which is familiar from fictional film, and which works to produce the consistency and movement of the narrative, placing the spectator in relation to it — the rhetoric, that is, of narrative realist film: eye-line match, field/reverse-field, point-of-view. This rhetoric centres the narrative: it establishes, within a world of events, scenes, characters, and little narratives, the line and the connections which are to be privileged. It orders the world into a readable hierarchy. It is worth noting that, made on film, documentary drama tends, within the articulation of its dramatic look, to have a more highly elaborated narrative rhetoric, with a more cinematic deployment of field/reverse-field or point-of-view, than the television drama which has its roots in the multi-camera techniques of the studio.

By the 'documentary look' I mean the system of looks which constructs the social space of the fiction, a social space which is more than simply a background, but which, in a sense, constitutes what the documentary drama wishes to be about, the 'document' which is to be dramatised. Thus, *Cathy Come Home* and *The Spongers* wish to be about the social environment of sections of the community and the bureaucracy which oppresses them; *Days of Hope* claims as its subject the whole of the labour movement from rural community to organised labour. This attention to the social environment and to the community is what connects documentary drama with the ideology of naturalism:

> We are looking for the cause of social evil; we study the anatomy of classes and individuals to explain the derangements which are produced in society and in man . . . No work can be more moralising than ours, then, because it is upon it that law should be based. ('To the Young People of France' in Zola, 1964.)

This connection with naturalism can be extended to the level of method: Zola's 'experimental method' consisted of observing the material world closely and then analysing it 'scientifically' by setting in motion an 'experiment', a narrative situation, to see what would happen. In a similar way, documentary drama seems to produce its analysis by setting in motion a dramatic experiment within the world observed and constructed by the documentary look.

Observed *and constructed*. The documentary look is not the perfect vision of an actual world, but operates, as does the dramatic, within a specific rhetoric which is not innocent, offering an objective, true social space, but which works within rules and strategies to produce a social space which is also a narrative, fictional space. What seems specific to documentary drama as compared with narrative realist film is that, whereas classical realist film depends to a greater or lesser extent on the illusion of unmediated vision, on a transparency of form and style, documentary drama operates a rhetoric of mediated style which is clearly marked, but which has a prior association with truth and neutrality. If classical realist film depends on a certain invisibility of form, and on a spectator who forgets the camera, the documentary look takes its appearance of objectivity from its place within the conventions of documentary: thus, the hand-held camera, the cramped shot, natural lighting, inaudible sound. The appearance in the fiction of the documentary look, easily visible but unsteady and apparently unpremeditated, establishes the impression of a basis of unproblematic fact on which the dramatic 'experiment' can be conducted, and which will guarantee its validity.

In one sense, the documentary look takes different forms, finding its guarantee in different sources, different documentary conventions. While black and white film was still acceptable for television. *The War Game* could rely on hand-held camera and grainy film, the conventions of immediacy, reportage, and *cinéma vérité*. *Law and Order*, particularly in the early episodes, works with the rhetoric of a concealed, investigative camera, spying on its object behind cover (cf. *Rome Open City*): it also depends on the illusion that, where sound is inaudible and language incomprehensible, they cannot have been created but must simply have been captured (cf. Robert Altman). *Days of Hope* has the problem of being visually beautiful, a quality which, for film, has an association with composition rather than with truth, but it seems to me to take its guarantee from a notion of 'old photography', the guarantee of which

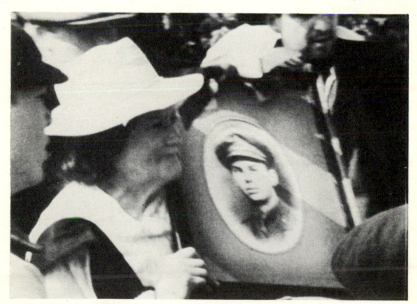

Fig. 4.1: Days of Hope

resides in its 'primitiveness' and naïvety. I am thinking generally of the compositions involving groups of characters, or involving characters positioned close to windows, naturally lit from the side. The point of interest is that all of these strategies of the documentary look rely less on the guarantees of their own reflection of the real world and more on a reference to other formal conventions which are associated with reflection. [See Figs. 4.1-4.3.]

At another, and I think more fundamental level, the documentary look finds its consistency in the rhetoric of the 'unplanned' or 'unpremeditated' shot: the camera surprised by the action.

> If you are making a documentary and there was just a cameraman in the room and he was following the conversation, he would never be at somebody when they started to speak. He would follow the conversation. That's what we tried to do really, to let the conversation call for the cuts, rather than the camera knowing who was going to speak next and, therefore always being in at the start of a sentence. (Ken Loach interview in *Cinema Papers*, April 1976.)

In the last episode of *Days of Hope*, Sarah and Philip are in a pub; Sarah raises her pint of beer and proposes a toast to the success of the General Strike; a voice off-camera responds, 'I'll drink to that'; Sarah, still in mid close-up, acknowledges the speaker, still off-camera; and only then does the camera pan round to look for the person who had taken it by surprise. The little scene denies a script, denies planning, denies rehearsal, and establishes in their place a complete world which the camera can only capture, cannot have constructed, a world which goes on beyond the fiction. This continuous world is the narrative space of documentary drama, a space which is familiar in its outlines from Bazin's celebration of Renoir. The truth of the world is discovered in the 'experiment', not produced but producing itself, organically, from the inside, in the absence of external interference, premeditated control, or prior knowledge. It is spontaneous, therefore true. [See Figs. 4.4-4.6.]

Figs. 4.2 and 4.3: Days of Hope

344

Now this could easily degenerate into a naïve critique of deception and cheating; or into the equally naïve assumption that the film-makers are not aware of what they are doing. Clearly they know, and, fairly reasonably, expect us to know that they are producing fictions, and exploiting certain conventions. My point is not to expose trickery, but to try to point to the bases and the determinations of conventions which are not innocent instruments, simply available for any use, but which come to documentary drama already weighted with significances and associations. More immediately, and more concretely, I am interested in what the articulation of the dramatic look and the documentary look does within the fiction.

Figs. 4.4-4.6: Days of Hope

I have already suggested that the dramatic look gives the narrative a centre, orders the heterogeneity of the world 'captured' by the documentary look, and establishes the privileged figures and events. Thus there is an easily discernible story running through the history of the working class in *Days of Hope*, and in *Law and Order* we have no difficulty picking out the figures of the Detective, the Villain, and the Brief from the total system of the institutions of the law. The problem is that, in the end, though documentary drama within its naturalist project wishes to be about the community and the social environment, there is always the risk that the balance will fail, the dramatic narrative will impose its resolutions on the documentary disorder, and the drama will end up being about the privileged, centred individuals. Thus, at the end of *Days of Hope*, we are as likely to be interested in whether Sarah and Philip will patch up the problems of their marriage, as to be interested in the future of the Party and its relationship to the working class. Within the terms of narrative resolutions this is an inevitable risk.

More than this, the rhetoric of the dramatic look inscribes the document into experience. Eye-line match, field/reverse-field, point-of-view are mechanisms which work within film and television to articulate the look of the viewing subject, and to construct a system of viewing places for the spectator within the fiction. The viewing subject identifies with the fictional world through identifying with the looks of the dramatic figures within it. By deploying this rhetoric of looks, documentary drama produces systems of identification which are specific to it as a televisual form and cannot simply be homogenised into a monolithic narrative system, but which nevertheless set in motion a play of sympathetic involvement for the spectator. The spectator experiences the drama. What documentary drama offers (like naturalism) is the experience of the drama, rather than the analysis of (or 'scientific experiment' on) the document. It is therefore vulnerable to the critique of Lukács that it is a 'subjective protest', or to the critique of Brecht that it fails to expose the spectator to the contradictions which have to be worked out. Thus *Days of Hope* offers the experience of history — memory — rather than its analysis; *The Spongers* or *Cathy Come Home* offers the experience of social injustice — bad conscience. The issue of experiences and analysis is clearly part of a wider debate, which will have to be picked up again in discussing documentary drama's 'progressiveness'.

If the rhetoric of the drama inscribes the document within narrative and experience, the rhetoric of the documentary establishes the experience as an experience of the real, and places it within a system of guarantees and confirmations. The look of the documentary is qualitatively different, lacking the reverse field of the dramatic look, its 'reversibility'. The documentary look is a look at its object, fixing the object rather than putting its look into play, the object looked at but only itself looking on: the figures of the drama exchange and reverse looks, the figures of the documentary are looked at and look on.

Within the conventions of documentary, the objectifying look is part of the support of truth and neutrality. For documentary drama, however, two looks are in play, and they come to constitute a hierarchy: the rhetoric of the drama operates an exchange of looks between the characters, dramatising their relationship, activating divisions between them and within them, putting them in doubt, giving them an incompleteness which can only be filled by the eventual plentitude of the narrative. The rhetoric of documentary, the fixed and fixing look, constitutes its object — the community, the social environment, the working class — as simply there, unproblematic, already completed, 'extras'. The working class, the community appears as a simple unquestioned presence, functioning to locate the dramas of others, but not themselves dramatised. I am thinking particularly of *Days of Hope* where the camera continually confirms the drama on the face of an extra who is looking on: the figures of the community — of the documentary look — function as a referent for the drama, guaranteeing its social relevance: but the attention is continually pulled back to the figures at the centre of the drama, to their play of looks, their struggles for knowledge and resolution. [See Fig. 4.7.]

The problem, then, is one of integration. The two discourses, of documentary and of drama, are integrated to produce a movement of

Fig. 4.7: Days of Hope

347

confirmations, guarantees and narrativisations back and forth between them. Each functions to support the other rather than to call the other into question; there is no contradiction for the spectator between the drama and the document, but only a confirmation; the tensions are all within the drama, rather than between it and its referent. The discourse is ultimately one of unproblematic truth. This is reinforced by the hierarchies established within the narrative, a narrative which, although it digresses to bring in the life of the community (the club scene in *The Spongers*, or the extended celebration dance at the end of the second episode of *Days of Hope*), nevertheless re-centres itself, pulling attention back towards narrative and resolution.

DOCUMENTARY DRAMA AND 'PROGRESSIVENESS'

All this, however, does not close off the question of documentary drama's progressiveness. On one level, the important question is not what the form has been, but what it could be. In this respect, there is a clear model of a potential development of documentary drama in the television production of *The Cheviot, The Stag, and the Black, Black Oil*. Colin McArthur has already commented on this in his monograph, *Television and History* [McArthur, 1978], and all I wish to add here (by way of bringing together again McArthur and MacCabe) is the relevance in this connection of the concept of 'separation' which MacCabe mobilises in his essay 'The Politics of Separation' [MacCabe, 1975/6]. MacCabe's interest is in the 'separation-out' of the filmic elements of sound, colour, writing, noise and music in the films of Godard, and he draws the concept of the 'separation of the elements' from Brecht's notes to the opera *Mahagonny*. It is worth quoting from these notes here:

> When the epic theatre's method begins to penetrate the opera the first result is a radical *separation of the elements*. The great struggle for supremacy between words, music and production — which always brings up the question 'which is the pretext for what?': is the music the pretext for the events on stage, or are these the pretext for the music? etc. — can simply be by-passed by radically separating the elements. So long as the expression *'Gesamtkunstwerk'* (or 'integrated work of art') means that the integration is muddle, so long as the arts are supposed to be 'fused' together, the various elements will all be equally degraded, and each will act as a mere 'feed' to the rest. The process of fusion extends to the spectator, who gets thrown into the melting pot and becomes a passive (suffering) part of the total work of art. Witchcraft of this sort must of course be fought against. [Brecht, 1977, pp.37-8.]

My argument against the documentary drama as it has been formulated has been that, though it is struggling on the right side, it produces itself

348

within a self-confirming integration, and produces a spectator who is also confirmed in an already determined position. As MacCabe argues, though it may expose contradiction, it is 'contradiction which it has already resolved', and it fails 'to produce a contradiction which remains unresolved and is thus left for the reader to resolve and to act out' [MacCabe, 1975/6].

For the development of the formal effectiveness of documentary drama, *The Cheviot* . . . represents a radical separation of the discourses of the drama and the discourses of the documentary: the television production is at the same time a drama, a documentary on the way in which the theatrical performance circulated in the Highlands, a historical reconstruction, and a documentary on working conditions in the North Sea oil industry. The elements are not integrated to confirm and support each other, but are clearly separated out and allowed to play against each other. The risk which the theatrical production always ran of being overwhelmed by the exuberance of its own performance is tempered by the possibility which the separation of discourses allows of continually unsettling the spectator's position. The documentary on the present oil industry produces a contemporaneity of history which both undercuts the romanticism of a 'Celtic twilight', and offers a way of seeing this struggle in terms of other struggles. It is the possibility of this collision of documentary drama, of the refusal of integration, which makes the documentary drama a potentially interesting political form. It also has to be said that, whereas *Cathy Come Home* started a tradition, the model of *The Cheviot* . . . has not yet been followed up.

At another level, progressiveness on television is not ultimately a question of form, of integration or separation, because television occupies a particular social space which makes its progressiveness or regressiveness more difficult to calculate. Thus, however much the ideology within which it operates may be characterised as reformist, the screening of *Cathy Come Home* is an event with material effects within the history of British social work; *Law and Order* is an event within the history of the relations between the police and one of the major media; the screening of *The Big Flame*, coinciding with the Devlin Report on the docks and the Upper Clyde Shipyard sit-in, occurs within a particular conjuncture of events and forces which makes the identification of its political effectivity more complex. Unlike films or plays, television programmes are seen all at once (and reacted to all at once) by a national audience. Because of this, it becomes difficult, and unrewarding, to establish the final conditions for the progressiveness of television. The conjuncture in which programmes are screened has to be critically identified; and because the programmes are made within basically conservative institutions which are both highly determined and highly determining, their place within the politics of the institutions has also to be brought into consideration. The political analysis of a television

349

programme such as *Law and Order* or *The Big Flame* has to go beyond the identification of the politics which it speaks, towards an analysis of the place which it occupies within the political forces and contradictions which are current at the time of its screening, and towards an understanding of its relationship to the other representations which television predominantly circulates and supports.

Also, to argue for the need to develop forms which will produce the spectator in contradiction implies a position within a wider political debate against the political effectiveness of notions of experience and solidarity. For television, I am less confident of this position. Under certain conditions, of which the present may be one, I want to be able to say that, *for television*, in its specific conditions, it may be politically progressive to confirm an identity (of sexuality or class), to recover repressed experience or history, to contest the dominant image with an alternative identity. Documentary drama seems to me to have occupied a progressive role within television insofar as it has introduced into the discourses of television a repressed political, social discourse which may contribute to an audience's political formation, and may increase its scepticism of the other representations which television offers. I want to

The Cheviot, the Stag and the Black, Black Oil

Figs. 4.8, 4.9: *drama*

Fig. 4.10: *historical reconstruction*

350

Figs. 4.11, 4.12: *theatrical performance*

Figs. 4.13, 4.14: *documentary*
i) *reportage* (4.13) ii) *interview* (4.14)

be able to say this at the same time as arguing for different ways of looking.

This, in a sense, is to collapse the whole notion of 'the progressive text', whose progressiveness can be measured against some scale of correctness. Within the social space of television, within the politics of its institutions, and within the way it circulates, television programmes have the capacity to be events as much as to be texts. But simply to leave it at that, is to accept a relativism which can only determine progressiveness after the event, and cannot influence the development of progressive forms of representation. Clearly, what is necessary, for a journal such as *Screen*, is to identify and give priority to areas of debate which can be effectively developed in terms of form and politics.

It is in this sense that I am arguing for the importance of documentary drama in particular, and drama in general: in the sense, that is, in which drama and documentary drama represent areas of tension and uncertainty for television, areas in which debate could be effective and in which institutional debates already exist. The question is one of privileging those areas as sites of critical and theoretical engagement: a question of how to respect those areas for their political progressiveness for television; a question, at the same time, of how to argue against them, for an extension of television's discourse in forms which will contest easy

351

images, unsettle its conventional patterns, and break up the homogeneity of its representations.

(First published in *Screen*, vol. 21, no. 3, 1980.)

References

Brecht, B. (1977), 'The Modern Theatre in the Epic Theatre: notes to the opera *Aufsteig und Fall der Stadt Mahagonny*' in Willett, J. (ed), *Brecht on Theatre*, London: Eyre Methuen.

Hall, S. (1976), 'Television and Culture', *Sight and Sound*, vol. 45, no. 4, Autumn 1976.

Heath, S. and Skirrow, G. (1977), 'Television: a World in Action', *Screen*, vol. 18, no. 2, Summer 1977.

Lukács, G. (1970), 'Narrate or Describe' in *Writer and Critic*, London: Merlin Press.

MacCabe, C. (1976), 'The Politics of Separation', *Screen*, vol. 16, no. 4, Winter, 1975/6.

Martin, T. (1964), 'Nats Go Home: first statement of a new drama for television', *Encore*, no. 48, March/April 1964.

McArthur, C. (1978), *Television and History*, London: British Film Institute.

McGrath, J. (1977), 'TV Drama: the case against naturalism', *Sight and Sound*, vol. 46, no. 2, Spring 1977.

Williams, R. (1974), *Television, Technology and Cultural Form*, London: Fontana/Collins.

Williams, R. (1977a), 'A Lecture on Realism', *Screen*, vol. 18, no. 1, Spring 1977.

Williams, R. (1977b), 'Realism and Non-Naturalism', Edinburgh International Television Festival 1977, Official Programme published by *Broadcast*.

Zola, E. (1964), 'Naturalism on the Stage' in *The Experimental Novel and Other Essays*, New York: Haskell House.

Film and Television Availability Note

FILMS

Films discussed in some detail in this book and available for hire are:
All About Eve, FDA, £11.50 (16mm)
Klute, Columbia-EMI-Warner, £17 (16mm)
Jaws, Rank Film Library, £75 (16mm)

TELEVISION PROGRAMMES

Television programmes discussed and available for hire are:
The Cheviot, the Stag and the Black, Black Oil, BFI, £20 (16mm), £12.50 (videocassette)
Culloden, BFI, £12.50 (16mm), £12.50 (videocassette)
Days of Hope, BFI, 4 episodes, each £20 (16mm), £12.50 (videocassette)
Gangsters, BFI, episode 6, 2nd series, £10 (videocassette)
Screening Nuclear Hazard, Open University (ref. U201/06), £15.50
The Spongers, Concord Films, £18.20 (16mm)
The War Game, BFI, £15 (16mm), £10 (videocassette)
Upstairs, Downstairs ('The Nine-Day Wonder'), BFI, £10 (videocassette)

Note that many editions of *Horizon* earlier than the ones discussed are available from Concord or BBC Enterprises, and more recent editions may become available in future.

Index of Names and Titles

Alice Doesn't Live Here Any More, 239
All About Eve, 259–60
Allen, Gracie, 29–31, 249
Allen, Jim, 296, 297, 302, 303, 305, 306, 315, 334
All in the Family, 28, 35
Allison, Malcolm, 151, 152
Alloway, Lawrence, 245, 264
All the President's Men 263, 265
Althusser, Louis, 69, 116, 231, 232
Altman, Robert, 238, 343
Alvarado, Manuel, 32, 73, 74
America, 285
Anatomy of a Murder, 9
Anderson, Lindsay, 234, 335
Andrews, Eamonn, 152
Animal Crackers, 11
Archers, The, 77
Are You Being Served?, 34, 37, 44
Army Game, The, 29, 35
Around the World in Eighty Days, 261
Arzner, Dorothy, 247
Ascent of Man, The, 285
Astaire, Fred, 10
Astor, Mary, 252
Attenborough, David, 178, 180

Backs to the Land, 34, 35
Bakewell, Michael, 334
Band Wagon, The, 10
Barker, Ronnie, 37, 38, 39
Barratt, Michael, 95, 120, 121, 122, 127, 129, 130, 131
Barthes, Roland, 15, 16, 79, 81, 82, 230, 233, 249, 256
Baxter, Anne, 259
Baxter, Raymond, 182
Bazin, André, 344
Beggar My Neighbour, 30, 36
Bellamy, David, 183, 184
Benjamin, Walter, 235, 270, 272, 317
Benn, Tony, 91
Benny, Jack, 24, 31
Bergala, Alain, 21, 22
Bergman, Ingrid, 244
Bertolucci, Bernardo, 261
Beyond a Reasonable Doubt, 22, 23, 247
Bierce, Ambrose, 221, 223, 224
Big Flame, The, 297, 341, 349, 350
Big Heat, The, 247
Big Match, The, 164
Birds, The, 254, 255
Body in Question, The, 172, 191
Boetticher, Budd, 209
Bogdanovich, Peter, 21
Bond, Ralph, 339
Bough, Frank, 140
Boulting Brothers, 29
Brando, Marlon, 238, 239, 250, 251, 261
Brass Tacks, 175
Braudy, Leo, 238
Brecht, Bertolt, 216–35, 247–9, 272, 313, 339, 346, 348
Bremner, Billy, 149, 154
Bridge Too Far, A, 322
Brody, R., 119, 120, 121
Bronowski, Jacob, 178, 180
Brooks, Cleanth, 242
Brothers-in-Law, 29
Brunsdon, Charlotte, 87
Buckman, Peter, 55
Buckman, Rob, 183

Bunce, Michael, 120, 131
Burke, James, 178, 191
Burns, E., 245
Burns, George, 29–31
Burns and Allen Show, The, 4, 29–31
Buscombe, Edward, 32, 73, 74, 142, 163
Bus Stop, 251
Butch Cassidy and the Sundance Kid, 209, 263, 264

Cain, Maureen, 69
Calder, Angus, 322
Calder, Nigel, 179, 180
Campbell Jones, Simon, 181
Cannon, 73
Capra, Frank, 11, 12, 24, 275
Carrington, Lord, 339
Casey, Luke, 129
Cathy Come Home, 225, 308, 329, 340, 341, 342, 346, 349
Caughie, John, 286–7
Channing, Carol, 266
Chaplin, Charles, 11
Charisse, Cyd, 10
Charlton, Bobby, 151
Charlton, Jack, 151, 156
Charlton, Michael, 98, 101, 104, 105, 106, 110, 111, 112
Chayevsky, Paddy, 337
Cheviot, The Stag and the Black, Black Oil, The, 298–301, 348, 349, 350
Clark, Lord, 178, 293
Clement, Dick, 33, 38
Clough, Brian, 151, 152
Coburn, Charles, 266
Colbourne, Maurice, 72
Coleman, David, 152, 156
Come Back, Mrs Noah, 4, 27, 31, 35, 37, 44–52
Coming Out, 329
Comolli, J.-L., 24
Connections, 191
Connell, Ian, 86, 118, 130, 131
Cook, Pam, 210
Cooke, Alistair, 178, 285
Corke, Hilary, 339
Costa-Gavras, 225, 308
Cox, David, 180
Coyne, Tom, 126, 129, 132, 136
Crawford, Joan, 244
Crerand, Paddy, 151
Critcher, Chas, 142
Croft, David, 34, 44
Crossman, Richard, 91
Cukor, George, 276, 278
Culloden, 285, 286, 294–6, 299, 331, 340
Curran, Sir Charles, 92, 93
Curti, Lidia, 86

Dad's Army, 34, 35, 44
Dallas, 179
Dance of the Vampires, 8
Davies, Barry, 188
Davis, Bette, 239, 244, 246, 253, 259, 260
Day, Robin, 95, 178
Days of Hope, 286, 287, 296–8, 302–18, 323–5, 327, 333, 339, 341, 342, 343, 344, 345, 346, 347, 348
Dean, James, 238
Death of a Princess, 285, 339
Deedes, William, 297, 339
Dickson, David, 174
Dick Van Dyke Show, The, 37
Dietrich, Marlene, 210, 211, 212, 246, 247, 261, 262

Dimbleby, David, 95
Dimbleby, Richard, 95
Dirty Harry, 56
Dishonoured, 212
Disorderly Orderly, The, 11
Dixon of Dock Green, 54, 55
Doctor on the Go, 37
Dr Who, 44
Donen, Stanley, 278
Don't Ask Me, 183
Don't Just Sit There, 172, 183
Dorfman, A., 132, 139
Dougan, Derek, 151
Douglas, Kirk, 245
Dracula, 8, 9
Drummond, Phillip, 32, 58
Dubroux, Danièle, 18
Duchess of Duke Street, The, 286
Dyer, Richard, 53, 56, 65, 145, 198

Eastwood, Clint, 246
Eaton, Mick, 4
Edward and Mrs Simpson, 285
Edward the Seventh, 288, 293, 297
Edwards, Blake, 17
Eisenstein, Sergei, 221–4, 246, 247, 254
Eliot, George, 218–9, 227
Elsaesser, Thomas, 198, 199
Explorers, The, 305

Fall and Rise of Reginald Perrin, The, 33
Farrow, Mia, 262
Fawlty Towers, 37
Figlio, K., 174
Fires Were Started, 339
Fonda, Jane, 219, 239, 243, 244, 249, 254
Fontaine, Joan, 247
Ford, John, 277
Forster, E. M., 60, 240, 241
Forsyte Saga, The 286
Fortini, Franco, 226
Foucault, Michel, 175, 322
Frankenstein, 8
Freud, Sigmund, 207, 209, 226, 314, 317
Friend, Martin, 186
From Here to Eternity (TV), 341
Fuller, Sam, 20
Funny Girl, 250
Funny Lady, 250

Gable, Clark, 253
Galbraith, J. K., 293
Gangsters, 5, 71–82
Garbo, Greta, 210, 239, 246
Gardner, Carl, 87, 188
Garnett, Tony, 296, 297, 302, 305, 306, 308, 315, 323, 331, 334, 340
Gentlemen Prefer Blondes, 266
George and Mildred, 36
Germany Year Zero, 228
Get Some In, 34, 35
Gillman, P., 120, 124, 125, 131
Godard, Jean-Luc, 229, 232, 249, 338
Going Straight, 4, 27, 33, 37, 38–42
Goldmann, Lucien, 231
Gold Rush, The, 11
Gombrich, E. H., 273
Gone With the Wind, 250, 263
Gorin, Jean-Pierre, 232
Grade, Michael, 26
Grahame, Gloria, 247
Gramsci, Antonio, 114, 115, 231
Grant, Cary, 244
Great Egg Race, The, 180
Great Gatsby, The, 262
Great Ziegfeld, The, 250
Grierson, John, 340
Gunplay, 71

Hall, Stuart, 55, 56, 86, 94, 121, 144, 335
Hann, Judith, 182
Happy Ever After, 30, 34
Hardcastle, William, 118
Hart, Richard, 55
Hart, William S., 246
Harvey, W., 240, 241
Haskell, Molly, 209
Hawks, Howard, 11, 21, 239, 276
Hawthorn, Jeremy, 241
Hazell: The making of a TV series (book), 73
Heath, Stephen, 7, 12, 14, 27, 31, 32, 35, 43, 80, 197, 198, 230, 311, 328
Hebdige, Dick, 61
Hedren, Tippi, 254, 255
Here's Harry, 28
Herzog, Werner, 8
Heston, Charlton, 267
Hill, Derek, 334, 340
Hill, Jimmy, 148, 151, 152, 153, 162
Hill, Lord, 130
Hitchcock, Alfred, 16, 77, 204, 211–13, 254, 276, 277
Hoggart, Richard, 134, 135
Holocaust, 333, 340, 341
Horizon, 172, 173, 175, 176, 177, 179, 180, 181, 182, 183, 184, 191
Howerd, Frankie, 28
Hugh and I, 30
Hurd, Geoffrey, 4, 65

Invasion, 340
Ireland: A Television History, 285
Iron Horse, The, 238
It Ain't Half Hot, Mum, 34, 44

Jakobson, Roman, 271
Jason and the Argonauts, 19
Jaws, 197, 200–5
Jay, Peter, 180
Johns, Hugh, 157
Johnston, Claire, 59, 210, 239, 247
Julia, 239

Kaplan, E. Ann, 260, 261
Kästner, Erich, 235
Kazan, Elia, 251
Keaton, Buster, 17
Kellogg, R., 254
Kerr, Paul, 5
Khalil, Ahmed, 72
King, 85
Klute, 219–20, 239, 254, 307, 308, 311
Kojak, 53, 179
Kuhle Wampe, 232, 233
Kuleshov, Lev, 246
Kumar, K., 95

Lacan, Jacques, 208, 226, 227
Lacombe Lucien, 322
La Fresnais, Ian, 33, 38
Lancaster, Burt, 245
Land of the Pharaohs, 21
Lang, Fritz, 16, 22, 247, 276, 277
Last, Richard, 75
Last Tango in Paris, 260–1
Latour, Bruno, 190
Law and Order, 333, 341, 343, 346, 349, 350
Laws, Frederick, 334
Leakey, Richard, 180
Lear, Norman, 42, 43
Léaud, Jean-Pierre, 261
Lee, Christopher, 246
Left-Handed Gun, The, 238
Leigh, Vivien, 251
Lewis, Jerry, 249
Likely Lads, The, 38
Lippman, Walter, 340

Lister, Moira, 36
Littewood, Joan, 336, 339, 340
Liver Birds, The, 44
Lloyd, Jeremy, 44
Loach, Ken, 296, 297, 302, 305, 306, 308, 315, 323, 334, 340, 344
Look Back in Anger (play), 335
Loos, Anita, 266
Lord Peter Wimsey, 34
Losey, Joseph, 276
Lovell, Alan, 56
Love Thy Neighbour, 35
Lubitsch, Ernst, 11, 23
Lugosi, Bela, 78
Lukács, Georg, 216, 337, 339, 346
Lynd, R. S., 288

McArthur, Colin, 87, 143, 151, 156, 267, 286, 303, 310–13, 327, 348
MacCabe, Colin, 74, 80, 198, 286, 297–8, 303, 304, 307–9, 324, 327, 348, 349
McColl, Ewan, 340
McGrath, John, 335
McIlvanney, Hugh, 167
McKenzie, Robert, 98, 104, 105, 107, 109, 110, 122
McLintock, Frank, 151
McMenemy, Laurie, 151, 153
McTaggart, James, 340
Magee, Brian, 178
Mahagonny, 348
Maltese Falcon, The, 78, 252
Man About the House, 36, 37
Man Alive, 175, 176
Mannoni, O., 23
Man Who Shot Liberty Valance, The, 263
Marnie, 212
Martin, Ian Kennedy, 60
Martin, Philip, 71, 72, 77, 78
Martin, Troy Kennedy, 334, 335, 336, 337, 338
Marx Brothers, The, 11, 24, 249
Marx, Karl, 316–17
M.A.S.H. (TV), 29
Match of the Day, 164
Mattelart, Armand, 132, 139, 173
Medical Express, 180
Meet the Wife, 34, 36
Méliès, Georges, 339
Mellencamp, Patricia, 17, 18
Mercer, Joe, 151
Metz, Christian, 3, 6, 18, 19, 201
Michelmore, Cliff, 122, 124, 130
Middlemarch (book), 218–19, 307
Midweek, 94
Mighty Micro, The, 173
Miller, J. A., 7
Miller, Jonathan, 178, 180, 191
Milligan, Spike, 5
Mind of Mr J G Reeder, The, 34
Minnelli, Vicente, 276, 278
Mr Deeds Goes to Town, 12
Mr Smith Goes to Washington, 12
Mitchell, Austin, 183
Mizoguchi, Kenji, 277
Moncur, Bobby, 151
Money Programme, The, 176
Monroe, Marilyn, 198, 239, 243, 244, 245, 250, 251, 259, 266, 267
Montand, Yves, 249
Monty Python's Flying Circus, 5, 31
Moore, Brian, 151, 153, 157
Moore, Dudley, 179
Moore, Patrick, 178
Morley, David, 87, 135, 136
Morocco, 212
Morricone, Enrico, 76
Mourlet, Michel, 267
Mulvey, Laura, 18, 81, 198

Murray, Don, 251
My Wife Next Door, 36

Nationwide, 47, 87, 95, 118–41
Neale, Stephen, 3, 4
Newcomb, Horace, 57
Niagara, 250
Nichols, Dandy, 36
Night Porter, 322
Noonan, Tommy, 266
North by Northwest, 16, 77
Nosferatu (1979), 8
Not the 9 O'Clock News, 5
Nova, 180
Nowell-Smith, Geoffrey, 87, 143
Now Voyager, 252, 253

October, 254
O Lucky Man!, 234, 235
On the Buses, 37
Onedin Line, The, 186
Only Angels Have Wings, 211
On the Waterfront, 261
Open Secret, 176, 177, 180
Ophuls, Marcel, 322
Oppenheimer, 172, 188–90
Osborne, John, 335
Oudart, J.-P., 7

Pakula, Alan, 219
Panorama, 86, 90–113, 121, 124, 125, 177
Paper Moon (TV), 29
Paris, B., 241
Parker, Charles, 340
Pateman, Trevor, 88, 89
Paterson, Richard, 5
Pennies from Heaven, 179
Perkins, Anthony, 254
Perry, Jimmy, 34
Pettifer, Julian, 118
Polanski, Roman, 8
Poldark, 323
Pollitt, Chris, 181
Porridge, 37, 38
Potter, Dennis, 334, 339
Poulantzas, Nicos, 114
Preminger, Otto, 276, 277
Prendiville, Kieran, 182
Price, Alan, 234
Prince, Peter, 188
Pringle, Ashley, 57, 65
Private's Progress, 29
Pryce-Jones, David, 336
Psycho, 8, 9, 254
Purser, Philip, 55
Pyke, Magnus, 178, 183

Queen Christina, 246
Q7, 5

Radek, Karl, 306
Rag Trade, The, 37
Ralling, Christopher, 186, 187, 188
Ramsey, Alf, 151, 157, 169
Ray, Nicholas, 276
Rear Window, 204, 212
Redford, Robert, 239, 243, 252, 262, 263, 264, 265
Red River, 263
Reflections in a Golden Eye, 250, 251
Reid, Elliott, 266
Renoir, Jean, 277, 344
Resnais, Alain, 338
Revie, Don, 152
Rise of the Novel, The (book), 236–7
Rising Damp, 37
Risk Business, The, 176, 180
Robins, Kevin, 173, 174
Robinson, Edward G., 247

Robson, Bobby, 151
Rock-A-Bye-Baby, 11
Rockwell, Joan, 242, 243
Rodd, Michael, 182, 183
Rome Open City, 343
Rose, David, 71, 72
Rose of Washington Square, 250
Rosemary's Baby, 8
Ross, Katharine, 263
Rossellini, Roberto, 228–9, 244
Rothman, Stephanie, 247
Rowbotham, Sheila, 133, 319, 320
Royal Institution Christmas Lectures, The, 180
Rudkin, David, 334
Russell, Jane, 266
Rutland Weekend Television, 5

Sands of Iwo Jima, The, 263, 264
Scholes, R., 254
Schreck, Max, 246
Scott, Terry, 30
Searchers, The, 263
Sexton Blake, 34
Shankly, Bill, 152
Sharif, Omar, 154
Sherlock Holmes, 34
Shockproof, 16
Shoulder Arms, 11
Shoulder to Shoulder, 286, 320
Singer, Aubrey, 182
Sirk, Douglas, 16, 276
Six Wives of Henry VIII, The, 285
Skirrow, Gillian, 27, 31, 32, 43, 328
Skolnick, J., 69
Smith, Anthony, 123
Soap, 179
Song of the Shirt, The, 188
Sorrow and the Pity, The, 322
Speight, Johnny, 36
Spongers, The, 341, 342, 346, 348
Stagecoach, 9, 76
Stanislavski, Konstantin, 337
Starsky and Hutch, 53
Star Trek, 44
Stein, Jock, 151
Stephens, Robert, 76
Steptoe and Son, 28, 37
Sternberg, Josef von, 211–12, 247
Stoppard, Miriam, 183
Strangers on a Train, 16
Strasberg, Lee, 337
Streetcar Named Desire, A, 251, 261
Sturges, Preston, 11
Sugden, Mollie, 44
Sutherland, Donald, 220
Sutton, Shaun, 306
Sweeney, The, 4, 53–69, 73, 179

Tashlin, Frank, 11
Taylor, John Russell, 333, 337
Television and History (book), 286
Television, Technology and Cultural Form (book), 26, 85
Testament of Youth, 285
Thaw, John, 54
Thief of Baghdad, The, 19
Thirty Nine Steps, The, 16
This is Your Life, 51
Thompson, E., 133
Thompson, E. P., 319, 320
Three Days at Szczecin, 285, 340, 341
Till Death Us Do Part, 28, 34, 35, 36, 331
Tinker, Tailor, Soldier, Spy, 179
To Be or Not To Be, 23
Todorov, Tzvetan, 22, 23
To Have and Have Not, 211
Tomorrow's World, 44, 172, 176, 180, 182–3
Tonight, 118, 122, 124, 297

Touch of Evil, 261, 262
Tout va bien, 232, 233, 234, 249
Train Now Standing, The, 34
Tribe, Keith, 285, 304
Trodd, Kenith, 334
Troubles, The, 285
Truffaut, François, 238
Tudor, Andrew, 87, 143
Tuohy, Denis, 98
Two or Three Things I Know About Her, 249

Up Pompeii, 28, 34
Upstairs, Downstairs, 286, 288–93
Up the Junction, 340
Ustinov, Peter, 179

Valentino, Rudolph, 198
Van Laan, T., 251
Varney, Reg, 37
Vaughan, Paul, 178
Vertigo, 212, 213
Vertov, Dziga, 246
Very Merry Widow, The, 36
Viva l'Italia, 228–9
Vlady, Marina, 249
Vodka-Cola, 180
Voyage of Charles Darwin, The, 87, 172, 184–8

Walden, Brian, 178, 180
War Game, The, 340, 343
Warner, Jack, 54
Warren, Robert Penn, 242
Washington: Behind Closed Doors, 333, 340
Waterman, Dennis, 54
Waterman, Jack, 54
Watkins, Peter, 295, 340
Watt, Ian, 236, 237, 238, 243
Way We Were, The, 252, 263
Wayne, John, 239, 243, 244, 245, 246, 250, 263–4
Webster, Frank, 173, 174
Wednesday Play (series), 331
Weekend World, 95, 177
Welles, Orson, 262, 277
Wellings, Bob, 127, 139
Wesker, Arnold, 335
West Side Story, 9
Westergaard, J. H., 68
Whatever Happened to the Likely Lads, 4, 33, 34
Wheldon, Huw, 332
Whitfield, June, 30
Whoops Baghdad, 28, 34
Widlake, Brian, 178
Wilkinson, Stuart, 119
Willemen, Paul, 11, 23
Willett, John, 248
Williams, Raymond, 26, 27, 28, 30, 85, 139, 297, 328, 338, 339
Williams, Tennessee, 251
Will Penny, 238
Winship, J., 134
Wollen, Peter, 58
Woman in the Window, The, 16, 247
Woodhead, Leslie, 341
Woodworth, J., 69
Woolgar, Steve, 190
World at War, The, 285
World in Action, 180, 328
World of Wodehouse, The, 34
World of Wooster, The, 34
Worth, Harry, 28
Written on the Wind, 9
Wyver, John, 32, 71

Yesterday's Men, 92
Young, Robert, 87, 174
Young Scientist of the Year, 180

Z Cars, 4, 53, 54, 55, 57, 58–69, 71, 73
Zola, Emile, 337, 338, 339, 342

DATE DUE

APR 1 6 1996